Women and Work in Britain since 1840

'A book that provides important insights into changes and continuities in the pattern and nature of women's paid employment.'
June Hannam, *University of the West of England*

This essential student resource is the first of its kind to study this period. Working chronologically from the early 1840s to the end of the twentieth century, it examines more than 150 years of women's employment history and the struggles women have faced.

With suggestions for research topics, an annotated bibliography to aid further research and a chronology of important events which places the subject in a broader historical context, Gerry Holloway considers how factors such as class, age, marital status, race and locality, along with wider economic and political issues, have affected women's job opportunities and status.

Key themes and issues that run though the book include:

- continuity and change in women's employment
- the sexual division of labour
- women as a cheap labour force
- women's perceived primary role of motherhood
- women and trade unions
- equality versus difference – the key feminist debate
- women's education and training

Students of women's studies, gender studies and history will find this a fascinating and invaluable addition to their reading material.

Gerry Holloway is a lecturer in Life History and Women's Studies at the Centre for Continuing Education at the University of Sussex. She has written extensively on women's history and the feminist movement and is on the Committee of the Women's History Network.

Women's and Gender History
Edited by June Purvis

Emmeline Pankhurst: A Biography
June Purvis

Child Sexual Abuse in Victorian England
Louise A. Jackson

Crimes of Outrage: Sex, Violence and Victorian Working Women
Shani D'Cruze

Feminism, Femininity and the Politics of Working Women: The Women's Co-operative Guild, 1880s to the Second World War
Gillian Scott

Gender and Crime in Modern Europe
Edited by Margaret L. Arnot and Cornelie Usborne

Gender Relations in German History: Power, Agency and Experience from the Sixteenth to the Twentieth Century
Edited by Lynn Abrams and Elizabeth Harvey

Imaging Home: Gender, 'Race' and National Identity, 1945–64
Wendy Webster

Midwives of the Revolution: Female Bolsheviks and Women Workers in 1917
Jane McDermid and Anna Hillyar

No Distinction of Sex? Women in British Universities, 1870–1939
Carol Dyhouse

Policing Gender, Class and Family: Britain, 1850–1945
Linda Mahood

Prostitution: Prevention and Reform in England, 1860–1914
Paula Bartley

Sylvia Pankhurst: Sexual Politics and Political Activism
Barbara Winslow

Votes for Women
Edited by June Purvis and Sandra Holton

Women's History: Britain, 1850–1945
Edited by June Purvis

The Women's Suffrage Movement: A Reference Guide, 1866–1928
Elizabeth Crawford

Women and Teacher Training Colleges, 1900–1960: A Culture of Femininity
Elizabeth Edwards

Women, Work and Sexual Politics in Eighteenth-century England
Bridget Hill

Women Workers and Gender Identities, 1835–1913: The Cotton Metal Industries in England
Carol E. Morgan

Outspoken Women: An Anthology of Women's Writing on Sex, 1870–1969
Lesley A. Hall

Women's History: Britain, 1700–1850
Edited by Hannah Barker and Elaine Chalus

The Women's Suffrage Movement in Britain and Ireland: A Regional Survey
Elizabeth Crawford

Women and Work in Britain since 1840

Gerry Holloway

 Routledge
Taylor & Francis Group

LONDON AND NEW YORK

First published 2005
by Routledge
2 Park Square, Milton Park, Abingdon, Oxon OX14 4RN

Simultaneously published in the USA and Canada
by Routledge
270 Madison Ave, New York, NY 10016

Routledge is an imprint of the Taylor & Francis Group

© 2005 Gerry Holloway

Typeset in Garamond Book by
Keystroke, Jacaranda Lodge, Wolverhampton
Printed and bound in Great Britain
by MPG Books Ltd, Bodmin

British Library Cataloguing in Publication Data
A catalogue record for this book is available from the British Library

Library of Congress Cataloging in Publication Data
Holloway, Gerry.
 Women and work in Britain since 1840 / Gerry Holloway.
  p. cm. – (Women's and gender history)
 Includes bibliographical references.
 1. Women–Employment–Great Britain–History.
 2. Women–Employment–Europe–History.
 3. Sex role–Great Britain–History.
 4. Sex role–Europe–History. I. Title. II. Series.
HD6135.H65 2005
331.4′0941–dc22   2004029363

ISBN 0–415–25910–X (hbk)
ISBN 0–415–25911–8 (pbk)

꙯

Contents

CONTENTS

ð

Tables

ଐ

Figures

ॐ

Acknowledgements

My interest in women's work began with my doctoral research on the Industrial Women's Movement before the First World War and I owe thanks to my supervisor Professor Eileen Yeo for her support and advice, based on her vast knowledge of nineteenth-century British women's history. I would also like to thank Professor June Purvis, the editor of this women's and gender history series, for her support of historians of women's history in general and of myself in particular. Parts of this book have been offered as papers at various conferences of the Women's History Network and I would like to thank colleagues from the network who have commented on my work, especially June Hannam who read a draft of this book. Thanks too to Vicky Peters of Routledge who waited patiently and supportively for the production of this book. Students on my post-graduate course 'The Social and Cultural History of Feminism in England' and students taking the undergraduate course 'Revolting Women: Women as Agents of Change in Britain' have discussed parts of this work in their seminars over the years and I thank them for their help in pitching this book at the right level for students new to this subject. Thanks, too, to colleagues at the Centre for Continuing Education at the University of Sussex who have given me the support I needed to carry on when my workload has been overwhelming. I would also like to thank my partner Ned Hoskins, who has provided emotional and domestic support throughout the years I have been working on this book, proving that it is possible to swap gender roles successfully; and my daughter Jessica Holloway Swift for sharing my interest in women's history and offering me a young woman's perspective on feminist issues. And finally, this book is dedicated to the late Vivienne Swift, a working-class woman and a pioneer who studied chemistry at university in the 1930s. She managed a pharmaceutical company during the Second World War but was replaced by a man at the end of the war. Undeterred, she became a postmistress whilst raising her children in the 1950s and 1960s and later supported me both financially and emotionally during my studies and research up to her death in 2001. To me, she represents the archetypal working woman who challenges the status quo and helps her younger sisters along the way.

Gerry Holloway

ॐ

Abbreviations

ASE	Amalgamated Society of Engineers
AUEW	Amalgamated Union of Electrical Workers
AUCE	Amalgamated Union of Co-operative Employees
CCWE	Central Committee on Women's Employment
CSCA	Civil Service Clerical Association
CWCS	Council of Women Civil Servants
DORA	Defence of the Realm Act
FWG	Fabian Women's Group
LNSWS	London and National Society for Women's Service
M-O	Mass Observation
NALGO	National Association of Local Government Workers
NAPSS	National Association for the Promotion of Social Sciences
NAWCS	National Association of Women Civil Servants
NFWT	National Federation of Women Teachers
NFWW	National Federation of Women Workers
NUGW	National Union of General Workers
NUPE	National Union of Public Employees
NAUSA	National Union of Shop Assistants
NUSEC	National Union of Societies for Equal Citizenship
NUT	National Union of Teachers
NUWT	National Union of Women Teachers
SPEW	Society for the Promotion of the Employment of Women
TUC	Trades Union Congress
UPOW	Union of Post Office Workers
WSS	Wartime Social Survey
WAAC	Women's Army Auxiliary Corps
WFL	Women's Freedom League

WIC	Women's Industrial Council
WLL	Women's Labour League
WLM	Women's Liberation Movement
WPPL	Women's Protective and Provident League
WRAF	Women's Royal Air Force
WRNS	Women's Royal Naval Service
WTUA	Women's Trade Union Association
WTUL	Women's Trade Union League

Chapter One

ॡ

Introduction

The study of women's history has expanded greatly since the rise of the women's liberation movement in the 1970s. This is not a coincidence as activists were acutely aware of the importance of understanding women's past for potential women's activism. For example, Sheila Rowbotham, in her groundbreaking work *Hidden from History* linked the question of women's liberation with the way that capitalism had affected women's independence through the economic opportunities allowed to them.[1] Since then, a vast amount of research has been undertaken into many aspects of women's lives, not least in the area of women's work. The sheer number of textbooks, pamphlets and journal articles on the subject can daunt the most enthusiastic student. One purpose of this book is to guide the reader through some of this material and highlight important texts. A second purpose is to chart and reflect on some of the debates, ideas and contests concerning women's work since 1840, and to evaluate the distance women have travelled towards a yet-to-be-achieved universal economic independence and equal opportunities. This road is not a straight one and women have experienced many setbacks as well as achievements on the way.

Choosing a date from which to begin a book of this type is a problem in itself and, ultimately, the choice tends to be arbitrary. Why pick the 1840s rather than the mid-eighteenth century when industrialization began to transform work in Britain? I chose to begin with the 1840s because to some extent this was another milestone in the history of women's relationship to work and also because I did not want to become involved in the debates about women and industrialization as these have been written about elsewhere.[2] My interest lies in the extent to which women have challenged dominant ideas about the work they should do and the conditions in which they should perform it. Further, I am interested in how women have worked together to achieve change. To this end, the 1840s are a good starting point. One can trace a growing awareness of women's economic position and the conditions in which they worked. For example, the First Report of the Children's Employment Commission in 1842 investigated the conditions of girls, boys and women working in mines and collieries and exposed not only the horrors of the coal industry, but also revealed in stark terms the contradiction between the way women were represented in Victorian society and the treatment many received by that society.[3] This was also the first time that women workers were classified with children and young persons. Questions concerning the morality of allowing women to work in areas deemed masculine were also highlighted in these discussions. Further, there was an increasing realization of what we would call today the feminization of poverty. Along with the growing concern about the treatment of women in industry, there was a corresponding awareness of the large number of working women, both middle- and lower-class, living in relative poverty.

Out of these concerns one can observe the seeds of discontent being sown – these would develop into a way of addressing 'The Woman Question' and the network of organizations that formed the first women's movement.[4] The foundations for this movement, which would challenge prescriptive limitations, seek to redefine gender roles, contest male dominance, yet make a case for special protection for women, began to emerge in the 1840s. Some of the issues that caused women to organize around employment at that time have continued to be issues of importance to this day. For example, current campaigns of the Fawcett Society in Britain concerning the under-representation of women in better paid and higher status work reflect the concerns of earlier organizations trying to open up new professional careers for women. Similarly, the question of employment rights, although different in the detail, can be traced back to earlier concerns about women's role as mothers.

The debate around continuity and change in women's history has been written about extensively.[5] However, many of these accounts, which often look at the notion of a golden age of women's work, tend to attempt to privilege one over the other, whereas I would argue that, while interesting, these debates mask the more important issue of how women have dealt with continuity and change. Understanding the issues around which women have organized, the responses they elicited and the limitations of their success, and the extent of their failure, help us to understand enduring attitudes towards women's employment and point to ways that might offer us solutions to our own problems. The study of history is important if we are to understand why society is organized the way it is and how we can use our understanding of the past to become agents of change in the present. This is not to argue that we can use simplistically examples of, say, how women responded to protective legislation in the lead industry in nineteenth century in the way we might organize around an issue today. Therefore, this book will not examine in detail the various areas of work in which women participated, although of course these will be mentioned and further reading indicated. Rather, it will focus on the interplay of continuity and change. That is, the ways in which dominant ideas concerning femininity, women's roles, gender, class and, to some extent, race, have dictated the types of work deemed suitable for women; the value placed on women's work, the status of women as workers and the strategies that women have employed to challenge these dominant ideas.

Several themes run throughout this book, so it is useful to draw these out from the beginning of this study. The first is the sexual division of labour. The question of what sort of work women should be undertaking is central to the whole debate around women's role in society and has affected all women. The sexual division of labour is not a recent occurrence forced onto the population by increasing industrialization. It has a much longer history than the period focused on in this book; it can be argued that there is a long history of women's work being accorded a lower social status and value than men's because of women's primary association with unpaid childcare and housework.[6] In Britain, Catherine Hall has led the way in arguing that an ideology of domesticity, reinforced by evangelical Christianity and the effects of industrialization, led to the sharply defined gendered roles of this period.[7] This ideology sought to elevate women's domestic responsibilities and condemn paid work that took women out of their so-called 'natural' sphere, that is, the home. Industrialization certainly made women's paid employment more visible as some forms of women's work moved from the home into the factory. Vickery, however, cautions against being too committed to the notion that the ideology of separate spheres developed in the late eighteenth century. She argues that there are problems with definitions of public and private and how the meaning of these concepts has changed over time. She calls for a careful reading of the contemporary meanings of these concepts and how people use the terms. Further, she argues that a close examination of particular individuals' and groups' activities rather than a focus on prescriptive literature undermines the notion that men and women of this period occupied different, self-contained spheres. She calls for a more nuanced approach to the exploration of the ways that gender, and indeed class, operated in the eighteenth and nineteenth centuries and argues that, if anything, women's sphere of influence increased in the nineteenth century especially in the field of philanthropy. Furthermore, she disputes that there was ever a golden age when men and women were held in equal worth in the world of work. She calls for more local case studies of how society operated at a micro level in order to test the separate spheres theory.[8]

Notwithstanding the concerns of Vickery and others who are calling for a more sustained critique of the separate spheres question, there is evidence in the nineteenth century of a changing attitude to women's paid employment. Women had, of course, always worked in a range of occupations. Sometimes, this was paid work and sometimes it was not. Some types of work took women away from the home while other employment could be undertaken at home. In this book, I shall focus on paid employment whether undertaken at home or in a public workplace. This does not mean that women's unpaid work was unimportant, whether it was the domestic labour that reproduced the workforce, philanthropic work or work that supported a family enterprise.[9] However, this work is outside of what is conventionally thought of as employment and it is the debates around paid work that are the focus of this book. Women's unpaid work will, therefore, only be discussed where it is suggested as being women's ideal work or where it impinges on their actual or perceived ability to do paid work.

Returning to paid employment, there was a significant and growing debate around women's work by the middle of the nineteenth century. For working-class women there was a growing public worry about the sort of paid work they were undertaking. It was not just women working in factories who were criticized, although they were probably the majority, as we shall see. Women working in agriculture and mining, for example, were also criticized for undertaking unwomanly work. The government intervened at several points to introduce legislation designed to protect women but which, in reality, excluded them from certain types of work. Consequently, during the nineteenth century, the types of work that were deemed suitable for working-class women were growing narrower over time and women's own attitudes towards work were increasingly shaped by their responsibilities and relationship to domesticity. Arguments centring on the exclusion of women from certain types of paid work drew on discourse that constructed women as wives and mothers and the guardians of Christian moral values. Women working outside of the home, especially in areas of work divorced from feminine pursuits, were increasingly seen as neglecting their primary role as homemakers and in danger of losing their virtue. This meant that women's employment opportunities, apart from domestic service, were funnelled into overcrowded sectors where they were ripe for exploitation. Against this background, campaigns to open up new areas of work to women exacerbated tensions by posing a threat to men and fuelling fears that the world was being turned upside down. For middle-class women, there was little concern about them undertaking unpaid work within their families and they were not discouraged from philanthropic work if it did not interfere with their domestic duties. Public anxiety about the type of work that women performed was a continuous thread throughout this period and will be examined in its various contexts.

Even without the campaign to remove women from certain employment sectors, there was widespread sexual discrimination within industries where segregation took place both vertically and horizontally. Segregation can mean the almost total separation between the types of work that men and women do. It is an ongoing phenomenon and is evident in many occupations and industries, although the form it takes differs over time and in differing work contexts. Women were, and still are to some extent, segregated into the unskilled, worst paid, most menial jobs and their pay was lower than men's even when they did the same work. Furthermore, women were usually denied any chance of extended training that might enhance their chances of promotion as they were regarded primarily through their ideological domestic roles whether these existed in reality or not. Either way, women's role in the workplace was not considered as a career nor were they considered the primary wage earner, although the reality often challenged these assumptions. Throughout the book, I shall examine various debates concerning segregation in the workforce.

The main types of work that were open to women at the beginning of the nineteenth century were agriculture, domestic service, textiles, needlework and governessing. Out of these, women's work in agriculture and textile factories was increasingly frowned upon, especially where married women were concerned. Various commissions investigated these occupations and sought to implement legislation that would regulate and consequently limit women's access to these areas of work. Working-class women and work became an increasingly problematic question and, apart from government investigations, was the focus of a range of literary and moral discourses. The danger of women's loss of moral character if they engaged in certain types of work was ever present in these texts. This will be discussed in Chapter One in respect of needlework, agricultural work, factory work and coal mining, and reviewed where appropriate in subsequent chapters. Up until the Second World War domestic service was seen as the ideal employment for working-class women and a great deal of effort was made by reformers, writers, clergymen and politicians to entice, or hector, women into this sector. For example, in the 1850s, J. D. Milne wrote of the 'charms' of domestic service:

> The situation of a domestic servant . . . is attended with considerable comfort. With abundant work it combines a wonderful degree of liberty, discipline, health, physical comfort, good example, regularity, room for advancement, encouragement to acquire savings habits. The most numerous class of depositors in the Savings Bank is that of domestic servants. The situation frequently involves much responsibility, and calls forth the best features of character. Kind attachment in return for honest service is not uncommon with the master or

> mistress: and honest pride in the relations springs up on both sides and lasts throughout life.[10]

This rose-coloured version of domestic service would probably have been unrecognizable to many domestic servants at the time who, in 1850, worked long hours, at the constant beck and call of their employers, for around £10 per annum; they were at the mercy of their employer if they fell ill and had meagre free time or holidays.[11] Further, it was not usual for domestic servants to stay with the same employer over a lifetime. Most domestic servants were young girls who left to marry or moved from position to position via the annual hiring fairs or employment bureaux.[12] However, cold facts were not allowed to dim the virtuous glow that surrounded the topic of domestic service for middle-class advocates of the work. Furthermore, despite these exhortations, the difficulties of finding suitable domestic servants and keeping them was a constant topic of conversation amongst the middle classes up until the First World War.[13] After the war, despite the best efforts of the government to coerce women back into domestic service, participation continued to decline. The notion of domestic work changed as more servants lived out and domestic appliances helped lessen some of the more tiresome aspects of domestic labour. After the Second World War, immigrant female labour from Europe and the Caribbean was channelled into cleaning work both in public institutions, such as hospitals, and in private homes. Race was an issue that shaped these women's employment opportunities, as we shall see in Chapter Thirteen.

Domestic service serves as an important example of a gender-segregated, idealized area of work but also as an area where class relations were sharply defined and class-based practices carried out.[14] For example, in 1899, the social investigator Seebohm Rowntree took the keeping of servants as the dividing line between the working classes and those higher up the social scale, thus setting out a clear demarcation between those who carried out the dirty, monotonous, low-status work and those who aspired to something better.[15] Class played an important part in the type of work women undertook, as did gender segregated employment. Loss of status through performing the 'wrong' sort of work was extremely serious. Conversely, like men, middle-class women wanted to ring-fence certain areas of work as their own and set up institutions that created indiscernible barriers that excluded working-class women from certain work. Consequently, the way that class operated in the employment arena and the implications of this will also be considered at various stages. Definitions of class are always problematic, however; Roberts has developed a rough rule of thumb: working-class women undertook manual work, were paid wages rather than salaries, and did not employ others. Middle-class women tended not to work but when they did were often not paid, or if they were, drew a salary; they did non-manual, often skilled, supervisory or professional work and employed people to do certain manual tasks. However, some areas of work fell between two stalls and their class status is less clear. Shop work, nursing and clerical work, for example, are not easy to define as, depending on the type of work under-taken, the work can be considered either working or middle class. For example, working as an assistant in a high-class dress shop would be acceptable to a middle-class woman, whereas being a general assistant in a general shop in a working-class area would not. Moreover, all women tended to be identified with the class status of their husband or father.[16] Therefore, although Robert's definition is a useful starting point, a more complex definition of class develops over time. Class status was particu-larly significant for middle-class women. Whereas working-class women were expected to work for money, middle-class women were regarded as losing respectability, and through this, status, if they worked for pay. This was a particular obstacle for the many middle-class women in the nineteenth century who needed paid work. It was a problem also for those women who did not need the money but wanted to be treated fairly in comparison with men. Consequently, the issue of middle-class women working for money was a continual problem for campaigners throughout the nineteenth century.[17] Class, the way it is defined and the implica-tions that this had on women's employment is considered throughout the book.

Another debate that is constant throughout the period covered by this book surrounds the issue of women being used as a cheap, flexible pool of reserve labour that can be brought in and out of the workforce to suit the requirements of capital and/or the state. Woman's ideal role of home-maker and mother means that women workers are not seen in the same light as male workers; they tend to be considered as temporary workers both before and after marriage. Before industrialization, family groups were often, although not always, regarded as work units with the male as the key worker and the family subordinate to him. Wives organized their work around their domestic chores and were consequently assigned jobs that could be easily interrupted. These jobs were considered as less skilled areas of work than men's work and consequently of lower value. These customary practices survived but were adapted during industrialization when the role of the male breadwinner and dependent unpaid, or low paid, family began to develop.[18] Much of the legislation of the nineteenth century that restricted the employment of women and children was based on the notion of the male breadwinner. This ideal strengthened as the century progressed even though, in reality, most working-class men did not earn enough to keep a family without the assistance of their wife and/or children. Moreover, many women did not have a man on whom they could depend for their support. The practice of paying women less and excluding them from trade unions that could fight for better pay, meant that women could be used by employers as a reserve pool of labour which could be brought in as the market demanded, but also to peg the wages of male employees or de-skill certain tasks.[19] The women's trade union movement in the nineteenth century struggled to organize working women so that they could resist this exploitation. This movement will be explored in Chapter Four. In the twentieth century women were actively encouraged to take up hitherto 'male' trades during the wars.[20] It is interesting to note how women's domestic responsibilities could be overlooked or taken over by the state if women were needed to fill certain roles outside the home. The issues of the male breadwinner and women as a reserve pool of labour will be discussed at various points throughout the book.

The issue of women being used as a cheap pool of labour is arguably a feature of middle-class employment too, where women have been employed in certain areas where demand has outstripped supply. Further, the employment of women in these sectors has also been seen to bring down the status of the work and has consequently been rigorously contested by male workers. Again, in these struggles, opponents of women's employment called upon the rhetoric of separate spheres which built on the ideology that condemned women to an idealized domestic sphere and elevated men to family breadwinners whether they had a family to support or not. Taken one stage further, when the employment of women was conceded to, the notion of separate spheres was used to segregate women into low-paid, low-status work with little or no possibility of promotion so that the victory in opening up new areas of work to women was tempered by the limitations placed on them once they entered that particular domain. An example of a practice that limited women's opportunities was the marriage bar that was often used in order to restrict numbers of women employed and to buttress the notion of a women's 'natural' role.[21] Although the marriage bar has long since disappeared, present-day practices in some sectors still ensure that women do not rise beyond certain levels in the career ladder. These often resolve around making it difficult for women to return to work after a period of maternity leave.

The final issue that will be discussed throughout the book, and was of great importance, is appropriate education and training for women. For working-class girls, there was an increasing emphasis on domestic training as the century progressed. Working-class education before 1870 was patchy. There was no obligation to send children to school and two economic factors impeded children's access to education.[22] First, payment had to be made and this was a deterrent to poor families; and second, children were important contributors to the family economy. Further, working-class girls were expected to help care for younger siblings and were taken out of school whenever their help was required at home. Schools often sanctioned this as they regarded acting as mother's help was the best training a girl could receive. Consequently, child labour and prevalent attitudes towards women's domestic role meant that many working-class girls received very little formal education. Ideologies about women's role in society also informed the curriculum, so that in later periods girls spent precious time learning domestic subjects rather than subjects that they needed to find more lucrative and satisfying types of employment. In turn, this lack of interest in girls' education did not encourage most young women to regard work as anything more than an interlude between school and marriage. This attitude existed well into the twentieth century.

As many reformers have pointed out, women could not participate in new areas of employment without sufficient education or training. As previously mentioned, in the nineteenth century, middle-class women were not expected to do paid work, as it would besmirch their family's reputation.[23] Their main goal in life was to marry well so, consequently, their education was focused on finding a husband rather than finding gainful employment. Most middle-class girls were either educated at home by governesses or sent to small day schools where they were taught accomplishments such as deportment, singing, drawing and conversational French alongside basic literacy. Often their education was inferior to that received by working-class girls as the attempt to recruit middle-class girls to train as elementary teachers demonstrated. If, in later life, they were unfortunate enough to need to work, the only avenues open to them were fancy needlework or, more likely, governessing. Consequently, governesses would replicate the vicious circle of the poorly educated passing on their sparse knowledge to the next generation of girls. It was the position of these governesses that contributed to the campaigns for women's education in the nineteenth century. This issue is discussed in Chapter One. Although the history of the campaign for women's education is beyond the scope of this book, it is important to note that feminists saw the campaign of improvements in education as going hand-in-hand with the campaigns to open up women's employment opportunities. Therefore, I shall discuss education at appropriate points in the book.[24]

For some historians, the concept of patriarchy underpins all these factors shaping the nature and availability of women's employment. Patriarchy, although a contentious concept, is crucial to our understanding why women have been regarded as inferior workers, useful for the most monotonous tasks, as a pool of casual labourers and the many other epithets that have been used to discriminate against women. Feminist theorists have defined patriarchy as a system of social structures and practices in which men dominate and exploit women. Some feminists have argued against using patriarchy as an interpretative framework because they see it as ahistorical, essentialist and universalist, asserting that patriarchy is just an ideology and subordinate to the capitalist economic system. However, others argue that it does not need to have such a narrow definition if one acknowledges that forms of patriarchy vary over time and in different social contexts. From this analysis developed the dual-systems theory, which suggests that in order to understand gender relations in the labour market, it is necessary to consider both patriarchy and class.

Using a Marxist feminist analysis as her starting point, Hartmann argues that patriarchal relations in employment cannot be understood only in terms of capitalism because they predate capitalism. She asserts that central to men's control over women in all spheres of society is job segregation. Excluding women from certain areas of work keeps them at a disadvantage. This exclusion takes place through a coalition of male interests – unions, employers and the state.[25] Sylvia Walby develops this theory further. She argues that rather than there being one source of male domination, patriarchy is present in six forms of social structures: patriarchal production relations in the household; patriarchal relations in paid labour; the state; male violence against women; patriarchal sexual relations and patriarchal cultural institutions.[26] This theory, which Walby calls the gender inequality theory,[27] is particularly useful in our context because she argues that individual experiences are mediated by the interaction of these structural forms so that over time, women's experience of patriarchy in the workforce will change but the underlying presence of patriarchy will be constant. For example, in the nineteenth century, we can see that the dominant domestic ideology, which was a variant of an earlier patriarchal construct, very strongly emphasized that women should ideally be confined to domesticity. This is a particularly intense form of patriarchal dominance that affected all areas of women's working lives. Walby calls this private patriarchy and the dominant patriarchal structure was household production. In this type of patriarchy, the dominant strategy was exclusionary. This belief has changed over time but has not disappeared. Today, public patriarchy is to the fore and its dominant structure is paid work and the state. The modern strategy is segregationalist and subordinating. Private patriarchy is much weaker today, but there is still an assumption that women have greater domestic responsibilities than men and this assumption affects women in a range of ways. Walby also places a strong emphasis on the ways that male-dominated trade unions sought to keep women out of certain sectors that they regarded as their territory. This might well be over-emphasizing the power that unions have to direct the economy, but it also highlights a contradiction where men have supported capital at the expense of women workers; for example, in the debates around protective legislation. More recently, feminists writing about women and paid work have focused on the centrality of sexual divisions at work and how gender is as important as class for analysing the capitalist system.[28]

In order to chart continuity and change in these debates around women's employment, this book is ordered chronologically. The book is divided into four parts and each part is divided into chapters that explore different areas of work and debates for a specific period. As the potential scope of each chapter is immense, each will give an outline of key areas of employment that I shall focus on, the most important issues at that time and a discussion of more recent historiographical debate. Recommended reading for undertaking further research will be offered at the end of the book.

Part One will focus on the debates around women's employment that occurred roughly during the period 1840–70. As previously mentioned, one of the milestones of women's employment history was the First Report of the Children's Employment Commission in 1842. This was just one of a series of reports which investigated the work of labouring women in this period. Restrictive and protective legislation was to be an area of contestation for the remainder of the nineteenth century. The debate divided feminists from feminists and other social reformers, women from men and working women amongst themselves. One focus of this part will be the findings of these various reports, the solutions they offered and the response these elicited from women. The question of what sort of work women should be undertaking was central to the whole debate of women's role in society and did not just affect the sort of work working-class women should do. Questions of appropriate feminine behaviour affected all women so the focus will also be on the struggles of middle-class women to open up new employment opportunities for the growing number of middle-class women who needed to support themselves and found their options limited. These struggles formed part of the larger 'Woman Question' and exercised the growing band of women who gathered around Langham Place from the 1850s onwards. On the one hand, they campaigned to improve women's education and training and, on the other, they sought to expand the sort of work middle-class women could undertake. The debates around women's employment featured large in the pages of their journal *The English Woman's Journal*, later retitled *The Englishwomen's Review*. The campaign was organized by the Society for the Promotion of the Employment of Women (SPEW) based at Langham Place. The second focus of this part will be on the activities of SPEW and the arguments that developed around work and how these reflect ideas of class and gender at the time.

The period 1870–1914 saw a huge growth in women's organizations as well as an expansion of women's employment in the retail and clerical sectors, the first tentative entries into professions such as medicine and the professionalization of other types of women's work such as nursing and social work. Langham Place had been the catalyst for many of these campaigning organizations, for example organizations around the issues of suffrage, married women's property, education, and importantly for this book, employment. Part Two will chart the development of various organizations around women's employment and will examine how they responded to women's needs and society's prescriptions. These organizations were largely concerned with expanding work opportunities, the unionization of women in order to protect their rights to work and employment conditions and investigation of the conditions of various trades open to women. The organizations that will be considered in particular are the continued work of SPEW; the Women's Protective and Provident League (WPPL), which became the Women's Trade Union League (WTUL); and the Women's Trade Union Association (WTUA) which was transformed into the Women's Industrial Council (WIC) in the 1890s. The way in which these organizations were shaped by different feminist ideas as well as by class and gender will be discussed.

During this period, women were employed in a whole range of work and were pushing gently on the boundaries of new areas, especially concerning the welfare of women and children. The Boer War raised questions about the health of the nation's children and women's role in improving this was considered as central. The question of whether married women should work was raised and resulted in a whole range of solutions to the problem being offered. Women were involved in this debate on both sides. Many working-class women insisted that their right to work should not be interfered with, but this was met by the concern of social reformers, many of them women, that a married woman's place was in the home. Consequently, the following will be considered: first, the debates around state intervention into employment practices; second, the concern around high infant mortality rates and their implications for married women's work; third, the way this debate offered increased employment for women in social and primary health work and education while attempting to limit the scope of work carried out by another group, working mothers. In addition, I shall assess the extent to which the expanding employment opportunities for women were opening up new fields of employment or were just offering more work in an enduringly limited sphere. A further issue examined will be the discussions around the consequences of educating young girls and the way that education would affect their prospects in the marriage stakes. This will include a discussion of the phenomenon of the *fin de siècle*, 'The New Woman'.

Part Three will examine the period from 1914 until 1945. One focus will be the effect that two world wars had on women's employment. We shall examine the extent to which the First World War opened up new employment opportunities for women and whether earlier notions of women's abilities and role in society shaped these opportunities. At the end of the First World War women were, at last, offered a limited franchise. This success was achieved at a time when women were being made unemployed in large numbers as their work in supporting the war was no longer needed and men were returning to take their places in the jobs that remained. It was, as Dierdre Beddoe has succinctly put it, 'back to home and duty' for large numbers of women.[29] Although some women were happy to return to domestic roles, many were either not in the position to do this or, having tasted the pleasures of earning a living, were reluctant to do so. The marriage bar was enforced to keep married women out of paid employment and, despite some campaigning for equal pay in the Civil Service, women found themselves paid much less than their male counterparts. Changes in technology also shaped the inter-war period with assembly line production being introduced and the ever-increasing mechanization of the clerical sector. These innovations, too, had implications for women's employment and will be considered in this part of the book.

When war broke out again in 1939, unlike in the earlier war, most single women were involved in paid work and not easily persuaded to move into factory production or the women's sections of the armed forces. For the first time women, as well as men, were eligible for conscription. The marriage bar was also lifted and some attempts were made to assist married women's double role as domestic worker and paid worker during the war. This need for women's labour during the war threw up some difficult contradictions for a society wedded to the belief that a woman's place was in the home. Many married women were loath to take on the double burden of paid work and domestic responsibilities and many employers did not want to confront the difficulties that this burden placed on women workers. Various attempts were made to assist women, for example nurseries, canteens and schemes to assist with shopping. However, the most successful scheme was the introduction of part-time work in key sectors. After the war women were, once again, expected to return to the home. However, the adaptations brought in to serve the country's wartime needs stuck. The marriage bar never returned, part-time work became increasingly popular and the debate around married women's work shifted once again to accommodate the nation's need to reconstruct a war-torn economy.

Part Four will focus on the period 1945 to the end of the century. The 1950s, like the 1920s, saw a society trying to return to normal after years of war. However, the 1950s were different in several respects. Women were sent conflicting messages: on the one hand, there was anxiety about the birth rate and women were exhorted to have large families and focus solely on the welfare of their families and their children in particular. These were the years when child psychologists rose to dominance and, through manuals and women's magazines, warned mothers of the dangers posed to children if they were subjected to 'maternal deprivation'. On the other hand, women – including married women – were needed in the workforce.

In 1947, the government had to launch a recruitment drive to encourage women back into the workforce in certain key sectors. Immigrant women were also brought to the country to help plug the labour shortage. This campaign will be explored in this section of the book. Another solution to the problem of labour shortage was the possibility of a bimodal work pattern. This meant that women would give up full-time work on the birth of their first child and return when the children were grown up. This was seen particularly as a solution in the professions, especially teaching. The debate around this new pattern of work and the increasing popularity of part-time work will also be explored.

The 1950s and 1960s were decades when a new generation of girls were raised to expect more than their mothers, being the recipients, as Carolyn Steedman has argued, of the free orange juice of the welfare state and widening possibilities for education beyond the age of fifteen.[30] Increased educational opportunities did not necessarily bring the widened employment prospects that young women educated to a high level might have expected. Just as employment had been an issue for women in the early women's movement of the nineteenth century, so too was employment an issue for women in the resurgent women's movement of the 1970s. In Part Four, I shall also examine the frustrations of young women who had been educated to expect more from life than their mothers, yet found themselves in dead-end secretarial work or consigned to the home and low-paid part-time work once they had children. Further, I shall focus on the initiatives taken by working-class women, frustrated by earning less than men, to bring about broader legislation to give equal pay and to end discrimination against women. This led to the introduction of the Equal Pay and Sex Discrimination Acts that women hoped would usher in a new era of employment rights for women.

The period from 1970 to the end of the century has, as Sue Bruley has commented, not yet been 'digested' and 'dusted over' by historians and is consequently difficult to analyse as history.[31] Therefore, the final chapter of this book will consider what issues characterize women's paid employment in the last third of the twentieth century and what issues still remain unresolved at the beginning of the twenty-first century. In conclusion, we shall consider the extent to which women's employment has been transformed in the 160 years that this book covers. What are the continuities and changes that have taken place over the period covered by this book and how might we reflect on the lessons of the past for our struggles in this new century?

Part One

1840–70

Despite the dominant ideology, which deemed that a woman's place was within the home, women worked in a wide range of occupations, much wider than can be discussed in detail in this book.[1] In this first part of the book, I intend to sketch out the terrain of women's employment and the debates that arose from it in this period. Following the mindset of Victorian domestic ideology, concepts of work and the developing economic structure of the period, this chapter is organized around the location of work, either in the public or private sphere, and the social class that workers occupied. Therefore, given the wide range of occupations that were available for working-class women, I focus on those occupations that employed large numbers of women, that were the subject of widespread public interest and reflected ideological constructions of femininity in a range of public texts. As I mentioned in the introduction, the largest sectors of employment for women in the first half of the nineteenth century were domestic service, needlework, agriculture, textiles, homework and teaching. Teaching was an option for both middle-class and the higher strata of working-class women so this sector is discussed in the chapter on middle-class women's work. Nursing was also a working-class occupation, but became an option for middle-class women towards the end of this period; as such, it is examined in the second part of the book where the increasing push to open up the professions to middle-class women is considered. In Chapter Two, I focus on domestic service and its allied trade, laundering, as well as needlework and other home-based work, factory work, agriculture and mining. Chapter Three focuses on the debate around surplus middle-class women needing, or wanting, to work and the discussions that emanated from the desire to open up suitable work other than governessing and needlework to women of this class. This chapter also encompasses a discussion of the debates around the need for training and education for women.

Chapter Two

ও

'Fit work for women'[2]

Working-class women and paid work in the mid-nineteenth century

Industrialization changed working patterns for women employed in areas affected by technological innovations. Before industrialization, most workers worked from home or in the homes of others, e.g. spinning, brewing, food production and clothes making.[3] During industrialization outwork, as it was called, became increasingly devalued and skilled areas of work, such as handloom weaving, were moved into factories and workshops and carried out mainly by men.[4] Further, since the seventeenth century, the practice of women undertaking skilled work alongside their husbands or in widowhood had declined.[5] Although women worked in factories alongside men, the work they undertook was regarded as less skilled and of less value than the work that men performed. So why were women less valued than men as workers during this period? Walby, focusing on the interplay between patriarchy and capitalism in the work-place, argues that shifting patterns of employment in the first half of the nineteenth century were the result of shifts in the accommodation of the needs of capital and patriarchy in certain key occupations. Trade unions and friendly societies in the early part of the century were largely skills- or crafts-based and used their ability to exclude women from apprenticeships and trade union membership to control the numbers of workers entering the trade which, in turn, kept up wages.[6] Women, from the sixteenth century onwards, were increasingly flexible, casual workers able to turn their hand to the particular task required rather than skilled workers. This was a weakness as it was impossible to organize workers not working in a recognizable trade at this time. However, women were unionized from the early nineteenth century in the cotton weaving industry. It is no coincidence that these women earned the best rate of pay and undertook similar skilled work to men in this sector. Walby further argues that capitalism and patriarchy do not always work in harmony over gender relations.[7] This is borne out throughout the period covered by this book. In the first half of the nineteenth century, there was a continuous struggle between the needs of capitalism for a cheap flexible labour force and patriarchal interests that wanted to maintain existing gender relations or, indeed, further the marginalization of women from the better paid sectors of the labour market.[8] This tension was played out in various arenas through a discourse of the domestic ideal. Women had very little formal power at the time. No vote, limited legal rights and limited access to education and training. All these factors contributed to the continuing and, indeed, growing limitations placed on women's employment opportunities. This was articulated in different ways in different employment sectors.

As previously mentioned, domestic service and its allied trade, laundering, needlework and other home-based work, factory work, agriculture and mining were the areas of employment where working-class women largely congregated. All these sectors were subject to public scrutiny to varying degrees and discourses developed which constructed ideal feminine types, which were used to dictate to working-class women what sort of behaviour and work was socially acceptable. Underpinning these discourses of women's work was the patriarchal assumption that a woman's primary role was domestic. Consequently, the further an occupation took a women away from domesticity and the behaviour associated in the public mind with domesticity, the more severely it was criticized. The language employed in these discourses did not always refer directly to a woman's domestic role. It was often expressed in terms of the moral danger women faced, especially if women worked alongside men or, as in mining, wore masculine work clothes. Working women's behaviour and demeanour was measured against norms expected of an idealized, leisured middle-class lady so any behaviour which was not passive or docile was deemed unfeminine, roundly condemned and used as a pretext to either limit or exclude women's participation in the occupation. This meant that domestic service and homework could be regarded as permissible areas of work but factory work and, more especially, working at the pit brow was not, especially if the woman was married.

Working women's responses to these public condemnations are difficult to ascertain as usually they were not asked for their opinion and the testimony we have is, of course, shaped by the context in which it was collected. Most of the testimony from working women concerning their work comes to us in the form of the government reports into women's work or from social investigators such as Henry Mayhew or Arthur Munby. As Hamilton, John and Sayer have demonstrated, testimony to Royal Commissions and other public investigations was shaped by the questions asked, the environment in which the evidence was given and how it was interpreted through the lens of middle-class investigators who had specific agendas.[9] Further, Walby has argued that the legislation produced by these commissions was the most organized form of patriarchal strategies of exclusion aimed at women during the nineteenth century.[10] Consequently, women's responses to these inquiries need to be analysed carefully as their replies might well have been shaped by the patriarchal mindset of the commission. Despite this, there are examples of women's resistance to the domestic roles assigned them. Both Sayer and John cite women who stated their preference for fieldwork or pit brow work over the only alternative available, domestic service.[11] Importantly, during the period 1840–70, there was no organized resistance by working women to the pressures exerted on them by social reformers and male trade unionists to work in certain gender-segregated or socially acceptable occupations, or to accepting whatever working conditions employers imposed on them. Consequently, we need to be especially wary of conclusions drawn from such scanty evidence. I shall now move on to examine the various sectors mentioned above in order to explore the range of work women undertook and some of the issues that these particular areas of employment raised.

Domestic service

In 1851, in England and Wales, more than one million women worked in domestic service and laundry work and more than 150,000 in Scotland. This figure increased to more than two million in England and Wales and 160,000 in Scotland by 1901.[12] However, these figures need to be treated carefully as Higgs has indicated that there have been problems over the definition of domestic work in the censuses.[13] As Horn has shown, domestic work took many forms, from the overworked maid-of-all-work in the household barely able to afford help to the hierarchical ranks of large country houses, so popularly portrayed in novels and television costume dramas.[14] Between these two extremes there was a wide range of work that fell into the category 'domestic service' and, consequently, the conditions experienced by servants were diverse. This range was huge from the housekeeper in a large house of the aristocracy to the scullery maid-of-all-work in a shop or private house. Furthermore, servants' status was linked to that of their employer and this affected the supply and demand for servants in diverse ways, depending on the location and social standing of the employer.

Living-in servants were usually girls and young women between the ages of 15 and 25. Older women living in were cooks, housekeepers or nannies. These groups were usually single women or, in the case of older women, possibly widows. Servants living out were chars and laundry

Figure 1 Nannies and fishwives.

Source: George du Maurier, *Punch*, 1866.

women, who tended to be married or widows. Servants who did not live in were renowned for their independence and would not tolerate the strictures of the living-in system. Although men were also employed in domestic service they were in a minority and domestic work was divided along gender lines. By the mid-nineteenth century women did most of the internal domestic work with male servants often in decorative roles, such as footmen, in large houses. Census returns indicate that certain members of households were categorized as servants of one kind or another, but the picture is more complex than it seems on first acquaintance. Higgs has shown that the number of women involved in domestic service recorded by the census is problematic, partly because of the varying definitions that covered the term 'domestic service' and partly because relatives employed to do domestic work were not always recorded as such. However, he also states that the blurring of boundaries between domestic and farm servants also makes precise figures difficult to ascertain. Only men were returned as farm servants, while women were returned as domestic servants even if they did farm work.[15] Of course, given the flexible nature of women's work, some women could have been employed as both, depending on the time of year.

Given the huge numbers of women employed in the sector and the variety of tasks it involved, domestic service is an important field in any study focusing on women's work. However, domestic service has not been an area that has produced a wide range of writing and Horn's 1975 study remains of central importance. There is plenty of scope for further research in this area, particularly local studies.[16] Most research around women's employment has focused on women's work outside of the domestic sphere, mainly in the factories. Labour historians of all political persuasions have seen this sort of work as the most important focus. An explanation of this might well be that historians specializing in women's history have tended to concentrate on areas where women have been ignored, even though present, and have sought to insert women's experiences into those areas. Gerda Lerner and others have called this type of research 'contributory history' and it is by far the most common approach.[17] As historians of men's history have not been particularly interested in writing about domestic service, there has not been a history that has needed to be rewritten to include women so domestic service has been, for the most part, overlooked. Furthermore, domestic service is largely absent from many of the archival sources that form the basis of a great deal of historical research; for example, in the large-scale reports and commissions that the state conducted in the nineteenth century into factory and other work. Moreover, as a predominantly unorganized sector, it is absent from the records of the Trades Union Congress. Choosing domestic service as an area of study entails researching alternative sources. Horn's study, for example, draws largely on the domestic archives of wealthy households, the census, written and oral sources of people employed in domestic service, life histories of employers and employees, household manuals, newspaper reports, letters to the press and advertisements placed by prospective employers – all fruitful sources for anyone embarking on a local study.[18] As Honeyman argues, it is an important area to study in furthering our understanding of the relevance of domestic service in women's social and economic standing at the time.[19]

Throughout the nineteenth century, domestic service was widely regarded as the ideal occupation for working-class women because the work satisfied dominant notions of the social order and the role of class and gender within it. Returning to Walby's six structures of patriarchy we can see why this was so. Women working in a domestic setting were firmly enmeshed in the Victorian bourgeois patriarchal family structure. The work they undertook was seen as of less value than the work male servants undertook and subsequently they were paid less. The work was strictly segregated so male workers did not feel threatened by women taking their jobs or being usurped as breadwinners. Women workers were under the strict control of their social betters and ultimately were answerable to the male head of the family or, in larger establishments, the butler or steward. Their sexual conduct was also regulated. Leisure time was very limited and the type of activity that was approved of by the employer excluded relationships with the opposite sex. The presence of 'available' young women within the household was morally problematic as there were instances of young women being sexually harassed by the male members of the employing family or their friends. Examples of these encounters were popular in nineteenth-century fiction and the story of the country servant seduced by the employer's son is a recurrent motif in a range of discourses, especially where class relationships were a focus. In most households 'followers', or boyfriends as we would call them, were at best discouraged and at worst forbidden. Servants were expected to follow their employer's instructions in most areas of life, including religion, though employers who were more liberal would not necessarily expect servants to follow the same denomination as them.[20]

However, this was the ideal and in reality working-class women resisted wherever they could, both within domestic service and by refusing to work as domestic servants if possible. Despite its popularity as suitable work for working-class women among middle-class commentators, domestic service was increasingly unpopular among working women, especially if there were other opportunities available in the area.[21] The 'servant question' was one that was hotly debated throughout the period before the First World War and returned as an issue after the war. So why were working-class women reluctant to enter domestic service? The industrial activist Clementina Black summed up the reasons why young, working-class women resisted domestic service. She suggests an alternative and less sentimentalized view of the work than that of Milne which was quoted in Chapter One:

> The conditions of domestic service are still those of an earlier industrial and social system, and this earlier form does not harmonize with the sentiments of today. In other employments, the person employed sells a certain number of hours of labour, and when those hours are over, all relations cease between employee and employer. The worker has, in short, a life of her own, absolutely apart from her industrial life. The servant has no such life of her own . . . She is at the beck and call from morning to night; her companions and her immediate supervisor are not of her choosing, and are not sympathetic. She is exiled from her family and from her personal friends. Smiles and civility are expected from her, whatever her mood or state of health, and whatever the conduct towards her of the persons with whom she is brought into contact . . . The domestic servant, in short, still lives under a state of total personal subservience. Now a feeling has gradually grown up that total personal subservience is intolerable and degrading; and it is this feeling which causes domestic service to be held in low social esteem by women who are often harder worked and less materially prosperous than most servants. The servant is despised, not because she cooks, or scrubs, or nurses a baby, still

less because she has to yield to orders – every factory worker has to do that in working hours – but because she consents to put herself permanently at some other person's beck and call.[22]

Horn largely concurs with Black's analysis of the 'servant problem' and points to the number of advice books and articles in journals that discussed the relationship between employer and domestic servant and tried to mediate in this problematic relationship. As the century progressed, employers increasingly had to look further afield for servants – to Irish immigrants, rural areas where there was a shortage of alternative employment or workhouse girls. Factory work, pit brow work and other manual employment all had their problems but many working-class women wanting a degree of autonomy preferred to work in these areas if they could, so the demand for servants often outstripped the supply. Moreover, Roberts notes that women who had been domestic servants tended to look for 'something better' for their daughters such as shop work or, if they could afford the training, elementary teaching. Higgs goes so far as to suggest that the rejection of domestic service by working-class women was also a partial rejection of the cult of domesticity and, one could argue, a challenge to the extreme forms of patriarchal control.[23] Whatever the reason for the resistance to domestic service on the part of working-class women, it was regarded as the most appropriate work for them to undertake. This resistance demonstrates that working-class women were not merely passive victims of patriarchy and capitalism but where possible made choices. Often these choices were limited, sometimes by location, i.e. living in areas where there was little other prospect of work; sometimes by low social status, for example girls from workhouses, or Irish or other immigrants.

Laundry work

Another area of work akin to domestic service was laundry work. Like domestic service, laundry work could be regarded as a feminine activity carried out in the domestic sphere. Malcolmson states that according to the 1861 Census more than 160,000 people were involved in laundry work in England and Wales and in some areas, 99 per cent of these workers were women. However, she goes on to point out that given the nature of the work, often seasonal and resorted to in times of need, the numbers of women involved in the work was likely to be far higher, since it was one of the occupations that was often not regarded as work when the census was completed. Also, category names and criteria changed from census to census so that it is difficult sometimes to separate laundry work from other domestic work.[24] Unlike domestic service, most of these women recorded in the census were married or widowed and, consequently, laundry work was one of the main paid occupations for older women. In the period analysed in this chapter, mechanization did not exist. The first mechanized laundries began to appear in London in the late 1860s.[25] Hand laundries were often small affairs requiring small capital outlay and therefore attractive to women either needing to supplement an inadequate male wage or, in many cases, to replace it. Hence, laundry women were often the main or sole breadwinners in the family. Other workers were itinerant, carrying out the work at the customer's home. Although laundry work was dispersed throughout the country, there were concentrations of the trade in large cities where a service industry was present: ports, university towns, spas and seaside resorts.

The public reaction to laundry work was mixed. On one level, like domestic service, it could be seen as appropriate feminine work, but on another level, it could be regarded as problematic because laundresses challenged normative feminine behaviour and the social order. First, they had a reputation for independence linked to their status as main or sole breadwinner and, even more worryingly they had a reputation for drinking and unseemly behaviour.[26] As the trade moved away from small workshops and individual laundresses to larger steam-driven laundries, regulation was seen as a way of not only regulating the trade but also regulating the behaviour of the women who worked in it. This move towards regulation led to a tense stand-off later in the century and will be discussed in more detail in Part Two.

Needlework and other home-based industries

Another area of work that was considered suitable for working-class women in this period was needlework, mainly dressmaking, tailoring and millinery. Again, the period 1840–70 was largely pre-mechanized and the needlewoman worked in a small workshop or from home. This added to needlework's suitability in the public mind. Hollis states that in 1861 it was estimated that more than 600,000 women were involved in needlework and dressmaking.[27] It was an overcrowded trade and, like laundry work, it is difficult to determine reliable statistics for the actual numbers of women involved. The work ranged from the high fashion apprenticeship-based dressmaking and millinery work, often pursued by lower middle-class women who needed to find paid employment, to slopwork, that is the cheap ready-made market, and rough work such as sack making.

The respectable end of the trade, dressmaking and millinery, required a period of apprenticeship and so was limited to the class of women whose family could afford to pay the premium of around £30–50 for a two-to-five-year apprenticeship.[28] Therefore, unlike laundry work, there were certain areas that were seen as suitable work for impoverished genteel women, such as embroidering and millinery.[29] However, like governessing, a lady would experience loss of caste by taking on paid work. Pennington and Westover argue that middle-class girls whose fathers could not afford to keep them before marriage, widowed clergymen's wives and clerk's widows were among the groups of genteel but impoverished women who surreptiously undertook sewing in order to keep their heads above water. They often sent their servants to fetch and return the work so that they could not be associated with the work they performed.[30]

The lower end of the trade was casual, seasonal and not unionized. Further, it was often associated with prostitution in the public's imagination.[31] Slopwork was carried out in small tailoring workshops or as outwork in the workers' homes; it is impossible to calculate how many women were involved in this type of work. During the nineteenth century needlework became synonymous with 'sweating', that is an area of work where 'a lack of capital investment, high rates and rents produced exploitation of an available pool of cheap female labour which helped stave off provincial competition'.[32] This made needlework one of the pressure points in the struggle between capitalism and patriarchy. Capital wanted a cheap, pliable workforce in order to maximize profits. Patriarchy, in the form of the male trade unions, wanted to protect their members against what they saw as a threat to gender order. 'Unskilled' women were seen by male tailors to be undercutting the wages of 'skilled' male workers. The unions further exacerbated this problem by banning women from their membership.[33] Pennington and Westover argue that although the invention of the sewing machine moved the mass clothing market into the factory in the last third of the century, there was still plenty of scope for sweating in tailoring and other specialist parts of the trade. Indeed, the invention of the sewing machine actually increased homeworking in this sector as the mass production of clothes meant that there was a great deal more complex finishing to do by hand by outworkers.[34]

Not all slopworkers were needlewomen but they were the most numerous and caught the attention of social reformers who, like the male unions, wanted to maintain the gendered status quo.[35] The exhausted, starving needlewoman became a symbol for the oppressed woman worker in the early 1840s following the report of the 1843 Children's Employment Commission, which drew a graphic picture of dressmakers as vulnerable, pathetic creatures enslaved by the whims of fashionable society and grasping middlemen.[36] This report caught the popular imagination and the plight of the needlewoman became the focus of discussion in radical and reforming circles, especially after Mayhew interviewed a range of needlewomen in his London survey.[37] Thomas Hood's 'The Song of the Shirt' conjured up an enduring picture of the poor, oppressed seamstress:

With fingers weary and worn,
With eyelids heavy and red,
A woman sat, in unwomanly rag
Plying her needle and thread
Stitch! stitch! stitch!
In poverty, hunger and dirt
And still with a voice of dolorous pitch
She sang the song of the Shirt:
"Oh, men, with sisters dear!
Oh, men, with mothers and wives!
It is not linen you are wearing out,
But human creatures' lives!
Stitch-stitch-stitch,
In poverty, hunger, and dirt,
Sewing at once, with a double thread,
A shroud as well as a shirt.
Seam, and gusset, and band,
Band and gusset, and seam,
Work, work, work,
Like engines that works by steam!
A mere machine of iron and wood
That toils for mammon's sake –
Without a brain to ponder and craze
Or a heart to feel – and break!"[38]

Like the investigation into mines, the Children's Employment Commission, which was supposed to report on child labour in workshops, warehouses and factories, broadened its remit to include women working in high-class dress shops and milliners. Rogers suggests that this was 'indicative of a wider infantilisaton of women workers as it sought to exclude women from certain types of work on the same grounds as children'.[39] There is no doubt that many needlewomen were exploited and lived either on or below the breadline. Rogers argues that the remedy in the 1840s was for social reformers and male workers, to speak on behalf of romanticized needlewomen in need of rescue rather than encourage autonomous workers to organize themselves. This was a convenient way to remove women from areas of trade that men inhabited and in which they were threatened by women undercutting their prices.[40] In other words, the figure of the downtrodden needlewoman was used as a trope for victimized womanhood in a society in need of reform rather than an oppressed worker in need of unionization. This powerful image drew attention to a much wider concern about working women and was arguably behind the moral anxieties about suitable occupations for all women. Behind the debates and handwringing about the downtrodden needlewoman was the fear that these women were a challenge to the idealized patriarchal social order.[41] This fear was two-pronged: first, women were not carrying out their natural duties of wife and mother if they were working all hours at slopwork and therefore presented a threat to the welfare of the working-class family; second, capitalists were using them as a cheap pool of labour. This undermined the honourable trade of tailoring, thus challenging the role of the male breadwinner. Added to these fears were Mayhew's revelations of the link between needlework and prostitution in slack periods. Inevitably, this heady cocktail of panics about the family, male roles and sexual morals made needlewomen obvious targets for state intervention in the form of state investigations and legislation to regulate the work.

Pennington and Westover state that the major home industries in the nineteenth century were clothing, boot and shoe making, glove making, hosiery, lace making, straw-plaiting, box making, carding, chain making, nail making and button making.[42] Statistics for these trades are hard to ascertain because, as with other trades, women did not necessarily declare the work on census returns and were not, especially during the period covered by this chapter, unionized. For example, Pinchbeck states that the census return for 1841 listed 1,638 women as button makers and 5,849 as glove makers but both these figures were an understatement. She also gives a figure of 10,564 for boot and shoe makers.[43] Pennington and Westover claim that there were 27,739 women involved in straw plaiting in 1861, rising to 45,720 in 1871.[44] This rise reflects the increasing number of women looking for work after the decline in women's employment in fieldwork following the 1867 Gangs Act, which is discussed in more detail later.

These trades tended to cluster in regions; for example, boot and shoe-making around Bristol and in Leicestershire, glove making in Dorset, Somerset, Herefordshire, Oxfordshire and Wiltshire, and straw-plaiting in East Anglia.[45] Pennington and Westover argue that there were four main conditions involved in determining whether women would be employed in one of these sweated home industries and where one or more of these conditions existed, employers found it relatively easy to employ a home-based workforce:

- They lived in an area where men's wages were especially low;
- Seasonal or casual work for men was common;
- There was no alternative work for women;
- There was a noticeable surplus of women.

They were also attracted to areas where there was a previously trained workforce.[46] Consequently, home-based industries tended to centre on rural areas although large conurbations, such as London, also had many women working in sweating trades. The work in London included clothing, box making, artificial flower making, matchbox making, sack making, fur pulling and umbrella making. In and around Birmingham there was the metal trade, including nail and chain making which was the main form of sweating, while in Leeds it was the clothing trade. As machinery took over certain processes, some of these industries moved into factories but, as previously mentioned, this did not necessarily mean that homework decreased. The mass production of some processes meant that more workers were needed to undertake others that were more complex, such as finishing in the tailoring and boot trades, at home. Also trades tended to run in families, with small girls learning the work at their mother's knee. As they took place in the home, most of these trades did not come under the scrutiny of the social reformers until later in the nineteenth century and where they did, it was under the auspices of the Children's Employment Commission of 1863. It was not until the 1880s that the conditions of homeworkers became more widely known and discussed so these trades will be discussed further in Part Two. However, the same cannot be said of the remaining groups of women discussed in this chapter, women whose work was considered unwomanly and consequently subjected to scrutiny and policing.

Factory work

From the early days of industrialization women worked in factories. Most were congregated in the textile mills of Lancashire and Yorkshire although they also worked in substantial numbers in other types of factories as mechanization progressed. According to Hollis, by 1851 635,000 women worked in textile factories throughout Britain, and textile manufacture was the second largest employer of women after domestic service.[47] Indeed, Walby states that in 1816 parliamentary returns indicated that men made up only 17.7 per cent of cotton operatives.[48] For women, work in the mills, although hard and the hours long, was better paid than anything else they could do. However, they were still paid less than men and were, therefore, a cheaper labour force to employ. Women had a long-standing involvement with textile production. In the proto-industrial period the work was segregated along gender lines with men doing the 'skilled' work and women doing the 'unskilled', lower-paid work.[49] The skill came not so much from the greater complexity of the work but from the authority that the man enjoyed over his family who were often his co-workers. The notion of the superiority of male workers and the focus on them as the main breadwinners was carried into the factory system and is another example of how patriarchy persisted in a modified form as the mode of production changed.[50]

27

Despite the gendered stratification of factory work, all sectors of the work were increasingly regarded as unwomanly.[51] Again, the principal reason given was that women were neglecting their domestic responsibilities by working in factories. In areas where the pre-industrial system of male handloom weaving was being replaced by factory-based female weaving, social commentators complained that the world was being turned upside down and a threat to the social order was imminent. Protestors were not only social commentators. Working men, evangelical Christians, a whole raft of social reformers and even women themselves attacked the practice of women working in factories. However, this attack was challenged. For a range of reasons, industrialists, liberals and working-class women and men defended working women, insisting that they were both necessary and needed to earn a living.[52] The low pay that women accepted pleased the factory owners. A sub-commissioner in 1833 justified the low pay of women thus:

> The low price of female labour makes it the most profitable as well as the most agreeable occupation for a female to superintend her own domestic establishment and her low wages do not tempt her to abandon the care of her own children.[53]

Women were also regarded as more docile than men who, in the early years at least, were not keen on the regulated atmosphere of the factory. Pinchbeck commented that 'Manufacturers seem to have been anxious to employ women wherever possible. According to Gaskell, men were "more difficult to manage", and more likely to cause trouble by their combination.'[54] However, the use of women's labour, especially married women's labour, destabilized the balance of capital and patriarchal interests. Pressure from male unions and social reformers keen on extending the ideal bourgeois family structure to the working class, meant that the government was forced to intervene. Walby argues that this tension between those who supported women working in factories and those who opposed the practice created a situation where access to factory employment became the source of a power struggle – between patriarchal and capitalist forces to control the sexual division of labour. Patriarchal interests prevailed, although there were concessions on both sides.[55] The resultant Factory Acts not only limited the number of hours women could work but also had the effect of further segregating them into the lower-paid sectors of the industry. This pleased both patriarchal and capitalist interests – working men had managed to exclude women from certain areas of work while securing shorter hours for themselves; and factory owners could still employ women at lower wages than men and have a stronger case for doing so. As they were refused entry to the skilled male unions, women had no real representation at government inquiries and the evidence produced reinforced the domestic ideal that privileged the model of the male breadwinner and his dependants. Walby argues that although the Factory Acts are usually seen as benign and progressive by historians, they enforced rather than diminished gender inequality. Further, Honeyman confirms this argument by claiming that the campaign for factory reform 'represents an early instance of the replacement of egalitarian strategies – which were constrained by sexual tensions within working-class communities – by a gendered rhetoric of domesticity in pursuit of working-class objectives.'[56] Protective legislation is discussed further in Chapter Six.

Importantly, these Acts only protected women in the factory workplace. As industrialization developed unevenly, many areas of production still took place in small workshops and workers' homes.[57] As mentioned earlier, Pennington and Westover argue that the transition from the domestic system to the factory system had significant implications for women, as outwork increasingly became an unprotected extension of the factory where women could be exploited beyond the reaches of the Factory Acts.[58] Consequently, thousands of women performed paid work within their own homes and this work had the tacit approval of social commentators and reformers for most of the century, as it did not take women into the public sphere. As Walby clearly argues, the exclusion of women from many sectors of the workforce and the disapproval of their presence illustrates that women's employment was located at 'the intersection of patriarchal relations and capitalist relations'.[59]

Let us look at the arguments leading up to one of the Factory Acts in more detail. The 1844 Factory Act limited working hours in factories to twelve hours and a further act in 1847 reduced hours to ten. These Acts affected the earning capacity of about 300,000 women and children.[60] Conditions in factories were not good for workers of either sex. Sanitation and ventilation were poor and accidents were common. The impetus for this legislation to restrict women and children's working hours was partly based in paternalistic philanthropy but was largely motivated by the prevalent idealized, domesticized image of women so dear to social reformers. It was also supported by male trade unionists fearful for their own jobs because women were paid half the male wage.[61] However, these reasons, poor conditions and women and children replacing male labour, were not enough to ensure success. Like the laundry women, female factory workers were regarded as de-sexed and likely to take on men's bad habits such as drinking. Lord Shaftesbury, in his speech on the Ten Hours Factory Bill declared:

> The females not only perform the labour, but also occupy the places of the men; they are forming various clubs and associations, and gradually acquiring all the privileges, which are held to be the proper portion of the male sex. These female clubs are thus described: – "Fifty

or sixty females, married and single, form themselves into clubs, ostensibly for protection; but in fact, they meet together to drink, sing and smoke; they use, it is stated, the lowest, most brutal and disgusting language imaginable" . . . What is the ground on which women says she will pay no attention to her domestic duties, nor give the obedience which is owing to her husband? Because on her devolves the labour which ought to fall to his share, and she throws out the taunt, "If I have the labour, I will also have the amusement".[62]

Note here that the work was not necessarily thought to be too hard for women. The message was that working in factories exposed women to influences that ran counter to dominant notions of correct feminine behaviour. Given that many of these women were married, they were also regarded as a bad influence on their children. This added fear of moral disintegration helped clinch public support for the Acts.

Patriarchal interests raised other concerns too. Sexual harassment of women by their male supervisors was widespread and it could be seen as another reason why it was felt that the factory was no place for a respectable working woman.[63] There was, however, no attempt to correct the behaviour of the men concerned. In a paradoxical twist, the sexual misconduct of one group of men, though not condoned, served the wider interests of the male workforce.

The Ten Hours Movement, ostensibly concerned with the exploitation of women and children, was also borne out of male fear that women and children were a cheap pool of alternative labour. The movement was also used as a lever for reducing male working hours as it would not be profitable to have employees working different hours in most factory production. Moreover, even though women gave evidence at the various commissions of the conditions in the factories, their testimony was used in such as way as to reinforce ideas that factory work was a threat to female virtues. Legislation could be justified as a tool for achieving an idealized, patriarchal status quo where men were the breadwinners and women stayed at home to look after the children and cater for their men.[64] As is discussed later, the early attempts to restrict women's work in certain areas would develop into an attempt to exclude them completely, especially if they were married.

Agricultural work

Women employed in agricultural work, especially fieldwork, were increasingly seen as a problem. According to the 1851 Census, 143,475 women were employed as agricultural labourers or residential farm servants. Women's participation in both agricultural work and as farm servants declined throughout the nineteenth century and had fallen to 58,112 by 1871.[65] These figures need to be treated as conservative. Like other areas of women's employment the actual numbers employed was probably largely underestimated in the censuses partly because of the seasonal nature of much of the work and partly because of the lack of clear definitions of the work performed.[66] The sector was segregated on gender lines and although women's dairy work was classified as skilled work, most women were segregated from male workers and were employed in unskilled fieldwork.[67] This work included fruit and hop picking, vegetable pulling, hoeing and haymaking. Much of this work was seasonal and therefore would not be regarded as employment for census purposes. Further, male wages were low so women were not seen as direct competitors.

The type of work undertaken and the conditions borne varied throughout the country. Women were regarded as a pool of reserve labour and different methods of drawing on this pool developed. For example, in East Anglia the gang system thrived while in Northumberland and southern Scotland bondaging was common practice. The gang system, which developed in the 1820s, involved groups of women and children, who were hired and supervised by a male overseer, working under contract to a farmer to complete a particular agricultural task. The gang usually had to work several miles from home and hours were long. Sometimes the gang would sleep in a barn on the farm if the work was particularly far away, but more often than not the gang had to walk several miles to and from work. Usually, the farmer paid the gangmaster who then paid the workers. Conditions were invariably poor and the welfare of the workers depended on the temper of the gangmaster. The work was done by the piece and if it rained, workers were not paid. The gang system was one of the issues that the Royal Commission on the Employment of Children, Young Persons and Women in Agriculture focused on and criticized. Although working conditions were harsh, the issues of immorality and women's absence from the home were particularly highlighted. Like factory work, fieldwork both in the gang system and as day labour was regarded as encouraging unfeminine behaviour. It was this as much as the severity of the working conditions that led to the 1867 Gangs Act which limited the employment of children, segregated the sexes and insisted that women's gangs were accompanied by a licensed female as well as the gangmaster. These limitations meant that the gangs eventually died out and patriarchal notions of suitable women's work prevailed.[68]

Sayer argues that, unlike the gang system, bondaging was not seen as an 'evil and corrupt' system even though the practice had connotations of serfdom. Bondagers were contracted to work by the farmer by the year and were often employed as a family unit where women's labour was part of the contract. Again, women were regarded as cheap labour but under the control of a male relative and therefore not a threat to the patriarchal order.[69] The different attitudes towards the gangs and bondagers can be seen from the way they are commented on in the reports of the Royal Commission, as the following extracts illustrate:

> In a gang of such a character it necessarily follows that even those who were steady and respectable when they joined it must be corrupted. When the gang is mixed, where I mean males and females work together, the evil becomes greater. The dress of the women is to a certain extent almost of necessity immodest. When the crops are wet they tuck up their dresses between their legs, often leaving their legs much exposed. . . . Thus a girl who is when she joins these gangs modest and decent gradually loses her modesty.[70]

Compare this extract with a description of women bondagers doing similar work, that is hoeing, picking crops, hay making, etc:

> The Northumbrian women who do these kinds of labours are physically a splendid race; their strength is such that they can vie with men in carrying sacks of corn, and there seems to be no work which affects them injuriously, however hard it may appear. . .[71]

Women's participation in agricultural work had been declining throughout the first half of the nineteenth century as farming practices changed and enclosure meant the loss of common land on which many poor people, particularly women, relied.[72] However, not all women who lived in the country worked in agriculture. As already discussed, many working-class countrywomen worked as domestic servants or in rural crafts such as straw-plaiting, lace making or glove making.[73] Most of these crafts were carried out within the home, away from the public gaze, to supplement rather than replace male wages. They could therefore be considered as suitable occupations and were encouraged by social reformers as an alternative to field work. They also represented the sort of rural idyll that informed Victorian romanticization of country life.[74] Consequently, these women workers did not constitute a threat either to dominant notions of femininity or to the male breadwinner. Many others worked in domestic service and often had to move away from their native area in order to find work. This became increasingly common as the century progressed due to the decline in women's participation in fieldwork and the increasing difficulty of finding urban working-class women willing to work in domestic service when other types of work were available. Consequently, rural women were forced by rural poverty into the towns to fill the shortage in the domestic service sector.

Like the urban factory worker, the fieldworker, especially if she was married, was regarded as a social problem. Fieldworkers were constructed as 'bold, wild and independent of their parents' in much the same way as factory girls were.[75] As Sayer argues, field women contravened middle-class notions of respectable femininity and consequently represented a threat. They swore, tucked their skirts up and laughed aloud. They also worked in public and preferred this work to domestic service. There was an implicit anxiety about fieldworkers' sexuality being out of control. Bondagers, however, were less visible and regarded as under male control.[76] The publication of the 1867 Report was accompanied by commentary in the press. The gang system was particularly reviled and notions of the rural idyll depicted in art and novels of the time were severely knocked by the findings of the Commission. However, in the end it was not necessary for the state to ban women from the work altogether as women's agricultural work declined throughout the second half of the nineteenth century and consequently became of less importance.

Mining

Of all the areas of work that were deemed unsuitable for women, mining was arguably the area that caused the greatest public uproar.[77] Not surprisingly, it was an early target of social reformers who sought to exclude women from working underground in the 1840s. As John has shown, women had worked in coalmines for hundreds of years without comment. Like other pre-industrial trades, the work was organized on a family rather than an individual employment basis and consequently women and children were a common feature underground. Although the practice was already in decline by 1840, the employment of women in the mines varied from district to district and it persisted in western Lancashire, parts of Yorkshire, South Wales and eastern Scotland.[78]

Working conditions were poor and the work was hard but, like other occupations deemed unsuitable for women, the moral risk to women and girls was emphasized in the Report of the Children's Employment Commission in 1842. This commission, which was ostensibly set up to report on children's labour, gave rise to all sorts of lurid fantasies about working underground. Not least were the references to hell and the likelihood of unimaginable (or all too imaginable) and unspeakable practices taking place in the subterranean tunnels of the coal mine. The work did not accord with public notions of femininity: it was dirty, often involved crawling on hands and knees and the heat meant that workers were often half-dressed. Illustrations accompanying the report showed women hauling trucks by a chain which passed between their legs. Such images shocked Victorian sensibilities and the language used to describe the work carried out by women was hardly objective:

> Chained, belted, harnessed, like dogs in a go-cart – black, saturated wet, and more than half *naked* – crawling upon their hands and feet and dragging their heavy loads behind them, they present an appearance indescribably disgusting and unnatural. [Emphasis in the original][79]

As Hamilton has argued, the tone of the report was one of brutalized, debased womanhood hardly thought possible in a Christian land which put woman on an ideological domestic pedestal and charged her with the guardianship of the country's morals.[80] Like the later report on field women, mining women were seen as bold and unwomanly and it was felt that even modest girls would be contaminated by the work. More importantly, mining women were seen as lacking the domestic skills to run a home and keep their husbands from the public house. An article that set out the thinking of social reformers and male trade unionists concerning future legislation appeared in the *Ten Hours Advocate*, the organ of the Lancashire Central Short-time Committee, a working men's organization, in 1846:

> Upon the passing of Lord Ashley's Act, [to exclude women and children working in mines] an almost instantaneous reformation took place. The women, being kept at home, have become tidy, respectable, and the colliers' houses are clean and comfortable. The taste for drink is gradually giving way. . .
> . . . a Scottish agricultural labourer, with his wife at home, and with two shillings a day, is infinitely more comfortable than a mill-spinner with double the amount of wages, but whose wife is engaged along with himself all day in the mill.[81]

Although women's testimony to the commission denied these accusations of domestic ignorance and sought to assure their inquistors of their moral probity, the overriding representation of mining women was at best unwomanly and at worse completely debased. Consequently, despite concerns about the lack of alternative work for women in many of the mining areas, and against the wishes of those concerned, who only wanted the worst of the employment conditions and practices removed, women and children were excluded from working underground in mines. This had dire consequences for families where no other work was available. As a result, in South Wales the law was sometimes evaded. In other areas, they were still allowed to work at the pit brow but this too was to become the subject of protective legislation later in the century.[82]

To sum up, patriarchal notions of gender roles in society underpinned the discourses around working-class women's paid work. Working-class women had a long history of work in the sectors discussed above. Industrialization had moved some areas of work out of the home and into the factory. Once this happened, the work was regarded increasingly as unwomanly, particularly if women were seen to be replacing male workers. Social investigators and male trade unionists often used the patriarchal discourse of the male breadwinner and the woman homemaker to justify excluding women from work that men perceived as theirs by right of their sex. Pressure groups formed and various investigations took place. These often lumped women's and children's work together. Rather than focusing on the poor conditions experienced by all workers, their reports were more concerned with fantasized moral dangers that women were purported to face. Increasingly, women were being urged to conform to social norms and restrict their field of labour to domestically situated work. If they needed to work in a factory, it was regarded as an unavoidable necessity to be undertaken before marriage, in segregated areas and at lower pay rates to the male workforce. Once married, a working-class woman was expected to concentrate on her family and, if obliged to work, undertake work in the confines of her home. It is telling that the only sector of work that escaped scrutiny in this period was domestic service as this was the sector favoured as suitable work for all women who needed paid employment.

ã▲

The problem of the 'superfluous women'

By the 1840s, the ideal role for women in British society was that of a wife. Girls' education was therefore focused on that goal. While it was acceptable for working-class girls to undertake paid work, especially in domestic service before marriage, the middle-class girl was expected to stay at home helping her mother with light domestic duties and visiting. So dominant was the idea that marriage was the middle- and upper-class woman's sole goal that single women were seen as failures, a social problem and labelled 'superfluous women'. The *Saturday Review* voiced colourfully, if somewhat provocatively, the views of many when it declared:

> Married life is a woman's profession; and to this life her training – that of dependence – is modelled. Of course, by not getting a husband, or losing him, she may find herself without resources. All that can be said of her is, she has failed in business; and no social reform can prevent such failures. The mischance of the distressed governess and the unprovided widow is that of every insolvent tradesman. She is to be pitied; but all the Social Congresses in the world will not prevent the possibility of mischance in the shape of broken-down tradesmen, old maids and widows. Each and all are frequently left without resources; and each and all always will be left without resources; but it would be just as reasonable to demand that every boy should be taught two or three professions because he may fail in one, as it is to argue that all our social habits should be changed just because one woman in fifty – or whatever the statistics are – is a spinster or widow without any resources.[1]

The *Saturday Review*'s unsympathetic view of women who had 'failed in their business' was harsh but not so far from the truth of how single women were regarded. For most middle-class women, the failure to find a husband did relegate them to an inferior position within their family where, if they were fortunate, they could play the part of companion to elderly parents, nurse to sick relatives and children and participate in some philanthropic work. If, however, the family could not afford to support an unmarried woman, she would have to find a way to support herself. The respectable occupation for women who found themselves in this unenviable position was governessing, or possibly working as a paid companion. Even so, undertaking these jobs would involve a loss of status because the woman would be working for money. This signified a double failure, first on the part of the woman to find a husband and second, a failure on the part of her family to provide for her and allow her to remain a leisured but respectable lady. Consequently, many regarded paid work as a last resort to be undertaken when all other avenues of support had been exhausted.

Some women would find work that could be undertaken within the confines of the home and therefore disguise the need for paid work as far as possible. For example, running a small girls' school in their home, needlework, other fancy goods work, literary work or taking in lodgers would fall into this category.[2] However, these occupations either required some capital or a home of one's own (for example, running a school or taking in lodgers) or the income would be so precarious that it would be impossible to live on (for example, needlework or literary work), especially if the woman had dependents.[3] Although single women usually engaged in these occupations, married, widowed or separated middle-class women also took them up in times of need. There is a need for more regional studies to ascertain the scope of middle-class women's paid employment especially in their own businesses.[4] However, whatever work middle-class women undertook, they had to maintain the semblance of a leisured existence to the public gaze. Other women, for example shopkeepers, farmers' or clergymen's wives and daughters, would be involved in family businesses. However, as they were not usually paid cash for this work, this group of women did not figure in the debate around whether women should undertake paid work and the sort of work that was acceptable, and so is beyond the scope of this book.[5]

The impetus to campaign to extend opportunities of work for middle-class women came from several sources. The 1851 Census revealed that as many as 30 per cent of all English women between the ages of twenty and forty were unmarried. Although some of these would eventually marry, it was estimated that around one million women would never marry. It was these women, who had 'failed in their business', who caused anxiety in the media.[6] The 'Redundant or Superfluous Women Question' was widely discussed at the time and an article by W. R. Greg set the anxious tone of the debate:

> There are hundreds of thousands of women – . . . proportionally most numerous in the middle and upper classes – who have to earn their own living, instead of spending and husbanding the earnings of men; who, not having the natural duties and labours of wives and mothers, have to carve out artificial and painfully-sought occupations for themselves; who, in place of completing, sweetening, and embellishing the existence of others, are compelled to lead an independent and incomplete existence . . .[7]

Greg felt that it was unnatural for women to work and those doing so were denying their true nature. Greg's answer to the problem was emigration of these 'surplus' women to the colonies to find husbands amongst the thousands of unwed male settlers. Some women followed this course, but their experiences are beyond the scope of this book.[8]

Both social reformers and feminists discussed the condition of those unfortunate women who found themselves unsupported yet unprepared for the world of work. Although these activists saw emigration as one possibility for single women they did not regard it as the only one, nor did they necessarily see marriage as the only alternative solution. They looked to improve women's education so that they would be equipped to participate in a wider range of suitable employment possibilities, i.e. those areas that were deemed respectable as employment for middle-class women. These women were the focus of a sustained campaign. However, before looking at the campaigns to widen employment opportunities, I shall look briefly at governessing and teaching, the main employment areas open to middle-class women, and why these occupations were regarded as problematic from the middle of the nineteenth century.

Suitable paid work for single middle-class women: governessing and teaching

The most important asset that a governess had was not her teaching ability but her status as a lady. This was her capital. The attraction of governessing was that, although the lady lost status through working for money, the work took place in the private sphere, under the patriarchal control of the head of the family and was therefore regarded as acceptable in times of acute hardship. Her main duty was to look after the younger children of both sexes and to instruct older girls in their role as young ladies.

Consequently, the cultural capital possessed by the governess was important, especially if the employers were the newly rich and lacked the cultural capital commensurate to their economic wealth.[9]

According to Neff, more than 20,000 women were listed as governesses in the 1851 Census.[10] Again, this was possibly a conservative figure as the role of governess could well overlap with other domestic work, or the governess could be a poor relation of the employer, and therefore not visible in the figures. The hours were long, the pay appalling – as little as £10 per annum plus room and food and not usually more than £20–30 – and job security was non-existent. Low pay was a particular problem if the woman had a dependant, such as an elderly relative to support. However, despite the conditions and low pay, governessing was an overcrowded occupation because there were hardly any alternatives and the skills required were generally minimal. In addition to low pay was the indignity of being too low in status to be part of the family and too high to participate in servant life. Consequently, the governess lived in lonely isolation, taking meals with the children and often undertaking other domestic work such as mending and nursing. Length of service depended on the caprices of the employer and there were cases of children harassing their governess out of her job. If the governess did not receive a good reference or as she aged, it would be impossible to find work and she was not entitled to a pension from her employer even if she had worked for the same employer for years.

Despite the article on 'business failure' in the *Saturday Review*, governesses evoked a certain amount of middle-class public sympathy. The image of the downtrodden governess caught the public imagination in much the same way as the victimized needlewoman. Because the work was womanly, the governess was regarded as a victim rather than an unruly hoyden. She was the heroine of novels such as Charlotte Brontë's *Jane Eyre* and the figure of the governess appeared in many other novels, such as Mrs Gaskell's *Ruth*.[11] The governess also caught the media's imagination and *Punch* led a campaign to relieve governesses of the exploitation they suffered.[12] Importantly, they were also the focus of some of the early campaigns of the Victorian women's movement.

In 1841, the Governesses Benevolent Institute was founded to assist older governesses who could no longer find work and who had no savings to support themselves. Women aged over fifty who were no longer able to find work overwhelmed the institute.[13] Moreover, it was soon apparent that the main problem for these women who drifted into the work because there was no alternative, was that they lacked not only teaching skills but also the education that would enable them to do any other suitable work. The feminist journal the *English Woman's Journal*, saw the governess question as a central plank in its campaign to raise the standard of women's education and broaden work opportunities. An article, based on evidence collected by the Governesses Benevolent Institute, set out the position clearly:

> What is the position of a governess? She has none. While engaged in a family . . . she is infinitely considered less than the servants; she has no companionship whatsoever; very frequently, not a syllable is addressed to her from week's end to week's end by the members of the family as if she were in disgrace. . . . The servants have their hall and their social pleasure; the governess is condemned to solitude . . . Let those parents who qualify a daughter for the *genteel* office of governess, reflect a moment on *how* she is looked upon by her superiors and inferiors. . . .
>
> At thirty-five or thirty-six she is cast aside like a blunt tool, young enough to see long years of penury ahead, yet too old to learn fresh employment . . . Servants are often pensioned off . . . not so the governess.
>
> Once more we earnestly entreat parents not to doom their daughters to the wretched life of governesses. Give them a trade. Do not be led away by insane ideas of silly pride.[14] [Emphasis in the original]

Campaigners wanted not only to open up new sectors to women workers, but also to improve the training in an area of work already open to women – teaching. Girls' education was seen as vital in the employment campaign and it was apparent to many reformers that existing educational methods were not giving girls an adequate education. Ill-educated governesses and teachers in girls' day and boarding schools were not able to raise educational standards. In response to this problem Queen's College was opened in 1848 and the more radical Bedford College in 1849. One of the paradoxes of the history of education is that the elementary education offered to working-class children was more closely scrutinized and the teachers better trained than the education offered in the fee-paying schools that middle-class children attended. As already mentioned, middle-class women in need of an income often opened small girls' schools in private houses. The Taunton Commission which investigated middle-class schools in the 1860s found that these schools were woefully inadequate both in the material conditions of the premises and the quality of teaching that took place. Like governesses, these untrained teachers were expected by parents to inculcate ladylike qualities in young girls rather than educate them for work. However, the Taunton Commission encouraged a new type of girls' school and more professionally minded teachers who were part of the campaign to transform girls' education in the latter part of the nineteenth century.[15]

The education of working-class children in working-class schools was one of the areas of employment to which some reformers turned their attention.[16] From the early nineteenth century, working-class children had been taught in Sunday schools, dame schools and monitorial schools. Daughters of the clergy often ran Sunday schools. Children were taught how to read the Bible and received general religious instruction. This sort of work was seen as philanthropic and therefore not paid. Dame schools were run by working-class women mainly as a childminding service for parents of children too young to work. For a small fee, children were taught to read and write and sometimes skills such as knitting and straw-plaiting. Monitorial schools were managed by religious societies. Classes were very large so the monitor system was used whereby older, bright children assisted the teacher as monitors. The teacher taught the monitors how to teach and they, in turn, taught the younger children. In 1846, a state-financed pupil-teacher system was brought in. Children aged 13–18 were trained to teach and those who passed the scholarship examination were offered subsidized places at elementary training colleges. This system was to open up the possibility for intelligent working-class girls, and boys, to train as teachers in elementary schools. Before the development of this system, child monitors usually left for other employment rather than train as teachers. The new system meant that students could attend college for as little as £3 per annum so girls from the better paid strata of the working class – daughters of skilled workers, small farmers, upper servants and trades people – could afford to send their daughters to these colleges.

Widdowson argues that the pupil-teacher system had the effect of moving the work of elementary teaching from a sector where a variety of social groups participated to one where the majority of teachers came from a working-class background. She argues that the system favoured working-class women. First, the system accommodated certain working-class traditions where young women, like their brothers, would be apprenticed at an early age. Working-class families would not object to sending their daughters out to work at thirteen, whereas middle-class families aspiring to gentility would not want to train their daughters until marriage was considered unlikely. Second, the work would be deemed too strenuous for daintily brought-up young ladies; and third, many parents would not like their daughters mixing with the labouring poor in the schoolroom as this could mean a further loss of status.[17]

In 1858, the Newcastle Commission investigated elementary education and began a debate about the class background of elementary teachers. Some reformers, interested in widening the employment opportunities for middle-class women saw the employment of middle-class teachers in elementary schools as having two advantages. First, the teacher would be properly trained and able to earn more than she could as a governess or teacher in a small girls' school. Second, she would be able to inculcate middle-class values into her charges and therefore 'raise' moral standards.

Angela Burdett-Coutts, the wealthy philanthropist, wrote a letter to the *English Journal of Education* making the case for more middle-class elementary teachers:

> from among that large and respectable portion of the middle class upon whose means the burden of education for their children presses heavily, few, comparatively, cause their children to be trained as National schoolmistresses. The government plan for educating and providing Mistresses for Elementary Schools appears generally overlooked, more especially by the friends and guardians of young persons left orphans . . . Not only is the remuneration larger, and the social position better, than that which many occupations confer, but there is in the Teacher's office a wide field for the exercise of ability for a good purpose, to promote which many young persons; labour at the expense of much self-denial.[18]

A reply in the *Journal* poured cold water on this idea and illustrates a wider attitude to middle-class women's employment, i.e. that it was always seen as a last resort:

> Excellent as the training colleges are, we doubt the wisdom of encouraging young ladies to seek entrance to them . . . They would marry the Clergyman or the Squire or their sons in nearly every parish they went to . . . The only obstacle to this now is the low birth of the present order of College trained schoolmistresses: and this Miss Burdett-Coutts' plan would remove. It would obviously be a great abuse to use public money to educate the future wives of men of fortune . . . Moreover her plan would deprive the girls of industrious poor parents of a post of usefulness . . . It is for the same homes and stations that they are intended to train their scholars; and they will do this all the more effectually because it is work in which their own lives have practically experienced them.[19]

Evidence given at the Newcastle Commission supported both sides of the debate. Patriarchal attitudes influenced these positions. Some witnesses felt the work unsuitable for middle-class ladies because it brought them into contact with the lower classes, others felt that working-class teachers offered a negative role model to working-class girls, encouraging them to pursue a career rather than follow a more domestic role as wife and mother.[20] The idea that pursuing a career might be a positive move was not discussed.

In the end it was the low educational attainments of middle-class girls which precluded them from entering teacher training colleges during this period. Following Burdett-Coutts' suggestion, an experimental examination was set up by the government to ascertain whether middle-class girls could pass the Queen's Scholarship that would-be elementary teachers needed to take. The results were disastrous and the idea was quietly dropped. However, as Widdowson points out, the experiment indicated the low level of education offered to middle-class girls in the mid-nineteenth century and this was brought sharply into focus ten years later when the Taunton Commission excoriated many of the schools catering for middle-class girls.[21] The opportunities for middle-class women to follow a career were so narrow, it is not surprising that paid work was one of the earliest foci for the emergent women's movement from the 1850s onwards.

Widening spheres: the opening up of employment opportunities for middle-class women

If the campaign to open up elementary teaching to middle-class women was unsuccessful in the 1850s, the women's movement was more successful at opening up the debate around middle-class women's education and campaigning to widen employment opportunities. As already mentioned, the campaign to improve middle-class women's education went hand-in-hand with the campaign to widen employment opportunities. The main instigators of these campaigns were a group of women who met at a house in Langham Place, London, or who were connected with its national network. These women became known as the Langham Place Group or Circle.[22] The group campaigned on a wide range of related issues but this chapter focuses on the campaigns around paid work. One of the leading campaigners was a young woman of independent means and radical ideas, Barbara Leigh Smith, later, following her marriage, known as Barbara Leigh Smith Bodichon.[23] In 1857 she wrote a seminal paper challenging patriarchal assumptions about women's relationship to work in which she made a claim for women's human right to work, denied that working for money robbed women of respectability and refuted the assertion that working women would take work from men. Subverting the dominant evangelical religious discourse on women's role, she made a case for work being a woman's duty as a human being and, in doing so, attacked attitudes towards gender difference of the day:

> Our duty in this world is to try and make it what God intends it shall become: we are his tools . . . To do God's work in the world is the duty of all, rich and poor, of all nations, of both sexes. . . . Women must, as children of God, be trained to do some work in the world. Women may not take a man as God: they must not hold their first to be towards any human being. . . . Fathers have no right to cast the burden of support

of their daughters on other men. It lowers the dignity of women; and tends to prostitution, whether legal or in the streets.

. . . Most of the work of the world must be done for money. It is of the utmost importance to make that work 'stuff of conscience'. To make all work done for money honourable is what we should strive for.[24]

Having made the claim that it was women's right to work, the activists associated with Langham Place set about developing a campaign to open as many suitable occupations for middle-class women as they could manage. They did this through articles in journals, including their own, the *English Woman's Journal*, which Bessie Rayner Parkes and Barbara Leigh Smith began in 1858, and through the organ of the National Association for the Promotion of Social Sciences (NAPSS), a progressive organization sympathetic to their cause.

In 1859, the Langham Place Group also established a campaigning organization, the Society for the Promotion of the Employment of Women (SPEW) situated initially at Langham Place. This eventually developed into a network of regional branches where they had sympathizers in provincial towns, such as Brighton, Gateshead and Nottingham. Jessie Boucherett and Adelaide Ann Proctor began this organization but Proctor soon retired because of ill health and Emily Faithfull replaced her.[25] SPEW had the support of NAPSS and by October SPEW had affiliated with it at the NAPSS annual conference in Bradford. This affiliation meant that men sat on the general committee which comprised twelve men and twelve women. Lord Shaftesbury was its first president. The women members included some of the leading names associated with Langham Place – Anna Jameson, Bessie Rayner Parkes, Adelaide Ann Proctor, Jessie Boucherett, Emily Faithfull and Isa Craig. Other prominent feminist activists sat on the committee over the years – Millicent Fawcett, the suffrage leader and Frances Buss and Emily Davies, educational campaigners, were all committee members at some point. Here they served their apprenticeship in platform speaking. For many years NAPSS was the only forum where women could speak in public as it was not considered a respectable activity for women. Contemporary journals, such as the *Saturday Review*, satirized women who dared to flout this convention.[26] However, this access to a public space gave women a wider platform than they could have otherwise hoped for and helped them to propagandize their causes. Women ultimately controlled this society: by 1867, 80 per cent of the society's subscribers were women. Men primarily lent it respectability by the weight of their names. This was so effective that Queen Victoria consented to becoming SPEW's patron.[27]

SPEW represented the first practical effort to prepare middle and lower middle-class and educated working-class women for wider employment opportunities and to provide apprenticeships and technical training for women in fields already open to them. This demonstrates that the Langham Place Group's interest extended to issues that concerned not only their own class but those of less privileged women and that activists appreciated the importance of training for all women. However, it also demonstrates that they were very sensitive to the nuances of class and that training had to fit a woman's social station. This strategy, they believed, meant that women would be able to find work fitting their social position and prevent overcrowding in 'genteel' occupations such as needlework and governessing.[28] Consequently, their attack was mainly focused on the patriarchal structure of employment practice and not on the class structure of the country.

Law copying was one of the first occupational experiments that SPEW set up. In 1860, Susan Maria Rye established a law stationer's office at 12 Portugal Street, Lincoln's Inn, to train women clerks in copying legal documents. Once trained, the women hoped to find work. This proved difficult because, predictably, male workers opposed the move and threatened to quit if women were employed.[29] Nevertheless, reports in the *Englishwoman's Review*, the successor to the *English Woman's Journal*, indicate that the operation continued, ultimately as a private concern, for at least twenty years.[30] Similarly, in 1861, Jessie Boucherett established and managed a business school for girls near Fitzroy Square to teach young women bookkeeping and accountancy to equip them with the skills they needed in work as cashiers in shops. The work was an uphill struggle because girls' numeracy was very poor, but added fuel to the campaign for the improved education of middle-class girls.[31]

Printing was the most publicized trade that SPEW engaged in. The NAPSS investigation into women's employment suggested that printing was a suitable employment for women but felt it might be too difficult for them even though there was a history of women working in the business.[32] Bessie Rayner Parkes did not agree and she bought a small printing press on which she and Emily Faithfull learned the rudiments of the trade. Faithfull resigned her post as secretary of SPEW and became the driving force behind this campaign. In 1860, she founded the Victoria Press with the practical help of Austin Holyoake, brother of the radical George Holyoake.[33] SPEW did not finance this enterprise but did provide the apprenticeship fees for five girls. Faithfull also employed some older women who were already skilled compositors.[34] She employed men to do the heavy manual work which fuelled the male printers' argument that women were not suited to printing and were cheating men out of their rightful work.[35] However, she also experimented in improving working and sanitary conditions to challenge the argument put forward to exclude women from the trade, namely that printing was an unhealthy occupation.[36] Women worked an eight-hour day and were paid £1 per week.[37] The commitment of feminists to improving working conditions indicates a determination that women should earn a fair wage for a fair day's work and that they were not against protective legislation per se but felt it should embrace all workers and not specifically women.

Despite, or because of, these improvements and the success of the Victoria Press, male printers were extremely hostile to the company. The print trade was an overcrowded one and men were fighting a battle to retain control of the trade by jealously guarding their skills. Further, the making of gender is a social process and, as Cockburn has argued, there was an ongoing social project in the nineteenth century to construct 'men as strong and capable, manually able and technologically endowed and women as technically and physically incompetent'.[38] It was a project to which most men and many women were prepared to subscribe. Consequently, the practice of employing 'girls to do men's work' undermined both their ideas of masculinity and, importantly, their bargaining power.[39] Emily Faithfull described some of the ways that male printers harassed girl apprentices:

> their frames and stools were covered in ink to destroy their dresses unawares, the letters were mixed up in their boxes, and the cases were emptied of 'sorts'. The men who were induced to come into the office to work the presses and teach the girls had to assume false names to avoid detection, as the printers' unions forbade their aiding the noxious scheme.[40]

The National Union of Printing and Paper Workers did not admit women members until 1904.[41] Such hostility to women workers in trades that men regarded as peculiarly theirs was not new and was to continue into the twentieth century.[42] Whenever men thought that women were trespassing on their territory, they would use all their powers to resist the incursion. Patriarchal interests consistently superseded class solidarity on these occasions.

Faithfull became the Printer and Publisher in Ordinary to Queen Victoria, but a divorce scandal severely hampered her work in the women's movement and from 1864 she played a low-key role. However, when Emma Paterson began her campaign to unionize women, Faithfull encouraged her and became one of the first women members of the Women's Protective and Provident League (WPPL). She also joined Paterson in setting up the Women's Printing Society which printed the *Englishwoman's Review*, the *Women's Union Journal* and *Transactions of NAPSS*. The movement of feminists into trade union organization is discussed in Part Two.

During the 1860s, the numerical influence of SPEW was small, but amongst the growing number of women concerned to open up women's employment and challenge stereotypes of femininity, it served to offer a beacon of hope for the future. Further, as Jordan has argued, even in areas that SPEW did not promote, employers came to recognize that employing women could be advantageous.[43] As in the debate about women working in factories, capital and patriarchy were in conflict over the issue of women workers. During this period, SPEW also continued to focus attention on the need for women's education and training and the problems that confronted women entering the male-dominated and male-defined public sphere of the workplace.

SPEW was not just concerned with opening up employment for middle-class women. Concern for more training for women pervaded the *Englishwoman's Review* whether the women were upper-class ladies wanting to use their artistic skills by taking up glass engraving or altar painting or workhouse girls being trained to be servants. Writers vigorously examined 'the servant question' and made interesting proposals to alleviate the problems of obtaining good reliable servants. In this debate the middle-class readership of the journal were employers rather than marginalized women workers. Writers observed that the daughters of skilled workmen, who formed the traditional servant class, became dressmakers or factory workers because the life of a servant no longer appealed to them.[44] Of course, as the employing class they did not celebrate working-class women's rejection of domestic drudgery or consider it as a step forward in the women's cause. Obviously, the lack of mechanical aids in housework at this time meant that no one would voluntarily give up servants to take on the work themselves. Further, little thought seems to have been given to new methods of domestic organization and this did not occur until the supply of servants practically dried up in the early twentieth century.[45] Instead, they looked to ways of improving working conditions for servants rather than questioning the ethics of servitude. Writers also cited cases of sexual harassment and cruelty and called for employers to regard young servants as apprentices. Throughout these earnest arguments, the writers viewed the work of the servant as an honourable trade and they castigated mistresses who treated their servants badly, in the same way as a bad industrial employer would have been criticized. This is interesting because, although the writers would not consider this work suitable for ladies, they regarded it as skilled women's work and demanded that it should be treated as such. This was an argument taken up later, for example, by the Women's Industrial Council, which established the Association of Trained Charwomen. When considering work for working-class women, the emphasis was on improving conditions and wages and the need for training to refute the argument that women were inferior workers.[46] However, class rather than ability, aptitude or gender, was the baseline for deciding which sort of work was suitable for women. In many ways, the constraints of gentility were as limiting as the constraints of femininity in the endeavour to open up areas of employment for women. However, just as men had more power to negotiate boundaries in patriarchal discourse, middle-class women had more power to negotiate the boundaries of class. This intersection of class and gender could have led to some interesting and radical thinking about how roles were defined. However, more conservative thinking dominated the women's movement,[47] a fact that becomes evident when examining debates about roles and who should perform them. This issue is discussed in Part Two.

Another area of concern for feminists was the increasing trend to group working-class women with children and legislate against them doing certain work or restricting the hours that they could work. As we have already seen, the effect of acts such as the 1842 Mines Act, the 1844 Factory Act and the 1847 Ten Hours Act was two-edged. The long working hours and horrific working conditions suffered by employees rightly appalled humanitarian reformers, but these conditions applied to both sexes. Feminists working for SPEW argued that legislation that restricted the working conditions of women only was prejudicial. They believed that this legislation prevented women from competing with men and deprived them of work opportunities. This was indeed true and male unionists were quick to realize that restrictive legislation based on sex was an effective way of excluding women from work they considered their domain.

The arguments put forward in favour of protective legislation were that legislation would exclude women from certain unsuitable work and reduce their hours in other jobs. As we have seen, supporters of legislation often sought to emphasize the moral danger for women when working in the public sphere and in 'unwomanly work'.[48] Taking an 'equal rights' stance, feminists pointed out the hypocrisy of these arguments. For example, in the debate around women agricultural workers the *Englishwoman's Review* rejected the arguments of moral danger that the protectionists made. One woman retorted: 'The occasional immorality of female workers in the field, in manufactories, in domestic service and elsewhere is preferable to the wholesale immorality of those who have no work, and consequently no honest means of earning their bread.'[49] Contributors produced statistics to show that female agricultural workers were no less healthy, more impoverished nor more likely to resort to crime than women in other work. For example, 1 in 556 agricultural workers against 1 in 313 seamstresses would go to prison. The article concluded:

> If then, legislative interference is required to abolish the employment of women in agriculture, on account of the danger of agricultural work to women, these other occupations [needle, domestic and factory work] require abolishing more urgently. If it is required on account of crime and immorality, there are two or three other occupations which require to be abolished previously. When seamstresses, the

shoemakers and bookbinders have been put an end to, it will be time to begin thinking how to prevent women from being employed as agricultural labourers. . . . we hope there will be no interference with the employment of adult women nor with the employment of girls, except such as may also be applied to boys with the view of obtaining for them the means of education. Any further interference would be an act of oppression towards the women.[50]

As stated earlier, although 'equal rights' feminists opposed protective legislation aimed specifically at women, this did not mean that they were against protective legislation per se. Instead they argued that women, like men, should organize to improve their terms of employment. This argument recurred at later points in the right to work debate and will be revisited in Part Two.

So how effective was SPEW in opening up new areas of work for women? In 1879, the annual report of SPEW claimed that the forthcoming census would show that the scope of women's employment had increased and they claimed responsibility for this increase.[51] It is indeed evident that some trades and the white-collar sector were beginning to open the door to women workers. However, it is difficult to claim that this was due solely to the efforts of SPEW. Some historians argue that all SPEW did was encourage young women to take up positions that employers were already offering.[52] However, Jordan suggests that SPEW also encouraged employers to use young women to fill the gaps created in the burgeoning white-collar sector. She uses the case of the introduction of women into librarianship to demonstrate that women's movement propaganda aroused employers' interest in women as employees. However, although librarianship was not one of the professions on which SPEW focused, the society's discussion of women's employment had raised consciousness about women as potential employees. This was felt most markedly in the field of commercial clerical work.[53] It does seem that the propaganda work of SPEW was important in influencing employers by encouraging them to think about new groups of workers. However, it remains difficult to substantiate its influence across the board. To do this, more research is needed both in the various trades and professions of mid- to late-nineteenth-century Britain and in local studies of SPEW's work.

Conclusion to Part One

As we have seen so far, during the period 1840–70 women's employment was in transition. The dominant assumption that women's role was domestic was gaining acceptance in some parts of society while, at the same time, was being challenged in others. Industrial reform meant that women's employment opportunities were being increasingly proscribed, or at best, limited to a narrow range of domestic-based areas. Patriarchal imperatives were restricting women's employment opportunities in several directions. The exclusion of women from trade unions meant that they were unable to challenge paternalistic state intervention in employment. This exclusion placed them at the mercy of well-meaning reformers who were so imbued with the patriarchal notion that women's work should be confined to the domestic sphere that they could not see that most working-class women needed their industrial position strengthened rather than weakened. Male workers were reluctant to intervene because they could see advantages in excluding women from areas of employment that they regarded as their own, although this meant that women were often used by employers as a tool to undermine male workers. Moreover, the concept of the male breadwinner and dependent wife and children bolstered their demands for higher wages and reinforced the notion that a woman's role was primarily domestic.[54] At the cultural level, women were bombarded with images of the domestic idyll and condemned as unfit mothers and wives if they left their homes to work. Unorganized, over-burdened working-class women found it difficult to resist this push to confine them to domesticity. Social reformers were keen to keep the lower classes in order and, working from an assumption that women's role was as guardian of family morals, they sought to replicate the middle-class patriarchal family structure and relationships within the working classes. Although it was not considered reprehensible for working-class women to earn money, the ways they did so had to be limited to certain areas which reflected their domestic roles. The ideal paid work for working-class women was domestic service or certain types of needlework. Very few people saw other work as desirable for them but among the dissident voices were some social activists who were part of the nascent women's movement. This movement was beginning to form a critical, if limited, analysis of women's position in society during this period. Consequently, alongside their campaigns to widen their own employment opportunities they spoke up against the limitations being placed on working-class women's employment.

Middle-class women who needed to work were in no better position than working-class women as they were mainly shoehorned into the limited but respectable field of governessing, whether they had the aptitude for teaching or not. Middle-class girls' education was focused on finding a husband rather than preparing for the world of work, although women still offered unpaid support to many family businesses. Those women who could not find a husband or who did not want to marry were in a precarious position if not economically independent. The 'superfluous woman' question was much debated during the 1850s and 1860s. Single women were depicted as surplus to society, a nuisance and a failure rather than an asset, so emigration was suggested as one way of eliminating the problem. However, many feminists and other radical reformers felt that the answer lay with offering girls a better quality education that would prepare them for work if they did not find a husband or preferred to work. Campaigners developed a two-pronged strategy to improve women's employment opportunities, first by agitating for improved education and training for girls by reforming secondary education and opening up college and university places to women and, second, by arguing for women to be allowed to take up positions in suitable employment sectors such as teaching, clerical work and the professions. One of the ways they did this was through the propaganda work of SPEW.

Part Two examines how increasing state intervention in the workplace affected working-class women's working conditions and the type of work that was available. The growth of women's organizations, which developed during the period, and the ways that they represented working women's needs is also considered. Finally, Part Two focuses on the implications of improving girls' education for employment issues and the types of work middle-class women occupied.

Part Two

1870–1914

So far as I remember in days gone by the only lines of employment open to girls and women were: teaching, assisting in a shop, dress-making; or bar-keeping. In these days, there is hardly an occupation, or even a profession, into which a girl may not aspire to enter. Typewriting provides a living for many thousands, perhaps hundreds of thousands. There are women newspaper reporters almost as numerous as men. Accountants and bookkeepers crowd the trains morning and evening, going to and from their work, while many branches of postal, telegraph and telephone work are entirely managed by women, as also are photographic studios. Sixteen years ago, the A.B.C. refreshment rooms were in their infancy. Now they are counted by the hundred, each with a staff of from ten to fifteen girls. Hardly a district but has a lady doctor, and some of these have risen to great eminence.[1]

Despite the upbeat tone of the above piece published in the *English-woman's Review* in 1904, it would be wrong to assume that the history of women's work in Britain is one of untrammelled progress and success. On the one hand, employment opportunities slowly began to open up for single middle-class women and the better-educated sections of working-class women. However, on the other hand, the growing influence of domestic ideology on workplace legislation and on working-class aspirations to a stay-at-home wife, meant that working-class women were seeing their range of work possibilities narrowing and that the numbers of married women participating in paid work was gently declining. As mentioned earlier, there are problems with using census returns and other official data relating to women's employment in this period because under-recording and changing job definitions skew statistical data. Sweeping generalized statements, based on national statistics, can also obscure regional variations and therefore need to be treated with caution.[2]

Overall, Roberts suggests that women's participation in paid work declined from 31 to 27 per cent in the period 1871 to 1891 in England and Wales and from 28 to 27 per cent in Scotland.[3] However, percentages do not demonstrate the actual increase in numbers of women working. In terms of recorded numbers, the main sectors employing women were still domestic service, dressmaking and textiles for working-class women and teaching for middle-class women. However, new sectors also came into the equation: nursing, shop work and clerical work in particular, and these were areas that attracted both working-class and middle-class women. Holcombe suggests that in England and Wales there was a huge increase in the employment of middle-class women in the period 1881–1911. This meant a rise of 161 per cent (from 427,000 in 1881 to 1,114,000 in 1911), whereas the increase in the employment of working-class women in the same period was 24 per cent (from 2,907,600 in 1881 to 3,687,000 in 1911).[4] Similarly, Rubinstein states that the number of middle-class women involved in paid employment increased from around 12.5 per cent in 1881 to around 23.5 per cent in 1911 and for working-class women there was a decrease from around 87.5 per cent to around 76 per cent.[5] The 1881 Census indicated that the number of women employed in textile industries had fallen. This does not necessarily mean that young working-class women were not working. The more ambitious ones might well have been turning to the increasingly popular occupations of shop and clerical work. In domestic service, the numbers of adult women servants was rising and the number of girls declining. However, although younger women were turning away from domestic service if they could, generally, most women workers were young and single. Clara Collet compiled an important report in 1896[6] which indicated that around 68.5 per cent of women in the workforce were aged between fifteen and twenty and overall women formed around 30 per cent of the total workforce,[7] a figure that Hakim asserts did not change for most of the twentieth century.[8] Holcombe backs these statistics by stating that in 1911 the percentage of unmarried workers over the age of ten was around 77.5 per cent, another 14 per cent were married and 8.5 per cent widowed.[9] As mentioned in the previous chapter, working-class girls living in northern industrial areas, where other work was more plentiful and often continued after marriage, regarded domestic service as an employment of last resort. In rural areas, where alternative work was less available, domestic service was the prime employer. Collett suggests that marriage was regarded as an escape from such employment.[10] Further, Jordan argues that in many regions women were enduring the worst of chronic underemployment, especially in areas of heavy industry.[11]

Part Two of the book focuses on some of the changes wrought on the terrain of women's paid employment from 1870 until the outbreak of the First Word War. The areas examined are the development of women's industrial organizations, some of the main debates and campaigns that they were involved with and how these affected some of the key employment sectors that women participated in. Chapter Four will focus on the development of women's organizations that focused on protecting women's work and investigating the conditions in which work was undertaken. These will include the Women's Protective and Provident League (WPPL) and its daughter and granddaughter organizations, the Women's Trade Union League (WTUL), the National Federation of Women Workers (NFWW), the Women's Trade Union Association (WTUA) and the Women's Industrial Council (WIC). The degree to which these organizations represented women's interests and helped women achieve economic independence and fair conditions is also considered.

Chapter Five will discuss some of the main issues that came out of the debate around women's work in the last third of the nineteenth century, focusing in particular on debates around equal rights, married working women, women factory inspectors and protective legislation. The question of whether women should campaign for equality with men or whether they should be treated differently in the workplace taxed feminists in these years. A movement that began to increase the range of work available to women developed, for some, into a crusade for equal rights, while for others it became a campaign to protect women from the worst excesses of a capitalist industrialized society. This equal/difference debate manifested itself in a range of issues and campaigns that affected all classes of women. The introduction of women factory inspectors was one instance of how women could be seen to be entering the male world. However, it was middle-class educated women who were employed, rather than working-class women with practical experience. So despite women's demands for equality, some women felt that class was an important difference too. As the earlier notion that marriage was the only career for women was slowly eroded, the right of women to work after marriage remained stubbornly contentious. Although marriage was still the ideal, the argument for the necessity of educating middle-class girls by those who had campaigned so vociferously in the preceding decades had largely won over enlightened circles. It was generally conceded that some women would never marry and might well need to work. However, women's right to work after marriage was problematic and was resolved in patriarchal terms by a marriage bar in most of the professions and in other areas of work too, if the market could stand it. Further, working-class women who needed or wanted to work after marriage increasingly became an issue of concern and a focus in the campaign to decrease infant mortality and morbidity. The question of married working women was also linked to the debates around protective legislation.

Chapter Six will survey the main occupations women undertook and examine some of the issues that arose for particular trades and occupations. Protective legislation, or the lack of it, is one particular issue;

sweated labour and girls' education were two others. Whether girls should receive the same education as boys or whether they should receive a different one was hotly debated. For example, this debate divided campaigners attempting to open universities to women and led to Girton and Newnham Colleges at Cambridge being established by opposing camps. By the 1890s, the position of unmarried women had changed to such a degree that a new stereotype of the 'New Woman', a liberated single woman who had a career and eschewed marriage, appeared. To what extent this stereotype existed in reality is questionable, but she was very different from the downtrodden governess of the 1840s and 1850s. The rise of the new middle-class woman worker employed in offices and shops and the way they were perceived by the public and state will also be considered.[12] For other groups of workers of this class, such as nurses, professional recognition was an issue that could divide or unite women. Finally, Part Two examines the new representation of single women that developed in the 1890s, the New Woman, and discusses the relevance this had concerning attitudes towards working women.

Chapter Four

ﻪ

Women organizing
Trade unions and other industrial organizations

Although there was sporadic union activity involving women before the 1870s, there were no systematic attempts to organize women in trade unions. The antagonism of working-class men towards women factory workers developed and hardened throughout the century. Women were increasingly regarded as a threat to male working practices and this perception was often justified when cheap unorganized female labour was used by employers to break a strike or simply to replace men. However, there are instances in the mid-nineteenth century of women supporting male workers during industrial action and sometimes this support involved campaigning for higher male wages so that women did not need to work.[13] As the 'woman question' became more prominent from the middle of the century onwards though, attention turned to the conditions of women workers as well as the rights of women to be able to work. SPEW was just the first of several organizations that emerged in the last third of the nineteenth century which focused on women's employment. The perception of a common bond with working women led some to form a movement that aimed to help the working-class woman fight for her industrial rights. This not only involved opening up new areas of work for women but also campaigning to ensure that women were treated fairly by employers. Further, as male workers were often antagonistic towards women workers and excluded them from unions or did not represent their interests even when they were unionized, some women decided that they needed their own unions, which not only represented women in trades dominated by women workers but also represented women's interests in male-dominated areas. The organizers in the early days concluded that women should protect themselves through unionization rather than protective legislation. The emphasis on women organizing to help themselves was common to all the organizations focused on in this chapter in the period 1870–1914. This changed after the First World War and the reasons for this will be discussed in Part Three. The Women's Protective and Provident League (WPPL) was the prime mover in putting the unionization policy forward. The WPPL was superseded by the Women's Trade Union League (WTUL), which was less sanguine about trusting to unionization to cure all working women's problems and looked to protective legislation to improve women's employment conditions. By 1914, women's organizations such as the Women's Industrial Council (WIC) were organizing surveys, collecting data and lobbying Parliament on a whole range of issues affecting women's work. In this chapter, I focus on the development of these organizations which sought to organize women workers, fight for women's employment rights and ultimately to investigate employment sectors in which women were already engaged.

Women's Protective and Provident League

The Women's Protective and Provident League (WPPL) was formed by a group of trade unionists and feminist sympathizers following the appearance of an article by Emma Paterson in *Labour News* in June 1874.[14] Paterson, who had already worked as a teacher and a bookbinder before becoming a speaker for the suffrage movement, was a secretary for the Workingmen's Club and Institute Union and had recently returned from a working honeymoon in America where she had seen some successful examples of women's trades unions.[15] In the article, Paterson cites the case of a woman who had starved to death despite being in work. She argued that blaming employers who paid starvation wages was counterproductive because they were just responding to market forces. It was 'the present isolation of working women [which] reacts injuriously on their prospects in many indirect, as well as direct, ways'.[16] Her remedy was unionization. Taking an 'equal rights' stance, she argued that until they organized, women would always be at the mercy of their employers and working men would continue to regard them as a depressant to men's wages. Further, she did not agree with male unionists and other 'benevolent persons' when they argued that women needed protective legislation like children:

> the idea that women are entirely unable to protect themselves, [is] a position to a certain extent, degraded and injurious.
>
> Women, more than ever, urgently need the protection afforded by combination, as it is possible that, if these suggested restrictions

become law [Factory Act], further legislation in the same direction may be proposed, and at present the women affected by it have no means of making known their collective opinion on the subject.[17]

The WPPL was to be a mixture of a friendly society and trade union. The aim was to educate working women in the benefits of union solidarity. Paterson argued that a general union was just a first step:

It must be borne in mind that the main object in view is to accustom women to the idea of union. If this object is once gained more elaborate plans may before long be found necessary, and, as a knowledge of the strength of each trade in certain localities is arrived at, classified unions of women will be more practicable.[18]

The WPPL was established with Paterson as its secretary. Several leading feminists, such as Millicent Fawcett and Emily Faithfull, were on its committee over the years and their views on women's work dominated the League's policy. In practice, the London-based WPPL never became a national general union; rather it developed as an umbrella organization to promote trade unionism among women working in a range of skilled activities, such as bookbinding, tailoring and upholstery work.[19] In fact, the committee assiduously omitted to use the words 'trade union' in its title to avoid antagonizing potential wealthy supporters. This act also engendered suspicion among some male trade unionists who were quick to dismiss the League as another middle-class philanthropic endeavour, a charge that Paterson would dispute fervently.[20]

During the next few years, Paterson held meetings among the skilled women workers in London and elsewhere. In a paper read at the Social Science Association Congress in Glasgow in 1874, she made a strongly feminist argument for women to receive equal pay for equal work with men:

It is said that men are PAID HIGHER WAGES than women because they have FAMILIES TO SUPPORT, but no one ever proposes to pay single men lower wages than married men. WOMEN ARE OFTEN LEFT the sole protectors of, and providers for themselves and their CHILDREN, OR THEIR AGED OR INFIRM PARENTS; yet their earnings are insufficient not only for the support of a family, but also, in many cases, for the bare subsistence of one person.[21] (Emphasis in the original.)

This was a persistent argument amongst feminists and one they repeated continuously. Further, Paterson refuted the usual reason given for women's low pay, that is, their lack of skill, by quoting a manufacturer whose evidence to the Home Secretary in a deputation in favour of the Factory Acts appeared in *The Times*: 'Skilled women whose labour required delicacy of touch, the result of long training, as well as thought-fulness, received from 11/- to 16/- and 17/- per week whilst the roughest, unskilled labour of a man was worth at least 18/-.' She also indicated that sexual harassment was a problem for isolated women and that unionization would give them the power to eradicate this 'evil'.[22]

So from the earliest days of the WPPL, its members were challenging patriarchal practices by calling for equal access to work, equal pay, a recognition of women's skills and an end to sexual harassment. All these were issues of concern in the twentieth century too. However, in the twelve years that Paterson led the WPPL, the League was never able to organize the mass of women workers into trade unions. There were several reasons for this. First, there was the problem of trying to organize women from above. Apart from Paterson and one or two of her co-workers, the committee of the WPPL was made up of well-to-do ladies who had little practical knowledge of the lives of women they sought to represent. This allowed male trade unionists to dismiss them as 'Lady Bountifuls' and, more seriously, gave the men an excuse to refuse representatives from the WPPL access to the Trades Union Congress for several years.[23] The composition of the committee also meant that they did not have any industrial experience nor did they consult with workers before forming policy, a fact that will be discussed more fully later. Second, women's wages were so low that it was difficult for them to fund even the smallest subscription. Third, many young women were influenced by the dominant patriarchal ideology and regarded work as an interlude between school and marriage rather than a lifetime career or trade. Consequently, they were not overly concerned about changing conditions if they felt that, personally, they were treated fairly.[24] Fourth, most women did not work in skilled trades, or rather trades that were recognized as skilled. As already discussed, many worked in small sweated workshops or from home, or changed jobs so frequently that it was hard to monitor them. These various factors meant that women were hard to organize into unions based on the traditional male union model and, like many unskilled male workers, remained beyond the scope of most trade unions during this period.[25]

Women's Trade Union League

After the death of Emma Paterson from diabetes at the early age of 38, the WPPL was adrift. The secretaryship fell to socialist women: first, tempo-rarily to Edith Simcox, the secretary of the Shirt and Collar and Underlinen Makers Society and then to Clementina Black.[26] These appointments indicate that the WPPL was trying to break with the liberal, 'equal rights' politics of Emma Paterson.[27] Black's involvement with the women's movement sprang largely from her interest in Fabian socialism.[28] However, Black's appointment was short-lived. Despite her energy and commitment to touring the country trying to drum up support for the WPPL, she left after two years to form the more socialist-leaning Women's Trade Union Association (WTUA), which is discussed later. For Black, unionization was not enough to change working women's lives. Her involvement with the Fabians and her career as a writer taught her that investigation and inquiry were the key elements in gaining theoretical knowledge of the conditions of workers and that without this knowledge change was impossible. Black's socialist ideas were anathema to those on the WPPL committee who still subscribed to principles of an entente cordiale between employer, worker and consumer and had taken exception to the word 'union', let alone socialism, even appearing in the name of the organization.[29] The WPPL had wanted to foster amicable relationships between the employer, employee and consumer and did not want to disturb the status quo at any cost. Black's involvement with the flamboyant socialist Annie Besant, during the Matchgirls' Strike in 1888, heightened tensions within the WPPL. The *Women's Union Journal* reported the strike and Black and the Reverend Stewart Headlam, another member of the WPPL, spoke at the initial strike meeting. However, the WPPL committee voted to take no active part in the campaign beyond boycotting the firm's matches.[30]

Despite this setback in challenging the old guard, the WPPL changed its name to the Women's Trade Union and Provident League (WTUPL) in June 1889 and soon dropped the word 'Provident'. Along with the change in name, there was a change in policy. In 1889, Lady Dilke, the League's president, sought to capitalize on her extensive political network and proposed a scheme for the affiliation of provincial unions to the WTUL. Under this scheme, the WTUL offered affiliation, for a small annual fee, to any trade union admitting women to its membership. Mixed unions took up this offer and the WTUL expanded steadily. By 1895, twelve unions had affiliated to the WTUL, which meant that 8,000 women were members.[31] However, this was still a mere drop in the ocean when it came to the total number of women members of all trade unions which, excluding teachers and professional workers, rose from around 37,000 in 1886 to around 118,000 in 1896.[32]

By the end of the century, the aims of the WTUL were very clear. First, it existed to support the organization of women's trade unions or to strengthen existing ones around the country. Second, it acted as a repre-sentative of women trade unionists at parliamentary committees and other legislative bodies. It also undertook to support members in complaints of breaches of factory and public health legislation. Finally, it offered members a social space by helping them to establish working women's clubs such as the Paterson Working Women's Club which met at the League offices in London.[33]

By 1899, the WTUL had moved away from the WPPL position on protective legislation, much to the chagrin of older feminists such as Jessie Boucherett and Helen Blackburn. However, the WTUL still pursued the social aims of the old WPPL and education remained central to its policy. The growth in organization in the provinces meant an increased demand for women speakers and organizers. The WTUL adopted a scheme of annual tours by which organizers could visit districts periodically where women were trying to organize, to offer help and encouragement. Sometimes, it would be the men's union who would approach the WTUL and, at other times, the women themselves. Less commonly, local reformers would approach the WTUL, especially when the workers seemed too dispirited to help themselves. The organizer would call a meeting at a local club or meeting room, and later, when working-class women were more commonly employed as organizers, at the factory gate. The organizer's task was to enumerate the benefits of unionization and help in the early stages of establishing a union.[34]

In 1892, the WTUL adopted the practice of employing working women as organizers. The first paid organizer was Annie Marland. These women were not elected representatives of unions but were appointed by the committee of the WTUL and later, the National Federation of Women Workers. This practice did nothing to enhance ideas of democracy and empowerment amongst union members. The choice of the committee would not necessarily reflect the wishes of the membership and later on led to the appointment of educated women rather than industrial women.[35] There had been an attempt in Paterson's day to pay her as a full-time organizer, but she had strenuously rejected this idea, arguing that it would undermine the personal commitment of the organizer.[36] No further discussion appears in the annual reports of the WTUL explaining why they adopted this new strategy, but the answer may lie in the problem of class tensions. Rubinstein suggests that Lady Dilke decided to employ Marland following a speech she made at the Women's Liberal Federation in 1891 in which she defended unions against the charge of trying to limit women's employment.[37] However, it is possible that Marland was employed as an experiment – one that was to prove successful and lead to the employment of more working-class organizers. First, the committee probably realized that there was resistance from working women in accepting advice from educated women who had no 'hands on' industrial experience. Nevertheless, unpaid middle-class women did continue to tour, but spoke to organized meetings in halls rather than at the factory gate. Second, the type of help given by some middle-class ladies was considered dubious. Ben Tillett attacked 'Lady Bountifuls', who took up disputes with employers and negotiated with them on behalf of their less 'able' working sisters, leaving the workers to feel grateful and dependent on the largesse of such women. Tillett's argument, like those of many supportive Labour men, challenged equality advocates, regarding them as at best rather misguided philanthropists. He argued that the methods of 'Lady Bountifuls' did not teach working women organizational skills and so they remained in the same vulnerable position they occupied before the dispute.[38] Following on from the older WPPL practice of trying to encourage able working women to become involved with the organization of unions, the committee of the WTUL was bound to be sensitive to such criticism. Under the leadership of Lady Dilke, it was increasingly willing to accept a certain amount of change, although the overarching hierarchy of a middle-class executive deciding policy remained in place.

Liddington and Norris make a further interesting point on this use of working-class women as organizers in the trade union movement. They argue that it proved a great help to the suffrage movement, as these women were often speakers for both causes.[39] Annie Marland does not appear to have been involved in any suffrage work but Helen Silcock, Julia Varley, Sarah Reddish, Sarah Dickenson and later Ada Nield Chew were all active trade unionists and suffragists.

Women's Trade Union Association

Olive Banks has argued that the late nineteenth century saw shifts in the ideas of the British women's movement as socialism re-emerged.[40] A new cohort of feminists developed which included women who were more interested in the ideas of the socialist Fabians than of liberalism. Of course, not all socialist women were feminists, for example, Beatrice Webb who was the leading British socialist woman writer of the time. However, many attempted to apply socialist ideas to women's issues, especially those around women's work. These social feminists, unlike equal rights feminists, developed a class analysis that denied the notion that women formed a class because they were all oppressed by men. They argued that the oppression of women was class-based.[41] That is, they tried to develop a class analysis of patriarchy.[42]

With her departure from the WPPL, Clementina Black became involved with New Unionism, which gathered force through the success of the Matchgirls' and Dockers' Strikes. Socialist women such as Black saw the possibility of organizing unskilled women in unions. Black reported:

A vast impetus to the cause of unionism among women was given by the success of the match-girls, and by the formation, under Mrs Besant's able guidance, of their numerous union.

Within the last month a new group of workers has arisen in this field. Some ladies anxious to take advantage of the interest created by the dock-labourers' strike in order to aid the working women of East

London, called together a little meeting and came to the conclusion that trade unions were the only remedy. They took counsel with the members of the Strike Committee [of the Dockers' Strike] and it was agreed to hold a large meeting in the East End to begin with.[43]

In October 1889, the Women's Trade Union Association was established along lines very similar to the WTUL. The aims of the Association were to establish autonomous, self-supporting Trade Unions that supported campaigns for protective legislation. However, after much discussion it was agreed that funds would not be used to support strikes.[44] At first glance, it would appear that the aims of the two organizations were the same and only differed in the type of worker they focused on, that is, the Women's Trade Union League concentrated on the more skilled trades. However, the real difference in the two organizations, and this may have been one of the reasons why they decided against amalgamation, lay in the WTUA's support of campaigns for protective legislation. This was a radical break. There was a vociferous campaign by the feminists linked to SPEW and the Vigilance Association against legislation that might hamper women's entry into the employment market. Paterson's adherence to the 'fair field and no favour' stance of equal rights advocates' opposition to protective legislation at the TUC blocked more interventionist members of the WPPL. As previously mentioned, the WTUL under Lady Dilke did support protective legislation but, in 1889, it was still adhering to its old policy. The debate continued over the years and two of the protagonists were the older equal rights feminists like Boucherett and the social feminist Black.[45] This debate is discussed later.

Mappen argues that the decision of the WTUA not to use funds to support strikes not only protected its meagre funds from depletion but also indicated the middle-class nature of the organization.[46] The latter part of her argument is true only up to a point. The committee of the WTUA largely consisted of working women representing unions, wives of union men and middle-class socialists as well as a few sympathetic men. Included in the first category were the Hickses, mother and daughter, and Clara James who were active members of the Social Democratic Federation as well as the WTUA and, later, the Women's Industrial Council. Amie Hicks, like Black, believed in the early days of the WTUA that it was possible to organize unskilled women provided they had the appropriate help – that help being 'hands-on' training in organizational skills.

In the *First Annual Report* of the WTUA Black wrote of some rope makers who had conducted what she described as an orderly and non-violent strike for higher pay:

It may be added that the women working in this factory have had the reputation of being some of the roughest workers among the east end workers but the members of the Association have found in them a most encouraging power of discipline, self-control, and quiet determination. Nothing indeed is more hopeful than the capacity for self-government, business management and orderly concerted action which the Association has found to exist among East End working girls. In the East End, at least, there is no lack of ability, but only of training.[47]

Like the WTUL and WPPL before it, the aim of the WTUA was to help women to help themselves. Strikes were not necessarily the best way to improve women's working conditions, but strikes did sometimes lead to organization.[48] However, it soon became evident to the organizers that although it might be possible to organize the militant rope makers, who tended to be concentrated in specific firms, it was impossible to reach the women scattered throughout the workshops and cellar rooms of the East End who were often working on a casual basis when the family fell on particularly hard times.[49]

Despite the enthusiasm of its organizers, the WTUA never succeeded in becoming anything more than an umbrella organization for a tiny number of women workers prepared to risk their jobs by joining a union. By the time the *Fifth Annual Report* was published the writing was on the wall for the WTUA:

> The WTUA has spent another year, the fifth of hard work; and the Committee in issuing their Annual Report, feel that they can point to valuable results. So far this is satisfactory; but honesty compels the admission that, though the work done has been good and useful, it has not been the specific work which the Association was formed with the object of doing. It must be owned, without any effort to minimise the facts, that the Association has tried during 1894, as during previous years to form Trade Unions of women workers, and that it has almost entirely failed.[50]

Such an admission of failure must have meant bitter disappointment for this small band of dedicated activists. However, in the same frank vein, the report continued to catalogue its list of failures for that year and some of the committee's conclusions on these failures. When the Tailoresses' Union was amalgamating with the Tailors' Union, the WTUA blessed this combination, arguing in a way contrary to their earlier thinking that:

> This form of Union is in the opinion of the WTUA, by far the most hopeful variety of organization for women. It is in the trades where men and women work together that women have the most opportunity of understanding the principles and details of Trade Unionism.[51]

On Clara James's futile attempts to organize East End box makers, the report concluded that although the girls were too afraid to join a union, her activities were not all in vain because her

> work among them has resulted in the accumulation of a mass of facts respecting the industry, and of the remedying of serious grievances not hitherto brought to light. . . . The collapse of the Union did not conclude Miss James' efforts among the boxmakers. She has constantly been among them as they go out to dinner . . . and gathered much information which will by-and-by be put into a systematic form.[52]

She was more successful with her musical drill classes at the Girls' Club. Consequently, the People's Palace opened a class two nights a week for factory workers. The report commented, "a little roughness and lack of discipline was somewhat feared by the founders, but such fears proved quite uncalled for. The class is overflowing, and is pronounced perfectly successful."[53]

Thus, the fate of the WTUA was sealed. The formation of women's unions was left to the WTUL, which was also rethinking its policy and would become less at odds with the leadership of the defunct WTUA. In future, investigative work, the promotion of Girls' Clubs, where breaches in factory laws could be monitored, and campaigning for amelioration of working conditions through state legislation became the priorities for the newly established Women's Industrial Council (WIC). However, placing women unionists at the mercy of their trade union brothers in mixed unions and relying on the patriarchal state where women had no formal representation to control work practices meant that the WIC was doing little to challenge the patriarchal order even if it was keen to confront capitalism.

Women's Industrial Council

At the inaugural meeting of the WIC in 1894, Frances Hicks suggested that one of the aims of the new body should be to establish specialized committees to organize inquiries into various industrial issues. In response, Clementina Black moved that

> in the opinion of this conference it is desirable that a central council shall be established to organize special and systematic inquiry into the conditions of working women, to provide accurate information concerning those interests, and to promote such action as may seem conducive to their improvement.[54]

A large majority carried the resolution and the WIC was born and con-tinued its work until at least 1917. The WIC had an explicit feminist aim. In 1914, Lucy Papworth-Wyatt, the WIC secretary, wrote an article survey-ing the twenty years of the WIC's existence. The WIC, she observed,

> continued the work of the Association [WTUA] on a broader basis, as a body whose aim was the welfare of all women engaged in trades and whose duty was to watch over all industrial matters concerning women. Interest in professional women, in the poor as such, and in children, except in so far as they either are or are being prepared for wage-earning occupations, being excluded, the Council had still an immense field of work before it, if it was to cope adequately with the improvement of all industrial conditions, whether general or special, which effect [sic] women.[55]

It did indeed 'watch over' the interests of working women but not always in such a patronizing way as that phrase suggests. As mentioned previously in discussing the WTUA, it had several strong-minded working-class women as key activists on its committees. It was no coincidence that they were all interested in the organization of girls' clubs and the training aspects of the WIC's work.

From the outset of the WTUA, the emphasis had been on self-managed unions and it is probable that women such as the Hickses would have had no truck with an organization that patronized working women and, indeed, they left when they felt that a radical restructuring of the organ-ization was going to give too much power to the executive committee.[56] This idea of self-management continued in the WIC, especially in the organizations and education committees, which the Hickses and Clara James dominated and which were the only sections of the WIC that main-tained direct links with industrial working women. Another interesting point about the aims of the WIC was that it did not follow the general mood of the time by privileging women's reproductive role over their industrial role.[57] Indeed, it concentrated on their role as industrial workers. Insofar as it was concerned with children as workers, it con-centrated on the training and education of girls, although appropriate domestic roles such as nursery nurses or charwomen were on the agenda before the First World War.

Lucy Papworth-Wyatt enumerated the aims of the WIC. These were:

I. The collection and publication of trustworthy information about the conditions of women's work;

II. The provision of remedies for such hardships as investigation revealed, by public action, whether legislation, administrative or voluntary;

III.   The education of the workers and of the public in questions affecting the interests of industrial women; together with such other propaganda of various kinds as circumstances might from time to time make desirable.[58]

Papworth-Wyatt noted that the WIC took up individual cases of hardship with government departments and helped women through its citizen's committee by acting as a poor woman's lawyer. This was particularly helpful for women who were not trade unionists and therefore could not turn to a union for help.[59] Although she did not mention it, the WIC, like the WTUL, worked closely with factory inspectors who often gave lectures at the Girls' Clubs. Further, it fostered good relations with 'friendly' MPs who would apply pressure in the House of Commons when necessary. This was particularly important as women did not have the vote at this time. A number of committees carried out the work of the WIC. Each committee developed its own programme of action which the general purpose committee co-ordinated. By the end of 1895, for example, the education committee had drawn up two programmes of lectures. One, consisting of thirteen lectures, focused on working-class life, and tried to impress on middle-class sympathizers the reality, as far as possible, of working life and the need for constructive help rather than philanthropy. They also had a programme aimed at working-class women and girls that focused on explaining rights and the benefits of trade unionism.[60] How successful this endeavour was is not recorded. Nevertheless, it indicates that the WIC perceived education as a two-way relationship and that both classes were in need of it, albeit in different forms.

The WIC was aware of the difference between organizations that worked on behalf of working women and those that were organized by working women themselves and it worked with both types. Lucy Papworth-Wyatt listed these organizations and noted that the WIC had been instrumental in the establishment of some and its members belonged to yet others. Consequently, being the elder sister, or at least first cousin to several organizations, the WIC had an octopus-like influence on the policy of diverse organizations.[61] Catherine Webb, the General Secretary, offers an example of their yearly work in a brief entry in the *Reformer's Yearbook* of 1902:

> The seventh Annual Report again shews good work done. Realizing that the inferior position occupied by women in the labour market largely rests upon the inefficient and untrained quality of their work, efforts are being made to discover what are the actual possibilities for training now existing for women, and to find ways of increasing opportunities for girls to acquire skills and training in industrial occupations. Specific enquiries have been made concerning season-

trades, domestic service, and the printing and kindred trades, the results of which will be shortly published. The lecture work of the Council has been well sustained.[62]

This example is typical of the way the WIC operated and echoes some of the concerns about the need for women to obtain good training in their chosen occupation that preoccupied activists in SPEW. However, unlike SPEW, the WIC emphasized thorough investigation by the appropriate committee, or committees, before choosing the action it would take and it would not hesitate to demand state intervention if it deemed it necessary. After investigation, they turned to propaganda work through lectures and political lobbying. In other words, they tried to rely less on the prevailing ideology and more on quantifiable facts, in deciding action. However, to what extent they were able to think outside that ideology is questionable. Further, the investigative methods used by the WIC excluded working-class women from much of its activity and led to them becoming merely the subject of its work rather than agents for change. Investigations were time-consuming and needed a reasonably high level of literacy. Literate working women found it difficult to spare the time to become too deeply involved despite being keen to do so.[63] This possibly explains the popularity of the Girls' Club work amongst working-class members of the WIC. Here they achieved results more speedily and, although the work could be time consuming, it was also pleasurable and positive. What is more important is that leaders such as Amie Hicks and Clara James understood the working-class way of life.

The WIC also ran its own quarterly journal, the *Women's Industrial News*. This publication reported the activities of the WIC and other organizations, for example, the Women's Co-operative Guild and, later, the Women's Labour League, and published reports of the findings of its investigations and the parliamentary progress of campaigns it pursued. The News reflected the differing views of the committee members who wrote the articles. However, the writers tended to be professional writers or graduates, and therefore lacked a working-class perspective. It is not possible to ascertain the composition of the readership but it is doubtful that many working-class women were among the number.

Money, or lack of it, was always a problem for all working-class women's organizations. The WTUL had the problem of women's low pay and job insecurity to contend with and, like the WPPL before it, relied heavily on the subscriptions of wealthy patrons. The WIC was in a similar position and many of its unpaid investigators were middle-class members of the Women's Labour League and Fabian Women's Group.[64] This reliance on unpaid investigators meant that workers would often leave when they obtained paid work and some possibly regarded the work as an entry into paid professional work.[65] Carrying on the tradition of optimism that had been part of the organization since the days of the WTUA, and by 1914 had some substance,[66] Lucy Papworth-Wyatt concluded:

> Although the day is still far distant the Council looks forward to the time when its services are no longer, when it and the kindred societies which have worked and are working zealously in one province or another of the great movement for better social and industrial conditions will be able to leave it in the hands of the workers themselves. Already the driving force is coming more and more from them; in their concerted and public action, rather than in work done for them by others, lie its best hopes for the future of this and all other countries.[67]

The WIC was predominantly a middle-class organization concerned to help working-class women improve their working conditions in any way that was within their ability. The presence of some working-class women in their number helped to prevent policy from drifting too far from these aims.

National Federation of Women Workers and the Women's Trade Union League

During the early years of the twentieth century, the WTUL grew steadily. By 1902 there were between 40,000 and 50,000 members of the League.[68] Lady Dilke's niece, Gertrude Tuckwell, was the honorary secretary; Mona Wilson the general secretary; and Ada Nield Chew was the full-time organizer.[69] The WTUL worked closely with the women factory inspectors whose prosecutions were published in the *Women's Trade Union Review*. Further, sympathetic MPs, such as Sir Charles Dilke and H. J. Tennant, the husbands of Lady Dilke and May Tennant (née Abraham) respectively, asked questions in the House of Commons on behalf of the WTUL and campaigned for various reforms. The WTUL was also represented on the Legal Advice Committee and referred cases to it. Like the WIC, the WTUL commissioned various inquiries into working conditions in various trades.[70] Further, a working woman usually represented the WTUL at the Trade Union Congress each year, although proportionately, there were fewer women representing women than in the latter days of the Paterson era.[71]

In 1903 Mary Macarthur, on Margaret Bondfield's recommendation, became the new general secretary. Then, in 1904, Lady Dilke died and Tuckwell became president. Under Macarthur's evangelizing secretaryship the WTUL flourished and within two years the membership had increased to 70,000.[72] Macarthur was a worker, albeit a white-collar one, and this contributed to her popularity with working women. She had been a bookkeeper in her father's shop, and was involved in trade unionism from an early age.[73] Therefore, unlike other leaders in the WTUL – Black, Lady Dilke, Abraham and Tuckwell for instance – she had practical experience of being a worker and member of a union at branch level. This probably led her to being less interested in the investigative and theoretical work than in propaganda and organization.

Despite the large number of women now affiliated to the WTUL, it was still a small proportion of the potential number of women who could join a union. In 1906, around 167,000 women were unionized, mostly textile workers and in mixed unions. As Drake points out, many of the non-unionized women were domestic servants (nearly 1,400,000 in 1911) or dressmakers in very small shops and therefore almost impossible to organize. She roughly calculated that about 20 per cent of women were unionized by the end of the First World War. Thom calculates that in 1906 the actual membership was 211,000 women out of a potential membership of just over 5,000,000, a density of membership of around 4 per cent. By the outbreak of war, this had more than doubled to 437,000 members or a density of membership of 8 per cent.[74] One problem was that women had been approaching the WTUL asking to join a union only to discover that their trade did not admit women or that there was no union at all for their trade.[75] Macarthur argued that a general union for women, as originally suggested by Paterson, would aid the organization of these women. She located two problems that hampered the successful organization of the majority of women:

> Firstly, the low standard of living may be stated to be at once the cause and consequence of women's lack of organization. This sounds paradoxical, but it is nevertheless true that, while women are badly paid because of their unorganised condition, they may be unorganised mainly because they are badly paid. The low rate of wages constitutes the most serious difficulty in the way of women's trade union organization. . . .
>
> This brings me to the second difficulty, which is found chiefly among higher grades. It is a narrow class prejudice which causes the semi-professional class of workers to look askance upon anything in the nature of trade unionism.[76]

These problems were not gender specific and she argued that men faced them too. To solve these problems for women, the WTUL formed the National Federation of Women Workers (NFWW) in 1906. The NFWW constituted a break with traditional WTUL policy because it was a general union rather than one tied to a specific trade.[77] The new union differed from other women's unions because the subscriptions were low, there was a strike fund, indicating that strikes were no longer the anathema they had once been; and the membership was open to all women workers regardless of skills. Macarthur was the primary mover behind this change, believing that unskilled women needed to identify and unite with a large organization that would have a more powerful voice than the small, localized unions that withered and died shortly after the organizer left the area.[78] Further, the employment patterns of women working in, for example, the semi-skilled trades in South and East London meant that women moved from factory to factory as work was available which made it difficult to organize them on traditional lines. Moreover, it was still necessary to circumvent male prejudice against women joining existing unions. On the second point, Macarthur was successful in organizing not only the unskilled factory workers, but also other groups that had been difficult to organize: white-collar workers such as telephone operators and postal sorters. As we shall see in Chapter Six, the number of women clerical workers was rising rapidly during this period. The National Union of Clerks took a progressive stance by recognizing women's right to work and sought to campaign for equal pay for equal work.[79] In practice, however, only a small percentage was unionized and as their work was segregated, equal pay for equal work was not an issue. Women teachers were also increasingly organized – mainly in the National Federation of Women Teachers which was founded as a pressure group within the National Union of Teachers in 1903.[80] These are discussed later.

The NFWW was closely linked to the WTUL. Until 1908 Macarthur was the secretary of both. Three members of the WTUL were elected to serve as advisory members on the NFWW's executive. Again, until 1908, Macarthur was the president, and then Tuckwell took over.[81] Nevertheless, the NFWW was a union in its own right and was affiliated to the TUC and the General Federation of Trade Unions. Despite the close relationship with the WTUL, the NFWW differed most markedly in the way it organized. Organization often first occurred when workers were on strike. The NFWW supported strikers much more actively than the WTUL, especially in 1911 when there was a flurry of strikes amongst London's hollow-ware workers. Drake argues that this was a deliberate policy of Mary Macarthur's, who asserted that a strike was the perfect opportunity to demonstrate to both women and employers the benefits of unionization. This was an argument that the WTUA had made nearly twenty years earlier but was then rejected by the WTUL. By the end of the first year of its existence (1907), the NFWW had more than 2,000 members and 17 branches in England and Scotland and by 1914 the it had 20,000 members. By 1909, the WTUL could boast an affiliated membership of 140,000 women.[82] By far the largest number of women organized were still in the textile unions who were not members of NFWW, and the largest number of unorganized women were in domestic service. The latter were not the focus of any recruitment campaigns.

The NFWW also concentrated on women's low pay rather than striving for equal pay. Macarthur was an advocate of minimum wage policy and used her position in both the WIC and the WTUL to campaign in the Anti-Sweating League for the Trades Board Act which was passed in 1909. However, not all activists supported this policy.[83] This Act established regulatory boards and minimum rates of pays in specific trades. At first, these were chain making, lace making, box making and readymade clothing – all areas that were notoriously underpaid – but more trades were later included. However, as Thom has pointed out, the minimum wage soon became the maximum and the Act in some ways undermined the notion that unionization was the way to strengthen women's bargaining power.[84] However, it could be argued that the Act strengthened women's ability to bargain, especially if they used it and strike action to increase their wage. For example, in 1911 chain makers in the Cradley Heath area of Birmingham struck for the immediate implementation of a pay rise although the Act gave the employers six months to implement the rise. Supported by the NFWW, WTUL and the Anti-Sweating League, women in small, scattered workshops were able to maintain a sustained strike to achieve their aims and, importantly, to encourage workers in other trades to follow suit.[85]

Boston argues that the early days of the women's trade union movement were a 'strange mixture of feminism, trade-unionism and middle-class attitudes', influenced partly by the ideas and character of Emma Paterson and partly by the ideas of the trade union movement at that time.[86] This characteristic was continued into the reigns of Lady Dilke and Mary Macarthur whose personalities shaped both organization and policy. However, it has been argued that this concentration of power at the top of the union hierarchy left the membership too dependent on charismatic or dominant leaders.[87] One problem for the movement was the tension between attempting to instil middle-class ideas of self-reliance on working-class women while wanting to continue to devise and shape policy. Thom has argued that the ideology of the leadership of women's trade unionism offered limited constructions of working-class women.[88] This meant that leaders failed to consult working women and often suggested policy that was not always in working women's best interests. Evidence of this can be seen in the debates around married women's work and protective legislation. Further, underlying class assumptions about working women's abilities to take on positions of responsibility meant that opportunities were missed for encouraging able working women to take more leading roles in the movement. The emergence of working-class women as leaders in the movement was therefore limited. These issues are discussed in Chapter Five. The feminist element also changed over time. Paterson's strong equal rights stance had been replaced, by the early 1900s, by Macarthur's more essentialist one. As a member of the Labour Party and the WLL, Macarthur supported Labour's position on the importance of the breadwinning male and the homemaking female. Despite being a working wife and mother herself, she believed that the wife's place was in the home and that women's domestic role was paramount, even though she ardently supported women workers. The shift towards a policy towards state intervention as the way to improve women's lives and the implications this had for the representation of women as workers will be discussed in the next chapter.

Chapter Five

੧ৄ

Equal or different?

Divisive issues in the industrial women's movement

As we have seen in the earlier period, much of the controversy around women's work opportunities centred on what was considered fit work for women. Women involved in the campaigns around work began to realize that, although improving women's education was vital, there were other issues that could both unite and divide women. In the campaign to improve women's education, divisions had occurred over whether women should be campaigning to have women and girls included in the education system as it stood, or whether women should join the campaign to reform the education system for both men and women.[1] Similarly, in the sphere of work, the question of equal or different was an issue for campaigners. Equal rights advocates challenged patriarchal norms because they wanted women to participate in the workforce on the same terms as men. There were problems with this stance, not least with men themselves who responded by accusing feminists of putting gender before class. The *Englishwoman's Review*, often the voice of equal rights feminism, followed closely the various strikes that involved working-class women during this period and stoutly defended the women against the chauvinism of male trade unionists who would not allow women to join their unions and then attacked them for working for less pay.[2]

For example, in 1875 the *Englishwoman's Review* followed the events around the Kidderminster Carpet Weavers' Strike. The employers were squeezing the carpet weavers to take a reduction in wages. Consequently, they employed women at lower rates than men. Rather than allow the women to join the union and fight alongside the men for a fair wage for all workers, the men attacked the women. This was a common reaction of male unionists. Their primary allegiance was to maintaining the patriarchal status quo rather than help women fight for their rights. Walby notes that male violence is a significant factor in patriarchal relations.[3] This strike offers an example to support this thesis. There was a report in the *Englishwoman's Review* of the explicitly threatening letters sent to women: 'they [the women] may think they are "doing something grand" by robbing men of their daily bread, but they are to be careful what they are doing, or they will very likely get their brains knocked out.' The report commented on one weaver who said:

> A weaver observed that he could now find plenty of young men from 18 to 25 who would be glad to be employed at the looms, and to get more wages than they were at present doing. But they were pegged back, and girls were getting looms in their place. He had a grown up son of 19, and it was hard to see a girl stepping before him. He had grown up daughters at work, but he should not like them to step in anywhere they would throw men out.

The *Englishwoman's Review* had little sympathy for the male weavers whose jobs were jeopardized by women's cheap labour and concluded:

> The carpet weavers of Kidderminster are a manly lot; they demand the exclusion of women from the privilege of earning a living at the looms. The struggle for existence must be pretty severe in which the male animal rends his female. Even a tiger suffers his tigress to hunt in the same jungle.[4]

Throughout the period 1870–1914, the antipathy felt by middle-class feminists and male trade unionists continued in various degrees of severity with claims of oppression from both sides. The clash is interesting because it can be seen as a patriarchal struggle expressed through a discourse of class. The equal rights advocates of this period tended to be women from the middle and upper classes. Some were wealthy, but others entered the debate because of their own need to work. All resented the limitations put on women because of their sex. Most had a reasonable amount of education and, if not, their class position gave them the cultural capital to be able to formulate and articulate their ideas and demands.[5] Further, their social and kinship networks gave them a sympathetic ear amongst their more liberal-minded menfolk. Moreover, they had seen that the inclusion of some working-class men into the body politic through the extension of the franchise and the growing power of the male unions demonstrated that it was possible to change prevailing conditions. Consequently, feminist activists began to perceive a connection between their oppression and the oppression of working-class women. Not having a worked-out theory of patriarchy, they used the language of class as a way of articulating women's oppression and organizing campaigns against gender-biased legislation and restrictive work practices. However, they did not treat working-class women as equals and working-class women did not always experience this sense of solidarity and, as we shall see, did not always reach the same conclusions about the need to campaign against gender-based legislation. Indeed, one of the main criticisms that middle-class activists made about working-class women was their apparent apathy towards organizing around campaigns for their rights.[6] Some women workers may well have been apathetic about joining a union, but others may have put class before gender by opposing women taking what they regarded to be men's work. Roberts points to the Preston spinners' strike of 1853 where women supported the male spinners' demand for a wage sufficient to support a family where the wife did not need to work.[7] These women obviously subscribed to the patriarchal view that insisted that a woman's place was in the home and were keen to let their views be known.

Married women's work

The position of married women was a sticking point between groups of women. Most activists were single women and they were campaigning for the rights of single women to work on the same terms as men. In the earlier period covered in Part One, the rights of married women workers were not of central concern. However, as we have seen, a large minority of working-class women workers were married. Consequently, they endured the double burden of paid work and domestic work and could not be expected to accept working conditions on the same terms as men. Activists, who had servants to deal with the domestic side of life, often ignored this double burden or took on board ideological assumptions that when a woman married she would give up any paid work to become a full-time housewife and, eventually, a mother. These suppositions ignored the experience of many working-class women who, although they might aspire to becoming a full-time housewife, in reality often found it impossible to give up paid work entirely. Whatever paid work these women performed, it was essential for many and they had an ambivalent attitude towards it. For some, it provided a degree of financial independence. For many, it was a wearisome necessity. No one, it seems, argued for men taking on board joint responsibility for domestic work.

Walby argues that state intervention on behalf of women should be understood as the result of an emerging contradiction between patriarchy and capitalism.[8] From the capitalist point of view the employment of cheap, unorganized female labour was preferable to the employment of militant, higher-paid men. However, the employment of women, especially married women, undermined a site of patriarchal control – the family. As discussed in Part One of this book, one of the main worries about women working in factories was that they were neglecting domestic duties and that this could lead to the breakdown of the country's morals. Married women's work intensified these concerns. The ensuing tension between the needs of capital and women's role in the family led to married women's work being the focus of much debate from the 1890s onwards.[9] First, a sizeable number of people were sufficiently interested in the question of women's work generally. This was borne out by the inclusion of the report of the Lady Assistant Commissioners to the Royal Commission on Labour, which firmly placed women's industrial role on the agenda. Second, the report drew attention to women's employment as an important issue, especially concerning high infant mortality rates. By the mid-1890s, the question of the state of the health of volunteers to the army had shocked the Establishment into asking serious questions about child mortality and morbidity.[10] Davin argues that in the latter half of the nineteenth century, Britain's increasing imperial responsibilities and the prevalent economic competition from America and Germany meant that population was increasingly regarded as a site of power. The nub of the argument was a racist one: the more white and, what was more important, the more *British* children born, the better it would be for Britain's position as an imperial and industrial power.[11] Unfortunately, for the proponents of this point of view, a high infant mortality rate coupled with a decrease in the birth rate meant that fewer babies were born but just as many were dying.[12] This added fuel to the prevailing eugenicist rhetoric fanning the debate into a moral panic that focused on the married working woman as the cause of 'race suicide'.

The focus of debate was not on the poverty that resulted in under-nourished mothers producing sickly babies, but on defective mothering. Fuelled by the consistent rhetoric that linked women's paid work with dereliction of domestic duties, politicians, medical practitioners, health and social reformers all looked to mothering as the source of the problem of infant mortality and morbidity. The need to improve infant health was deemed by all sides to be a women's issue but, like most other issues of concern at this time, was divided on class lines. Middle-class professional health and social workers were the advisors and working-class mothers were the recipients of that advice. The working-class home was subject to inspection and comment by single middle-class women who had no experience of the poverty that characterized working-class married lives. Advice and information was communicated to working-class mothers through mothers' meetings and home visits. The advice given reflected middle-class notions of childhood and childcare; all other practices were measured against middle-class norms and inevitably found lacking. Working-class mothers were accused of neglect because they did not live up to middle-class notions of good childcare practices. Further, mother-hood was considered a great leveller and there were calls to middle-class married volunteers to take on this work by visiting working-class homes and speaking at working-class women's groups. Mrs Sumner, a leader of the Girls' Friendly Society and Mother's Union appealed to middle-class mothers to become involved in this work through the Mothers' Union which, she argued:

> includes all classes of mothers . . . in as much as the duties of mothers are the same to a certain extent in every rank. We feel strongly that if mothers in the upper classes will lead the way by joining this movement, we may be able to win all sorts and conditions of mothers to see their responsibility. . . . May we not as mothers, combine and unite together, for the good of our homes . . . by laying as far as we can, the foundation of strong principle and good habits in the hearts and lives of our children?[13]

The message could not be clearer. Sumner believed that middle-class women were needed to instruct working-class women in how to bring up their children. This instruction was to be moral as well as practical and was aimed at further embedding domestic ideology in the working-class world view. However, despite the large number of working-class women who joined the Mothers' Union, there is evidence that working-class mothers resented these interventions, because of the organizers' patronizing attitudes and in some cases obvious lack of knowledge of working-class life.[14] Further, all the advice in the world could not address the underlying economic problems that were the basis of many of the problems that married working-class women faced and some activists began to point this out by either drawing on their own experience[15] or by initiating investigations into the reality of working-class life.[16]

In 1903, the Inter-departmental Committee on Physical Deterioration was established to investigate the perceived deterioration of the race. Again married women's work was seen as the main problem although women factory inspectors were not convinced that this was the case, arguing that factory work could be beneficial to working mothers if the working conditions were good. Hilda Martindale, a factory inspector, commented that it was hardly surprising that women preferred to work in factories when domestic life took place in such squalor.[17] However, despite the growing evidence to the contrary and no firm statistics in support of it, the prevailing message was that working mothers were the root cause of the high infant mortality rates. John Burns, who had worked with Clementina Black in the trade union movement in the 1880s and 1890s, was of this opinion. Like the male trade unionists who used protective legislation as a way of excluding women from the industrial workplace, he wanted married women to stay at home. In addressing two national conferences on infant mortality in 1906 and 1908, he blamed women's paid work for a whole range of childhood illnesses and even for idle husbands.[18] For Burns and others, paid work was primarily for men and unmarried women. At the 1906 conference, despite there being no substance to support claims that working mothers were the main cause of infant mortality, resolutions were passed to prohibit women from returning to work until three months after childbirth by extending the provision of the 1891 Factories and Workshop Act.[19] As there was no provision for maternity benefit, women would have no income so the benefits to children of having a stay-at-home mother would be negated by the lack of income.

In spite of these often clumsy attempts at social control, not all reformers had such reactionary views of motherhood. Social investigations, similar to the sort carried out by the Women's Industrial Council or the Fabian Women's Group (FWG), began to demonstrate the stark reality of working-class life and some activists began to focus their attention on the problem of poverty. The FWG were, for the most part, concerned with women's economic independence and they focused on the economic independence of married women.[20] Their work highlighted the lack of control women had over the family's income and the answer, as they saw it, was to trans-pose the concept of state intervention in the industrial workplace to the working-class home.[21] They focused on low and irregular pay, lack of rights to the family wage, bad housing and homework as contributory factors to working-class women's inadequate care of their children. Their work generated a variety of responses and proposals.

Margaret Llewellyn Davies concurred with the FWG. She went further by challenging the dominant domestic discourse by arguing:

> Writers on infant mortality and the decline of the birth rate never tire of justly pointing to the evils of which come from the strain of manual labour in factories for expectant mothers. Very little is ever said about the same evils which come from the incessant drudgery of the working-woman at the stove, at scrubbing and cleaning, at the washtub, in lifting and carrying heavy weights, is just as severe manual labour as many industrial operations in factories.[22]

Others adhered to the male breadwinner argument. They argued that low pay and irregular employment were the root of the problem and that the solution was to pay men a decent wage so that their wives would not be obliged to work. Moreover, women would have more time and money to care for their children properly. This was the line that many trade union-ists and Labour Party men took and, given the hegemonic sway of the domestic ideology discourse, it seemed the most obvious solution. Some feminists also followed this argument, basing their beliefs on socialist as well as feminist thinking. For example, Anna Martin, a district visitor in South East London and a committed suffragist, saw her role as a defender of the married woman. Martin noted perceptively, and at odds with many of her fellow investigators, that commentators on the working mother regarded her as

> a creature of limited intelligence and capacity, who neither has, nor ought to have, any desires outside her own four walls. She is not so much an individual with interests and opinions and a will of her own, as a humble appanage of husband and children.

This representation, she argued, was untrue. She defended the working mothers by arguing that it was wrong to judge working-class women by middle-class standards. She went on to discuss at length the practicalities of combining domestic work with homework and the problems of rearing children on an inadequate and irregular income in defective housing which did not have even the basic amenities such as running water or a proper range to cook upon.

> Of course, the homemakers of the mean streets are not to be judged by middle-class standards . . . most people . . . fail to see that a code which works well enough in the household of a prosperous professional man would often prove disastrous in the household of a dock labourer.

Martin argued that working mothers worked for practical reasons: 'a very common reason for a wife's going out to work, perhaps the most common is that the man's wages alone are too small and too irregular for the family to live upon.'[23] Martin, though, believed that excluding married women from paid work would not be the answer, indeed it would make matters worse:

> The proposal . . . which strikes most terror to the hearts of the working women of the district. . . . They did not realise the political danger of such a prohibition, which would inflict a serious disability on their class and come perilously near repealing, as far as they are concerned the Married Women's Property Act, but they know from their own life experience the wholesale ruin that would result, under the present industrial system, from the passing of such a law . . . the women are appalled at the idea of their liberty of action in this matter being forcibly taken from them. To do this, and to leave untouched the causes which drive them into the labour market seems to them about as wise as a proceeding as trying to cure a broken leg by removing the splints.[24]

She thought that the only way to solve the problem would be by paying the husband a living wage. To achieve this, the government would need to

PART TWO: 1870–1914

intervene by bringing in minimum wage legislation supported by state insurance against unemployment and the establishment of fair rents courts.[25] This would lead to women voluntarily absenting themselves from the marketplace. However, her argument was based on two suppositions rooted in middle-class domestic ideology: first, she assumed that working-class men would use the extra money to benefit the family, and second, she assumed that working-class women did not object to being totally dependent on men. Not all social feminists were convinced that men would be so ready to turn over their extra pay to their wives and they backed their argument by facts garnered either from social investigations or from personal experience. Further investigations into working-class life showed that there was no guarantee that men would hand over the extra money to their wives.[26] Some advocates argued that men should be legally obliged to hand over a specific percentage of their wage to their wives. However, this would be difficult to enforce, particularly as so many men did not earn adequate amounts in the first place.[27]

Many activists advocated some form of endowment of motherhood.[28] Mabel Atkinson of the FWG regarded it as the only way that women could obtain respite from paid labour during the early months of a child's life and then return to her previous job. Deflecting any argument that might be forwarded by equal rights advocates that endowment would give men the excuse to expel women from the labour force, she argued that only in a socialist system where women were guaranteed certain rights to return to the labour force would this be possible.[29] This argument ignored the patriarchal attitudes of many on the left and assumed that under socialism women would be treated equally with men.

Other more radical women were nervous about the endowment question because they felt that the system could easily degenerate into a 'wages-for-housework' scheme and relegate women to domestic drudgery. Ada Nield Chew was a vociferous supporter of the right of the working-class mother to financial independence. However, unlike Anna Martin, she was no advocate of the minimum family wage which she suspected would not help women and children; neither did she support the campaign for the endowment of mothers as the way to secure women's financial independence. This she regarded as a retrograde step. Presaging later feminists by some sixty years and taking the equal rights argument to its logical conclusion, she saw domesticity as the main source of women's oppression. In an article in the *Common Cause*, a suffrage newspaper, she argued:

It is desirable that married women should be economically independent, and free to develop their humanity on lines best suited to that object. The bondage of the married workingwoman is twofold: the dependence of her young children, and the primitive stage in

82

which domestic industry still remains. In other words, her babies and her domestic jobs are the chains which bind her; and it is these chains which must be broken before talk of human development for her ever becomes more than talk.[30]

Chew insisted that, in reality, domestic responsibilities were too great a burden for one individual to bear, especially if the children were small and the income inadequate. She went on to make two feminist and extremely radical suggestions. First, she argued that state-run nurseries should offer places to all children so that women were free to work and be economically independent of their husbands. To counter the rejoinder that babies needed their mothers, she added that middle-class mothers did not spend all their time with their babies. They left their children with nurses without being labelled as bad mothers. Second, and most controversially, she contested the essentialist argument that domestic work was intrinsically women's work and that all women shared this calling. Like childcare, domestic work would become a paid job. Chew wanted women to rebel against prescribed femininity and to become 'human', as domestic slavery was uncivilized:

Rebellion, refusal to do and submit, are the first steps to progress; and if we consciously discourage the domestic ideal in our girls, domestic work will of necessity have to step out of the painfully primitive stage into line with progress generally.

This rebellion, she asserted, should take the form of married women 'demanding the right to paid work and refusing to do domestic work simply because they are wives'.[31]

In holding these views, Chew was more in line with the American radical feminist, Charlotte Perkins Gilman, whom she admired. Gilman advocated communal childcare as part of her feminist vision. Similarly, the socialist Social Democratic Federation made similar arguments and Chew was conversant with their ideas too. This suggestion would be regarded as quite outlandish to the reformers who read the *Common Cause* or, indeed, the Labour Party which was more concerned with the male breadwinner rather than the needs of working-class women.[32] Domestic ideology was too ingrained in cultural practice for Gilman's and Chew's ideas to be taken up seriously and the patriarchal assumption that women are primarily responsible for domestic work has persisted, with little modification, to the present day.

More recently, Barrett and McIntosh have argued that men in the labour movement defended the campaign for a family wage as a way to increase incomes. But, like Walby, they believe that this was also a way of strengthening patriarchal structures. They argue that men made this choice and it was not something foisted on them by the 'needs of capitalism'.[33] Rowan has extended this argument by adding that although working-class men tended to hand over their wages, or the bulk of them, to their wives to manage, they were structurally in a position of power over their wives.[34]

The ties with the Labour Party and trade unions made it especially difficult for affiliated women's organizations to argue against entrenched patriarchal attitudes. As with other debates, feminists who wanted economic independence for women, whether through endowment of motherhood or wage-earning, were accused of putting gender interests before class interests, whereas it would be equally valid to argue that working-class men, despite their protestations, put gender concerns before class interests. Consequently, Labour and trade union men stood in an uneasy alliance with certain middle-class reformers, such as Millicent Fawcett, who believed that the endowment of mothers would undermine the man's role in the family, and those who believed that working-class married women should not work at all, rather than be allied to radicals like Chew. Further, some of the middle-class women leaders did not regard working-class women in the same light as themselves. Mary Macarthur was a leading figure in the WTUL, NFWW, WIC and the Women's Labour League, the women's wing of the Labour Party. However, although she was a working mother, she was no feminist, and argued that:

> We are familiar with the old ideal what woman's place is the home, and I am sufficiently old-fashioned to agree that there is something to be said for it. In the ideal world as I conceive it a woman would not be driven by economic necessity, and her home would be a home in every sense of the word, and not a mere shelter from which she might quite justifiably desire to escape on every possible occasion.[35]

Macarthur did not believe that men and women were equally entitled to economic independence and she regarded the man's role as provider as paramount. This attitude meant that she brought little force to bear in negotiations around NFWW munitions workers' employment rights during the First World War as she did not regard working women's claims to employment to be as legitimate as men's.[36] Similarly, Margaret MacDonald of the WLL and WIC argued that a 'Right to Work' Act for men would be a charter of the 'Right to Leisure and Home Comfort' for their wives.[37] She was horrified to discover that some women preferred to leave their children with their mothers and work for a pittance rather than stay at home and be a 'good mother'.[38] Consequently, it can be argued that some of the leaders of the industrial women's movement were colluding with labour men to preserve patriarchal notions of femininity rather than asking women what they wanted and pressing for their demands.

Clementina Black was not one of these women. Like Chew and some other more progressive feminists, she advocated co-operative housekeeping.[39] In 1908, the debate around the effects of married women's work and the campaigns to control sweated labour prompted the investigation committee of the WIC to initiate a nation-wide investigation into married and widowed women's paid work. In a letter circulated to both national and local newspapers in their search for help, the WIC claimed that:

> This subject is of immense interest at the present time, the more so because the driving of these people into the labour market has done so much to create the demand for women's suffrage. The lack of authoritative and exact statistics and general information, such as is to be collected, is always commented upon whenever anything related to working women is publicly discussed.[40]

This call aroused great interest amongst social reformers throughout the country.[41] There was a collaboration of WIC members with members from the WLL, Fabian Women's Group and National Union of Women Workers, many of whom were also members of the WIC. Because only expenses were paid and the very nature of the investigation meant that a large amount of amount of time and a high degree of literacy were required, these investigators were mainly middle-class and many were already actively involved in the industrial women's movement. Dissension and splits in the WIC meant that the book itself was seven years in the making and was not published until 1915.[42] The war radically altered the lives of many people and the legislation that Black had been seeking, the Trades Board Acts, had long been implemented. As Mappen has argued, the survey represented the conditions of thousands of women's lives in Britain. It covered the type of work they did, their wages, health, home conditions, and their relationships with their husbands and with their children.[43] Drawing on the experience of their investigation committee, the WIC was in a good position to know which questions to ask to elicit useful information for its cause. Mappen suggests that this work and the conclusions that were drawn from it are important because they provide a summary of some of the major concerns of social feminists at the time.

In the introduction to the book, Black, like Martin, rounded on those who criticized working-class women for the way they conducted their lives. She divided the women interviewed into four categories. The first group were women who did no paid work even though their family income was insufficient. Black obviously had little time for these women who seemed to spend their days gossiping on the doorstep. These women were grist to the mill of both the family wage and endowment of motherhood campaigners who could argue over the best way to help these women. The second group were the women who worked because their family income was inadequate. These, she claimed, were 'the most overworked, the hardest pressed, and probably the unhappiest of working women'. However, she continued, 'the very act of earning money, no matter how little, gave them 'the sense of partial freedom and independence by which their hearts are thus warmed'. She agreed that the children of these women often suffered, but argued that they would suffer more if their mothers did not work and that it 'would be rash' to prevent these women from working. She called for the establishment of more nurseries and refers to Chew's articles in the *Common Cause* as an example of working women seeking their own solutions to their childcare problems. The third group were not included in the study because these were the working-class women who did not work because their family income was adequate. However, she combined them with women in the fourth group who did work even though they had an adequate income. She commented that these classes 'belong [to] that great body of intelligent, able and efficient mothers, examples of whom may be seen at the meetings, large and small, of the Women's Co-operative Guild'. Black could relate more readily to these women and they won her admiration rather than sympathy. They were, she wrote ironically, 'those reprehensible women who could if they chose afford to live upon their husband's earnings but devote many of their hours to paid work'.[44]

None of the women, she argued, wanted any restriction on married women's labour. Like Chew, she believed that wage earning was beneficial to women. The thrust of her argument was against low pay and the primitive conditions in which working-class families lived. She also believed that the lack of training for girls condemned them to low paid work for the rest of their lives. On the whole, the investigators agreed with her and thought that women took pride in their ability to work although they concluded that many worked only because of economic necessity. Importantly, they concluded that infant mortality was a result of poverty and poor living conditions rather than caused by married women working. Most investigators agreed with Black that preventing married women from working would only increase hardship. Black felt that the whole question was complex and that there was not one simple solution to family poverty. She summed up the situation:

> In one direction lies the effort towards the establishment of a minimum wage, in another the tendency to introduce improved methods of child nurture and saving of domestic labour, in yet a third the demand for endowment of mothers and the rights of wives to a fixed share of their husbands' incomes.

She then outlined her own preferred socialist vision of the future family:

> It is possible that society is evolving in the direction of a family supported by the earnings of both parents, the children being cared for meanwhile and the work of the house being performed by trained

experts. To me personally that solution seems more in harmony with the general lines of our social development than does any which would relegate all women to the care of children combined with the care of households.[45]

It is incongruous that some of the women most opposed to working-class mothers working were working mothers themselves, for example Mary Macarthur and Margaret MacDonald. As Chew pointed out, middle-class women left their children in the care of others and no one criticized them. The focus on the perceived defects of working-class mothering cloaked the poverty that so many women battled against every day of their lives and the views of working-class women went largely unheard. Chew, who was a working mother, revealed that she used part of her wages to pay other women to do her domestic work.[46] She argued that until

> women see that it is within *their* province not only to bear and nurse, but to provide for their young will women recognise their glorious duty to the race and act to end starvation of the minds and bodies of themselves and their children.[47]

All fine sentiments, but as I have shown, the debate around the married working woman was controversial. Whether working mothers were blamed, problematized, praised or seen as a progressive force, there was no agreed solution and the desires and hopes of working-class women were largely absent from this debate.

The debate around protective/restrictive legislation

As already discussed, when there was a clash between the needs of capital and patriarchy, there was an increasing willingness for the state to inter-vene throughout the nineteenth century. However, although this led to improvements in working conditions and pay, the patriarchal stance of legislators meant that legislation restricted women's access to employ-ment.[48] Further, it could drive the trade out of the factory and into the unprotected realms of the small, unregulated workshop or the employee's own home. Homeworkers are the most difficult group to quantify, as they do not show up easily in the census or other statistics and conditions could be far worse than in any factory. However, homework had appeal to both patriarchy and capital as it kept women at home and prevented them organizing for better pay and conditions.[49] Homework is discussed in more detail in the next chapter. State intervention into employment practices grew apace in the last decades of the nineteenth century as laissez-faire policies of earlier decades, which only sought intervention by the state in order to preserve the free market, gave way to increased surveillance and regulation. Gendered ideologies, the failure of trade unionism to reach large groups of workers, especially the majority of women workers, rising unemployment and the consequent poverty it brought, the need for increased efficiency and the increasing concern about the perceived physical deterioration of the 'race' all culminated in the development of systematic investigations into social and economic problems. This trend led to a growing demand for legislation that would address these issues.[50] Indeed, by the end of the century there emerged a systematic attempt to gather data to inform legislation; the WIC was just one of the voluntary organizations involved. More formally, in 1893, the Department of Labour was established to provide empirical data for policy making and the factory and workshop inspectorate was enhanced, employing women inspectors for the first time, in order to facilitate the implementation of new laws.

Hall and Schwarz argue that this increasing emphasis on state intervention, together with new forms of political representation, resulted in new political formations and coalitions increasingly replacing the previously class-based ones. These coalitions tended to pit skilled workers against unskilled workers, or male workers against women workers. Feminist activism fell into these new coalitions as the campaigns instigated by activists often worked across class lines.[51] Increasingly, diverse groups such as trade unionists, social reformers and feminist activists etc, called upon the state to intervene in the workplace, to make laws and enforce them. Groups who still maintained that laissez-faire was the best way of regulating the economy or refused any legislation that treated people differently because of gender, in turn, opposed them but became more marginalized. Consequently, in this period protective legislation was increasingly turned to as remedy to employment problems with each side arguing about the lives of women who had little or no say in what would be implemented. As already discussed, women rights advocates were divided on the issue of protective legislation. Fuerer suggests that there were two types of feminists: equal rights feminists who were against legislation aimed only at women; and social feminists[52] who supported some forms of legislation directed at women if it made women's lives less burdensome.[53] Levine divides activists into three groups:

> the outright laissez-faire opposition to any proposals as a restriction on women's freedom; those supporters who saw restriction as a progressive and humane response of the state; and those – more numerous than the unqualified supporters – who applauded the principle of protective legislation but only where it was not on the basis of gender.[54]

Women associated with the Langham Place Circle through SPEW or the Vigilance Association for the Defence of Personal Rights fell into the first category and, indeed, many of their activists belonged to both organizations. Their ideas were disseminated in the *Englishwomen's Review* and they were key to the development of the Women's Protective and Provident League (WPPL).[55] Jessie Boucherett and Helen Blackburn, both Langham Place habituées and editors of the *Review* were ardent opponents of protective legislation and they carried on their campaign long after the WPPL became the Women's Trade Union League (WTUL) and had begun to support legislation where appropriate.[56] As we have seen in the previous chapter, equal rights feminists felt that protective legislation made women dependent and defenceless and that the only way for women to protect themselves was to come together in unions. The more strident of them opposed all forms of control that made women economically dependent on men. One of their most well-known campaigns was against the attempts to remove women workers from pit brow work.[57] Further, if the equal rights advocates were suspicious of male motives in supporting legislation, male trade unionists saw this opposition as an example of middle-class ignorance of industrial life, a tendency towards 'do-gooding' to appease their consciences, and ideological dogma.[58] Male trade unionists argued that the Factory Acts were protective rather than restrictive, a defence against the worst excesses of industrial capitalism and that equal rights supporters were blinded by their own experience of oppression by middle-class men who thought that women should not work at all. Ray Strachey summed up the situation succinctly when she wrote: 'The men's very genuine fears were put aside by the feminists as plain sex selfishness, while ideals of the women were derided as middle-class ignorance by the men.'[59]

Both arguments have certain validity but they took place mainly between middle-class equal rights feminists and working-class men and other social reformers including, later, social feminists. What did working-class women think about legislation that intervened in their working life? As we have seen, many working-class women had no alternative but to work and to take whatever work they could get and on whatever terms offered. Notions of 'the right to choose' were meaningless to them even if, as Levine argues, feminism offered them 'an alternative and realistic solidarity between women'.[60] The male trade unions' response, which barred women from membership or only allowed them in on very limited terms, also increased their exploitation.[61] Restrictive legislation was often used to impose certain ideals of femininity and moral codes on women and could be a bar to finding work.[62] This in turn fuelled anxieties about women being forced into prostitution. Further, Fuerer notes that along with their interest in opening up the labour market and suspicion of legislation that made gender distinctions, equal rights feminists had a philanthropic concern for working-class women and this led to them seeking to represent working-class women rather than enabling working-class women to represent themselves. For example, many of the women that the WPPL represented at the Royal Commission on Labour in 1875 did not oppose legislation that improved their working conditions, yet Paterson, rather patronizingly, attributed this to a lack of education on the women's part. The pervasive idea was that working-class women only needed the 'right' education that is, the education middle-class reformers deemed suitable. This was a form of silencing. The assumption was that working-class women's opinions lacked informed analysis and that they needed help from more educated and privileged women. Of course, these educated women considered themselves suitably informed or able to gather the necessary facts to help working-class women. This placed these feminists in a similar position to male trade unionists, each side thinking they had the right to talk on behalf of working-class women. Consequently, surprise was often registered by middle-class women when working-class women expressed opinions contrary to those expected. What working women felt about state intervention is hard to establish as they were seldom asked and rarely left records of their feelings on the issue. There are instances though that can give us some idea of their response and I will address some of these below and in the next chapter. However, usually, it was the spokeswomen of the industrial women's movement that tended to decide what policy would be and felt it was only a matter of educating women workers into supporting their argument.

An example, already mentioned, of how equal rights activists sought to represent working women occurred when members of the WPPL gave evidence to the Royal Commission on the Factory and Workshops Acts in 1875. Mrs Heatherley, the secretary of the Dressmakers, Milliners and Mantlemakers Union and Mrs A. B., a working bookbinder, gave evidence with Paterson. On being asked whether the members of the League objected to an act that would limit their working hours, Paterson replied:

> I do not say that they all object; our league committee thinks that it is objectionable, but I do not think that the workers generally at present do, although I believe that they are now beginning to see the great value of combination for these purposes, and that very soon they will be in such a position as not to require legal interference, and not to wish for it.[63]

Later in the proceedings, Mrs Heatherley said

> But with respect to the season's hours I was very anxious not to give my opinion but theirs therefore I wrote down what they had told me and read it to them and asked all those that I had seen whether they agree to this and these are all their own sentiments.[64]

Although we cannot generalize on scraps of evidence like this, it does raise the possibility that in certain circumstances, women workers were not against state intervention. What they appear to have objected to is legislation that prevented them from working altogether rather than legislation that ameliorated their working conditions.[65] This indicates that there were obviously tensions between the feminist ideology of the middle-class executive and the more pragmatic, personal views of the membership of the unions involved. More dialogue and a willingness to listen to workers might have overcome these differences and permitted an informed debate around state intervention.

Even though social feminists were not against legislation per se, most feminists were wary of restrictive legislation aimed solely at women as they suspected the motives behind such legislation, fearing that it was instigated by men in order to protect their own jobs. However, after the death of Emma Paterson in 1886, the balance shifted towards state intervention. As mentioned in the previous chapter, the new President of the WTUL, Emilia Dilke, was not opposed to legislation where appropriate, nor was Clementina Black, leader of the WTUA and the later WIC. They both knew how difficult it was to organize women into unions and accepted that legislation was often the only practical solution to some of the exploitation women faced. In her essay supporting the Factory Acts, Black argued that there was no place for the individualism advocated by some feminists in working-class life. Individualism, she argued, meant long hours and low pay, in short, sweated labour. By the time she wrote this essay she also believed that it was not possible to organize all workers in unions and she cited casual workers and those whose employers enjoyed a monopoly in the trade as impossible to organize.[66] Mappen has shown that, as activists carried out investigations, they became more familiar with the reality of the experience of working-class women's lives and were less likely to put their faith in unions as the answer to women's problems. Activists were, in turn, viewed as experts and served on many government committees and gave evidence at various commissions.[67] One of the most important instances of contestation over the implementation of protective legislation was the case of the laundry workers. Chapter Six focuses on areas of women's employment that were subject to public scrutiny and attempts to regularize the work during this period.

The campaign for women factory inspectors

Social feminists supported state intervention in the workplace as the best way to curb exploitative practices, especially after the formation of the WIC in 1895. They also advocated the employment of women factory inspectors, some even calling for these to be working women who had hands-on experience of factory life.[68] Equal rights feminists also wanted women factory inspectors. The WPPL fought consistently for women factory inspectors. From 1878, Emma Paterson argued pragmatically, if somewhat paradoxically, that if there were going to be laws protecting women workers then there should be women factory inspectors to ensure their efficient operation. The Trades Union Congress (TUC) passed her amendment each year, but its lukewarm reception at the Parliamentary Committees of the TUC ensured that the resolution got no further. The Factory Inspectorate was less supportive. In 1879, Alexander Redgrave, the chief factory inspector, reiterated some old arguments in his annual report:

> I doubt very much whether the office of Factory Inspector is one suitable for women. It is seldom necessary to put a single question to a female [worker]. Possibly some details, here and there, might be superintended by a female Inspector, but looking at what is required at the hands of an Inspector, I fail to see advantages likely to arise from her ministrations in a factory . . . so opposite to the sphere of her good work in the hospital, the school, or the home.[69]

This report encapsulates dominant patriarchal opinions on women entering hitherto male employment domains. On entering the public sphere the woman factory worker was unsexed and, as we have already seen, this was an argument put forward for excluding women in the first place. Consequently, in the workplace, her needs were regarded as the same as men and therefore there was no need to ask her opinions. This attitude reflected the common belief that women's interests were subsumed in the interests of men. Feminist supporters of women factory inspectors exploited this dichotomy between the public and private to gain access to the inspectorate by arguing that women's 'natural' role as carer could be employed in gaining the confidence of the woman factory worker and ensuring that her moral as well as physical welfare was safeguarded. They emphasized the difference between male and female factory workers and stressed women workers' presumed special needs. For example, women were more likely to discuss delicate issues, such as lavatory arrangements, with a woman rather than a man. Both arguments made large assumptions about women. Predictably, the chief inspector trotted out the cliché that a woman's place was in the home, while feminists assumed that factory women would be more likely to confide in an educated lady. There was also an implicit understanding in the debate that female factory inspectors would be middle-class. This both served the feminist demand for more careers for middle-class women and their assumption that supervisory work was their domain.

Labour unrest in the 1880s resulted in the establishment of the Royal Commission on Labour between 1891 and 1894. Its brief was to investigate the conditions prevailing in factories throughout the country. At the beginning, it seemed that female witnesses would not represent women. The Commission had sent a questionnaire to the secretaries of all trade organizations, but Lady Dilke argued that because most women were unorganized they were not being represented and that women were a special case and needed representation before the Commission.[70] The Royal Commission capitulated and appointed four women to act as Lady Assistant Commissioners to investigate the working conditions of women: Eliza Orme was the Senior Lady Commissioner, a feminist and a member of SPEW who supported the pit brow women in their struggle against their exclusion from pit brow work. She also wrote for the *Englishwoman's Review* and was a friend of Lady Dilke. Clara Collett was a graduate who had worked with Booth on his investigation of the employment conditions of women in the East End. Margaret Irwin was the secretary of the Scottish Council for Women's Trades and finally, May Abraham of the WTUL.[71] Surprisingly, although they were investigating women's work, the only working women who appeared before the Labour Commission were Elizabeth Mears, the Bookbinders' Union secretary and, from the WTUA, Clementina Black, Amie Hicks and Clara James.[72] Interestingly, in 1891, Hicks and James had asked that the women commissioners should be working women, not ladies because ladies would misrepresent the facts. Predictably, their request was ignored.[73] The Lady Assistant Commissioners' findings and the increased pressure applied by women's organizations made the appointment of women factory inspectors more appealing and eventually inevitable.[74] Petty objections, such as women's clothing being hazardous in factory conditions indicated that the battle was almost won.[75] Isabella Ford, a trade union activist, commenting after the introduction of women factory inspectors wrote:

> The idea that it was not right that it was unjust and sometimes even cruel, for women to have no one but men to whom they can appeal against any sort of abuse, had been steadily growing in people's minds. It was an idea that appealed to everyone, both rich and poor.[76]

This was probably true. However, who these women should be was an issue. For some, it was purely a question of gender and there was no question raised about who should be employed because they assumed that only educated, middle-class women need apply. For others, the class of these women was important and they argued that the work should be offered to women with experience of working in a factory. Emma Paterson had argued at the 1879 TUC that women inspectors should be 'practical working women', not ladies.[77] Further, as late as 1891, Miss Miller of Glasgow was arguing for working women to inspect women's workshops.[78]

In August 1892, the Liberals came into power. In January 1893, following increasing pressure from a variety of women's organizations, a deputation of women's organizations, including the Women's Liberal Federation, the Scottish Liberal Association, SPEW and the WTUL met Asquith to argue their case for women inspectors.[79] Sprague Oram, the new Chief Inspector of Factories was more sympathetic to the idea of women inspectors. The time was ripe for Asquith to comply with women's demands. It was the first commitment to allowing women to enter the higher ranks of the Civil Service. Naturally, given their arguments over the years, trade unionists wanted working women to be appointed. Lady Dilke even entertained a few, a form of informal interview, but decided 'that their backgrounds had not prepared them to take the initiative or to organize, or to grapple on their own responsibility with work'.[80] When appointing women, the standard of education required for inspectors was different to that expected of men. The men were usually expected to have 'hands-on' experience of the trades they inspected. Women were usually university graduates.[81] The previous Home Secretary had advised that mature women were more suitable as factory inspectors. The title 'Lady Factory Inspector' was revealing in itself. The first woman inspector with experience of a factory working life was Vera Chinn. She was not appointed until 1930.[82]

So why were middle-class educated women chosen over women with workplace experience? Jones argued that by employing 'middle-class women, a compromise was reached with those who fought shy of an explicit commitment to labour'.[83] Lady Dilke was a liberal reformer rather than a feminist or socialist. She did not want to change the power relations between patriarchy and capital, rather she wanted to ameliorate some of the injustices that tensions between them created. Further, the essentialist idea that women were different to men and therefore only women could understand and assist women evoked a form of social maternalism where women factory inspectors took on the mantle of protector of their vulnerable sisters/daughters. This mimicked patriarchal gender relationships that regarded women as dependent on men. Working-class women did not usually employ this rhetoric and would be more likely to use a class analysis of women's working conditions. This emphasis on women's special qualities led to gender differences in the work lady inspectors undertook and the work these women performed possibly accentuated the differences.

Although the inspectors were working for women's welfare, factory workers sometimes resisted the lady inspectors' attempts to enforce the law. One of the continuous complaints of the lady inspectors was that factory girls seemed willing to collude with their employers to evade the

Factory Acts and deceive the inspector. This was partly due to the working-class tendency to thumb their noses at any figure of authority. However, the exclusion of experienced working women from a job performed by experienced working men and the appointment of educated ladies to the inspectorate instead, might have been a factor. Workers possibly resented these young ladies descending on them in their workplace and disrupting their work and saw them in a similar light to charity workers and home visitors who interfered in their private life. Piecework was prevalent and therefore any disruption meant a loss of wages or the need to make up lost time. This might have contributed to collusion with the employers. Amie Hicks, in her evidence to the Royal Commission on Labour arguing for women inspectors, had pointed out that women were reluctant to report abuses to officials.[84] She might have added that an older, more wily factory hand might have been more successful than an educated young lady in winning the confidence of the workers and might have offered a figure of authority that the workers could respect as one of their own rather than resist because of what she represented.

Therefore, as early as 1893, a potential class problem developed between the lady factory inspectors and the women they were employed to help. Indeed, based on the diaries and other writings of the first cohort of women factory inspectors, Livesey argues that they fall within the wider context of the professionalization of social work and the formation of an elite group of women workers. She also focuses on the conflict between the professional and the women she is employed to help.[85] As Livesey argues, little or no attention was paid to power inequalities between different classes of women. Traditional ideas about class were used to empower some women at the expense of others. Activists argued that women should enter the public sphere and be employed in the same fields as men, but the assumption was that middle-class women, particularly those with professional expertise, led and working-class women were led. Consequently, middle-class activists expended more energy in attempting to mould working-class women into acceptable feminine roles than in enabling them to think and act for themselves. These women did not breach the class gap, instead they papered it over with a rhetoric of gender unity, a unity that was constantly under pressure and often cracked. Sisterhood was permeated by inequality.

ë▲

Women's work before the
First World War

This chapter will focus on some of the main employment sectors for women and, specifically, those that came under public scrutiny during the period 1870 to 1914. Laundry work, domestic service and manufacturing still continued to be important employers of working-class women, although agricultural work and pit brow work was in decline. Changing aspects of these sectors will be examined later in this chapter. New opportunities were appearing for the better educated working-class and lower middle-class young women with shop work and clerical work increasingly needing vast numbers of low-paid, low-status assistants and clerks to carry out the tasks of an increasingly consumerist and administratively based economy. Professions, too, were beginning to open up and nursing joined teaching as a respectable occupation which employed women in large numbers.

The 1890s saw the invention of a new stereotype, the New Woman. The New Woman was the product of new ways of thinking in which marriage was no longer seen as the only occupation for young middle-class women. Better quality education and the chance for some to attend university; the opening up of new areas of work for women; the acknowledgement that not all women would marry and a general relaxing of some of the more restrictive rules of etiquette meant that young middle-class women appeared to be very different from their mothers' generation.[1] However, the reality of working life for young working women was often very different from the cheery bravado of the New Woman stereotype. Just because some young women had a modicum of financial independence did not mean that they had unbridled freedom to live as they wished. Long hours, low pay, interference in private lives by employers and family and a lack of promotional prospects did little to allow young women to emulate the New Women depicted in fiction of the period.[2] Most were employed as shop workers or clerks or, if they had a better education, as teachers. All these occupations were characterized by long hours, low pay and limited career opportunities for the girl who did not marry. The marriage bar was also used to ensure that married working women did not become a norm. By focusing on some of the new occupations opening up to young, moderately well-educated young women in the final decades of the nineteenth century and up until the First World War, that is shop work and clerical work and the more established occupations of teaching and nursing, a more realistic picture of the New Woman should be possible. However, I shall begin by focusing on the employment that was limited to working-class women.

Laundry work

Malcolmson asserts that in the period from 1861 to 1901 the numbers of laundrywomen rose from around 167,000 to 205,000[3] and that this period was the heyday of the laundry trade, the third largest employment sector for women and the second largest for women over 45.[4] This was because washing was such an onerous, messy business that anyone who could afford to do so would either employ a laundrywoman to do their washing or send it to one of the new mechanized laundries.[5] However, Lucy Papworth-Wyatt and Dorothy Zimmern, in one of their numerous surveys for the Women's Industrial Council, calculated that as mechanization increased, the percentage of women in the trade decreased from 99 per cent in 1860 to around 93 per cent in 1911.[6] Census returns, again, are on the conservative side. Malcolmson notes that a survey undertaken by the Women's Trade Union League in 1891 uncovered 67,500 bona fide laundresses in London whereas the census of the same year put the figure at 51,000. Moreover, although mechanized laundries began to appear in the late 1860s, hand laundries were still common in London as late as 1901 and would be hard to enumerate. Elsewhere, mechanized steam laundries were gradually becoming more common.[7]

As discussed in Chapter Two, public opinion concerning laundry work was ambivalent and a similar attitude was apparent when it came to the law. From 1895 up to 1920, a series of Acts were formulated which sought to regulate the trade. This was a successful enterprise and Malcolmson argues that these Acts, as much as capitalization and mechanization, transformed the trade from a hand trade to a modern industry. Further, she asserts that the trade was changed from a sweated trade or domestic by-employment dominated by drunken, slatternly workers to an orderly, respectable occupation with regulated wages and working conditions.[8] However, she argues the path to modernity was not a straightforward one and the battles that occurred on the way were a struggle between the forces of reaction and reform and emerged from the wider debate around protective legislation.[9] There were diverse groups who participated in the debate around protective legislation concerning laundry work. This debate is of particular interest because this was a trade dominated by women workers and therefore it was not tenable to argue that legislation was being used as a ploy to exclude women from the workforce.

Malcolmson states that much of the laundry trade was excluded unintentionally from the 1867 Factory and Workshop Act because the industry was offering a service rather than producing new goods. In 1876, the Royal Commission on the Factory Acts noted this and recommended that the trade should be included in the Act.[10] Opposition to this recommendation was strong. Employers, free traders and the equal rights advocates attached to the women's movement all protested. Employers, naturally, baulked at state intervention in their businesses, arguing, in the case of large employers, that fluctuations in the trade would make regulation an unbearable burden and small employers feared that they would no longer be able to compete with large, modern establishments. Equal rights advocates, such as the Executive Committee of the WPPL, took a libertarian stance, protesting against any legislation that might interfere with personal freedom or access to employment. Malcolmson states that one of the leading campaigners against the inclusion was the MP Henry Fawcett, husband of the suffrage campaigner and advocate of equal rights feminism, Millicent Fawcett.[11] For some years the anti-legislation lobby prevailed and the trade continued to be excluded from the Factory Acts. However, as the mood in the industrial women's movement became more inclined towards supporting appropriate protective legislation, the focus turned to the laundry workers once more.

Laundry work was included in the 1895 Factory and Workshop Act but not without a struggle that involved reformers, equal rights advocates and the laundry workers themselves. Malcolmson argues that this struggle threw into focus the differences that had been simmering for some time between equal rights advocates and those who favoured regulation. Jessie Boucherett and Helen Blackburn established the Women's Employment Defence League in 1891 to fight any attempts to extend the Acts.[12] They argued that any extension of the Acts would mean that women were replaced by men or machines and would wipe out the small hand laundries that were large employers of women.[13] Malcolmson asserts that Boucherett was selective in her facts and inflated statistics to support her argument, especially in the struggle to include laundry women within the provisions of the 1891 Factory Act. This Act proposed to make it illegal for an employer to employ a woman within four weeks of a confinement.[14] The battle was long and hard, with the Laundresses Co-operative Union supported by the equal rights advocates on one side, and the Amalgamated

Society of Laundresses supported by the WTUL and others campaigning for protective legislation on the other. Investigations carried out by the WTUL and WIC offered quantifiable facts rather than the rhetorical hyperbole of the equal rights advocates. In 1891, a huge survey of London laundresses carried out by the Amalgamated Society of Laundresses claimed that nearly 60,000 out of 67,500 laundrywomen were in favour of protective legislation being applied to their trade.[15] The League and sympathetic MPs, factory inspectors and male trade unionists coupled this with an effective lobbying campaign. Both sides in the debate made good points. The laissez-faire feminists, such as Boucherett and Fawcett, rightly argued that women's exclusion from paid work during this period after childbirth would cause real economic distress as many laundry-women were the main breadwinners in the family. More controversially, they also challenged arguments about the detrimental effects of working after confinement by arguing that women who were used to hard work were not adversely affected and that it was their right to choose whether to work or not. Of course, the main problem was that there was no welfare safety net for women and therefore they had very little choice in the matter. Poor women returned to work, whether paid or not, as soon as they possibly could after their confinement and this often affected their health and that of their baby and subsequent babies.[16] Beatrice Webb, in a series of lectures delivered to women's groups and the Fabian Society insisted that the freedom of the individual argument was flawed. She argued that the regulated woman textile worker enjoyed more personal liberty than the unregulated laundry worker. She saw regulation as a prerequisite to successful unionization:

> Before wage-earners can exercise the intelligence, the deliberation, and the self-denial that are necessary for Trade Unionism, they must enjoy a certain standard of physical health, a certain surplus of energy, and a reasonable amount of leisure. It is cruel mockery to preach Trade Unionism, and Trade Unionism alone, to the sempstress sewing day and night in her garret for a bare subsistence; to the laundry woman standing at the tub eighteen hours at a stretch or the woman whose health is undermined with 'Wrist-drop', or 'Phossy-jaw'.[17]

Webb had a valid point but it does not account for the general hostility on men's part to women workers or their consistent refusal to allow women access to the trade unions that already existed. Malcolmson observes that laundry women were divided over the question of regula-tion. Regular workers tended to favour inclusion whereas casual workers, taking on work to supplement husbands' irregular or non-existent earnings, were more likely to be against regulation.[18] The protests of the coalition of employers, laissez-faire sympathizers and casual workers paid off. Although the 1891 Act was passed, the laundry women were excluded from its terms.

The struggle to exclude laundrywomen from the Factory Acts continued with the laundrywomen being represented as 'independent', and 'able to take care of themselves'. Malcolmson argues that the equal rights advocates underplayed the structural changes to the economy that were undermining the values of individualism and self-help that underwrote their rhetoric.[19] The move to mechanization of laundry work was inevitable and most laundrywomen would eventually be employed in steam laundries rather than as independent workers and, as employees, would be better off if protected by factory legislation that limited the hours they worked and generally regulated the conditions in which they worked. Many women involved in the trade union movement appreciated this. Following the death of the equal rights advocate Emma Paterson, the WTUL moved towards supporting appropriate protective legislation. Malcolmson locates this shift to the contest around including laundrywomen in the 1895 Factory Act and argues that the difficulty of organizing workers in casual, unskilled work led trade unionists to decide that it was easier to organize workers in a regulated workplace than in an unregulated one. She also argues that the establishment of the Department of Labour and the introduction of women factory and sanitary inspectors played their part in getting recognition for the real needs of women laundry workers.[20] However, things did not all go the way of the reformers and when the Act was passed in 1895, the government had compromised over the laundrywomen and the Act did not apply to all laundries. Thus the most overworked of laundry workers were the ones not covered by the Act. It was not until 1907 that all laundries were finally included in factory legislation.

Domestic service

The number of women involved in domestic work continued to rise in this period but its percentage share of the female workforce fell slightly. Roberts states that in England and Wales over 1,500,000 women worked in domestic service in 1871. This had risen to 1,600,000 in 1911 but as a percentage of the total female workforce had fallen from almost 13 per cent to 11 per cent. In Scotland the percentage drop was greater. Domestic service accounted for over 150,000 or almost 9 per cent of the female workforce in 1871. It had slightly risen in numbers to 160,000 in 1911, but dropped as a percentage of the female workforce to 6.5 per cent.[21] This rise in numbers but drop in percentage share suggests that the opening up of other types of work was having a detrimental effect on domestic service as the prime employer of women, a gradual trend that continued after the

First World War. As an unregulated industry, domestic service continued to be one of long hours and low pay. Roberts states that in 1873 it was calculated that a housemaid's day was 16 hours including two half-hour breaks for meals and an hour and half 'break' in the afternoon for needle-work.[22] These figures indicate longer hours and possibly heavier work than most factory workers would undertake and, as this was an average, some women, especially lone maids-of-all-works, were possibly working longer hours.

As well as the lack of legislative check on the amount of hours women worked, the conditions in which they were worked were also unmoni-tored. Very few reformers bothered to investigate domestic service, even though it was promoted as suitable work for very young girls and the largest sector of working women in the country. Harrison has identified some attention paid to domestic service in the Royal Commission on Labour and an article in the progressive journal *Shafts* in 1893. Nothing came of this and the next mention was in Thomas Oliver's investigation into Dangerous Trades in 1902 where it took up all of two pages. Even the Women's Industrial Council (WIC), which carried out investigations into all manner of trades, did not turn its attention to domestic service until the end of the period under discussion.[23] One of the issues that the WIC report confirmed was that there were few changes in patterns of employ-ment in domestic service earlier in the nineteenth century. The sector was still hierarchical and, although some of the more prestigious jobs in better class houses had status and were often less onerous, overall, domestic service was viewed as low status. Former servants were not keen on letting their daughters enter the sector if they could find them other employment such as shop work, clerical work or, in some cases, elementary teaching – all occupations aimed at by aspiring working-class families for their daughters.[24] The WIC report also highlighted the limitations on personal freedom imposed by the living-in system. One servant complained:

> I am very often shut right indoors from one week to another, Tuesday to Tuesday. I never have a day out . . . I consider all maids should have two hours each day to call their own. . . . Domestic service would not be nearly such a monotonous occupation if a little variation were included. A good home and good food *is not all* that is required by a servant. [Emphasis in original.][25]

Others expressed a desire to be included in the Factory Acts. The report recommended that domestic servants should be given two hours off duty each day, excluding mealtimes and a half-day holiday per week as well as Sundays. However, there was no need for the government to intervene here as domestic service was not viewed as part of the capitalist economy. As Harrison has noted, because domestic service was carried out in the privacy of the employer's home it was considered improper to legislate and monitor the work in the ways that the Factory Acts did.[26] Consequently, these recommendations were not taken up by the legislature and conditions did not change until employers were forced by the shortage of servants to change the conditions of service. This occurred mainly after the First World War.

Manufacturing industry: factories, workshops and home-based industries

As the regulations affecting factory life became more focused and more stringently policed, less scrupulous employers moved their production to small workshops and then, where possible, to homework. Therefore rather than heading this section factory work, I refer to manufacturing so that the full range of the work can be discussed. Under this rubric I include textiles, clothing, pottery, metal work, engineering, chemicals, paper and fancy goods, food and drink and other sundry manufactured goods produced either in a factory, small workshop or in the worker's own home. Again, statistics on women's work in this sector must be regarded as conservative, especially in relation to home-based work. For example, in textiles, probably the easiest of these trades to enumerate, Roberts states that in 1871, 460,000 women in England and Wales and over 59,000 in Scotland worked in textile factories. By 1901 Hollis, who tends to be less conservative, states that there were 795,000 women textile workers in Great Britain as a whole, the number having risen by 160,000 since 1851. Drake puts the figure at 863,000 women textile workers for the whole kingdom by 1914.[27] Whichever figures are used, the textile industry was one of the main employers of women and the number of women employed in this sector was steadily rising throughout the period. Further, it was the sector claiming the largest number of women members of trade unions. Drake put a figure of 19,000 women trade unionists in 1876, rising to over 143,000 by 1906 and over 250,000 or one third of all women workers in the trade by 1914.[28] However, despite the large number of women involved in the sector and the large numbers of women who were trade unionists, they were segregated into the lower paid weaving work. The higher paid spinning work was regarded as male work despite the pre-industrial tradition of spinning being woman's work. Walby argues that it was the better-organized male workers who were able to 'cherry pick' the best textile work early in the nineteenth century. This, together with the prevailing patriarchal ideology concerning the primacy of the male breadwinner, meant that men were able to exclude women from the best-paid work rather than the issue being the question of strength needed to perform the task.[29]

Figure 2 Homeworkers, early 1900s.

Source: By kind permission of The Salvation Army International Heritage Centre.

The clothing industry was also a large employer of women workers. From the 1870s the industry started to be mechanized and factories began mass-producing clothing, although the small dressmaking and tailoring workshops continued to flourish, especially in the bespoke end of the trade. Further, Pennington and Westover state that, in spite of mechanization, many women continued to be employed as outworkers well into the twentieth century. Sewing processes were separated out and outworkers could do finishing more cheaply.[30] The nature of the work and the structure of the sector (i.e. it could include part-time and casual workers so many workers could be homeworkers who did not specify their employment in the census) make it very difficult to ascertain how many women were employed in this industry. Nevertheless, Hollis states that in 1851 there were 491,000 women working in the clothing industry, including those in the shoe industry and that this had risen to 792,000 by 1901. Drake says there were 612,000 women involved in the clothing trade in 1914 but does not indicate whether this figure includes the shoe and boot trade.[31] The increase in trade union membership for this sector demonstrates the success of the women's trade union movement in this period. Membership was 100 in 1876, rising to more than 5,000 by 1906 and almost 26,000 by 1914, although this was still a tiny proportion of the possible number who could have joined and it was impossible to organize the masses of outworkers.[32]

However, it was not always easy to unionize women, even when they were working in a factory and, consequently, as mentioned in the previous chapter, protective legislation was important to protect workers from the worst abuses of factory work. All jobs have their dangers, but some types of work are more dangerous than others. Harrison points to the lead industry, matchmaking, fur pulling, rubber making, tinplate making, asbestos manufacturing and a whole variety of other trades that involved the production of large quantities of dust, all of which were the focus of the women inspectors; however, they had no powers beyond informing their male counterparts.[33] Harrison argues that despite all the fuss made about women carrying out certain types of work and the panic around married women working, the connection between accidents and women workers was not easily recognized. Discourses around accidents tended to focus on the male worker because accidents were associated with machinery and machinery with male workers.[34]

As I have previously mentioned, it was very difficult for factory inspectors to encourage workers to report infringements of the law. The WIC, through their work with Girls' Clubs, tried hard to encourage young women to report infringements but many were reluctant if it would either affect the amount they could earn, or worse, result in the loss of their job. It is useful here to mention the aims of one particular organization. The Clubs' Industrial Association was formed to organize Working Girls' Clubs in London. Its objectives were:

1   To affiliate Working Girls' Clubs together, with a view to studying Industrial Law, doing Investigative Work, reporting infringements of Factory Laws, via the Women's Industrial Council, to the Home Office.
2   To unite clubs in different districts of London by making them realize the common aims of good citizenship.
3   To stimulate the sense of responsibility amongst wage-earners (a) towards themselves; (b) towards their employers; (c) towards each other; (d) towards posterity.[35]

The Clubs' Industrial Association was successful in London but did not develop in the rest of the country, although Working Girls' Clubs were established in other industrial areas. The WIC and the Girls' Clubs associated with it were also keen to encourage young women to train at technical colleges.[36]

However, one young woman did challenge her employers and it is to her I shall now turn. We do not have many examples of factory life by women employed in the work, but an excellent exception to the rule are the letters of the Crewe Factory Girl, which appeared in the *Crewe Chronicle* between May and September 1894.[37] These letters were written anonymously by the 24-year-old Ada Nield, before she began her career as a trade union and suffrage organizer. Nield's letters give us an extraordinary insight into the daily life of a clothing factory making uniforms for the army. She alleged that women were doing the men's work for less money than men were paid but that when the factory inspectors visited, the work was given to the men. Life was a continual struggle for survival and, she argued, women were paid so little that:

> we cannot be said to "live", we merely exist. We eat, we sleep, we work, endlessly work from Monday to Saturday night, without remission. Cultivation of the mind? How is it possible? Reading? Those of us who are determined to live like human beings and require food for the mind as well as the body, are obliged to take time which is necessary for sleep to gratify this desire. . . . "A living wage!" Ours is a lingering dying wage![38]

Nield's depiction of factory life paints a very different picture of women workers than that usually found in middle-class observations. Nield describes young women wanting more out of life than the unremitting grind that they were subjected to. She details the work the women undertook and the exploitative practices that the employer used to maximize profits while keeping wages low. She also highlighted unfair practices carried out by foremen, which today we would call sexual harassment or discrimination. Unionization was, she argued, the only way that women would be able to fight the discrimination that they suffered in factories. Encouraged by the editor of the *Crewe Chronicle*, she wrote in total twelve letters to the paper, describing to an astonished readership the lives of young women like herself and the problems they endured whilst trying to earn a living. Her writing was so good that some people doubted that she was really a factory worker or they believed that left-wing sympathizers were coaching her. These doubts she rebutted, but they demonstrate that most people had extremely negative images of working-class women and found her a challenge to these. Finally, her identity was exposed and the newly formed Independent Labour Party employed her as one of their itinerant speakers, although what happened to the other workers who had supported her and were sacked, too, is not reported. The letters are a wonderful source as their vibrancy and immediacy speaks of the humanity of the young women who worked in factories, the way they were treated and one young woman's desire to speak up and challenge the employer. For this alone, they are an important source for the historian.

If life was tough for the Crewe Factory Girl and her contemporaries, there was at least a semblance of protection by the law. It was often much worse for outworkers who were not protected by the Factory Acts. As Harrison has pointed out, the 1891 and 1895 Factory Acts brought workshops within regulation and this was likely to have increased the amount of work that was contracted out to homeworkers.[39] Outwork or homework was prevalent in a range of urban and rural settings. Homework meant piecework distributed either from the factory or workshop or by a subcontractor acting as an intermediary between the factory owner and the workers. Its main characteristics were that it was unregulated, casual and low paid. It was usually classed as sweated work because it could be defined as low paid, involving long hours and carried out in poor working conditions.[40] Bythell summed up the main features of homeworking as work carried out in the home, producing goods of low value and using processes where few skills were required and simple equipment used. Finally, he stated that the goods produced were consumer goods destined for the mass market.[41] As mentioned in Part Two, the major homeworking industries were clothing, boot and shoe making, glove making, hosiery, lace making, straw plaiting, box making, carding, chain making, nail making and button-making.[42] Estimating the numbers of women engaged in homework is difficult. First, the problems of categorization in the census and the casual nature of the work means that both under- and over-representation in the returns could occur. Second, it was not necessary for employers to register homeworkers as employees until 1901, so they were doubly invisible. Third, women had their own reasons for not making public work they undertook in the privacy of their own home. Harrison states that it was not until 1901, when employers were required to register outworkers, that there was any real sense of how many workers were involved in outwork. These returns showed that there were around 50,000 outworkers in Britain as a whole but, Harrison observes, this would have been only a small proportion of all homeworkers and it is not possible to ascertain from these figures whether the work would be defined as sweated or not.[43] However, the 1890 House of Lords Select Committee deemed low wages as the primary factor in sweating and this was to be the focus of various campaigns to eliminate the practice.[44]

Pennington and Westover argue that outwork would continue to prevail, even after mechanization, if it was still profitable because low wages and a desire to circumvent the factory regulations outweighed the benefits that mechanization offered.[45] Indeed, Mrs Heatherley had been quite prophetic when she stated at the Royal Commission on Factories and Workshops in 1876 that 'If the people are prevented from working at the workshop they take homework to do, and if you stop the working in the workshop you only make the work get done under more unwholesome conditions.'[46] Women in particular were vulnerable to sweating. Domestic ideology encouraged the notion that a woman's place was in the home and that respectable men should not let their wives go out to work. As we have seen, women needed to work for a whole host of reasons, not least because their husbands did not earn enough to be the sole provider for the family. Legislation restricting women's access to work could also exacerbate the problem as it could make it even harder for women to find paid work outside the home. Consequently, working at home was the only viable option for many women. As the clothing industry was one of the main employers of women, it is not surprising that many sweated outworkers worked in this industry and that homeworking was particularly prevalent in the London tailoring trade.[47] Other London trades, including fur pulling, pen making, French polishing, artificial flower making, millinery and box making to name but a few, were all subject to investigation by various groups of social reformers, especially the WIC.[48]

Concern about sweated labour grew out of the increasing interest in working-class life generally and is linked to the various campaigns around protective legislation and anxiety about the deterioration of the 'race'. Social feminist groups, like the WIC and FWG, were central players in the debate and wrote widely on the issue.[49] Various solutions were suggested but the contentious issue was how to remedy it. The WIC drew up a bill for the better regulation of homework. The main thrust of the bill was to improve working conditions for homeworkers by extending the protection of the Factory Acts to home workshops by a licensing system. This was introduced many times between 1899 and 1907. Margaret MacDonald of the WLL and WIC and Ramsay MacDonald, her husband, were leading campaigners for this Act, making a case for it at the Select Committee on Homework in 1907. Margaret MacDonald's testimony at the Committee suggests that she was more concerned to inculcate bourgeois domestic ideology through a licensing system that would give factory inspectors access to the homes of the poor.[50] However, this remedy was not widely accepted by many related associations. The Committee recommended the establishment of Trades Boards that would focus on the wages of all workers in a particular trade whether they worked from home or in a factory or workshop.

Following the various investigations instigated by social reformers and women's organizations, the *Daily News* organized an exhibition in 1906 to expose the sweated conditions in which many workers earned their wage.[51] After the exhibition the Anti-Sweating League was formed to take forward the momentum of interest inspired by the exhibition. The main focus of the League was to campaign for minimum wage legislation although the licensing proposal was part of its remit too. However, this caused tensions between the promoters of the two schemes, with Black and Macarthur supporting the Trades Boards and MacDonald supporting the licensing system. This disagreement spilt over into the WIC.[52] Black felt that it was not enough to focus just on homeworkers but that low pay in certain trades was the main problem. MacDonald was more con-cerned with homework and the impact it had on the living conditions of the poor. She also believed in paying the male breadwinner an adequate wage so that his wife would not need to work. Despite these tensions, the Trades Boards were established in 1909 and initially covered four trades: box making, chain making, lace mending and finishing, and ready-made clothing.[53] The Boards were later extended by legislation in 1918 and were eventually renamed Wages Councils. These lasted for most of the twentieth century.

A new sector that was beginning to emerge in this period, and which became a major employer during the First World War, was engineering. In this period, the number of women participating in engineering increased from 5.5 to 6.2 per cent of the total engineering workforce.[54] Most of these workers were employed in the metal trades in the Black Country. Walby argues that male workers were able to exclude women from the skilled areas of this work because of their control of the apprenticeship system from which some men and all women were excluded. This meant that women were excluded from the skilled engineering trades unions. Consequently, women working in the metal trades were obliged to join a general union such as the NFWW.[55] However, Wightman, writing about a later period contests this, arguing that the sector was less organized than generally reported and that the gendered nature of the work is more complicated than the triumph of patriarchal interests.[56] I shall return to this debate in Part Three.

Shop work

Shop work grew as an employment sector for women in the last third of the nineteenth and early part of the twentieth century. Further, it was a sector that was deemed suitable employment for middle-class and working-class women. Like domestic service, the sector was highly stratified from the lowly assistant in a corner shop in a poor district to well-groomed young ladies, or those aspiring to be ladies, in the large new departmental stores in town and city centres. Like domestic service the trade also operated a living-in system. Hollis states that the number of women shop assistants rose from 87,000 in 1861 to 250,000 in 1901.[57] Holcombe estimates that by 1914, the number of women working in shops had risen to nearly 500,000 in England and Wales and the sector was the largest employer of middle-class women at that time.[58] These figures probably exclude female members of shopkeeping families, especially those working part-time; as Roberts points out, it is hard to ascertain whether those counted are assistants or shop owners, dealers or people engaged in producing goods for sale.[59] What can be said is that retail was a growing employment sector for women although participation rates varied throughout the country. One of the reasons for this increase in women's employment in retailing is the change that was occurring in the sector. Earlier in the nineteenth century, the retail trades were seen as skilled. Young men were apprenticed to work in, say, grocery or drapery and had to learn a whole range of skills that applied to that particular section of the trade.[60] Shops were small, specialized and did not employ a large number of workers from outside of the family. Consequently, retail work was not seen as a viable option for many women unless they were working in the family business.[61] However, the retail trade was transformed in the last decades of the nineteenth century. Holcombe argues that:

> the later nineteenth century saw a revolution in the distributive trades which paralleled the contemporary trend in industry towards large-scale organization, specialization and the division of labour. An enormous increase in both the quantity and variety of goods to be channelled to the public by retail traders followed naturally upon industrialization with its mass production and new inventions and processes, upon improved methods of transport, and upon British dominance in and dependence upon a world market, accompanied as it was by a policy of free trade.[62]

As mass production and consumerism took hold in society generally, Holcombe states there was an increase in the number of shops from 295,000 in 1875 to nearly 459,592 in 1907, an increase of 56 per cent.[63] Not only were there more shops, there was also an increase in the size of shops as this period saw the emergence of the department store, co-operative retailing and the start of chains. Many of the skills relating to the retail trade in the early part of the century were redundant as factories increasingly turned out standardized goods. Consequently, a few skilled managers and buyers could run the newer larger stores with a host of relatively unskilled assistants working under them. As the sector grew women were increasingly looked to as a source of cheap labour. Holcombe argues that gender segregation took place. Women tended to feature in the less skilled, lighter end of the trade where employers could justify lower wages. For example, they were clustered in women's clothing, bakery and confectionery, dairy, flowers, stationery and tobacco shops.[64]

However, Jordan suggests that although this employment pattern might be true for large stores selling clothes and household goods, there were still plenty of smaller shops where a more expert knowledge of the trade was important; yet these shops were employing young women too. To demonstrate this using census information, she has compiled a table of the main retail occupations of women aged 15–24. Part of this is reproduced in Table 6.1.

Interestingly, these statistics indicate that women were already present in shops, even though in small numbers, as early as 1850. Jordan suggests

Table 6.1[65] Women's work, 1851–1911

Occupation	1851 number employed/ % of occupation	1871 number employed/ % of occupation	1891 number employed/ % of occupation	1911 number employed/ % of occupation
Draper	2,750/6	10,458/14.1	26,307/24.6	50,475/33.4
Hosier, haberdasher	789/13.8	1,602/18.8	3,221/25.8	782/8.03
Butcher	140/0.23	685/0.9	977/1	1,996/1
Fishmonger	439/4	408/2.7	963/3.2	1,693/3.8
Baker	575/1.11	1,393/2.4	3,263/3.9	20,860/2.8
Grocer	1,464/1.3	3,244/2.9	9,068/5	10,959/5.2
Greengrocer	580/4.3	939/3.6	2,614/6.4	5,566/7.7

that the reason for women's presence in shop work increasing was that the sector was moving away from employing family members who, presumably, did not appear as employees on the census returns, to employing local young women. This she attributes to the growing aspirations of gentility amongst the shop-owning classes who wanted their own daughters to attain ladylike qualities and therefore do no work, in public at least. The young women employed would most likely have come from a background where they would have been servants in an earlier generation and this, in part, explains the living-in system operating in the retail sector. The long working day was another reason for the living-in system, which meant that workers had little time for any life outside of work. The retail trade is an area that needs further research so it is difficult to be definite about why it became a major employer of women in this particular period. Although Jordan doubts that deskilling was the reason for women being employed in the first place, she concurs that deskilling contributed to the increasing feminization of the sector in some areas, especially in drapers' shops.[66] Several writers have commented on how women tended to be clustered in employment sectors where workers were considered transitory and where there was little prospect of promotion, and shop work is one of those areas.[67] Jordan argues that it was in the larger stores that women were employed because they were less skilled, likely to leave through marriage and did not expect a large wage. This is borne out in the statistics, which show a huge increase in women working in drapers, which tended to be large enterprises, whereas grocers and other food shops tended to be small-scale. In conclusion, Jordan argues that women working in shops did not disturb patriarchal notions of gender segregation in the workplace. The living-in system meant that young women were still under patriarchal control, there was a history of women working in family businesses and rules and regulations concerning dress and demeanour meant that women shop assistants did not offend middle-class sensibilities. This made work in the large stores ideal for middle-class women in need of earning a respectable living and for aspiring, present-able working-class girls wanting to avoid less attractive work in factories and domestic service.

However, the sector had its own problems for workers. The 1876 Royal Commission on Factories and Workshops noted that shop workers worked up to 85 hours per week. Not only were hours long but assistants had to stand for long periods without breaks and were fined for a variety of petty infringements. However, as Holcombe points out, opening hours varied hugely from 56 to 97 hours per week depending on the trade, area and size of the business.[68] Again, equal rights advocates, such as Jessie Boucherett, firmly opposed legislation aimed at restricting working hours. Boucherett argued that not only would restrictions on women's working hours mean that employers would not employ women but that it would, adversely affect poor women generally, not just those working in shops:

> In the cheap shops in the East and South of London, large numbers of women are employed, and it is in these poor localities that the sales are chiefly effected in the evening. The servant-girl goes out in the evening . . . to make her purchases; the charwoman goes out after her day's work is done . . . the man, woman or girl employed in a factory or handicraft goes out after taking supper and making a change of clothes. At nine o'clock the shops are still busy, busier indeed than in the middle of the day.[69]

As Jordan has pointed out, shop work generally had a genteel public representation and many women were prepared to endure poor con-ditions because the work had higher status than domestic service or factory work. However, various investigations into the sector demonstrated that the work could be equally arduous despite its claim to respectability. Clara Collett included shop workers in her study of London in 1892–3[70] and the WIC sent Margaret Bondfield, a former shop worker, underground to report on the conditions of shop workers.[71] Living in was regarded as particularly unpleasant and was cited as one of the reasons why young women wanted to leave the work.[72] The living-in system meant that illegal overtime was prevalent and, even if employees did not live in, they often had to take part of their wages as meals even though the standard of food was usually very poor. Similarly, an investigation in Edinburgh found that very few shops in the city had seats for assistants and even if seats were available in the shop, the girls were forbidden to use them.[73] Consequently, campaigns to improve working conditions took place during this period. These were for shorter working days; abolition of fines and the living-in system; and a call for a minimum wage.

Holcombe notes that it was very difficult to organize shop workers, as they tended to think of themselves as above unionization.[74] However, in 1891 the National Union of Shop Assistants (NAUSA) was formed and, in 1895, Co-op workers formed the Amalgamated Union of Co-operative Employees (AUCE).[75] Although women were not well represented in the early years, it is no accident that Margaret Bondfield and Mary Macarthur, both leaders in the industrial women's movement, started their activist careers in NAUSA, a union more welcoming to women than the average trade union. Women's membership of this union grew from 2,000, out of a potential membership of more than 22,000 in 1910, to more than 22,000 out of a potential membership of more than 81,000 in 1914.[76] Of course, given the wide range of types of shops in existence it was more likely that union members would emanate from the larger places of employment and it would always be difficult to unionize isolated workers in small establishments. However, some of the larger employers were very anti-union. They would actively discourage employees from joining a union in the instances when shop workers were persuaded that unions were not beneath them.

The first reform on NAUSA's agenda was shorter working hours. This affected both male and female workers and was a culmination of more than fifty years of campaigning. The Shop Act of 1886 restricted working hours to 74 hours a week but, Harrison reports, there was no provision for enforcement. Unions continued to press for a 50-hour week with fixed closing times and a half-day holiday per week, but to no avail.[77] Improvements did take place over the next twenty years or so, although Harrison argues that the unions largely failed to improve the conditions that shop workers laboured under.[78] In 1896 Sir Charles Dilke, the husband of Lady Dilke of the WTUL, managed to get the Truck Bill through Parliament. This Act made it illegal to pay shop workers in kind rather than in cash and consequently assisted in the dismantling of the living-in system.[79] Further, in 1899 the Seats for Shop Assistants Act was passed although there were no fines for employers breaching the Act. This series of acts passed between 1886 and 1911 were all incorporated in a single act of 1912. By 1914 the retail trade was becoming a major employer of women and was to retain that position for the rest of the century, although its status was eroded as the education level of young women rose. Another sector that was to become an increasingly popular choice for young women was clerical employment, discussed below.

Clerical work

In some ways the development of office work in the nineteenth century followed a similar trajectory to the development of shop work. Both sectors were male-dominated areas focused on by women's rights advocates; both were rapidly developing in response to industrialization and the burgeoning empire; both offered a respectable alternative to the narrow range of work previously available; and both were looking for a cheap alternative to highly trained, specialized male workers for the more mundane tasks in the sector. However, it is useful to take a closer look at the development of this sector rather than just comparing it with shop work. Holcombe explains that in the first half of the nineteenth century business establishments were small, often family-run, employing indentured apprentices to learn a particular aspect of business. There was no great demand for clerical labour and what was required could easily be obtained from among young, reasonably educated men.[80] However, Anderson argues that in the last third of the nineteenth century there was a rising demand for clerical work as the economy shifted towards service and finance industries. In addition, manufacturing industries were increasingly employing clerical workers. He states that by 1911, 42 per cent of all Britain's commercial clerks were employed in the manufacturing sector. There was also a huge increase in the Civil Service. In 1881 there were more than 208,000 commercial clerks and more than 46,000 clerks and officers in the Civil Service. By 1911 this had expanded to almost 547,000 and 118,000 respectively. These figures do not include those in banking, law and insurance.[81] So how many of these clerks were women and what sort of work did they undertake?

SPEW took up clerical work as one of the sectors it wanted to open up to women as early as the 1860s. Jordan argues that this project was one of SPEW's more successful endeavours, although she suggests that women's rights advocates were pushing at an opening door.[82] The campaign to open up clerical work to women dovetailed with the need for more clerical workers. The opening up of the Civil Service to women in 1871 also assisted in the increase of women workers in the clerical sector. Roberts states that the number of women clerks increased by 400 per cent in the period 1861 to 1911.[83] Anderson argues that in this period women were being recruited into clerical work at a faster rate than men. By 1881 there were almost 7,500 women employed in the commercial sector and more than 4,600 in the Civil Service. Numbers had risen to more than 146,000 and 27,000 respectively by 1911. This meant that women had taken over more than 25 per cent of the sector.[84] However, although women had campaigned for years for equal access to higher-grade work in the Civil Service, they were barred from sitting the examinations for the administrative grades, despite favourable evidence to the Royal Commission on the Civil Service in 1912–15.[85]

As always, it is difficult to acquire hard statistics concerning numbers employed in the sector, especially as the census categorized clerical workers differently over time. Zimmeck includes commercial and government-employed workers in her figures and states that the overall numbers of workers employed in the industry in England increased from 95,000 in 1851 to 843,000 in 1911. Of this figure, the number of women increased from 2,000 to 160,000 or, as a proportion of the clerical workforce, from 2 per cent to 20 per cent.[86] Roberts, using figures for Scotland and Wales too, states that there were almost 150,000 women clerical workers in England and Wales and 33,500 in Scotland by 1911. Holcombe puts the figure for England and Wales at almost 125,000 by 1911. According to Holcombe, in 1911 most women clerical workers in England and Wales were employed as commercial or business clerks (almost 94 per cent). The Civil Service employed almost 40,000 (21 per cent) women mainly as Post Office clerks, telegraph or telephone operators.[87] Other clerical work included local government work. Jones states that almost 20,000 women were employed as Poor Law, municipal and parish officers.[88] In the vast majority of cases, women occupied the low-grade, low-paid jobs in the sector and seemed grateful to do so as clerical work was deemed a clean, safe, respectable occupation for middle-class women and better-educated working women looking for an alternative to factory or domestic work.

Overall, during the latter half of the nineteenth century, clerical work was transformed from a small-scale, male-dominated, unmechanized sector to a major employer of both men and women. The sector was beginning to take advantage of new technology, such as typewriters, and other office machinery dealing with bulk processing; telegraphy, and towards the end of the period, the telephone; and an improved postal service. In addition, the work was increasingly subdivided, simplified and streamlined so that the office at the end of this period was a very different place to the office of the first half of the nineteenth century. The amount of paperwork produced to sustain the economy and public services had increased exponentially. Furthermore, the improvements wrought in the education system generally and the increasing acceptance that middle-class girls needed to be educated for work as well as marriage meant that there were plenty of young, reasonably well-educated women looking for employment, yet who were still restricted by a limited range of options open to them. As educated young men had a wider range of white-collar work available to them and could demand higher wages, employers turned to a less mobile, more docile group of workers – young women – to fill low-grade jobs. Zimmeck argues that Victorian society operated a test of less eligibility to work, in which the objective of middle-class women working was to allow them to earn a subsistence wage and not be better off than they would have been had they married or stayed at home. Consequently, wages were offered at just the right level to encourage those who needed to work to apply but deter those who did not strictly need to work. To this end, clerical work fitted the bill for many middle-class women who needed to earn a living.[89] The desirability and respectability of clerical work meant that employees were difficult to organize in unions, despite poor conditions and pay in some areas of the sector. Although emphasis in the literature is placed on clerical work for young middle-class women, it was also a sector in which better-educated, respectable working-class women could aspire to work.[90]

The Post Office was the first and largest of the government departments to employ women clerks. Mr Scudamore, in a report on the re-organization of the telegraph system, summed up the employers' views on women clerks:

> In the first place they have in an eminent degree, the quickness of eye and the delicacy of touch which are essential qualifications of a good operator. In the second place, they take more kindly than men and boys do to sedentary employment and are more patient during long confinement in one place. In the third place, the wages which will draw male operators from but an inferior class of the community, will draw female operators from a superior class. Female operators thus drawn from a superior class, will, as a rule, write better than male clerks, and spell more correctly; and where the staff is mixed, the female staff will raise the tone of the whole staff. They are also less disposed than men to combine for the purpose of extorting higher wages, and this is by no means an unimportant matter.
>
> On one other ground it is especially desirable that we should extend the employment of women. Permanently established civil servants invariably expect their remuneration to increase with their years of service . . . Women, however, solve these difficulties for the department by retiring for the purpose of getting married as soon as they get a chance . . . if we place an equal number of females and males on the same ascending scale of pay, the aggregate pay to the females will always be less that the aggregate pay to the males; . . . and further, there will always be fewer females than males on the pension list.[91]

As clerical work was usually segregated along gender lines, access to higher-grade and better-paid work could easily elude women. Supervising other women was probably the highest prize that a women clerk could aspire to and these jobs were rare. Zimmeck suggests that this segregation was modelled on dominant notions of male and female roles at this time, in which men were ascribed roles that involved the intellect and decision-making and women were given the mechanized work which required attention, dexterity but above all an imperviousness to monotony – all attributes, as Scudamore suggests, that women were supposed to possess. This segregation also meant that men and women were separated physically. Female supervisors managed women workers and a separate salary scale for women was easily operated.[92] The marriage bar, that is the practice of dismissing women on marriage, was usually in place and again could be used to steer women towards domesticity and the view that work was an interlude between school and marriage rather than a lifetime career. Class stratification meant that women from the upper working class and lower middle classes congregated in the low-status end of the sector with very little chance of advancement. However, despite low pay and lack of career structure, clerical work was very popular. Zimmeck states that in 1901, when there were alternative jobs available, there were 329 candidates for just 25 posts in the Post Office.[93] Anderson also argues that typewriting had quickly become synonymous with women's work through the late-nineteenth-century use of typewriting agencies which employed large numbers of women trained in the skill in commercial schools.[94]

When compared to other sectors, the working conditions of clerical workers were usually tolerable, although Harrison mentions some reports of overcrowding, unhygienic conditions and overwork.[95] However, employers competed for staff by offering reasonable conditions. Low pay was a problem and women maximized their potentialities by changing jobs frequently. The Civil Service lost many workers when commercial companies offered better salaries and terms. Overall, the larger companies offered the better terms and conditions. However, women's mobility could also be read as lack of commitment or loyalty and supported the view that most women only worked in the interlude between school and marriage.

The relatively fair conditions and the aura of respectability that surrounded clerical work meant that it was a difficult sector to unionize, although there were several other reasons why it was difficult to organize women clerical workers. First, women regarded the work as an interlude before marriage rather than a career. Second, apart from the large organizations, many clerical workers were employed in few numbers and the different types of work, grades and status militated against unionization. Third, they met with the usual opposition from male workers. Walby has demonstrated that there was considerable male hostility to women clerical workers throughout the last third of the nineteenth century. The usual arguments around the patriarchal discourses of the male breadwinner and the work making women unfit as homemakers were employed.[96] She also argues that some parts of the sector were more successful at excluding women than others. Although women constituted around 40 per cent of the Civil Service and around a third of commercial clerks in 1911, they had made very little impact in the railways and in banking where their numbers represented less than 2 per cent. However, Cohn finds little evidence that male workers had much influence over employers' recruitment practices.[97] There is plenty of evidence to suggest that men were no keener on women entering the clerical sector than any other sector but it seems that the needs of capitalism won out, possibly because women were not in direct competition with men in most areas of work. Nevertheless, Walby argues that 'job segregation was a negotiated outcome of a three-way struggle between male clerks, employers and women'. Segregation was an outcome of competition between men and women and employers used it as a way to placate male workers. She concludes:

> The outcome was the entry of women to the new occupational slots not already monopolized by men and the rigid sex segregation of the workforce. These new slots were created at lower levels of pay and status than the old. Thus while men won their struggle not to have women in direct competition with themselves, employers won theirs to employ women at cheap rates of pay. The result should be seen as the negotiated outcome of a struggle between these patriarchal and capitalist forces.[98]

She does not mention that it was also a victory of sorts for feminists who wanted to open up this particular area of work for women.

Men may have resisted women entering the sector but they do not seem to have refused them access to the unions. Indeed, equal treatment for men and women was the policy of some of the unions. In 1890, the National Union of Clerks was established and included women workers from the outset. Although women had equal membership to men, the latter were disproportionally represented on the executive. Other unions also appeared during this period, such as the Association of Shorthand Writers and Typists. This was established in 1903 and changed its name to the Association of Women Clerks and Secretaries in 1912. Another union that included women clerical workers was the Railway Clerks' Association, which was formed in 1897.[99] Civil Service unions included the Association of Post Office Women Clerks, established in 1897; the Women Sorters' Association and the Civil Service Typists' Association, both formed in 1903. Membership of these various unions grew slowly and was never large during this period. Overall, women's membership of clerical unions grew from 920 in 1896 to almost 15,500 in 1914. Most of these workers were Civil Servants.[100] The main campaign for these unions during this period was around the National Insurance Bill of 1911, although low pay and equal pay were also important issues.[101]

Clerical work is an area that needs further research. Walby cites regional variations on the numbers of women employed in the commercial sector.[102] Local variations in women's employment in this sector would make an interesting research project.

The professions

The opening up of higher education to some women in the last third of the nineteenth century meant that the push to open up more of the professions to women was supported by their proven intellectual ability.[103] Jones states that by 1900 women comprised 16 per cent of university students.[104] Although increased education opportunities meant greater employment opportunities, they did not necessarily mean new areas of work were becoming available to women on a large scale. Consequently, women's moves into the professions were largely limited to the caring professions such as nursing and teaching. Some professions were just beginning to open to women; for example, medicine and the professional grades of the Civil Service. Others such as law were still closed to women. There were also areas where the willing amateur still gave service for free, for example, social work. Levine suggests that there were around 170 women doctors by 1894.[105] However, Jones states that by 1911 this had increased to 477 general practitioners and surgeons.[106] Jones also argues that women employed in senior government positions, such as factory or workhouse inspectors, were rare because the appointments were made on an ad hoc basis; therefore, no system was put in place for other women to follow and create a recognizable professional career path.[107] Jordan points out that women hardly figured in any of the independent professional categories in the 1911 Census, except for medicine. She states that there were 200 registered pharmacists, 19 accountants and 12 dentists but no lawyers, engineers or surveyors listed. This she puts down to women becoming increasingly diverted into the suffrage campaign which meant that they did not concentrate on professions other than medicine.[108] Consequently, this section will focus on the two areas where women made most progress in the professions during this period: nursing and teaching.

Nursing

Like teaching, nursing was always considered to be women's work and was, moreover, exclusively a woman's occupation, so mid-Victorian feminists did not have to make out a case for the suitability and desirability of women's employment. Rather, nurses, like governesses, had fallen upon evil days and women reformers faced the same problems that they did in the case of teaching, that of raising a depressed class of women workers to the status of true professionals. This goal was triumphantly achieved, and no aspect of the women's movement is more striking or important than the transformation of nursing from a refuge for the outcast into an honourable and skilled calling, and a very popular one as well.[109]

Holcombe's rather rosy picture of the professionalization of nursing needs closer examination. Whilst it is true that in the mid-nineteenth century nursing was transformed from its Dickensian 'Sairey Gamp' image (from *Martin Chuzzlewit*) into that of the 'Lady with the Lamp', the triumphalism of Holcombe's assertion needs to be treated with caution. Jordan states that between the 1851 Census and the 1891 Census, nursing had been transformed from an occupation largely occupied by elderly widows without training to an occupation for young educated unmarried women. Although she also points out that hospital nursing before the Nightingale era did not relate to the 'Sairey Gamp' stereotype, she also suggests that apologists for the new system wrote much of nursing historiography. The new system, she argues, owed as much to the work of St John's House, a pioneering nursing institution as to Nightingale's methods.[110] Whichever narrative is supported, it is evident that middle-class women had been involved in nursing but usually in a philanthropic way. This unpaid labour was transformed, in part, into nursing sisterhoods from the 1840s. The structures developed in these institutions formed the model for later hospital nursing.[111]

One reason given for the increase in the number of nurses was a large increase in hospital accommodation, which took place during the 1880s. This, too, contradicts dominant narratives, which attribute the expansion solely to the reform work of Florence Nightingale. Jordan suggests that changes in medical knowledge and practice meant that it was necessary to employ nurses who were able to understand and carry out doctors' instructions.[112] Jordan argues that hospital nursing was like teaching and shop work in the second half of the nineteenth century. It was a labour-intensive sector in need of a cheap, docile but educated workforce. Marriage would mean that many young women would leave before they started demanding promotion. In addition, the need for a trained workforce meant that it was also an occupation that was encroaching on work that men had previously done. Tasks that male medical students and dressers undertook in the early years of the century, such as dressing wounds and making beds, became part of the female nurse's job.[113] Jordan argues that romanticized media representations of Nightingale nursing in the Crimean War in the 1850s encouraged young middle-class and upper-middle-class women to want to enter a hitherto working-class, low-skilled occupation. Dominant notions of middle-class women as caring and morally superior, together with the work of the philanthropic nursing sisterhoods, increased the push to open up nursing to well-educated women.

The history of nursing in the nineteenth century reflects the class and gender attitudes of that society. As previously stated, women of all classes had always undertaken nursing. Philanthropic ladies visited the poor or cared for relatives; working-class women were employed by their peers to help as midwives and wise women. As middle-class women sought to find a place for themselves in the public sphere of paid work, rather than the private sphere of home nursing and philanthropic visiting, through their inclusion in the reformed medical profession, they moved to professionalize nursing so that it complemented the doctor's role. In fact, the reformed hospital resembled the bourgeois family to some extent with paternal doctors, maternal nurses and the patients as children. The role of working-class women in this model was as servants. They were nursing assistants carrying out all the heaviest domestic work, just as they would in the bourgeois home. Lower-class women, often daughters of small farmers or better-educated domestic servants, entered the profession as probationers for a year while they learned the work; they then became paid nurses contracted to the training institution for a further three years. These women lived in the Nurses Home where the domestic set-up was akin to the middle-class home.[114] However, there were also higher-class young women, influenced by religious fervour and the 'Nightingale effect', wanting to train as nurses too. These women paid between £30 and £50 a year and although they were relieved of some of the heavier work and worked less hours, they undertook a very similar training to the lower-class women, although their ultimate position in the sector would be different. The training of all hospital nurses led to them campaigning for professional recognition at the beginning of the twentieth century.[115] Lady nursing sisters were important as a tool for inculcating bourgeois values. Despite their training, they were employed as much for their moral influence as their nursing skills. Vicinus argues that they used their superior moral influence as a way of making the work appear respectable to doubting middle-class parents reluctant to let their daughters embark on the work. These middle-class nurses worked mainly in the military and civilian hospitals.[116] They were not so prevalent in smaller cottage hospitals or district nursing, which remained the domain of educated lower middle-class and working-class women.

Despite the transformation of nursing into a profession, both Vicinus and Harrison argue that by the 1880s nursing was characterized by overcrowding, wage stagnation and variable local standards, as in other women's occupations.[117] The work was hard, often unpleasant and the pay was low. Harrison argues that these were the issues most complained about in the evidence to the Select Committee of the House of Lords on Metropolitan Hospitals in the early 1890s.[118] In addition, the practice of living-in meant that nurses' private as well as working lives were under continuous scrutiny. Although nursing employed a large number of women (53,000 in 1891 according to Jordan, 64,000 in 1901 according to Hollis and 77,060 by 1911 according to Harrison[119]), its popularity is in doubt as recruitment was always a problem and the drop-out rate was constantly at around 30 per cent up until the First World War.[120] As in other occupations, exact figures are difficult to ascertain due to problems with census categories. The term 'nurse' covers a wide range of activities from nurses based in large civilian or military hospitals, nurses in asylums and workhouses, district nurses, midwives to nurses working in private homes looking after individual patients.

Because nursing was a divided profession, both in terms of class and a complex internal hierarchy, it was very difficult for women to demand their rights as workers. Vicinus states that understaffing and poor pay were justified by the employers who argued that the wrong type of woman would be attracted if conditions were improved.[121] The inference being that if a nurse left the work because of the conditions then she was not suited to the work anyway. This demand for strong moral integrity was coupled with a strict militaristic discipline that only the strongest characters could endure for long. Although the reformation of nursing was necessary and improved the care that patients received, there were structural weaknesses in the new system. Imbuing the role with an almost unattainable saintliness in which the class of the nurse was of paramount importance meant that it was difficult for women to live up to the ideal expected. Even the most dedicated nurse needed a decent salary and reasonable working hours and conditions. However, any complaint was seen as the nurse not living up to the impossible ideal that had been constructed around the occupation, an ideal that was not found in any other job except, of course, motherhood. Very few women could expect to make a decent career, culminating in the position of matron, and those who did maintained an iron control over their subordinates, resulting in the high turnover of probationers and nurses in their early years.[122] Consequently, it is not surprising that the demand for nurses always exceeded the supply, especially when other work, teaching or clerical work in particular, offered better prospects and a chance of an independent social life.

The emphasis on the vocational element of the work, coupled with the links to philanthropy and the employment of lady nursing sisters, militated against the organization of nurses in unions to protect their interests. Again, this led to a high turnover of probationers and newly trained nurses. Apart from long hours and low pay, the lack of pensions and the living-in system were also causes of disagreement among the lower ranks. Nursing associations were formed but they were more concerned with the professionalization of the sector than the pay and conditions. The British Nurses Association was formed in 1891 and this organization was successful in getting nursing recognized as a bona fide profession when it was awarded a royal charter in 1893. In 1894, the Matrons' Council was established and this, in turn, introduced the National League of Certificated Nurses in 1900, although full state registration was not accepted until 1919.[123] Midwifery, too, was transformed from a working-class community role to a profession as exams were introduced in the last third of the nineteenth century.[124] However, underlying the changes to the sector was an unchanging relationship with the wider patriarchal structure of the medical profession.[125] Women were welcome in the subordinate position of nurse, and even the most powerful matron was subordinate to male physicians, but patriarchal interests bitterly opposed women training as doctors in this period. There were 25 women registered as physician, surgeon or registered practitioner in 1881. This had risen to 477 by 1911, 2 per cent of the whole profession.[126] Clearly, the medical profession was still regarded as a male domain and a battle still to be fought.[127]

Teaching

Like nursing, teaching was becoming increasingly professionalized in the last third of the nineteenth century. The training of teachers had moved from the pupil-teacher system to the college-trained system. Holcombe states that in 1890 there were 49 training colleges with accommodation for 3,700 students. This had increased to 89 training colleges and 22 council colleges with nearly 11,000 students in 1914.[128] She also argues that the college culture engendered a spirit of solidarity which, in turn, facilitated strong unionization. However, even a strong union representation did not undermine the prevailing ideology that men should be paid more than women and had a better claim to better career prospects. Teaching continued to be one of the main areas of work that respectable upper working-class and middle-class women flocked to, especially as the demand for teachers increased dramatically once schooling became compulsory. Holcombe states that there were 13,200 elementary schools with 1,873,200 pupils in England and Wales in 1875. This number had increased to 21,000 schools and 5,392,600 pupils in 1914. In the same period, the number of women teachers rose by 86.21 per cent and where women had represented 54.3 per cent of elementary teachers in 1875, by 1914 they represented 74.5 per cent.[129] Holcombe states that in the 1871 Census there were 94,029 women teachers and this rose to 183,298 by 1911.[130]

In the 1870s, the sector was still largely divided on class lines, with working-class women working in elementary schools and middle-class women working in private schools or still as governesses. However, this pattern began to change as the sector expanded. Following on from Burdett-Coutts' campaign in the 1850s to open up elementary teaching to middle-class women, Louisa Hubbard began a similar campaign in the 1870s.[131] Widdowson argues that by the 1870s it was easier for middle-class women to enter the sector for several reasons. First, the demand for elementary teachers was increasing. Second, it was becoming easier for people who had not been pupil-teachers to become assistant teachers. Third, the way for Hubbard's scheme had been opened by feminist propaganda in the 1860s. Thus the work of feminists was beginning to have an effect on the way the public viewed training for middle-class girls.[132] Hubbard's aim was to encourage middle-class women, the daughters of clergymen, army officers and doctors, into the profession. She was keen to counteract the predominance of lower middle-class women in teaching. Widdowson suggests that the reasons why Hubbard wanted to open up elementary teaching to a higher class of women were:

1 This group of women would be less demanding than lower class women who might be ambitious for promotion and higher wages;
2 As they were less well trained than ex-pupil teachers they would be suitable for teaching in rural areas where lower standards of teaching were more acceptable;
3 They were suited to living in small communities and would reinforce traditional expectations in their charges.[133]

Bishop Otter College was established to carry out the project, but Widdowson suggests that the scheme reached very few of the women that Hubbard had wanted to recruit and that the majority of women who passed through the college were not of that class. However, Widdowson concludes that the campaign had two positive effects. It boosted the status of elementary teaching and it encouraged other colleges to offer greater comfort and privacy to its students.

The structure of the pupil-teacher system changed radically during the period covered by this chapter. The change encouraged middle-class parents to allow their daughters to train as teachers. There was a move away from young children being apprenticed as pupil-teachers at age 13 to a more college-based system. Young women would receive secondary education up to age 16 or 17, then spend a year as a student teacher and attend college. The implementation of this system was uneven, with the old system surviving for longer in rural areas than in urban areas. The changes occurred in several stages. However, Widdowson argues that the changes improved the standard of training that pupil-teachers received.[134] This led to a shift in the class of women training as teachers, although the majority were still from lower middle-class and artisan-class students.

There are several reasons why teaching proved to be such a popular occupation for reasonably well-educated women. Oram states that these included the attraction of combining a professional occupation with one that reflected dominant notions of women's role in society; the appeal that working with children had for women; the possibility of having a relatively well-paid and secure career; and the pride to be felt in professional achievements.[135] One could add to this that if a woman was working in one of the new girls' grammar schools or private schools, she would feel pleasure at being part of a woman-only community which valued the individual for her intellectual prowess rather than her ability to catch a man. However, Harrison points to the social isolation of teachers in remote rural schools compared to those working in elite girls' grammar schools.[136] Teaching took place in a variety of settings, from elementary schools in poor working-class areas to elite private schools. Consequently, conditions of employment were also varied. Long working hours, equal pay and promotion were issues that the unions focused on during this period.[137]

The National Union of Teachers was established in 1870 and Widdowson argues that it was instrumental in raising the status of elementary teaching by negotiating pay settlements and a pension scheme for certificated teachers.[138] By the outbreak of the First World War it had a membership of more than 80 per cent of the 109,000 certificated elementary teachers in the country.[139] Oram states that women outnumbered men in this union from about 1904 and that women's membership steadily increased in the next twenty-five years, while men's membership was virtually static.[140] Given the dominance of women in this union, it is hardly surprising that it was one of the first unions to be interested in equality issues. Oram argues that these campaigns were closely related to wider feminist politics, especially suffrage. Many teachers, both in the NUT and other teaching unions, were involved in the suffrage movement in the years preceding the First World War.[141] However, teaching should not be regarded as a site of women's emancipation during this period. Women undertook the same work as men but received around 75–80 per cent of men's wages, although there was less vertical and horizontal segregation in elementary teaching than in, say, clerical work.[142] This was not true in secondary schools. Oram argues that men's promotion opportunities were twice as good as women's and the marriage bar meant that married women were increasingly likely to lose their job on marriage during this period.[143] Further, Harrison argues that the campaigns for equality with male teachers often obscured issues of health in the workplace.[144]

Conclusion to Part Two

For most working-class women, the same occupations were on offer in the last third of the nineteenth century as were available earlier in the century. Vast numbers were still employed in domestic service, factory and homework although the better educated of the younger working-class women, like their middle-class sisters, were turning to teaching, clerical work and shop work if they could. For most working-class women, paid work was seen as necessary at certain times of their lives: when schooling ceased and before marriage or in times of family hardship. These factors were recognized by the new women's organizations that sought state intervention to ameliorate working conditions in factories, workshops and shops. So to what extent were the women's organizations that developed during this period successful? On many issues women were divided over what was the best action to take. The shift from laissez-faire approaches to women's work to a more interventionist approach caused splits between older liberal feminists and younger women more inclined to social feminism. Those who had joined the campaigns to limit excessive hours by the implementation of the Factory Acts were successful in bringing about improved conditions for those women covered by the Acts. However, they did not include the huge numbers of women who worked at home or in domestic service. Further, although the introduction of Lady Factory Inspectors to enforce these laws opened up a new area of professional work for middle-class women, it did nothing to bridge the gap between classes of women. Factory workers regarded lady inspectors in the same light as other middle-class social reformers so, paradoxically, workers often colluded with the factory owners rather than working with the inspectors. The WIC responded to this by organizing Girls' Clubs that sought to teach girls about citizenship and encourage them to seek further training for employment at technical schools rather than focusing on domestic skills. It is hard to gauge how successful these clubs were as there has been little research into the movement during this period.[145]

Social feminists were not always united over the best strategies for tackling a particular issue. For example, in the debate around married women's work, activists could not agree whether the emphasis should be on campaigns against the exclusion of married women working outside the home or whether encouragement towards economic independence, through allowances, better pay or nurseries, should be given. This split also informed the debate around the Trades Boards, where some felt that the emphasis should be on better pay for husbands so that women did not need to work and others wanted a minimum wage for all workers in sweated trades so that women would not be so economically dependent on their husbands. The dominance of the domestic ideal could not suppress economic imperatives that compelled women to work whether they wanted to or not. However, during this period the investigative work of organizations such as the WIC, the WTUL and the FWG meant that discussions were more informed than they had been in the earlier period between 1840 and 1870. Several women, such as Lady Dilke, Amie Hicks, Margaret Bondfield and Mary MacArthur to name a few, were invited to report to government inquiries into industrial issues. Their work not only informed public policy but offered a more nuanced understanding of the material lives of many women that did not necessarily reflect their own experience.

Attempts to unionize working-class women were problematic partly because of male resistance to women joining existing unions, partly because working women were usually in short-term jobs rather than long-term trades or careers and partly because the leadership failed to give them an adequate voice in making union policy. All these points are generalizations and more local research is needed to explore the complexities of work patterns for women. What were the differences between employment patterns in large cities and industrial centres, small country towns and isolated rural areas? Were women's employment experiences in Scotland and Wales different to those in England? How did women's work patterns change over their life cycle? These are all areas that need more work, as do some of the trades that employed smaller numbers of women.

The opportunities for middle-class women in the period were more positive although still limited. Education and employment were opened up to a large number of women who, a generation earlier, would be consigned to a life of dependency or, if they were unlucky, work as a governess or companion. However, there were no serious inroads into male domains. In clerical work and shop work women found themselves corralled into low-paid, dead-end jobs with no prospect of career progression beyond supervising other women. Even in teaching where women teachers dominated, women were clustered towards the lower end of the career ladder. Patriarchal ideology continued to promote women's economic dependency on men but was tempered by an acknowledgement that some women would need to work. Moreover, the demands of capital for the services of a docile, transitory workforce for certain types of work ensured that women would be able to find work in specific sectors of the market.

During this period, society also continued to benefit from women's unpaid philanthropic work. This meant that jobs such as nursing were regarded as a vocation and consequently women were not expected to demand high pay or good working conditions. However, careers could be carved out of areas of work and campaigns around professionalization both in teaching and nursing and later in social work assisted in turning these sectors into ones that were regarded both as satisfying careers for educated women and as work that did not challenge normative ideas of femininity. However, the development of careers for women in male-dominated professions was less successful at this time as male resistance to women's entry into, for example, the legal profession was as strong as ever. The development of careers for middle-class women is now a focus for research and is a worthwhile area to pursue both at a local and national level. It was not until the outbreak of the First World War that women began to make serious inroads into male territory. In Part Three of the book we shall examine how two world wars affected women's paid work and what happened when peace returned.

Part Three

1914–45

The war revolutionised the industrial position of women. It found them serfs and left them free.

Millicent Fawcett, 1920[1]

As this part of the book spans both world wars, the focus will be on the effect that two world wars had on women's employment. Summerfield states that there are two broad readings of the effect that the wars had on women's employment opportunities. First, there are the accounts, like Fawcett's, that suggest that war brought in significant changes and second, there are others that throw doubts on these claims.[2] Although the circumstances of the two wars were very different, they both raised discussion around equality and difference and the debates around these issues reflect the time in which they were conducted. Summerfield states that Titmuss in 1958 argued that war defined women more emphatically as dependent on men through the implementation of allowances for the support of service men's wives and children.[3] Men were regarded as the breadwinner and while the breadwinner was away fighting for the country the state stood in for him. These allowances were often more generous than the housekeeping given by the breadwinner to his wife and so, Titmuss asserted, benefited poorer families. However, this benefit was short-lived as it ceased at the end of war and was not always adequate given the soaring cost of living during the war. Family allowances only became a permanent benefit with the introduction of the Welfare State after the Second World War. Further, Summerfield argues that during the First World War, allowances were also used to regulate women's sexuality whilst their husbands were away. If a woman did not conform to the dominant sexual mores of the day then allowances could be withdrawn. Summerfield concludes that war work and the higher standard of living that wages brought to a family probably accounted more for the better health of women and children rather than allowances but this is an issue that will continue to be debated.

The issue of motherhood was a continuing preoccupation during both World Wars. As we have seen, before the First World War there was an ongoing anxiety about the quality of childrearing in Britain. The war did nothing to allay these anxieties. The prospect of working mothers was still frowned upon even though both personal hardship and the needs of the country meant that mothers were being channelled into paid work. This move was countered by propaganda such as the National Baby Weeks that sought to encourage full-time motherhood.[4] During the Second World War anxiety was focused on low birth rates and the emphasis was on people having larger families although, again, this was in conflict with the country's need for women workers. Summerfield argues that motherhood continued to be viewed as women's primary role and that the call for women workers during the wars was regarded at most as unavoidable.[5]

Wars also challenge sexual norms and, during both of the World Wars, fears were expressed about the laxity in sexual behaviour. This arose out of young women working long hours alongside men and often living away from home and therefore out of parental control. Welfare workers and women police officers were brought into being during the First World War to act to some extent as *in loco parentis*. Further, the Defence of the Realm Act (DORA) was implemented in 1916 and extended over the period of the war. This Act echoed the earlier Contagious Acts and was not welcomed by all, especially women's organizations.[6] The regulation of women workers' private lives in this way could hardly be used as an argument for their liberation as they were still regarded in relation to men and seen as victims of male lust rather than as active agents in their own lives.

The fact that is most used to argue that women lives were transformed by war is the extension of the franchise to women over the age of 30 who were already, or were married to, local government electors.[7] However, others dispute this argument. For example, Pugh argues that because reform to the franchise was needed to enable servicemen to vote and that the suffrage movement had persuaded many MPs that women should be enfranchised, their inclusion was inevitable.[8] To what extent women's war work transformed ideas about their rights as citizens is disputed. As the franchise was limited to women over 30, it cannot be argued as anything but a marker on the road to equality.

So to what extent can we say that women's lives changed during and after the First World War and how permanent were these changes in the inter-war period? Part Three will explore these questions. Chapter Seven will focus on the First World War period. First, it explores the changes in women's experience of work during the war. Second, it focuses on the debates around whether the First World War opened up new employment opportunities and if so, whether this signalled new thinking about women's employment or whether any expansion in opportunities was merely expediency on part of the state and employers. Chapter Eight will focus on the inter-war period. Starting with the abrupt demobilization of huge numbers of women and the pressure on women either to get back to the home or return to women's work, such as domestic service, the chapter then focuses on some of the new areas of work opening up for women. Further, it focuses on some of the issues raised concerning women's work in the inter-war period. These include a return to the issue of married women's work and differing interpretations of what strategies were best for improving women's lives. Chapter Nine will concentrate on the Second World War period. Women's experience of this war was quite different to the first. Not only were civilians caught up in warfare, but women were conscripted into war work for the first time. One of the results of this policy was that married women workers were officially condoned and throughout the period there were debates on how women could be both workers and homemakers. The consequences of war work for single women and whether war did in fact find women serfs and 'left them free' is also examined.

Chapter Seven

ﻚﻫ

Out of the cage?[9]

Women's experience of work during the First World War

When war broke out on 4 August 1914 women formed around 30 per cent of the workforce in England and Wales. In Scotland, it was nearer 25 per cent.[10] The number of women recognized as workers had increased since the beginning of the century and as we have seen in the previous chapter, the scope of women's work had widened, especially for middle and lower middle-class women. However, we have also noted that despite the widening opportunities and rising numbers of women participating in paid work, women were segregated into sectors which offered lower pay and less possibility of promotion.

So, what impact did the war have on women's employment opportunities? Were the effects mainly positive or were there problems too? Did women's work during the war change public opinion, as Fawcett suggested? Were their contributions to the economy recognized or were they merely regarded as a reserve pool of labour, employed when needed, then exhorted to return to 'home and duty' when no longer required? Did sex segregation in the work place disappear and were women paid the same rate for the job as men? In order to address these questions this chapter begins by assessing the impact that war had on the major employment sectors that had employed women before the war and new areas that opened up to them. The second part of this chapter will focus on general attitudes towards women and work during the war and to what extent these attitudes changed. This section will examine substitution, dilution and questions of equal pay. Finally, I will examine the legislation brought in during the war years that was concerned with women's work in munitions. How far did this legislation challenge normative perceptions of women and paid work or how far were conventional perceptions reinforced by legislation?

The impact of war on women's employment

Braybon argues that in 1914 there were 3,276,000 women working in the enumerated industries, that is industries that could be readily quantified and therefore did not include homeworkers or women working in small workshops. There were a further 1,658,000 women working in domestic service.[11] Countless other women would be working on a casual basis, doing a wide range of unrecorded, unskilled tasks. The outbreak of war had an adverse effect on women's employment, with possibly up to 44.4 per cent of all women unemployed for a brief time in September 1914. In Chapter Six we saw that the numbers of women employed in domestic service was declining in the decade before the First World War but that it was still a major employer.[12] The war offered many women in this sector the opportunity to leave for better-paid work. Braybon states that 16 per cent of the factory workforce had left domestic service to work in industry and the domestic sector never recovered from this loss. By 1918, the number of domestic servants had shrunk from 1,658,000 to 1,258,000.[13] However, this move from domestic work to factory work was not altogether voluntary. The war had an immediate and serious effect on the economy. The cotton trade, traditionally a large employer of women, was seriously affected when cotton exports slumped and many women employed in the 'luxury' trades fell foul of the middle-class urge to economize. Consequently, the wealthier sectors of society stopped buying clothes, fancy goods and jewellery and laid off surplus domestic staff. Further, Braybon states that the Central Committee on Women's Employment (CCWE), a body made up of representatives from the WTUL, NFWW and WLL, claimed that short-time working was a problem too. Their figures showed that only 24 per cent of dressmakers were working full-time in large businesses and this figure dropped to 13 per cent in smaller firms. In other trades that had employed large numbers of women full time before the war, the figures were equally bad if not worse. Only 13 per cent of women workers in the shoe manufacturing trade were full time; 26 per cent in printing and bookbinding; 39 per cent in jam and pickle making; 18.5 per cent in furnishing and upholstery; and 33 per cent in furs and skins.[14]

In the first months of the war, the main war work to be had was voluntary and many women in the financial position to do so spent their time knitting and sewing for the troops. This was not an option for most working-class women and domestic servants were prevalent among the 190,000 registered unemployed women by the end of September 1914.[15] Women's organizations swiftly set up relief workshops to help destitute women. Domestic servants and laundry women fell into this category because National Insurance, which had been introduced in 1911, only applied to a limited number of industries. One of these workshops was the

Queen Mary's Workrooms which was funded by Queen Mary's Work for Women Fund set up by the CCWE. The wages paid by these workrooms were very low, about 10 shillings (50 pence) a week, and Sylvia Pankhurst labelled the workrooms as 'Queen Mary's Sweatshops', although unemployed women were probably grateful for any work they could get.[16] Furthermore, this initiative of the CCWE was probably the first serious attempt to address the problems of unemployed women. Pugh argues that unemployment was seen as a male problem at this time, although he argues that the CCWE was more in the tradition of Victorian philanthropic schemes that did not compete with normal employment opportunities.[17] SPEW also set up a fund for non-manual workers, the Educated Woman's War Emergency Training Fund which sought to retrain women for clerical positions.[18] The situation of large-scale under- and unemployment changed quickly in some sectors as the government geared up for war production. Although dressmaking was slow to recover, the market for military clothing and supplies (uniforms, boots, medical equipment and other kit) opened up to absorb workers, especially women. Further, by early 1915, women were increasingly needed to fill the places that men were leaving and to satisfy the growing need for munitions.[19]

Munitions was not the first sector to experience a gender shift in its workforce but it was the largest. The engineering industry was loathe to lose its skilled male workers and resisted attempts to replace them with unskilled female labour. The first areas in which the gender shift can be seen were in the non-industrial sectors such as retail, clerical work and transport where male employees were not considered to be performing essential work. This process was called substitution. Arguably, this process has led to the common reading of the period as a time when employment opportunities for women widened. Pugh provides a useful table that demonstrates the increase in the number of women working in various industries and occupations. There are some interesting facts to pull out of this table, both expected and surprising. For instance, it is not surprising to learn that women in the metal industries increased in number from 170,000 in 1914 to 594,000 in 1918 but, given the need for uniforms, it is surprising that women employed in the clothing trade decreased from 612,000 to 568,000.[20] Apart from these trades, it is useful to see which industries and occupations were affected by the war. Pugh, using the figures supplied by the Board of Trade *Report on the State of Employment in all Occupations in the United Kingdom in July 1918* (see Table 7.1), shows that there were gains in the number of women employed in the metal industries, chemicals, food, drink and tobacco and other miscellaneous industries. Domestic service was omitted from the list but as previously mentioned, the numbers of women involved in domestic service decreased from 1,658,000 in 1914 to 1,258,000 by 1918, a loss of 400,000 workers. There were losses in textiles, the clothing trades and paper and printing. In all, however, there was an overall gain of 565,000 women or an increase in almost 25 per cent in industry.[21] Braybon argues that many of these women were not new to the workforce but were transferring from other less popular trades, such as domestic service, laundry work, other factories or dressmaking, or were married women returning to work. Further, she points out that the increased wages and better opportunities of war work meant that even the relatively well-paid cotton industry could not compete.[22]

Table 7.1 Increases in women's employment, 1914–18[23]

Occupation	Number of women employed in July 1914	July 1918 gain (+) or loss (–)
Metal industries	170,000	+ 424,000
Chemicals	40,000	+ 64,000
Textiles	863,000	– 36,000
Clothing trades	612,000	– 44,000
Food, drink and tobacco	196,000	+ 39,000
Paper and printing	147,000	– 6,000
Other industries	89,500	+ 61,000
Government establishments	2,000	+ 223,000
Agriculture	80,000	+ 33,000
Transport (including municipal)	18,200	+ 99,000
Banking, finance and commerce	505,000	+ 429,000
Professional occupations	50,500	+ 69,000
Hotels, pubs, cinemas and theatres	181,000	+ 39,000
Civil Service including Post Office	66,000	+ 168,000
Local govt including teaching	196,200	+ 30,000

In the non-industrial sector, the increases were even more spectacular. It could be argued that if there was any change in perception of working women it was amongst this class of worker, although Thom points out that many of these workers were extra workers rather than just substitutes for men.[24] Clerical work was particularly impressive. Local government, which included teachers, increased from 196,200 to 226,200; in banking, finance and commerce numbers increased from 505,500 to 934,500 and in the Civil Service, including the Post Office, from 65,000, of whom 58,000 worked for the Post Office in 1914, to 170,000 working across Whitehall in 1919. However, Jones argues that the women employed in the Civil Service during the war years were employed on a temporary basis to perform war-related work and usually at a level well below their capabilities, although she concedes that often they were given responsibilities that they would have been denied before the war.[25] Other non-industrial sectors increased the number of women workers dramatically too. For example, women were encouraged into agricultural work via the Women's Land Army. When war broke out, some 80,000 women worked on the land. By the end of the war this had increased to 113,000, with women participating in all areas of agricultural work. Women also made inroads into the service industries: the number of women working in hotels, pubs, cinemas and theatres increased from 181,000 before the war to 220,000 by the end and in transport the numbers rose from 18,200 to 117,200, an increase of almost 550 per cent.[26] Women also joined the armed services, though not in the large numbers that characterized the Second World War. Pugh states that although 35,000 women put forward their names for the Women's Army Auxiliary Corps (WAAC) in 1917, only 18,000 actually joined up.[27] Both the Women's Royal Naval Service (WRNS) and the Women's Royal Air Force (WRAF) accounted for even fewer women. Generally, their work in the forces tended to replicate the sort of work women did in civilian life (clerks, domestic workers, cooks), although others took on more male-defined work such as drivers, welders, fitters and carpenters.

Overall, the number of women employed increased from around 4.9 million in 1914 to around 6.2 million in 1918, an increase of around 24 per cent.[28] These figures are likely to be conservative as there was a whole range of women employed in unregistered home-based occupations or working for their family.[29] The work available to women during the war was more varied and sometimes better paid, but they were nowhere near to achieving parity with male workers. It is clear that more women were participating in paid work, but how was this viewed by society and what impact did these attitudes have on women's employment opportunities?

Attitudes towards women's work during the First World War

On the face of it, the figures given above suggest that Fawcett's comment at the beginning of Part Three was correct. However, we need to move beyond the bare statistics offered in government reports, which Thom argues had a certain agenda, in order to ascertain whether the war had permanently changed society's views of women's work.[30] There seems to be a consensus in more recent historical work that the war offered some temporary benefits to working women but also posed problems for them. Braybon's doctoral thesis overturned the classic reading that women were welcomed by employers with open arms and gave up their jobs at the end of the war without a murmur.[31] Subsequent writers have agreed with her to a greater or lesser extent.

First, the question of whether women were welcomed as workers will be examined. As mentioned earlier, in the early months of the war women experienced a sharp rise in unemployment. At this time, unemployment

Figure 3 Female attendant working in a bacteriological laboratory at Messers Lyle & Co, 1918.

Source: Photograph courtesy of the Imperial War Museum, London, Q106592.

was seen as a male problem.[32] Although women could receive benefits if they had been in an insured industry before the war, and there was a sharp increase in the number of women working in insured industries during the war, their unemployment rights were whittled away after the war. Married women were supposed to return to domestic duties and single women lost benefit if they refused to take up domestic service and other so-called women's work. This suggests that ideas about women's work had not changed much during the war years. The needs of women as workers, outside of munitions work, went largely unnoticed and it was assumed that all women had, somewhere, a male relative who could offer support in times of need. This notion that women worked for pin money rather than as a main source of income prevailed throughout the war and can be traced through writings in the media, government reports, comments by social commentators and trade unionists, both male and female, all of whom stress the pre-eminence of the male breadwinner model. At the end of the war, the pin-money epithet was used in the media to criticize women who had the temerity to carry on working in male-defined industries once the war was over.[33]

From early 1915, the pressure for women to replace male workers and the need for munitions increased. The government had no alternative but to turn somewhat reluctantly to women. Extraordinarily, an alliance

Figure 4 Women labourers clearing firebricks at the Glasgow Gas Department, 1918.

Source: Photograph courtesy of the Imperial War Museum, London, Q110142.

between the Pankhursts and their old enemy Lloyd George developed, with Lloyd George using the Pankhursts' campaigning skills to encourage women to sign up for war work.[34] Within a few months, 50,000 women had registered as available for war work. Employers were faced with the inevitable. They had lost many men to the war in the first months of patriotic fervour and, although conscription and the ring-fencing of essential workers stemmed the flow to some extent, there was a large shortfall in available labour which had to be addressed urgently. In many cases, even in heavy industry, the work that women took up was not necessarily heavy or skilled work; it was labelled men's work just because men had always done it. Pugh cites examples in the steel industry where women initially took up clerical work, in the railways where they moved from clerical work to ticket issuing and portering, and in munitions where they initially worked in the packing room only. However, as the army consumed more men, women moved more firmly into male territory and this is where the tension was felt most strongly although all-male unions were resistant to women workers to some extent.[35]

Nevertheless, this influx of women workers was not greeted with open arms. Braybon and Walby assert that employers were reluctant to employ women largely because they were imbued with prejudicial, patriarchal views on women's role in society. This led them, often unfairly, to

Figure 5 A woman working in an electrical sub-station in Glasgow, 1918.

Source: Photograph courtesy of the Imperial War Museum, London, Q110153.

conclude that women were inferior workers to men.[36] Pugh argues that it was in the industries where the government intervened most markedly that most women were employed. Consequently, far more women were employed in government-controlled munitions works than in the uncontrolled ones. He reports that by October 1916 women workers had increased by almost 300 per cent in government-controlled munitions works but by only 36 per cent in the uncontrolled ones. This, he asserts, meant that when government control was withdrawn at the end of the war, women were likely to lose their jobs. He goes on to discuss how, usually without evidence, women were perceived as poor timekeepers, sickly and not as productive as men.[37] Braybon takes this one step further and argues that patriarchal attitudes shaped all men's attitudes about women's role in society and their capabilities.[38] This is certainly borne out by the literature of the time. However, Wightman argues that one cannot take the whole of the engineering industry as a homogenous mass. She argues that women's participation in the industry varied for economic reasons as well as gender prejudice. Because jobs were diluted in order for the new workers to be able to pick up necessary skills as quickly as possible, women were rarely the fully skilled workers that the men they had substituted were. Resistance from trade unions, concerned to protect skills from dilution, meant that dilution was always partial and hemmed in with conditions that made the practice temporary. In this argument, the need to meet the extraordinary demands of the munitions industry and the protection of a skilled trade is emphasized rather than male prejudice against women. Wightman does concede that gender did play a part in pay and conditions in munitions; she argues that it is equally important to consider employers' concerns about the viability of mass production and the unions, anxieties over competition from cheap unskilled labour.[39] Wightman raises an interesting point when she states that engineering cannot be taken as a homogenous mass. More research needs to be done at a local level to ascertain the ways gendered ideas of women workers and economic imperatives shaped policy.

One of the main preoccupations of government, employers and trade unions was the question of substitution. Braybon states that substitution occurred in all major industries and that dilution, where the less skilled parts of a job were given to women, in the engineering trades was just one form of this. She goes on to enumerate the different forms of substitution as:

1   Complete or direct substitution where a woman undertook all of a man's job;
2   Indirect substitution where a woman replaced an unskilled or semi-skilled worker so that the man could be transferred to more difficult work;
3   Group substitution where a group of women replaced a smaller group of men;
4   Substitution by rearrangement where processes where changed and women used new machinery to undertake men's jobs.[40]

Consequently, most women were not strictly doing men's work; rather they were doing part of a job. This move underlined the temporary nature of women's employment where there was no commitment to teach them the whole job. Moreover, the understanding that dilutees would be the first to leave their jobs was formalized in the Treasury Agreement of 1915.[41] This made it easier for employers to claim that women were not doing the same work as men and therefore should not be paid the same rates. Unions were keen that women should be paid the same rate for the job because they did not want employers to undermine negotiated pay agreements by employing women after the war so this was part of the dilution deal. However, despite paper agreements, employers found a loophole by paying women hourly rates rather than the usual piecework rates that men commanded. Thom states that by 1916 pay was already being decided by gender. She argues that these rates were established to appease the unions rather than as an acknowledgement of equality between the sexes or to encourage women into the workplace. The unions held a contradictory position: on paper, equality was espoused; in practice they were content to allow employers to pay women less. Employers were also satisfied with this arrangement. Again, it can be argued that patriarchal and capitalist interests merged over the issue of pay. However, employers were less happy when, in 1917, Circular 447 was brought in to fix a minimum rate for women's work.[42] These laws were aimed only at munitions industries, however, and women undertaking other types of work had no such entitlement to protection and were reliant on negotiations undertaken by employers and trade unions on their behalf.

The trade unions were opposed to women being employed because there was a long history of women being used to undermine hard-won industrial rights and pay levels. The Amalgamated Society of Engineers (ASE) was particularly resistant to women workers and, as Wightman argues, an elite craft union had reason to fear that they would cause the erosion of pay rates and loss of status. After initial resistance, the union realized that the government would impose agreements if it did not negotiate and the ASE made an alliance with the NFWW in the summer of 1915. A policy towards women workers was developed during 1915 but it is important to note that women were not represented in these negotiations. The unions came to an agreement that employment restrictions for women would be relaxed but only for the duration of the war. Mary Macarthur supported this although it is difficult to see how she could have refused to agree. It was also agreed that women would be paid a special women's rate which, of course, was less than the men's.[43] Although women's membership of unions increased greatly during the war years, 358,000 women were union members at the beginning of the war and this had risen to 1.2 million by 1918, Pugh asserts that others were put off partly by male hostility but also because women regarded the work as temporary. Indeed, the ASE excluded women from membership. However, Pugh argues that the National Union of Clerks encouraged women to join the union because they feared that employers would outflank union members by taking on even more women.[44] It seems that the National Federation of Women Workers was the only union to welcome women warmly, but even in this union, the leadership subscribed to the male breadwinner theory.

It is possible to make some assessment of what women thought about working during the war as their stories have been recorded both in written texts[45] and in the sound archive of the Imperial War Museum.[46] Using life histories told or written years after the events need to be read cautiously, however, as these are no more likely to be 'the unvarnished truth', overlaid as they are by popular memory and coloured by dominant ideological readings of the events. As the title of Braybon and Summerfield's book suggests, some women found war work liberating. Some moved from an existing occupation to one of war work as a patriotic gesture. Many had husbands, lovers, brothers and other friends and relations fighting and dying at the front and they wanted to 'do their bit', although Thom states that very few of the women she interviewed mentioned patriotism in the interviews.[47] Munitions work was particularly popular because it freed up men to fight and produced the means to do the fighting. It also paid reasonably well despite the long hours, monotonous work and dangerous conditions. Others, doing paid work for the first time, were struck by the sense of community they found in the workplace and the sense of purpose it gave to their lives. For some women it was the first time they had had the opportunity to earn a living wage, live away from home without marrying and, as their labour was in high demand, shift from one type of work to another as it suited them.[48] It also seems that although many women did not want to lose their jobs at the end of the war, it was impossible to resist the changing needs of the nation. Patriotism, a sharp decrease in demand for munitions, agreements made with male unions, an enduring patriarchal view of the gendered nature of work meant that many women lost their jobs as the war drew to a close. As we shall see in the next chapter, the institutions of the state media and popular opinion allied to ensure that women went back to home and duty wherever possible.

If working-class women were liberated from domestic service or low-paid needlework by their substitution in traditionally male-defined work, middle-class women found their own benefits during the war. The war tended to make it more acceptable for middle-class women to work, although as we have seen, acceptance was slowly growing before the war. The main sector that middle-class women entered was the clerical sector. Women were usually employed as substitutes for men although there was an overall increase in the need for workers. Wages in the clerical sector were relatively good, too. A government typist earned around £1 per week and telegraphists between £1 and £2.[49] Pugh argues that the Land Army was also a popular choice among middle-class women despite entrenched prejudice from farmers who thought that they were expensive and not up to the work.[50] A few middle-class women worked in factories and some left memoirs.[51] Others joined the forces, becoming nurses or ambulance drivers. However, as Pugh argues, with the exception of clerical work where extra workers were needed anyway, there was a sense that most of these workers were only employed for the duration of the war.

Working conditions for women in the First World War

Braybon argues that although life for women workers was hard during the war, it had been equally hard for most women workers before.[52] However, war work did raise its own issues, especially in the munitions factories and it is to these issues we now turn. Most concern, as before the war, was focused on women doing so-called 'men's work' so government policy focused largely on women working in munitions and where women replaced men in other sectors. Braybon reports that women involved with traditional women's work, such as the clothing industry, who were working long hours and in poor conditions aroused little concern. Further, although, as previously mentioned, pay in the clerical sector was relatively good, Braybon states that there was 'little interest in their work or health. Priority was given to the health of those whose efficiency at work was vital to munitions production'.[53]

During the war, the Factory Acts were suspended so that women in munitions often worked night shifts and 12-hour shifts, although girls under 16 were not allowed to work at night. Long hours took their toll on women's lives, especially those who had the double burden of paid and domestic work to contend with. Furthermore, the Defence of the Realm Act (DORA) meant that no employee could leave a job without a leaving certificate.[54] Early in the war the conditions in the factories were also usually poor. However, as factories expanded, working conditions gradually improved, especially as the government laid down rules for minimum standards. One of the issues that continued to concern the government was the 'mother of the race' debate. Braybon argues that it was concern for young women as future mothers of the race, rather than for their health per se, which underpinned much of the government discourse around workers' welfare.[55] The government formed three committees to deal with this issue. The Health of Munition Workers Committee was set up in September 1915, the Women's Employment Committee was established in August 1916 and the War Cabinet Committee on Women in Industry was set up in 1918.[56] These committees dealt with aspects of health and welfare, women's pay and the future of women's work after the war. Focus was on the health and efficiency of munitions workers to the neglect of other areas. The moral as well as physical well-being of munitions workers was also considered and, as Braybon points out, this concern was focused on women and boys, not workers generally, and was reminiscent of pre-war legislation.[57] Some of the changes that came about in the munitions factory (but not necessarily elsewhere) were improved sanitation, seats, lifting apparatus, rest rooms and canteen facilities, medical facilities and better ventilation. All these were advances that were normalized in the post-war factory. Although Thom, writing about the Woolwich Arsenal, says that it was infested with rats, had inadequate lighting and ventilation and that the medical centres dealt with the health of applicants rather than the ongoing needs of workers.[58] Welfare supervisors oversaw many aspects of the improved environment. These women tended to be middle-class and, originally, were volunteers.[59] However, Thom states that Lillian Barker, the Chief Women's Welfare Superintendent at the Woolwich Arsenal, herself an elementary teacher from a working-class background, rejected amateurism and sought to employ women with experience of controlling other women.[60] The work of the welfare supervisors was to administer canteens, toilets and other welfare issues but also to watch over the behaviour of the workers. This meant that they kept employment records, investigated absences, supervised night work, checked accommodation, set up thrift schemes, arranged educational classes and provided recreation.[61] Many workers were unhappy with these supervisors, tending to see them as spies for the employers. There was also a tendency by supervisors, which was criticized by Barker, to divide workers into 'nice girls and rude girls'. Commenting on some volunteer welfare workers in a report to the War Cabinet Committee on Women in Industry, she remarked:

> I do not think women like voluntary workers. They are such busybodies. They always sum up the girls into the nice girls and the rude girls and the nice girls get attention and the rude girls get nothing. It makes some girls who are not rude, rude.[62]

Braybon argues that interference in their private lives certainly annoyed women workers mainly because men were not subject to the same scrutiny. Surveillance of women workers infantilized them, denied them the same liberties as men and was seen as undermining the work of the unions. She quotes one journalist:

> Factory girls are just as sensitive to home truths as other women. They object to comments on their dress and their domestic arrangements from the welfare worker as much as she would object to similar comments from them. One lady made her debut in the factory where very rough girls worked by saying to them 'you want a club, you come from such overcrowded dirty homes,' and then she was astounded when they threw their lunch at her!'[63]

How far this article is based in fact or is an anecdote to make a point is difficult to ascertain but it does indicate that the way welfare was provided in the munitions factories reflected normative notions about working-class women and how they were in need of guidance from the middle-classes. However, welfare supervisors were very different to the Lady Factory Inspectors. They were more aligned to the needs of the employers than the protection of the workers' employment rights. They were also part of a growing tendency to supervise and thus control poor women. The women's police controls were also part of this trend, maintaining a watchful eye over workers outside of the workplace in ways similar to the welfare supervisors inside it. Both indicate a general wariness of working-class women in the public sphere and a sense that women workers could not be trusted to manage their own affairs.[64] Both Braybon and Thom argue that although women workers disliked the interference from welfare workers, they welcomed many of the benefits of welfare provision. These included social clubs, canteens and being provided with protective clothing.

The most serious issue that faced some women workers was health problems arising from the particular work that they were doing. Working in factories had always been dangerous but the risks involved in handling explosives increased this dramatically. The ever-growing demand for munitions led to long shifts and speeding up of work processes which, in turn, led to accidents. Usually these involved individuals caught in machinery or succumbing to TNT or other poisoning, but occasionally there were explosions that resulted in fatalities. Workers' actions, in the form of refusal to work with TNT, absenteeism and moving jobs played their part in encouraging the government to take health risks seriously, although the need for fit workers meant that the government was willing to act. However, both Braybon and Thom discuss how the health issues of individual war workers were lower down the priority list than the general conditions of women as mothers and, of course, the war effort generally.[65]

Chapter Eight

ஜ

Women's work in the inter-war period

Of all the changes wrought by the War, none has been greater than the change in status and position of women, and yet it is not so much that woman herself has changed as that man's conception of her has changed.

Mary Macarthur, 1918[1]

By the end of the First World War there was no doubt that women's participation in the workplace had been crucial to the war effort. We have seen in the previous chapter that women had been present in the workforce in large numbers at the outbreak of the war.[2] By the end of the war, the figure stood at 4,940,000 or 37.7 per cent of the total workforce. Bruley has argued that war was, indeed, a golden age for women's trade unionism, with the number of women members increasing threefold from 433,679 in 1914 to 1,209,278 in 1918.[3] However, we have already seen that women were often encouraged to join a union for expedient purposes, rather than because male trade unionists wanted to see women as their equals. We have also noted that male workers were often extremely hostile to women entering their trade as they felt that once there, they would be hard to remove. Consequently, deals were drawn up with the government and without women's representatives being present to ensure that women would be the first to lose their jobs in munitions when they were no longer required. Further, the dilution of the more skilled work and strategies to ensure that women would not earn as much as men, even when lip service was paid to equal pay, all indicate that women were accepted reluctantly into the workforce and that male opinions of women workers had hardly shifted at all.

The most telling negation of Macarthur's naive optimism about male attitudes to women workers can be found in what happened to women as the war drew to a close and after it ended. The first part of this chapter will explore what happened to women as paid workers during demobilization and it will assess how much attitudes had altered concerning women as workers. The second part will examine to what extent women's employment changed during the inter-war period. Finally, the last section will consider the extent to which women's organizations were able to shape policy aimed at women's employment in the inter-war years.

Demobilization, 1918–20

Demobilization, and the discussions about what would become of displaced men, began before the war had ended. Once the Eastern front had collapsed, the demand for munitions decreased. It was generally accepted that women would step down from work where they had replaced men but would they be content to return to their old pre-war roles? It was by no means a foregone conclusion that women would meekly return to domestic service or other lower paid work. During the war there had been some militancy amongst women workers, especially over unfair discrimination against women. For example, in the Woolwich Arsenal in 1917 women agitated for equal pay just as the lay-off began; in August 1918 female London tram workers went on strike against a bonus being made only to male workers.[4] Even before the war ended, there was a demonstration of 6,000 munitions workers who marched on the Houses of Common two days before the Armistice and a 'Right to Work' conference was organized in September 1919 by the Women's International League.[5]

Others groups of women used less militant tactics. Some, who considered engineering as a legitimate career choice for women, founded the Women's Engineering Society in 1919.[6] Others also wanted to continue in the work they had been doing during the war. The Society of Women Welders, women who had literally made the trade, wanted to continue with this work but, Thom argues, class and gender interests prevented them from doing so. The job was considered part of engineering and, therefore, men's work. The welders were middle-class and therefore the women's trade unions put working-class men before middle-class women.[7] Demobilization was, as Zimmeck succinctly suggests, 'not so much a relaxation into "normalcy" as an attempt to recreate it by main force'.[8] Further, Braybon states that discussions on how the workplace should develop after the war suggest that there was no clear-cut decision about the role women workers should play in the post-war era. I.O. Andrews identified three positions on women's future employment:

1 Those who wanted a return to the status quo in industry and the home;

2 Those who wanted radical changes for men and women in industry;

3 Those who believed that there should be some changes, but that society should remain fundamentally the same with regard to its treatment of women as industrial workers.[9]

It appears that although most commentators and the government would have liked the first option, pragmatism, in the face of opposition from women workers and their supporters who had no intention of returning to pre-war conditions, meant that they opted for the third option. It had soon become obvious that women would not be prepared to return to pre-war industrial conditions. This is particularly true of the clerical sector where women had been appointed to positions that they would never have achieved in peacetime. In many sectors women had enjoyed the comradeship of the workplace; others who had worked before the war realized that trade unions were a benefit; and many had no male dependent who could allow them the privilege of returning to the home, even if that is what they wanted to do. However, despite the differing needs and desires of women workers, the notion of the male breadwinner with a dependent family still held hegemonic sway and had been present in the thinking behind all the legislation that had been passed during the war. Pugh argues that this was inevitable given that there were 4 million men wanting to return to their homes and work. He notes that the expulsion of women from work not only occurred in workplaces covered by the Restoration of Pre-War Practices Act but also in new establishments that had not existed before the war, and that women were also being replaced by men who had not seen active service. Some women leaders challenged these practices. For example, Lady Rhondda led a deputation from the Association of Women Clerks to Lloyd George, resurrecting the pre-war feminist arguments that not all women had men to rely on and that the women clerks were better trained and more efficient than the men who were replacing them.[10] However, arguing that not all women had a breadwinner to depend on, whilst true, also meant that feminists were supporting the view that married women should be economically dependent on their husbands. For some, for example the Labour women Mary Macarthur and Susan Lawrence, this was what they believed; for others, such as Lady Rhondda, it was more a case of expediency, where she used the contemporary dominant discourse to make a case for women without the recognized breadwinner to support them. The question of women's economic independence in the inter-war years will be discussed again later in this chapter.

Of course, some women were content to stand down. For example, not all munitions workers wanted to remain in the industry. Married women with children, burdened as they were with domestic as well as employment responsibilities, and middle-class women doing their patriotic duty, would not want to work such long hours by choice. However, there was little attempt at retraining beyond traditional women's roles, and married women could only receive training if they had no children. Some women might well have wanted to retrain for other types of work but were disappointed when they saw what the government was offering them. The government made its position clear on the type of work they wanted women to undertake:

> Industrial training will for the present be confined to normal women's trades, for example clothing manufacture, in the processes known as women's processes before the war in which recent inquiry has shown there is a need for skilled workers.[11]

The other work on offer was mainly domestic service and laundry work. However, many women were not content to follow the government's wishes. Government reports into women's work in the post-war years indicate that women were refusing jobs in domestic service, laundry work, dressmaking, millinery and tailoring, even if refusal to take such positions meant that they would lose their out-of-work donation.

Although, the government had hoped that women would quietly return to their homes or be content to take up domestic service again, they did not rely on goodwill alone. The Restoration of Pre-War Practices Act (1918) which restored jobs to men, plus the dwindling demand for munitions, meant that some three-quarters of a million women had left their wartime work by the end of 1919. How many of these women were 'willing volunteers' is hard to assess. We do know, however, that many women still regarded themselves as workers because by March 1919 there were 494,000 women registered as unemployed.[12] Feminists demanded that work was found for these women. Lady Rhondda wrote to the *Daily News*:

> There are over half a million women workers at present receiving unemployment allowances, and there are probably an additional million of industrial women at present out of employment. . . . A period of unemployment on the cessation of war contracts was recognised to be inevitable, but what is the government doing to find employment for this great army of efficient women workers in peacetime occupations?[13]

The government's reply was to remove vast numbers of the women from the unemployment register. As discussed earlier, unemployment was regarded as a male issue and the notion that a woman could be un employed was an alien one. Unemployed women were encouraged to take unpopular women's work such as domestic service. If women refused the work offered, their benefits were withdrawn and they were removed from the register. The government was supported in this purge by the media, which began a hysterical anti-woman worker campaign that labelled unemployed women as parasites and scroungers.[14] The number of unemployed women had fallen to around 29,000 by November 1919. The NFWW challenged the more damning reports appearing in the media, organizing a public meeting with the *Daily Herald* to demand 'The Right to Work; the Right to Life; the Right to Leisure', and producing a report in its organ the *Woman Worker*, which declared:

> They do not ask their country to maintain them in idleness. They ask to be set to productive work. . . . They merely plead for a minimum of security, comfort and leisure; not for any distant Utopia, but for a means of escaping from the grinding poverty, the overwork and the desperate uncertainty of their pre-war lives.[15]

Thom argues that although the Wages (Temporary Regulation) Act was supposed to offer women some protection, there were no women representatives on tribunals that dealt with disputes, no representation on the Select Committee on 'out-of-work' donations and employers were able to lay off experienced women and replace them with cheap young trainees.[16]

In the two years following the war a range of acts of Parliament were instituted aimed at improving women's social, political and economic position in society. The Representation of the People Act 1918 gave the vote to women over the age of 30 who satisfied the property requirement or who held a university degree. Later in 1918 the Eligibility of Women Act allowed women to stand as MPs, and in 1919 the Sex Discrimination (Removal) Act was supposed to remove barriers to women's entry into the professions. However, these Acts had little effect on the thousands of young munitions workers who were now told that the only work they could do was domestic service or needlework. Thom argues that the leaders of the women's trade union movement were keener on integrating women trade unionists with their male counterparts than securing women's rights to equality in the workplace. This argument seems to be pausible. The protest from women's organizations was more concerned with the way that demobilization took place than women's innate right to work.[17]

By December 1919, Mary Macarthur had lost some of her enthusiasm for the new post-war world order. As Thom explains, Macarthur was seriously ill, recently widowed and had failed to win a seat in Parliament but her bitterness also reflected the way all industrial women workers felt by the end of that year:

Reconstruction has been for some time our favourite shibboleth. Shall I be accused of faintheartedness if I say that, at this moment, the new world looks uncommonly like the old one, rolling along as stupidly and blindly as ever and that all it has got from the war is an extra bitterness or two?[18]

The gains that women had seemed, tentatively, to have made during the war years looked as though they might swiftly be eroded.

Women's occupations in the interwar years

Although thousands of women were demobilized and public opinion seemed to have turned on women workers, women as a percentage of the British labour force had hardly changed from the pre-war position. Pugh states that women formed 29.6 per cent of the British labour force in 1911. This dipped slightly to 29.5 per cent in 1921 and rose to 29.8 per cent by 1931. An assessment of participation rates for work undertaken outside the home indicates that women's participation was 35.3 per cent in 1911; 33.1 per cent in 1921 and 34.2 per cent in 1931. This meant that 6,265,000 women were in quantifiable paid work in 1931. Many more would have been working in the black economy or did not identify themselves as workers despite undertaking paid work.[19] There were also regional variations, participation rates being lowest in rural Wales and highest in Cheshire and Lancashire where the textile industry was largely situated. Numerically, the highest number of women workers lived in London and the south-east of England. According to Glucksmann this indicates that higher participation rates were increasingly concentrated in the areas of industrial growth where new jobs for women in the mass assembly factories and associated clerical and sales work were being created.[20] Pugh concludes that the lack of overall increase in participation 'explodes the notion that the First World War represented a revolution in Britain'.[21] However, Pugh concedes that statistics conceal the changes in the type of employment women were undertaking. As discussed in Part Two, before the war the main occupations for middle-class women were occupations they shared with aspiring upper working-class women: shop work; clerical work; elementary teaching and nursing. Some taught in the new girls schools and colleges and a tiny minority managed to break into other professions such as medicine.[22] Before the war, the largest group of working-class women workers were domestic servants or those who worked in textiles or the clothing trades. Overall, the female workforce tended to be young and single. So, to what extent had these features changed after the war?

The age profile of women workers did not change significantly during the inter-war period. Hakim has shown that more than two-thirds of women workers between 1901 and 1931 were under 35 and that more than three-quarters of women workers were single (see tables 8.1 and 8.2 below). It is important to note that there was no census in 1941 so it is difficult to ascertain any changes in the late 1930s using the census as a source. Hakim's figures demonstrate that the female workforce was mainly young and single. Glucksmann states that:

> An ever-increasing number of women in the younger age groups went out to work so that by 1931 half of all 14–15 years olds and three-quarters of all 16–17 year olds were in the labour force. The 18–20 year old group had the highest participation rate (79 per cent) but after the age of 24, the rate fell dramatically.[23]

Table 8.1 Age profile of female working force in percentages, 1901–31[24]

Date	Under 35	35–69	60+	Total number of working women (millions)
1901	73	22	5*	4.2
1911	71	24	5*	4.8
1921	69	26	5	5.0
1931	69	26	5	5.6

Note: *Figures for 1901 and 1911 are estimations.

Table 8.2 Marital status of the female labour force in percentages, 1901–31[25]

Date	Single	Married	Divorced or widowed
1901	78	13*	9*
1911	77	14	9
1921	78	14	8
1931	77	16	7

Note: *Figures for 1901 are estimations.

Despite this decline in participation in the older age ranges, there were still a large number of working women in the over-35 age group. However, after 1931 the trend began to reverse.[26] If single, these older women would be unlikely to marry and were therefore likely to work until retirement, although they did not have the same opportunities as their male colleagues. They were usually segregated into 'women's work' which meant that they were paid less than their male counterparts and were denied promotion to better paid work.[27]

Pugh states that although the war had highlighted the issue of equal pay, there is little evidence to show that women's wages greatly improved in relation to men's. On average, women in industry earned 43.7 per cent of the male wage in 1901. This had increased to 48 per cent by 1935.[28] This was hardly a huge improvement. When looking at the breakdown of women's wages as a percentage of men's wages in different industries, one can see that the position declined in textiles from 58.5 per cent in 1906 to 55.9 per cent in 1935. However, in the metal industries the percentage rose slightly from 38.1 per cent in 1906 to 47.6 per cent in 1931, only to fall back to 45.7 per cent in 1935 as the impact of the Great Depression was felt. As many women workers were young girls, with little formal training, who were working in non-unionized jobs where it was easy to dismiss workers and replace them with a new batch of inexperienced workers, it is not surprising that wages remained low. Further, Summerfield suggests that many employers used ageist practices so that it was difficult for any woman over 35 to find a new job. She states that unemployment hit women disproportionately once they entered their 40s and 50s and often they were unable to claim unemployment benefit.[29]

According to Pugh, equal pay was only on offer to a tiny number of women in professions such as law, medicine, the press, the stage and Parliament. From the 1920s, feminists concentrated their campaigns for equal pay on the Civil Service because they felt they were more likely to succeed in this sector.[30] The feminist groups behind the campaign for equal pay were the National Union of Societies for Equal Citizenship (NUSEC), the Women's Freedom League (WFL), the Six Point Group, the Open Door Council and above all the London and National Society for Women's Service (LNSWS). All these groups had strong links with the earlier suffrage movement. Whereas Pugh suggests that equal pay was the concern of a few professionals and did not affect women generally, Smith argues that these groups regarded equal pay as a gender rather than a wage issue and that sex-differentiated pay symbolized women's subordination.[31] He differs from Pugh in his interpretation of the campaign, arguing that it was concentrated on the Civil Service because many of its female employees were interchangeable with male colleagues and therefore the argument that women did different work to men was not tenable. Further, he argues that the groups also worked with two of the women's unions that had a feminist orientation, the National Association of Women Civil Servants (NAWCS) and the Council of Women Civil Servants (CWCS) although the trade union movement generally was less supportive.[32] Union support would of course have been desirable, as it would have helped the campaign be more effective if the there was a common mindset. The strategy employed was the 'thin end of the wedge' – activists felt that if they managed to obtain equal pay for women civil servants then teaching and other public service workers would follow. A Royal Commission on the

THE YOUNG WOMAN IN BUSINESS.
THE MANAGER AND HER PRIVATE SECRETARY.

Figure 6 'The young woman in business'.

Source: A. Wallis Mills, *Punch*, or the London Charivari, 21 January 1931.

Civil Service reported in 1931 and the treasury made two arguments for resisting equal pay. First, they claimed that men were better employees and less likely to leave and, second, that a gendered pay policy was consistent with practice outside the Civil Service.[33] The feminists' response was that the reason women often left work was the marriage bar and that the commonly made argument about the need for the breadwinner to earn more than the single person only held if the argument was gender blind, that is if women with dependants were paid the same rate as men. The commission made no recommendation on equal pay although it acknowledged that women had a case and noted that there were some groups of women who received equal pay, notably medical women and scientists. The government chose to ignore this and even reversed the policy of paying women scientists the same rate as men.[34] In 1934 the feminist groups and unions organized an Equal Pay Rally and from this sprang the campaign. Smith argues that although feminists saw equal pay as a gender issue they chose to run the campaign as a wage issue, arguing that equal pay would preserve men's jobs.[35] The campaign was successful up to a point – in 1936, the government was defeated and had to provide equal pay for women in the common classes of the Civil Service. However, rather than accept the defeat and implement an equal pay policy, the government chose the well-worn but effective tactic of calling for a vote of confidence and the bill was defeated on the second vote. Consequently, the government did not bring in an equal pay policy for the Civil Service at this time.

There was also little change in the number of married women involved in the labour force. The figures for married, divorced or widowed women have to be treated with caution as they are not likely to include the vast number of women who worked in their homes or in the black economy, especially in cleaning and laundry work.[36] Further, there were regional variations in the proportion of married women who worked. Before the war, many women in the textile industry of the north-west had worked after marriage. However, after the war, the textile industry went into decline as it unsuccessfully struggled to maintain its hegemony against the opening up of competing markets elsewhere in the world.[37] Glucksmann argues that in the inter-war period there was a trend for married women to work in the expanding new industries of light engineering, chemicals, synthetic fabrics and food processing, etc. in London and the south-east. These new industries were organized differently to older forms of factory work in that they involved mass-assembly production lines. The work was also deemed unskilled, monotonous and therefore ideally suited to women. Glucksmann argues that this new production process created a new set of relations between labour and capital through the creation of the 'collective worker'.[38] As a result of the falling birth rate, fewer women were spending less time childrearing. However, some of the work that women did undertake would have been seasonal and therefore did not show up in census returns.[39] Glucksmann also states that married women worked in a hostile environment and were often blamed for taking single women's jobs.[40] However, the lack of part-time work in most industries made the work unattractive to many married women who needed to fit work around domestic duties.

More generally, ideological factors were at play both in attitudes about the male breadwinner and women's role in society. These attitudes allowed employers to use the marriage bar when it suited their purposes without initiating too much protest from the unions and other organizations. This bar was informal in the private sector, especially during the Great Depression, but legally enforceable in the public sector, that is in all local government and Civil Service employment including teaching.[41] However, the bar was met with resistance from workers and was overturned occasionally. Bruley states that teachers campaigning in the NUWT in London were able to persuade the government to overturn the London County Council marriage bar in 1935. This affected doctors and nurses as well as teachers.[42] So, if the age and marital profiles of women workers had changed slightly but not significantly, to what extent had the type of work women undertook changed?

Table 8.3 demonstrates that although domestic service and personal service, which included outdoor domestic workers and other groups such as waitresses, were still the major employers of women between 1901 and 1931, the percentage of women participating in these areas was declining. It seems that women's reluctance to return to domestic service, especially indoor service, is reflected in these figures as personal service and indoor domestic work fell from 75 per cent of the workforce in 1901 to 56 per cent in 1921 and rose slightly to 59 per cent in 1931. The Women's Advisory Committee Report of 1919 concluded, after its investigation into the decline in domestic service, that lack of social status, the long hours of work expected by employers and the lack of companionship were the reasons for the reluctance of women to work in this sector, especially if the job involved living in.[43] However, women were increasingly employed in hotels and catering and commercial cleaning rather than domestic. Textiles and the clothing trade also declined as an employer of women and other manufacturing sectors remained static. Moreover, as the Great Depression deepened, factories brought in the marriage bar as a way of reducing employees. Pennington and Westover argue that changing trade conditions and the greater efficiency of mechanization reduced the need for homeworkers in several trades.[44] This, of course, would affect married women workers particularly. However, Wightman shows that numbers of women in engineering steadily increased over the inter-war period. In 1920, 58,320 or 8 per cent of the total female workforce were employed in the various engineering sectors. By 1939 this figure had increased to 167,403 or 14 per cent of the sector. However, the type of work women performed shifted from general heavy (18,737) to general light (10,486) and telephones (10,354) in 1939. Electrical engineering remained a constant employer during this period (15,709 in 1921 and 19,380 in 1939).[45] Gender segregation in factory work is discussed in the next part of this chapter.

The sectors that expanded were the ones that upper working-class and middle-class women tended to occupy. Clerical work, commerce and finance increased as a percentage of women's employment quite substantially. In 1901, clerical work was only 1 per cent of the market. By 1931 the market percentage had increased tenfold to 10 per cent, the same as textile work. Commerce and finance had increased from 7 per cent to 11 per cent. Of the better-paid, higher-status work only the professions stayed the same, although the numbers of women entering the professions was rising. In 1921 there were nearly 350,000 women employed in the professions. By 1931 this number had increased to nearly 390,000. Women formed a large proportion of teachers in the inter-war years. Beddoe states that there were 203,802 women teachers or 58.5 per cent of women in the professions in 1921 but these figures had declined to 199,560 or 51.3 per cent of the total number by 1931.[46] Nursing was the second largest

Table 8.3 Occupational distribution of women in major occupations in
percentages, 1901–31[47]

Occupation	1901	1911	1921	1931
Personal service	42	39	33	35
Indoor domestic	33	27	23	24
Other	9	12	10	11
Clerks, typists, etc.	1	28	10	–
Commerce and finance	7	9	10	11
Professional and technical	7	8	77	–
Textile goods and dress	16	14	11	9
Textile workers	14	13	12	10
Metal manufacture and engineering	1	23	2	–
Storekeepers, packers, etc	–	–	2	3
Transport, etc	–	–	2	3
Paper, printing	2	2	2	2
Food, drink, tobacco	1	1	2	1
Leather, fur	–	–	3	1
Agriculture	1	2	2	1

employer of women in the professions, numbering 94,381 or 27.1 per cent
of women professionals in 1921 and 118,909 or 30.5 per cent in 1931.
Table 8.4 shows how few women were represented in other professions.
Overall, we can see that access had improved slightly in the white-collar
and professional sector[48] and in engineering and other factory-based work,
but the numbers of women employed in domestic service and textiles had
fallen slightly. Equal pay and promotional prospects were still elusive and
the marriage bar affected many women's access to work, especially in the
better-paid jobs. We shall now turn to the social, political and economic
barriers that prevented women's progress in these areas.

Table 8.4 Women in the professions[49]

Occupation	1921 (percentages in brackets)	1931 (percentages in brackets)
Subordinate medical services	6,585 (1.88)	11,989 (3.07)
Librarians	832 (0.23)	3,439 (0.88)
Physicians, surgeons, registered medical practitioners	1,253 (0.35)	2,810 (0.72)
Social welfare	1,863 (1.13)	33,389 (0.87)

Issues in women's employment in the inter-war years

So how can we account for the nature of women's employment in the inter-war period? Walby argues that the popular notion that women were content to return to 'home and duty' after the war is incorrect.[50] If we consider the figures mentioned in the previous section, there is not much evidence that single women felt this, but the picture is more complicated when we consider married women. As most paid work was full-time, we can surmise that many married women, especially if they had young children, were not keen to participate unless their husbands were not able to support them. This supposition is supported by oral history research carried out by Elizabeth Roberts.[51] Further, Strachey differentiated between married women in professional, well-paid work where women would gain from having interests and contacts outside of the family and the majority of married women in low-paid, industrial work that added to their burdens.[52] However, some women wanted to continue work after marriage whether in the professions or industry and the marriage bar that operated in many sectors certainly suggests that married women had to be forced out of certain jobs rather than leave voluntarily.

The question of married working women was crucial in restoring the pre-war status quo as far as was possible. Employers, male-dominated trade unions and even single women workers colluded to keep married women out of 'white blouse' occupations and some factories also followed this practice, especially if they were looking to reduce the workforce. Equal rights feminists, however, did offer some support for the married woman's right to work. If the marriage bar is seen as the stick, then the question of the endowment of motherhood can be seen as the carrot in the project of restoring the status quo. Underpinning both was the perennial patriarchal assumption that all men were breadwinners and consequently all married women were dependents rather than individuals who had a right to work if they so wished. There was an acknowledgement, amongst feminists and social reformers, that stay-at-home women needed some degree of financial independence but only if they had children. The worries about the decline in the birth rate and the standard of mothering continued during and after the war.[53] As discussed in the previous section, various schemes for allowances for mothers were mooted; none of these were adopted until after the Second World War, but the issue grabbed the attention of many activists aligned to the New Feminism of the inter-war years.[54] Pugh argues that most of the issues that feminists pursued regarding employment failed to translate into legislation because the government was wedded to the notion that women's role in society was tied to their biological role as mothers. Consequently, demands for equal pay, the elimination of the marriage bar and the removal of gender-biased protective legislation as well as other demands not related to employment were ignored by the government during this period.[55]

Alongside the ideological reasons for discouraging married women from working were the economic ones. Pugh argues that:

> The extension of legal restrictions on female employment, the endless prevarication over equal pay for teachers and civil servants, and the maintenance of the marriage bar were all symptoms of the defensive mood engendered by the prolonged economic depression.[56]

The economy was indeed in decline for most of the inter-war period and women, like men, formed part of the unemployment figures. Women's unemployment, however, was never regarded as a problem, but more a need to redirect women either into the home or into domestic service.[57] This meant that struggles over the issue of women's employment were both ideological and pragmatic. Ideological considerations meant that men were always put before women in considerations concerning employment, even though these were tempered by pragmatic considerations. However, long-term male unemployment meant that many women had to work in order to feed and clothe their families. In doing so, they took on the role of breadwinner. This subverting of normative gender roles led to public denouncements of women workers for depriving men of work.[58] This, in turn, hardened attitudes towards encouraging women to stay at home and letting men take up available jobs. The marriage bar was crucial to this endeavour.

The notion of the male breadwinner also played a part in the debate over equal pay. Oram argues that during the First World War regulations for employing married teachers were relaxed and that women even taught in boys' schools. This threw the notion of the male breadwinner into disarray and, in turn, strengthened women teachers' demands for equal pay.[59] Teachers were at the forefront for the demand for equal pay. It had been part of their platform since 1903 when they set up the Equal Pay League, which became the National Federation of Women Teachers (NFWT) in 1906. Oram states that this organization became the focus for feminist issues both within and outside of the National Union of Teachers (NUT), especially after the male members of the NUT refused to support the campaign for equal pay.[60] The war fanned the campaign and it spread to other women workers outside of the teaching profession but it stalled against the brick wall of the family wage argument. Even when women received equal pay during the war years, it was just for the duration.[61] As mentioned previously, after the war the campaign for equal pay was focused on teaching and, especially, the Civil Service. Pugh argues that this is because women in these professions had a strong case and that because the state was the employer it could legislate to make equal pay happen if it could be persuaded to do so.[62] However, resistance to any attempt to get legislation through was effectively maintained, despite Ellen Wilkinson managing to win the support of the Commons for an Equal Pay Bill. The notion of the male breadwinner persisted throughout the period even though Eleanor Rathbone produced figures to show that more than 60 per cent of male workers over the age of 20 were either unmarried, widowed or had no dependent children.[63] Suffice to say that no legislation sanctioning equal pay was passed in the inter-war period.

One of the problems for the equal pay campaign was that women were still in segregated areas of employment. This was particularly true of the clerical sector where a panoply of strategies were employed to keep women in low-paid unskilled work.[64] Women continued to be segregated in most parts to lower-status and, consequently, lower-paid work. Table 8.5 indicates the gender distribution of occupations in the Civil Service at this time. It is apparent that women are found mainly in the low-paid sectors of the Civil Service even though the equal pay campaign selected the Civil Service because there was interchangeability between men's and women's work. Further, technological innovation assisted in this segregation as typewriters, adding machines and the like were seen to de-skill the work. This meant the work was downgraded and seen as more suitable for women to perform.

Table 8.5 Employment of women in the Civil Service, 1928–34[65]

Government staff	January 1928 Men	January 1928 Women	April 1934 Men	April 1934 Women
Administration	1,131	19	1,210	25
General executive	4,002	137	4,034	225
Other executive	10,243	480	11,123	519
General clerical	27,442	6,961	32,938	8,007
Other clerical	19,206	2,503	18,319	3,480
Writing assistants	–	4,914	–	7,336
Typing grades	120	6,980	76	8,904
Totals	62,144	21,994	67,700	28,498

Glucksmann argues that the introduction of new technologies meant that the existing divisions of labour could be transformed but they would also be enmeshed with ongoing notions of women's subordination and gendered ideas of work.[66] This affected different industries in different ways, depending on the previous history of the industry. In manufacturing the outcome was women doing work that could be described as routine, repetitive and needing manual dexterity. Men's work meanwhile was heavy and labour intensive, needed extended or formal training and often involved positions of authority. This had always been the case and with the advent of new technologies and manufacturing processes, these gendered notions were carried over into new work practices. However, in the new industries this often meant that there were many more 'women's jobs' than men's jobs. Focusing on different industries, such as electrical engineering, clothing and food processing, Glucksmann concludes that there were three common characteristics in the assembly line process. First, the division between direct and indirect producers was reproduced as a division between the sexes. Women were the direct workers making the actual goods; men were indirect producers, e.g. electricians, machine setters, belt feeders, etc. She cites companies such as Siemens, HMV and GEC as demonstrating this characteristic. Second, women in these industries formed a large homogenous group who were all on the same grade, had the same level of skill and earned the same wage for similar tasks. Men were in a more heterogeneous position, spread through a wide range of occupations at different grades and in work involving different levels of skill, and they were paid accordingly. Third, women were subordinate to men in the hierarchy of the workplace. Once again patriarchy had adapted to suit a particular form of production.[67] Glucksmann concludes:

> The traditional exclusion of women from control of technology, technical knowledge and skill, effected in the past by exclusion from craft apprenticeships, was perpetuated in assembly line industries as a consequence of the combination of the technical and sexual divisions of labour. The skills that women brought to assembly work or learned on the job (dexterity, attention to detail, speed) went unrecognised and were discounted as innate sexual characteristics. A long term form of gender inequality involving male power and female subordination in relation to machinery was thus created anew in new circumstances.[68]

While women were segregated in work that was considered low-skill and low-status because it was women's work, it is hard to imagine how any equal pay strategy might be put in place. A further factor in the maintenance of this inequality was the attitude of the trade unions.

As mentioned in previous chapters, trade unions reflected the dominant patriarchal ideology and supported the notion of the male breadwinner and dependent wife. Even the NFWW and WTUL had supported this stance before their amalgamation with the male unions in the early 1920s. Mixed unions did little to help women.[69] As Pugh has pointed out, even the NUT, a union that had a majority of women members, failed to protest against poor post-war wage scales for women.[70] Rising male unemployment fuelled adherence to the dominant patriarchal ideology, even though women did not usually perform the same work that men undertook. As

Glucksmann notes, this was a particular failing of the trade unions. Rather than encourage women to join unions, especially in the new assembly line sector, which was conspicuously under-unionised,[71] most unions ignored women or only took a token interest in them.[72] Focusing on the notion that women should stay at home and that it was a slight to a man's masculinity if his wife worked, meant that an opportunity to transform the traditional economic and social position of women was lost. Of course, it can be argued that it suited both capitalist and patriarchal interests to continue the subordination of women in the workplace. Capitalists wanted to exploit women as a cheap, pliable labour force; men generally wanted comfortable homes at a minimal cost to themselves or the state. Even many women in the labour movement and beyond failed to appreciate how far they colluded in their own subordination, preferring to vest their interests in Victorian ideology rather than work for something fairer.

A further issue that had dogged equal rights advocates for years was protective legislation. Indeed Smith argues that this more than any other issue precipitated the break between new and equality feminists in 1927.[73] NUSEC had adopted an equal rights policy towards women's employment which meant that they felt that protective legislation should not be based on the sex of the worker. During the inter-war period, more employment measures were introduced that put women and young people and children in the same category of worker. Pugh suggests that the politicians and trade unionists were taking advantage of the economic slump to impose more restrictions on women's employment opportunities. Whatever the purpose behind the legislation, these proposals led to a split in the women's movement as Lady Rhondda, and other equal rights feminists, formed the Open Door Council to oppose sex-based legislation and other gender-based inequalities. Despite women proving their capabilities during the war and the protestations of the Open Door Council, gender-biased restrictions were placed on the maximum hours a woman could work, they excluded women from work involving lifting heavy weights and handling dangerous substances. None of these restrictions applied to domestic service. However, Pugh argues that the Open Door Council's middle-class credentials meant that it was not taken seriously within the wider labour movement.[74] Indeed, within the women's movement equal rights feminists were accused of being opposed to all protective legislation. However, Smith argues that this was not the case and that they supported maternity rights for women workers while opposing gender-specific protective legislation.[75] As the notion that women's real place was within the home and that the main breadwinner was the man regained its foothold after the turmoil of war, there was very little opposition to this legislation from activists in the industrial women's movement. These activists, together with adherents to new feminism, pragmatically agreed to legislation that would protect women from the worst excesses of industrialism when it seemed unlikely that it would be extended to men. This pragmatic acknowledgement of the difference between men and women could be used against women in the workplace and reinforced their subordinate position to men.

The push to send women back into the home was never achieved in the inter-war period. Despite the marriage bar, the Anomalies Act, restrictive protective legislation and, most importantly, the growing cult of domesticity, women continued to work outside the home. Interestingly, too, despite the lack of any real commitment on the part of the trade unions, women's participation in trade unions remained constant during the inter-war period. Table 8.6 shows that although women's membership dipped, it was climbing back to the same level by the time the Second World War began. It closely followed male participation, rising and falling at the same points. Moreover, the approaching Second World War, like the First World War, would overturn all normative assumptions about women's role in society as women were called on once again to replace men in the workplace.

Table 8.6 Trade union membership:
men and women, 1918–39
(in millions)[76]

Date	Men	Women
1918	5.3	1.2
1920	7.0	1.3
1921	5.6	1.0
1925	4.6	0.8
1933	3.6	0.7
1936	4.5	0.8
1939	5.2	1.0

Chapter Nine

ೱ

Women's employment in the Second World War

The Second World War was a very different experience to the First World War. However, like the first war, historians have differing views on how it affected women's lives and, for our purposes, women's working lives. There is an enduring assumption that the Second World War had a deep and lasting affect on British women's lives. Arthur Marwick, in particular, subscribes to this view. He argues that the war affected women's lives because the disruption it caused shook women out of long-established patterns of behaviour and this caused them to question assumed gender roles. There is a point to this argument, but it is questionable whether the overarching threat of death or personal injury that many civilians experienced during the war would induce a yearning for change or whether it would encourage people to return to the old ways even if those ways were less than satisfactory.[1] Others, in particular Penny Summerfield and Harold Smith, question whether this disruption offered permanent changes to women's role in society.[2] This chapter focuses on the arguments about whether the Second World War meant continuity or change for women's working lives. How did women respond to the war? Did they rush to fill the places that men left or was it necessary to coerce women into their wartime roles? Did new opportunities open up for women as they had in the First World War? Were there restrictions placed on women which suggested that any changes that took place were only for the duration?

One of the reasons why Marwick is so sanguine in his analysis is that he focuses on the number of women who worked during the war. As Smith states, more women were mobilized during the Second World War than the first and Britain took the lead over all the participants in the war in recruiting women from the outset.[3] By 1943, the number of women engaged in paid employment was 7,258,000. This meant that 38.8 per cent of women were in the workforce (excluding the military) in 1943, an increase from 29.8 per cent in 1931.[4] Smith argues that if one considers the figures for 1939, and includes women in the armed forces, there were around five million women employed; so by 1943 the number of women workers had increased by almost 50 per cent.[5] Whichever way one analyses these figures, it is obvious that there was a huge increase in women working during the war period. However, can we then follow Marwick's assumption that employment was a new experience for all these extra women workers or that all these women entered the workforce voluntarily?

Conscription

First, as discussed in the previous chapter, many young women worked after leaving school but gave up working, voluntarily or otherwise, after marriage. The removal of the marriage bar and conscription of married women, especially those without children, meant that many of the extra women workers during the war had some sort of pre-war work experience, even if the work they undertook during the war was different to that they had performed earlier in life. For some married women, inadequate separation allowances made the return to work imperative. The allowance for a private soldier's wife with two dependent children was £1 13s or £1.65 in 1940,[6] which was not enough to maintain a family without falling into debt. This suggests, therefore, that many of the extra women workers who appear in the figures for 1943 probably had experience of work before the war and, rather than rushing back to work in a fit of patriotic fervour, many returned for more pragmatic reasons – they needed the income. Second, the fact that conscription was introduced suggests that not all women took up the call to work voluntarily. This is not surprising as the government were offering few details concerning pay and conditions of war work.

So, what can be said about women's employment during the Second World War? As at the beginning of the First World War, unemployment rose, especially in the consumer industries. Summerfield states that female unemployment in 1940 was higher than it had been in 1939 but male un-employment declined.[7] However, the situation was soon changed as men were called up and the munitions industry needed huge numbers of employees to meet the demands of war. Of course, munitions was not the only industry that needed women to replace men but it certainly was the primary focus for the government. At first, the Ministry of Labour relied on propaganda to stir up feelings of patriotic duty among unemployed women.[8] However, it was soon clear that propaganda alone would not attract enough women into the workforce. Smith states that the Manpower Requirements Committee projected that an extra two million women would be needed in industry to support the war effort.[9] Consequently, the government brought in two measures to ensure that women participated directly in the war effort. First, there was the Essential Work (General Provisions) Order that allowed the Ministry of Labour to assign certain areas of work as essential. This meant that employees could not leave this work without permission from the Ministry. This was hardly an incentive to opt for that work so there was a second measure that enforced compliance. In December 1941 the National Service (No 2) Act became law and included the Registration for Employment Order. This required that certain groups of women had to register for work with their local labour exchange.[10] Initially, all women aged 20–30 were obliged to register at labour exchanges.[11] This was widened to include the 19–41 age group in 1942 and was eventually increased to age 50. Conscription posed an interesting dilemma for the Government – how could it square its need for women's labour in industry with its concern for the primacy of women's domestic role? Summerfield argues that the government constantly worried that by conscripting women it was changing gender roles in the workplace irrevocably and it sought ways to modify any radical shifts.[12] Consequently, the rules around registration were carefully framed so that women with children under the age of 14 were exempt from compulsory registration. Married women who did not fall into this category were classed as immobile and were found work locally, although in the early days it was fairly easy for married women to avoid being called up at all by citing domestic responsibilities. Some feminists wanted a more radical approach to married women workers. An article appeared in the feminist journal *Time and Tide* which, taking an equality stance, argued:

> There is every reason for going carefully with compulsion in respect to the women with infant children. But there is no more reason that the childless married woman or the one with children of school age should be left outside the national effort than the widow in the like case should be. Incidentally this dispensation to married women as such is likely to encourage the making of irresponsible marriage contracts.[13]

These words fell largely on deaf ears. The government had no intention of treating married women in the same manner as single women. Married women's first responsibility was still perceived as being their home and family. National interest had to come second, but the complexity of the conscription issue highlights the government's ambivalent attitudes towards its need to call on married women at all. Single women with no dependants were considered mobile and were directed to wherever workers were needed. Through these measures, minimal disruption to patriarchal gender relations was caused. Women were once again given the signal that their participation in the workplace was secondary to their domestic responsibilities and it was a temporary participation at that.

Conscription was at first focused on industry. By August 1941, two million women had registered but only 500,000 had been interviewed and only 87,000 had joined the Women's Auxiliary services or gone into industry. Military conscription was extended to women in December 1941. This meant that more pressure could be placed on women to comply because they were given the choice of working in industry, in the women's services or civil defence. About a third chose to accept employment in industry. Women who resisted the call to conscription were vilified. Summerfield states that women who worked in station kiosks were particularly singled out for criticism.[14] These women would be seen every day selling luxury goods such as cigarettes and chocolate and could therefore be identified as serving no useful purpose and deliberately evading their patriotic duty. This was a negative attitude towards women workers that was reminiscent of the 'pin money' girls during and just after the First World War.

Another consequence of conscription was the subverting of normative notions of what constituted women's work. As in the First World War, the carefully gender-bounded spheres of men and women's work were disrupted by the conflict. Some feminists rather naively thought that conscription would guarantee equality after the war.[15] Others were less sanguine and believed, rightly, that women would still be discriminated against. Pay was a particular concern as women were not receiving the same rate of pay as men. Edith Summerskill pushed for equal pay for equal work, as did the Woman Power Committee, arguing that conscription would only be acceptable if women were treated equally to men.[16] However, the government had no intention of introducing legislation that would acknowledge that women had equal employment rights to men. One of the ways that women's pay was checked was the re-introduction of the practice of dilution. In contrast to the First World War, dilution was achieved through voluntary agreements rather than government legislation, although the Restoration of Pre-War Practices Act was passed in 1942 to ensure that women surrendered their jobs to men after the war.[17] However, although many skilled occupations, especially in the engineering trades, were designated as reserved occupations, there was still a skills shortage, so jobs were broken down into unskilled or semi-skilled tasks. Women were conscripted into this work in large numbers to undertake diluted jobs. The proportion of women workers in 'male' jobs varied from sector to sector. For example, in industries where relatively few women were employed before the war, the percentage participation increased from 27 per cent to 52 per cent in chemicals; 32 per cent to 46 per cent in metals and 10 per cent to 34 per cent in engineering.[18]

Debates about the practice of dilution are interesting as they reflect more generally the attitudes towards women as workers and how they would be recompensed for their labour. Summerfield argues that, as in the First World War, the potential influx of large numbers of semi-skilled female labour threatened the status quo and the response was varied and subject to intense negotiation.[19] Furthermore, she argues that dilution served patriarchy well. First, the government could free up some of the manpower for fighting and increase the overall size of the workforce. Second, employers could capitalize on a cheap labour force by arguing that women were not doing the equivalent of a man's labour and should therefore be paid a lower rate than the men. Third, unions could make a case for the inclusion of women in certain work on a temporary basis only and ensure a return to the status quo once the war was over. Fourth, dilution was used to allay male fears about women taking what they perceived to be their work on a permanent basis. Women's trade unionists tried to resist different pay rates for women but it was a battle they lost. The government and private employers consistently justified unequal pay to women for equal work, citing women's inability to perform as well as men, a claim refuted by women workers and trade unionists. Women were also paid lower war bonuses than men and here there was little or no justification for the practice. It seems that paying women less than men was seen as the norm and that any objection from women could be dismissed as un-reasonable. The bottom line was that women continued to be perceived primarily as wives, mothers and dependants of men rather than as workers in their own right and, consequently, not deserving of the same rights and privileges as male workers.[20]

Importantly, Wightman argues that dilution shaped women's attitudes towards engineering as an employment option after the war.[21] However, Wightman does not agree that patriarchal interests were the root cause of the resistance to women working in 'male trades'. She agrees that the unions were defending themselves, but argues that this was not so much a gender issue but rather a defence against competition from a growing body of semi-skilled workers over whom they had no control.[22] She argues that the unions were keen to protect hard-won pay and conditions from employers who wanted to keep wages down and profits high. To achieve this end, like the women on the Woman Power Committee, the unions wanted women to receive equal pay for equal work but only for work that was performed by both sexes. However, work undertaken only by women was not considered part of their quest to protect and improve conditions for their workers. Wightman also argues that most of the work undertaken by women in the engineering trades continued to be perceived as women's work; for example, the largest increase in women workers was in electrical engineering where they had been a substantial presence before the war and, therefore, the pay women received was not of primary importance to the engineering unions.[23] However, Wightman does agree with Summerfield that dilution agreements were constructed in such a way as to restrict women's work and pay and to minimize any threat to the usual peacetime practices of the sector. Consequently, women's pay changed very little and was usually between 50–70 per cent of men's wages.[24] As women's work continued to be regarded as less skilled and women as workers of secondary importance in her argument, it is difficult determine much difference between the conclusions drawn by Wightman and Summerfield. Whichever way the evidence is examined, women's domestic role continued to have primacy.

Boston argues that women did not accept unfair treatment passively. She notes that women trade unionists pushed forward motions at TUC conferences to demand equal pay and to abolish the marriage bar. The issues of childcare, school meals, canteen provision and laundries were also on the agenda during the war years. However, women trade unionists were realistic and expected and received little meaningful support from their male colleagues. The only campaign that women could call successful was the campaign for equal compensation for women injured or disabled by enemy action.[25]

Women in the armed forces fared no better than their civilian sisters. Many men were against women joining the services, especially through conscription. Pugh states that fathers and husbands were opposed because these were the women that they were fighting to protect.[26] Further, the official role of women in the services was to help the men and consequently, as in the factories, women found themselves doing very similar work to that they would have done before the war: clerical work, catering and nursing in particular. The Women's Land Army also employed over 80,000 women during the war. These women worked in all areas of agriculture. Yet, in both the armed forces and the Land Army there was no question that women were employed permanently. Their inclusion was accepted as being only for the duration of the war. Even so, around half a million women were in the armed services by the end of the war.[27] Oral histories of women's experiences in the services, as in other forms of war work, form a complex picture. For some women, the services represented a certain amount of freedom even though discipline was strict and life regulated. There were also more opportunities for training than in civilian life. Bruley cites oral history evidence of young women being taught to drive and maintain their vehicles in the WAAF, something they would not have had the opportunity to do in civilian life. However, overall, the Ministry of Labour was reluctant to offer much more than essential training for a specific job as it viewed extensive training unnecessary if women were only in the job for the duration of the war.[28] On the other hand, Higonnet and Higonnet have argued that even where women directly replaced men in the workplace, any relative advance they might have made was cancelled out by the corresponding advance in men's status resulting from their combat role, thus maintaining the gendered status quo. Higgonet and Higgonet called this phenomenon 'the double helix' effect.[29] This idea of the double helix has credence and has been used by other historians. For example, Bruley states that women ferry pilots could transport aircraft but could not carry passengers. Also, women were not able to participate in combat, at least, they were not allowed to fire guns but could work out the calculations that decided when the gun should be fired.[30] However, Stone has demonstrated that the issue is more complex than this and that women in the WAAF, at least, were not automatically subordinate to their male colleagues. Gender was less an issue than the type of work undertaken. Non-combatant men were lower status than those who flew fighter planes. There was no simple division between fighting men and non-fighting women and more complex definitions of male and female work is needed in the case of the Royal Air Force.[31]

As the need for female labour increased during the war, further stringent measures were brought in to compel even more married women to participate; many were directed to specific essential war work that they could not leave without permission from the Ministry of Labour.[32] All this suggests that women were less than willing to take up war work and that the government had to devise a number of strategies to compel them to comply. However, statistical evidence only tells part of the story. What did women think about being forced into essential war work? There are other ways that we can assess women's response to conscription. For example, there were organizations surveying public opinion at this time, in particular, the Wartime Social Survey (WSS) and Mass Observation (M-O) which focused on women and conscription.[33] In October 1941, the WSS undertook a survey of 1,000 women who were classed as free to take employment. Of these, 32 per cent stated that they did not want to undertake any war work, many citing domestic responsibilities or not wanting to leave home as their reason. Uncertainty about what type of work they would be directed to, the pay, conditions and whether they would be posted far from home were the main concerns.[34] M-O found that less than half the women they surveyed concerning military conscription were in favour. None of this is surprising given that most women, even single women, had domestic responsibilities that increased rather than diminished during wartime. Other personal evidence collected from women at the time suggests that many women were prepared to take up part-time work but found the idea of full-time work too much.

Figure 7 Land Army recruitment poster from the Second World War.

Source: Courtesy of the Imperial War Museum, London, PST0146.

The double burden

Braybon and Summerfield demonstrate that personal testimonies give a variety of complex responses towards war work. Young women with small children often found that leaving them with others was trying. One young woman told a Mass Observer that leaving her children with her sister was hard:

> I know she does everything for them, but I never seem to see my babies now. I miss it, dressing them and feeding them, and I sort of feel they will forget their Mummy. . . . Starting at six in the morning and getting back at nine, all I see of them is when they are asleep.[35]

Part-time work would have made this young woman's life a lot more bearable but the government was concerned that the availability of part-time work might be more popular than they would wish it to be. However, when it became impossible to recruit the numbers of women needed on a full-time basis, part-time work was reluctantly introduced.[36] From 1943 onwards, various part-time schemes were introduced and, by 1944, 900,000 women were working part-time.[37] Although Summerfield suggests that many women were ambivalent about working, for some married women part-time factory work was a welcome break from the drudgery of domestic labour. M-O testimonies indicate that women enjoyed the companionship that factory work brought and, revealingly, some even felt that married women would not want to return to full-time domesticity after the war:

> I thoroughly enjoy my four hours working in the afternoon. I'm all agog to get here. After all, for a housewife who's been a cabbage for fifteen years – you feel you've got out of the cage and you're free. Quite a lot of the part-timers feel like that – to get out and see some fresh faces – it's all so different, such a change from dusting. I think the war has made a lot of difference to housewives. I don't think they'll want to go back to the old narrow life. Another thing, they enjoy earning a little money for themselves, of their very own, even if it all goes on the children.[38]

This testimony reveals not so much a feeling of patriotism but it is interesting in its resistance to the dominant acceptable role of the housewife. Obviously, it depended on women's circumstances whether they found war work liberating or not. The question of part-time work was a two-edged sword. In the short term, part-time work suited women who would otherwise be compelled to either juggle the burdens of domesticity and a long working day; on the other hand, the practice confirmed the primacy of housework and that women were low-status workers.[39] For Summerfield, there was an alternative outcome, if there had been the collective will, and that was to focus on the collectivization of housework and to employ women on the same terms as men.[40] Focusing on women as workers rather than as homemakers would have meant a revolutionary change in the way both the government and society generally perceived women. If this had happened, then Marwick's assertion that the war permanently changed women's perception of themselves and their relationship with paid work would be vindicated, although one can argue that some married women had always wanted to work but were prevented from doing so by the marriage bar and assumed threats to the status of their husbands as breadwinners. However, the government did not intend to change women's role and ensured that any moves made to encourage women to work were only for the duration of the war.

An example of the temporary nature of government policy towards women is the issue of childcare provision. Although not conscripted, many women with small children were obliged to work during the war. Most, like the young woman quoted above, were forced to rely on relatives to care for their children. Summerfield argues that nursery provision was, at best, patchy during the war but at least some women were enabled to work because they had such provision.[41] Summerfield suggests that there were two approaches to childcare provision detectable in government policy. One favoured a universalist approach where, for the duration of the war, provision would be available for those who needed it. The other approach inclined towards selectivity and was based on concerns that some children, specifically the urban poor, were not being reared in an appropriate manner and were therefore best removed from parental influence for at least part of the day. The first approach meant that nursery schools for working mothers were seen as a departure from the norm to satisfy wartime needs. The second approach meant that what provision there was would be child-centred and focused on respite from a dysfunctional family unit, that is, provision was part-time and not designed to fit in with women's employment needs. Whichever the approach, there was no discernible move towards a changing attitude to women as workers.

Shopping was also a problem for many women. In the early days of the war, there were no provisions made for women's need to shop and consequently levels absenteeism and lateness soared as women tried to juggle a long working day with domestic responsibilities. M-O interviewed women about their work and reported that at least half were responsible for shopping for themselves and their families.[42] The government and employers agreed that something needed to be done because production was affected but, as Summerfield argues, neither were willing to accept responsibility for enabling women to have the time to shop. Various schemes were suggested, including schemes where women would shop for each other, although as Bruley points out, there was never any suggestion that men should take responsibility for shopping.[43] Canteens and British Restaurants offered cooked meals for the middle of the day. However, many women had to use their lunch break either to rush home and cook for the family, as was the practice then or queue to shop for later meals. Summerfield quotes a journalist from the *News Chronicle* which illustrates the problem women faced. These women started work at 7.30 am and worked until 5 pm which meant that shops opened after they started work and closed shortly after they finished:

> Yesterday I joined a stream of women leaving a group of factories at noon for their midday meal break. Many were folding paper carriers and made a dash for a bus to take them to the nearest shopping centre. There they scattered along the street making their purchases; then several hurried into a tea-shop. Here I managed to talk to a couple while they ate a hot meal in record time.[44]

Summerfield goes on to point out that in many areas shops closed for lunch at midday too and were reluctant to change their practice, thus compounding the problem for married women workers. Summerfield concludes that, unlike childcare where the government made some concessions to women's needs, shopping largely remained in the private sphere. Nothing was done either to alter the practice of shopping or its gender identification. This was another indication that women were regarded as primarily homemakers not workers. Consequently, the collision of the two worlds was regarded as a domestic problem not an industrial one.

War work and the single woman

Of course, most women workers during the war were single women whose experiences were very different to the harassed working mother. Some felt that war work was the making of them. A bank manager's daughter who joined the WRNS as a flight mechanic, rather than as a clerk which was the normal work for a girl of her class, wrote:

> The War really did a lot of good to girls like me, who had previously been privately educated, it really did. It taught me that working-class people could have emotions, and that they could be bright, really bright, because my goodness some of those girls were clever. These were things that I had simply never considered before.[45]

However, several historians have questioned the notion that the war was a great leveller. Marwick argues that the war tended to class levelling, again a claim that was made about the First World War. However, Smith argues that women often voiced their support of conscription in ways that suggest that class tensions had not been abandoned. He cites the M-O surveys in which some opined that conscription would force idle rich girls to work. This view was also supported by women trade unionists and the London Women's Parliament,[46] and is further supported by women's testimonies. Many found that the mixing of the classes heightened class tensions. Even when classes mixed, people quickly recognized class difference and labelled accordingly. Nina Masel, a WAAF member, noted:

> The moment you entered the room, you knew exactly which group to join, almost instinctively. The noisy group in the middle was the working-class one: barmaid, waitress, mill-girl, domestic servant and a few others. At the side, the Colonel's daughter was surrounded by an admiring semi-circle of actresses, a dress designer and 'ladies of leisure'. A hairdresser, accountant's clerk, schoolteacher and mannequin formed another group. Others paired off, skirting one or other of the main groups.[47]

Braybon and Summerfield add that there was job segregation too. In the WAAF, working-class women were more likely to be cooks, sparking plug testers, general duty hands; lower middle-class were orderlies, teleprinters, clerks, while middle-class and above were administrative workers, radio operators, and plotters.[48] However, it was not just class that divided women. Braybon and Summerfield found that the women's testimonies also demonstrated that women were divided by education, regional differences and urban and rural origins. Therefore, the issue of whether war work was a social leveller is complex. Although the war potentially threw together women of all classes, oral history testimony and auto-biographies demonstrate that it is hard to generalize on this issue and serve as useful sources in gaining a richer perspective on women's work and women's attitudes to work and each other.[49] However, it is possible to speculate that for many young women, especially those in the armed forces and who lived away from family influence, war work offered them a glimpse of a world that they would otherwise not have seen.

Continuity or change?

So did the war change society's perceptions of women as workers or women's perceptions of themselves as workers? Summerfield thinks not. Throughout her book she examines official policy beyond the rhetoric that exhorted women to enlist in war work and unpicks the patriarchal thinking that underpinned much of official thinking. She argues that official policy reinforced gender inequality rather than removed it. She notes that there was the potential for change, especially around housework with, for example, a scheme being suggested to employ otherwise unemployed women to take on the domestic work of working mothers (note that men were not deemed suitable for this type of work). However, she concludes that very little was done during the war to ease women workers' domestic responsibilities – most women just had to cope with the double burden – and therefore it was unrealistic to hope that anything radical would occur after the war. Consequently, whatever women might have wanted, society's attitudes towards women as workers had not changed perceptibly. Focusing on the engineering industry, Wightman argues that skills dilution meant that women were never given the opportunity to regard the work as a long-term prospect. Like Summerfield, she agrees there was no evidence that employers had changed their opinions on women in the engineering industry. She states:

> The war failed to produce any radical revision in the pre-war arrangements for women's work. Practical constraints, conservatism and the idea of women workers as a temporary, emergency measure were important reasons. But the main cause . . . was the determination of employers to limit the costs of female labour both during and after the war. This meant that the employment of women was expanded on work already recognised as female, and that new and sectionalised work tended to be redefined as female with female rates of pay.[50]

However, Pugh is slightly more optimistic in his conclusions. He argues that, unlike at the end of the First World War, women had made gains in terms of employment. Women at the end of the Second World War, although urged to return to the home, were not subject to the marriage bar. Part-time work in the post-war years became more acceptable and debates around equal pay had been raised again if not resolved. These were tangible gains that enabled more women to continue working after marriage and raised questions about the quality of women's work, but did little to address the primacy of women's domestic role.

To what extent women had changed their perceptions of themselves as workers is more difficult to ascertain. As previously mentioned, some married women found war work liberating after domestic drudgery but others found the disruption to their homes and families unbearable and we must assume that the latter returned to their domestic work, pleased to lose the double burden of paid and domestic work. In January 1944, the M-O issued a directive to its panel members, asking the question: 'Should married women be able to go out to work after the war?'[51] Replies from both men and women were varied, although Sheridan points out that women were more ambivalent than men about returning to the home. An older married woman wrote:

Speaking for myself, I shall be sorry to leave my job, and the part-time hours I work could be continued ad infinitum as far as I am concerned . . . but I think it is usually a mistake for women with children to go out to work.[52]

However, a single woman wrote, 'Married women well trained and fitted for their job will be allowed to continue – i.e. teachers and nurses etc, where there is need of them. But going out to work is incompatible with the proper care of children.'[53] Moreover, a young married professional woman wrote:

Where women have had careers, and where they are more suited to continue working than to spend time housekeeping and baby minding, I think they should work. Far better for a woman to continue with the job for which she is suited, and to pay the right type of person to look after her home and children, than to become a drudge herself, if housework is drudgery to her.[54]

As Summerfield has argued, personal testimony can certainly offer a wider perspective on an issue, but we must also remember that historians use these selectively to support a particular argument and that no consensus for the 'truth' can be obtained through this methodology alone or from one that relies solely on quantitive data.[55] That women differ in their responses to the M-O question is not surprising. Their answers reflect age, social class, education and the type of activity they carried out during the war. Furthermore, their responses also reflect the way that individuals perceive women's role in society and how they respond to these perceptions. This in itself is particularly interesting as the varied responses from these women indicate that not all women accepted the primacy of domestic labour and were looking for ways in which they could negotiate normative gender roles with their own particular needs and desires.

Conclusion to Part Three

To what extent did attitudes towards women working change in the period 1914–45 and how did this affect women's opportunities to be economically independent? The simple answer is that there was both continuity, in the sense that patriarchal attitudes towards women still prevailed, and change present throughout this period. Continuity was evident in the assumption that women's role was primarily domestic. This was underlined in every government report on women that assumed that women's work was always an unavoidable necessity rather than something desirable. The conflicting demands of a patriarchal, yet capitalist, state meant there was a continual push/pull effect concerning policy relating to women as workers. The two wars highlighted the impossibility of a purely domestic role for women, even if this was considered desirable. The need for women in the labour force in order to free up men for fighting was tempered by patriarchal concerns about the damage this might cause to women's roles as wives and mothers. This concern is made clear in the attempts to force women back into 'women's work' at the end of the First World War.

The anxieties concerning the restoration of patriarchal values were justified. Although women had always worked in a variety of occupations before the First World War, the war had meant that women were drawn into a range of industrial and military positions that they did not usually occupy and this had brought women workers to the nation's attention. Moreover, women gained an insight into a different sort of world of work than they had previously known, and for some, the first chance to participate in work at all. Although many women were content to settle for domesticity after both wars, as many oral history testimonies and autobiographies attest, the camaraderie of wartime work and the satisfaction of mastering difficult work was remembered fondly. Further, women who had not experienced managing their own money before also cited this as one of the privileges they had enjoyed. Leaving home and living independently was a new experience for many women and this also gave them insights into other women's lives that were very different to their own. It is not surprising then, that coercive measures were used to attempt to return women to their perceived proper place. Propaganda against women workers in the media, the changing rules for benefit claimants, the insistence that the Restoration of Pre-War Practices Act should be fulfilled to the letter and the reinforcement of the marriage bar all militated against women who wanted to continue to work in jobs outside their given sphere after the First World War. Any fears that the war had opened the floodgates for women workers keen to oust men from their rightful place in the workforce were quickly allayed by the imposition of stern measures that sought a return to the status quo where possible. Consequently, it is depressing to read women's narratives of the Second World War in which they reveal how the war had opened up new horizons for them in ways that are reminiscent of women's accounts from the previous war.

Throughout this period, women's organizations continued to work to improve women's lives. During the First World War, women's unions flourished as membership hit an all-time high. However, it was difficult for women's organizations to make permanent progress in employment opportunities. The emphasis on patriotism made it difficult to argue in terms of women's rights. Even the suffrage campaign had been put on hold for the duration of the war and was split by disagreements between those who supported the war and those who opposed it.[56] Braybon argues that from the outset, the government had been reluctant to take the advice of women's organizations about mobilization and other issues.[57] Further, the Restoration of Pre-War Practices Act, 1918, compelled women to leave employment that had been defined as men's work before the war and there was no move to challenge the introduction of this Act. The Committees formed at the end of the war, such as the Women's Employment Committee of the Ministry of Reconstruction and the War Committee on Women in Industry, recommended amongst other things that training opportunities, such as apprenticeships, and equal opportunities to enter local government work should be given to women at the end of the war. They also advocated encouraging women to join trade unions. However, despite some radical recommendations, these committees asserted that women's primary function was childrearing and that married women should not work outside the home. By the time the recommendations were published, women were already being laid off in large numbers despite protests from some women's groups, and little was done to retrain women beyond offering them training in the detested domestic service.[58] During the 1920s women's organizations continued to be split or were merged with male organizations. The merger of the NFWW with the National Union of General Workers (NUGW) was less a celebration of women being recognized as workers than a silencing of a militant organization. As Boston points out, by 1930 the NUGW no longer sent any women representatives to the TUC.[59] The WTUL became the Women Workers' Group of the TUC and was soon being criticized for not representing women's interests adequately at the TUC. Similarly, the Women's Labour League became the Women's Section of the Labour Party and was therefore more wedded to mainstream labour policy. The Women's Industrial Council ceased to exist after the war. The women's movement generally was split over which issues to prioritize in the inter-war period. Some took an equal rights stance and wanted women to compete with men on equal terms. They wanted equal access to the professions and equal pay for equal work. Equality was, however, a problematic issue in the inter-war period as there was no political will to accommodate women's demands and little progress was made along these lines despite the introduction of the Sex (Disqualification) Act in 1919. Others regarded women's domestic responsibilities as primary and sought ways to ameliorate the worst aspects of employment through protective legislation that limited women's working hours and through campaigning for the endowment of motherhood that would give women a measure of economic independence without undertaking paid work.

However, it would be wrong to interpret the inter-war years as a period of regression for women workers. Despite attempts to force women back into domestic service, it was always the least favoured occupation and young women actively sought work in shops and offices and the new assembly line factories rather than work as a maid in someone else's house.

The role of the live-in domestic servant was in decline, although women were still employed in large numbers to clean offices, shops, factories and other public buildings as well as the homes of the well-to-do. Going to work continued to gain respectability for middle-class girls in the inter-war years and they entered the ever-expanding clerical sector in their droves. However, the marriage bar meant that the inter-war workforce largely consisted of young women working in the period between school and marriage. Older working women were mainly single or widowed, and vertical and horizontal segregation of the sexes meant that women were usually clustered in low-pay work with very little prospect of promotion within their own sphere and no cross-over into male-defined work. Married women were supposed to be happy with their domestic lot but, of course, as in earlier periods, many working-class women continued to work in low-paid, low-status work. Middle-class women and those working-class women who were not compelled to work, were often less than satisfied with a purely domestic role and a new problem was identified as housewives were diagnosed as suffering from 'nerves'.

By the outbreak of the Second World War, the number of women working in Britain had increased slightly. The government called on women again to enrol in war work, but women were more reluctant this time, partly because most single women were already employed and were not keen to enrol in work that might offer less favourable conditions. Conscription was introduced for women for the first time. This was accompanied by a return of anxieties about women preferring work to housekeeping. Married women were also conscripted and the demonstrable double burden of domestic work and paid work led to part-time work being introduced in factories, a practice which continued after the war. Further, new working practices such as canteens and crèches were introduced, although crèches soon disappeared when the war ended. Women also joined the armed forces in large numbers during the Second World War but again this was regarded as a temporary aberration and women were expected to leave when the conflict was over.

Overall, the period covered by this section of the book indicates both advances and reversals in women's accessibility to paid work and decent conditions. The needs of war gave women the opportunity to demonstrate their capabilities and raised their expectations. The end of each war was marked by a desire of the state to return women to their earlier roles. Each time it was only partially successful. After the First World War women filled the lower strata of clerical, shop and factory work which they left only on marriage, largely because of the marriage bar and the effects of the prevailing domestic ideology. Part Four of this book examines what happened to women workers in the years after the Second World War up until the passing of the equality legislation in the early 1970s and the effects this had on women's opportunities as workers.

Part Four

1945 to the end of the century

The conclusion of the Second World War took place over a protracted period and although some women feared that their employment prospects would end as abruptly as they had at the end of the previous war, the reality was more complex. The lay-offs in munitions factories began quite a while before the end of the war and, even then, women were re-directed into other work, such as aircraft construction where production was still increasing.[1] However, again, the general expectation was that married women would want to return to the domestic sphere and that young single women would return to 'women's work' in the interlude before marriage and starting a family. Many women expected only to be employed in the particular work they were undertaking for the duration of the war. They remembered what had happened at the end of the First World War to them or to their mother's generation and had few illusions that anything had changed, although some did not necessarily want to lose their wartime work. Braybon and Summerfield cite a woman in a M-O survey undertaken in 1942:

> Look at the last war. Those hundreds of women ran our trams and did a wonderfully good job. When the war was over the Transport Department snarled at them, "You're doing a man out of a job" and they were flung into the streets without a word of thanks.[2]

However, history did not repeat itself. The context following the Second World War was quite different, although the underlying patriarchal imperatives remained. Returning soldiers would not be able to fulfil all the employment requirements of a country that needed massive reconstruction, both of its industries and its infrastructure, so women, including older married women, were soon urged to do their duty and return to certain types of paid work. Further, the introduction of the Welfare State meant that thousands of new jobs in the clerical and service sectors were created. This meant that there was, once again, a conflict between ideological notions of women's proper place and the economic need to fill employment vacancies throughout the rest of the 1940s and into the 1950s. The impact of this conflict persisted throughout the period, albeit to greater or lesser extent.

Jane Lewis argues that the three most significant social changes to affect women in the post-Second World War period were the increase of married women in paid employment; the dramatic increase in the divorce rate; and the steep rise in illegitimacy.[3] The changing structure of the family certainly contested the dominant notion of the male breadwinner with dependent wife and children to an extent. However, simply reading off from these factors an assumption that women were becoming more economically independent or able to exercise more choice in these matters is unwise. First, women were still perceived primarily as homemakers and, consequently, bore the double burden of paid work and unpaid domestic work. This fact alone would limit women's choices and opportunities as they were expected to fit paid work around childcare and housework. Further, during this period there were fears that working mothers endangering their children's well-being. In earlier generations, discourses around married women focused on the physical neglect of children by working mothers. In this period, the worry was more around the psychological damage done to children deprived of their mothers' attention. So married women's presence in the workforce was, and is, always hedged around by fears about the damage this might cause to children. These fears, coupled with a lack of childcare facilities of course, encouraged women to try to fit paid work around school hours, an issue still pertinent at the end of this period.

The post-war period was also a time when women's participation in trade union activity decreased. Soldon states that female membership was 1,010,000 in 1939 and reached a peak of 1,790,000 by 1951.[4] However, following the war, male trade unionists only paid lip service to women's issues, regarding women as temporary employees and therefore relatively unimportant. They were not interested in equal opportunities for women and only made, at best, lukewarm responses to women's issues generally. Unsurprisingly, by the mid-1950s, women's union activity was declining and unions were resorting to fashion shows in a vain attempt to attract women members.[5] Despite this half-hearted attempt to appeal to women workers, the unions made little attempt to encourage women to attend meetings. These were often held in the evenings when it was difficult for married women to attend, although some unions, such as the National Union of Public Employees (NUPE) and the Amalgamated Union of Electrical Workers (AUEW), set up women-only meetings in order to solve this problem.[6] However, women took the initiative into their own hands from the late 1960s onwards and this time they found support from feminists rather than male trade unionists. The event that marked this change occurred in 1968 when nearly 200 women machinists working at Ford's car factory in Dagenham successfully struck for recognition as skilled workers in order to gain a wage increase. They also paved the way for a renewed interest in the campaign for equal pay for women.[7] The 1970s saw several examples of women's militancy in the trade union movement. There was the night cleaners' campaign to unionize women cleaners in London to campaign for higher wages in 1971. This campaign linked working-class women with the newly revitalized women's movement but was not vigorously supported by male trade unionists.[8] Moreover, for the first time, West Indian women played a key role in a strike.[9] Women at the Trico car component factory in Brentford also struck successfully for equal pay in 1976.[10] Further, an Asian woman, Jayaben Desai, led the Grunwick strike in 1977. Bryan *et al.* argue that this strike in particular showed that the trade union movement was guilty of both sexism and racism.[11]

Beyond the trade unions, class and race were factors that affected women's opportunities. As in previous generations, middle-class women were more likely to work for personal fulfilment and to have received adequate education to achieve interesting careers. During the 1950s, these women were the focus of studies that explored women's dual role. We shall examine this debate in more detail. Working-class women and immigrant women tended to continue in low-paid, low-status monotonous work. The introduction of the Welfare State meant there was a great deal of this type of work available on both a full- and part-time basis. Moreover, immigrant women, in particular, were disadvantaged because the official view towards them was that they were allowed in this country as workers. Consequently, scant attention was paid to their domestic role. In the 1950s and 1960s, economic independence was still a dream for most women. Single women found it difficult to leave the family home because women's wages were still significantly lower than their male counterparts and married women's earnings were still regarded as a supplement to that of the male breadwinner. Little change in the attitudes of policy makers was apparent until the 1970s when the attitude towards women shifted somewhat with the introduction of the Equal Pay Act 1970 and the Sex Discrimination Act 1975, and the establishment of the Equal Opportunities Commission in 1975. Women were able to take advantage, albeit painfully slowly, of the opportunities this legislation allowed but to this day women still earn less than men in comparable work and the so-called glass ceiling acts as a brake on women's ambitions.

The test of women's economic independence in the post-war years is also complicated by the way the Welfare State was structured. Wilson

181

suggests that the Welfare State created a new patriarchal relationship between women and the state, where the state stands in for the husband in cases where women had no male on whom to depend for financial support.[12] This relationship was hardly liberating for the increasing numbers of women who had no male breadwinner to rely upon as the patriarchal state placed limitations on the way women dependant on benefits could live. Indeed, the benefit system militated against single mothers taking on paid work as they lost benefit and were obliged to pay for childcare. This meant that many single mothers were worse off in paid employment than they were living on state benefits.[13]

This part of the book focuses on a rather under-researched era in terms of historical research. However, although the sources are limited at present there are discernible themes and debates emerging. These include what happened to women workers after the war? How did the Welfare State create a particular way of constructing women as workers? What were the differing experiences of black and white women as workers? Why was equal opportunities legislation introduced and what has its impact been? What are the issues for women in the twenty-first century? It is to these issues we now turn.

Chapter Ten

ૐ

Back to home and duty again?
The women and work debate,
1945–50

The social, economic and political context of the post-Second World War period was very different to the 1920s. Although the Allies were the victors, Britain's economy was drained and the empire was slipping from its grasp. Further, there was no clear-cut conclusion to the war. The men in the forces slowly returned home, rationing carried on into the 1950s and there was a huge price to pay in terms of reconstructing bomb-damaged cities as well as returning the economy to peacetime production. Added to this, shortly after the Japanese surrender in August 1945, the withdrawal of the American Lending-Lease Agreement meant that the country was plunged into an economic crisis. The new Labour Government was interventionist by nature and decided that the over-riding priority in the post-war years was to boost exports and therefore it kept wartime controls over the economy. This meant that workers were still controlled by law, which, of course, affected men and women differently. In these new circumstances, male workers were expected to stay in work permanently and, in some occupations, this meant they were trained to do new work, often by the women they were replacing, or were returned to their previous trades, again often at women's expense. Women were expected, and indeed many wanted, to resume family life. However, no sooner had women returned to the home when the government, perturbed at the apparent labour shortage, called them back to work. As usual, the work they were required to undertake was focused on 'women's work', mainly in unpopular sectors such as textiles and, of course, domestic work of various kinds. Commentators have mixed views on how women were treated at the end of the war and, indeed, on what women expected to do. This chapter explores the government's expectations of women in the immediate aftermath of the war, how this related to the expectations of society more generally and what women wanted for themselves. In conclusion, it assesses the affect that post-war expectations and policies had on women's work in the longer term.

Demobilization

As previously discussed in Chapter Nine, many women were in diluted work during the war. This meant they were only expected, and expecting, to be in those jobs for the duration of the war. The government certainly assumed that married women would return to the home at the end of the war. To this end, it began closing down the few nurseries that existed as early as 1944 and the nursery wartime funding grant was removed in April 1946, making it clear that married women workers were expected to return to the home once the war was over. How women felt about this, of course, varied from person to person. Most young married or soon to be married women were happy to leave dirty, low-skilled monotonous work in order to start or pick up family life or to move into work that was more 'feminine'. A survey carried out for the Ministry of Reconstruction in 1944 indicated that a high proportion of women who had entered the sector because of war wanted to leave at the end of it. The report indicated it was young married women employed in low-skilled work, such as packing, who wanted to leave the sector. Women in professional or administrative work were more inclined to want to remain in the work.[14] Not surprisingly, most women who wanted or needed to continue working preferred to work in more interesting, cleaner work than factory work, which had always had lower status than shop and clerical work. The rapidly increasing number of available jobs, largely created by the Welfare State, meant that there was plenty of choice.[15] Consequently, many women who needed to continue to work returned to so-called 'women's work' although not to domestic service which suffered a further decline compared to the pre-war years. Indeed there was a concerted campaign in the immediate post-war years to encourage women into domestic service.[16] The distribution of residential domestic servants varied from region to region, but while 24 per cent of the female labour force remained in domestic service in 1939, this figure had dropped to 11 per cent by 1951.[17]

After a short period when unemployment rose slightly, there was plenty of work available for women who wanted it, because it was in the areas that were designated 'women's work' that the economy was expanding. For example, between 1931 and 1951 the number of women clerks and typists rose from 657,000 to 1,408,000.[18] There was also an increase in the number of posts available in nursing and teaching, again traditional women's work with higher status than factory work.[19] Pugh argues that this increase in women workers had little to do with changing ideas about women's role in the workplace. Rather, it reflected the needs of the economy. Most of these extra jobs continued to be low-paid, unskilled or semi-skilled occupations with no career structure, that is, they had the typical characteristics of women's work. However, Braybon and Summerfield also argue that there was an increase in women in male-dominated professions too. They cite the numbers of women doctors increasing from 2,580 in 1928 to 7,198 in 1945 and women dentists increasing from 82 to 549 during the same period. Women solicitors, barristers and architects had increased too and the marriage bar in these professions had disappeared.[20]

Women in the services had little choice about the future although women continued in the Land Army until 1950.[21] Braybon and Summerfield state that this was the same for most of the half a million women employed in the services. Most returned to civilian life soon after the war ended although some were able to stay on to serve in the continuing war in the Pacific and others were sent to Europe to help in the reconstruction process. Married women were the first to be demobilized. Age and length of service were taken into account. Notwithstanding whatever work they had undertaken in the services, these women were expected to return to 'women's work' or marry on leaving the forces. The official advice to ex-servicewomen seeking work was to retrain as a teacher, nurse or clerical worker even if women had engineering skills. Like other women who had enjoyed their wartime work, some women in the forces would have liked to continue in their trade but knew they would not be able to.[22]

Although it was generally accepted that women who continued to work would return to their old pre-war occupations, some women were squeezed out of their wartime roles rather than giving them up willingly. This seems to have been a particular problem in the retail and clerical sectors. Here, women had been undertaking higher status and higher paid 'men's work' during the war, often without any extra pay. This work was often very similar to the work women did but because it was deemed to be 'men's work' it was part of a career structure that allowed for promotion. For example, Braybon and Summerfield recount the story of one woman who worked in a bank and, during the war, was expected to do men's work (cashiering) without being paid the male rate for the job. At the end of the war this work was offered to inexperienced men whom she then had to train up for the job before being relegated to lower status machine work that was designated as 'women's work'. The woman was quite rightly unhappy and did not surrender the higher status work willingly.[23]

For those women who wanted to continue in 'men's work' the transition to peacetime was not always easy. Wightman states that a survey carried out amongst women members of the Amalgamated Engineering Union indicated that out of the 2,000 women (7 per cent of the total female membership) who replied, 79 per cent wanted to continue in their jobs provided that they were not depriving a man of a job. Most of the women who wanted to continue were dilutees.[24] The closure of nurseries was only one factor preventing women from continuing to work. However, male workers and trade unions also applied pressure on women to persuade them to give way to male workers. Both these groups had their own reasons for wanting to see the Restoration of Pre-War Practices Act carried out to the letter. Braybon and Summerfield cite one woman who said:

> [I] was made redundant . . . this displeased me very much, so straight round to the union representative we went and discussed the matter with him. And he said that the jobs were for the men coming out of the forces and that we had to leave them. And I understood it perfectly, but I didn't approve.[25]

Other women met opposition from their husbands who did not want them to continue working, feeling that a working wife undermined their position as breadwinner in the family. There are many oral histories testifying to the fact that a fair proportion of women were not keen to give up their 'male' jobs at the end of the war but often were resigned to the inevitable.[26]

Despite the assumptions that women's involvement in the workforce would return to pre-war levels, this was never the case. In fact, by the end of 1947 there were more women working than in 1939.[27] Pugh states that women, as a percentage of the workforce, had risen from 29.8 per cent in 1931 to 30.8 per cent in 1951. This was in spite of the baby boom after the war.[28] However, Summerfield states that the number of women working fell sharply after the war, having increased from around 6,250,000 in 1939 to 7,750,000 in 1943, it had shrunk back to 6,000,000 by 1947. However, she suggests that the shrinkage was partly due to the higher school leaving age, which meant that there were less young women available for work, and also due to undercounting because many women left insured wartime work to take up casual, unregulated post-war work.[29] Part-time work, which became popular during the war and continued its popularity during the post-war period, would often fall into this unregulated sector.[30] Further, Pennington and Westover state that in 1948 in the shoe industry, which was one of the industries suffering from labour shortage, there were 600–700 homeworkers in one shoe-making centre alone. In the hosiery industry there were 12,000 homeworkers; they were also common in the clothing industry.[31] Homeworking is notoriously difficult to quantify so official surveys and the census possibly continued to underestimate considerably the number of women involved in paid work in the post-war years.

Although the Ministry of Labour planned the return of men from the forces, little thought was put into planning for post-war women's employment beyond persuading them to give up work that was deemed male and returning to more 'feminine' work. The question of whether there would be enough men available to fill the gaps in production was also not properly considered. The necessity of boosting post-war production, coupled with the continued maintenance of a large army, meant that there was a severe labour shortage in some sectors in the late 1940s.[32] This was particularly acute in the engineering sector where, between 1943 and January 1947, the female engineering workforce was nearly halved but had not been replaced by sufficient numbers of men because the school leaving age had been raised to 15 and conscription of men into the forces was still continuing.[33] The shortfall was so large that during 1946–7 the government was obliged to restore employment controls so that they could direct workers into essential work. This was seen in a campaign to persuade women to return to work in key industries again.

The government's return to work campaign

The new Labour Government sent out mixed messages to women about their role in the economy. On the one hand, they needed women to stay in the workforce, but on the other hand, they wanted women to concentrate on rebuilding the family. So what sort of work were women encouraged to take up and how successful were the government's contradictory campaigns? Were there any long-term changes to assumptions about what constituted women's work and any moves towards equal treatment for women?

Croft and Carruthers argue that the government had known that they would need to keep women in the workforce long before the war ended. Indeed, the situation on the industrial front was regarded as a national emergency.[34] Carruthers points out that a gendered appeal to workers was not restricted to women, as men were being encouraged to apply for 'men's work' in unpopular industries.[35] In October 1947, the government issued an order giving it power to compel unemployed men aged 18–50 and unemployed women aged 19–40 to work in certain industries where the need for labour was deemed the greatest.[36] One of the main problems for the government was that women were either not working in the industries most affected by shortages or they wanted to leave these sectors for more attractive work once conscription was lifted. Wightman states that in the engineering trades the problem was not so much encouraging women to leave the trade but persuading them to stay in sectors that were suffering shortages.[37] So how did the government set about encouraging women to fill the sectors where there were shortages and how successful were they?

The government's campaign to encourage women to work in the employment sectors suffering from labour shortages began in June 1947, despite it having known for three years that there would be shortages.[38]

" I started training to become a nurse—but the work was too exhausting."

Figure 8 'I started training to become a nurse – but the work was too exhausting'.

Source: 'NEB' (Ronald Niebour), *Daily Mail*, 12 September 1947. *Daily Mail*/Solo Syndication.

Originally, the government had wanted to conscript young women for two years' service in employment of national importance but this idea was rejected as being too costly to implement for the number of young women it would reach. In the end, the campaign was specifically aimed at women in the 35–50 age group, including married women who had worked during the war. This helped to partially solve the government's dilemma about whether women should focus on childrearing or work, as women in this age group were unlikely to have small children. The government calculated that there were 300,000 married women working during the war. It also estimated that there were another 600,000 women who would be potential recruits if nurseries and part-time jobs were offered.[39] So, what was the work that the government wanted women to take up?

Many women workers were employed in catering or the distributive trades, whereas the government wanted workers in footwear, clothing, laundries, domestic work, rubber, iron and steel, transport, agriculture, cotton and textiles.[40] Later there was a drive to recruit more into teaching.[41] The target was 6,000 extra women teachers but only 4,000 were actually found.[42] The textile industry is an interesting case given that it was one the main areas of employment for women before the war. During the war many of the Lancashire mills had been closed and their employees transferred to war-related work. Croft argues that the conditions in this new work were superior to the old mills and the work had higher status. Consequently, women were not keen to return to millwork after the war. Some remained in engineering, others found cleaner work in retailing, catering and public transport or they remained at home.[43] The government decided to focus the campaign on the sixty districts where they were most needed. Women's organizations, such as the Women's Institute, were used to transmit the message and encourage recruitment.[44] There was also a nationwide campaign to alert and educate the public, and women in particular, to the fact that there was a crisis and how it should be addressed. The rhetoric of the campaign continued in the discourse of war. Croft quotes George Isaacs, the Minister of Labour, who in a broadcast message attempted to invoke the Dunkirk spirit: 'In the battle for recovery there are still many frontline jobs for women to do.' However, the work they were being offered was not men's work but women's work, the sort 'which has always been usual for women to do'.[45] Other catchy phrases such as 'Birmingham's bread hangs by Lancashire's thread' were used to encourage women back to these less popular jobs. Domestic service (particularly hospital domestic service) and nursing were also part of the campaign's focus.[46] Giles argues that as early as 1941 the Ministry of Labour had been thinking about setting up a National Service Orderly Corps to provide not only hospitals and other caring institutions with domestic help but also private households, although the latter was soon dropped from consideration.[47] The minutes from the discussion argued somewhat optimistically that:

> the formation of a Corps would raise the status of domestic work in national services and might improve recruitment by attracting women who at the moment were not subject to any form of compulsion from the Ministry of Labour and National Service (such as women with young children) and might also encourage women who registered to opt for domestic work.[48]

The corps was never established and the status of domestic work remained low. However, in 1947, Violet Markham was asked to write a report on the future of private domestic employment. Giles argues that this report contributed in important ways to the debate around femininity and class in the post-war years.[49] One of its recommendations was the establishment of the National Institute of Houseworkers. This aimed to improve the pay, conditions and status of domestic work.[50] Briar argues that this project was under-funded and quickly undermined by another government scheme to use immigrant women workers as domestic workers.[51] This issue is discussed further in the next chapter. The caring professions also featured in the government's sights. Teaching and nursing had always been regarded as suitable work for women and the Welfare State created demand for women workers in both of these professions.

However, there was little to tempt women back to work in these under-staffed sectors, as there was no attempt to offer women equal pay. The main argument against equal pay was that women would be doing women's work, not men's. Consequently, women were back to the pre-war situation in which with certain areas of work were designated as women's work and consequently worth less pay. Furthermore, there was an assumption that women were only working during the emergency period and would return to the home when they were no longer needed.[52] Apart from being offered only low-paid 'women's work' Croft argues that the government's propaganda was 'austere and unglamorous, a restoration of the prototype wartime woman, dressed in dungarees and headscarf, rolling up her sleeves for the next gruelling battle on the factory floor'.[53] This image was hardly likely to attract women back into low-paid mill or factory work when it was in competition with more glamorous office and retail work or the prevailing ideology that a woman should aspire to build the post-war home. As Pugh argues, women were willing to work after marriage but not on any terms.[54] Consequently, women were less driven by patriotic fervour than by earning a reasonable wage and experiencing good working con-ditions. The government acknowledged this and revamped the campaign by offering certain incentives. To encourage women back to the mills, incentives included the opportunity to work part-time, the provision of laundries at the mills, shopkeepers delivering fresh food to the mill, priority given for the building of nurseries and after-school and holiday care for older children. Further, Croft suggests that working conditions at the mills were improved and higher rates of pay were offered, making millwork above the average for pay.[55] However, the campaign only attracted about a third of the total number that the government had hoped to attract. At least 92,000 jobs were advertised and only around 31,000 were filled.[56]

It may be that some women had imbibed the 'back to home and duty' message too well and did not want to undertake the double burden of paid and unpaid work. For others, the improved conditions experienced in their war-time employment and the expansion of available work for women may have meant that they were not prepared to return to old-fashioned mills or low-status domestic work. In 1947, G. D. Cole observed perceptively that:

Experience of these factories [munitions] made many people reluctant to return, or send their children, to the textile mills. This attitude was reinforced by the bad repute into which the cotton industry had fallen because of the high rate of unemployment that had prevailed in it year after year. In these circumstances, it was evident that the industry would not get or hold the labour it needed without a substantial improvement in wages even though its output were to fall a long way short of what it had been in the bad times before 1939.[57]

Evidently, there was to be no return to the pre-war working patterns. The trend for women to want clean, respectable work with a reasonable wage and working conditions would continue into the 1950s. Domestic service, textiles and the clothing industry all declined as the main employment sectors for indigenous women, while clerical work surged in popularity and women were outnumbering men in this sector as Table 10.1 shows. By 1951, women constituted 49 per cent of clerks, cashiers and office machine operators of which 30 per cent were married and 6 per cent worked part-time. Typists, shorthand writers and secretaries were virtually all women – 97 per cent in 1951.[58] These figures represent by far the largest groups of clerical workers. However, women were over-represented in low-paid, low-status work in the sector. In factory work, women were found in light unskilled and semi-skilled work. In engineering, women constituted around 10 per cent of the workforce but by 1951 this had risen to 22 per cent, which reflects the expansion of light engineering such as electrical engineering.[59] Women were also to be found in the food and drink and tobacco industries as well as the clothing industry. How the government sought to deal with the problem of recruiting women into the unpopular sectors of work will be discussed in the next chapter.

Table 10.1 Clerks and typists in Britain, 1931 and 1951[60]

	England and Wales		Scotland	
	Male	*Female*	*Male*	*Female*
1931	795,486	579,945	69,272	77,451
1951	861,676	1,270,456	70,485	138,699

Women and work in the post-war period

There were many influences at play affecting women's preferences. Some wanted to return to a purely domestic role. The war years had shown them how difficult the double burden of full-time work and domestic responsibilities could be. New labour-saving domestic appliances had not yet appeared and continued rationing meant that shopping was still a time-consuming chore which meant queuing for even basic commodities. Many of these women also subscribed to the dominant ideology that stated that men were the breadwinners and women and children their dependants. They saw this as the natural order and wanted to return to this status quo as quickly as they could. They also felt that women should not take 'men's jobs'.[61] Women were unlikely to develop a permanent or engaged interest in engineering in peacetime because their experience was shaped by wartime experiences, which included skills dilution, the negative attitudes of the male workforce towards women and meaningless and monotonous work.[62] Universally, patriotic propaganda had told women that the war work they were undertaking was of a temporary nature and had encouraged them to believe that it was really 'men's work'. Towards the end of the war and after, women's magazines largely focused on the reconstruction of the traditional home and nuclear family. This also enforced the 'return to home' message. However, despite the propaganda, many women found that they still needed to work after the war because the cost of living was rising faster than their husbands' wages. Others wanted to continue to work because, despite the barrage of propaganda on the joys of domesticity, they enjoyed the relief from the loneliness and boredom of full-time housewifery.

Women's views on whether they should work and what sort of work was appropriate in the post-war period is still an under-researched area although some work has already been undertaken.[63] Of course, there are problems with using oral history as a method of finding out about people's views on past events and issues. For example, how can we determine the difference between views held then and views held now – what part does popular memory and today's attitudes towards women and work play in constructing life histories?[64] However, these testimonies give us some idea of women's views on whether the war had changed them and how this affected their attitude to work in the post-war years.[65] When M-O surveyed women at the time on their attitude to work in the post-war years,[66] it claimed that most women who had worked during the war wanted to return to domesticity but they qualified this assertion by differentiating between different age groups and occupations. They found that women under 25, especially service women, were less likely to want to settle down than slightly older women. Older women, in their 40s and 50s were less inclined to be restricted to the home.[67] It is not surprising that service-women were less enthusiastic about domesticity than other women. They had left home to enter the forces and were generally more independent than women who stayed at home even if they were going out to work.[68] Summerfield interviewed twenty-two women who had served in the forces during the war, most of whom said that their wartime experiences had changed them and made them more independent and confident of their abilities.[69] Summerfield reports that although some women in civilian war work felt like the servicewomen, in that they felt they had improved their social consciousness and developed a sense of feminine citizenship, the majority of servicewomen's stories were what she calls 'heroic' in their narrative style. Civilian workers, on the other hand, felt less sure that the war had changed them in any way, and they told their stories in a 'stoic' style.[70] Summerfield states that the women who felt that the war had not changed them were conscripted and viewed their war experiences as an unfortunate necessity.[71] Women's feeling about whether the war had changed them might well indicate whether or not they were keen to return to the pre-war status quo. For some women, the war offered them the opportunity to do something other than work in 'women's work' in the period before an anticipated marriage and possibly to combine work and family in the future. For others, it might well have postponed the pleasures of marriage and setting up a family. Interestingly, the subsequent life experiences of both groups shows that most of the women who married combined work with family life no matter whether they felt that the war had changed them or not.

Like the First World War, the Second World War gave women the opportunity to experience different types of lives than they had lived before the war. For many this difference was explicitly related to their experience of work. For the first time women were conscripted, married women's work was formally acknowledged and, to some extent, their needs catered for; for example, the introduction of nurseries and canteens to lighten, albeit marginally, the domestic load. Significantly, part-time work became a possibility for a substantial number of married women. However, the continuing primacy of women's role as homemaker and mother meant that the changes were tempered by the continual channelling of women into low-paid, low-status work that offered very little chance of progression. It is difficult to argue that the war had substantially challenged normative assumptions about women's role in society. What it did achieve, however, was the acknowledgement that women did play a significant role in the economic as well as the social interests of the country and consequently crushed the hackneyed legend that women's place was solely in the home. After the Second World War, young middle-class single women no longer had to justify to their family the desire to take paid work. The situation had completely reversed. It was still considered desirable for married women not to take paid work, but the marriage bars that had eliminated any possibility of choice were never re-introduced. Briar, however, suggests there is anecdotal evidence to suggest that an informal marriage bar continued to exist in some middle-class occupations, even in the Civil Service, into the 1970s.[72] This is an area for further research. However, the debate about women's work, and married women's work in particular, continued into the 1950s and 1960s and it is this period that is examined in the next chapter.

Chapter Eleven

હ

Women's employment in the 1950s and 1960s

The 1950s and 1960s is regarded as a period dominated by the centrality of family life. This was formalized through the Welfare State with its dominant model of the male breadwinner with dependent wife and children. Some historians also regard the period as the 'nadir' of the feminist movement when little progress was made and when any advances could be attributed to forces outside of women's agency.[1] As we have seen in the previous chapter, there was a desire amongst many people to 'get back to normal' as soon as possible after the war, implying that 'normal' for women meant marriage and domesticity. However, this 'return to normal' was tempered by wider economic and social changes that occurred in the post-war world. The focus on the family was accompanied by an increase in marriage generally, and a lowering of age at marriage. However, there was also an increased use of contraceptives and family planning generally which meant that child-rearing years were compressed, allowing women to return to work as their children grew older. The 1949 Royal Commission on Population confirmed that the average size of a family was 2.2 children.[2] It also underlined the official line that raising a family was a woman's primary responsibility.[3] As previously noted, after an initial rise in unemployment following the war, the demand for women workers was high. This occurred not only in the areas into which the government wanted to channel women in order to support the recovery effort, but also in the new areas of employment stimulated by the development of the Welfare State and the burgeoning consumer market. The period was characterized by the centrality of the family, the notion of the companionate marriage and the reinforcement of the notion of the male breadwinner. However, it was also punctuated by the debate around equal pay as well as the debate around married working women. Further, changes in the education system meant that the school-leaving age was raised, more girls were being educated to secondary level and more were progressing to colleges and universities and, consequently, these women were looking for more fulfilling jobs than their mothers had engaged in. There was also a new group of women to consider when researching women's work in the 1950s: the new intake of immigrants, largely from the Caribbean and other parts of the Commonwealth but also migrants from European countries affected by the Second World War. These issues are considered in this chapter.

The campaign for equal pay

Equal pay had been an ongoing issue for feminists throughout the twentieth century. Sometimes the campaign lay dormant because economic and social conditions meant that the idea was a non-starter. However, there were some periods when feminists thought that prevailing conditions meant that women had a chance of success. Feminists tried unsuccessfully during both wars to establish an enduring principle of equal pay for equal work as did the feminists involved in the campaign for equal pay in the Civil Service in the 1930s. Throughout the Second World War, the Woman Power Committee, an official advisory body, campaigned for equal pay. Following a strike at the Rolls Royce factory in Glasgow, a new equal pay campaign was formed in 1943[4] but met with mixed success. The teacher's unions were successful in getting equal pay for women teachers written into the 1944 Education Bill. However, echoing the government's earlier reluctance to act in the 1930s campaign, Churchill foiled this by making the issue a vote of confidence and offering a Royal Commission on Equal Pay instead. This enabled the government to shelve the issue until after the war when, it presumably hoped, women would have less of a case. In that hope, it was correct. The report was published in 1946 at a time when the tide had turned and most women had left 'men's work' and were either working in 'women's work' or had given up paid work altogether. The commission argued for equal pay for commensurate work and found this applied only to teaching, the Civil Service and local government. However, despite this narrowing of the field to these areas, the Labour Government rejected the commission's findings, stating that although they agreed on principle, the effect would be inflationary.[5] This was not the end of the issue and women trades union activists in the Civil Service Clerical Association (CSCA), the National Union of Teachers (NUT), the National Union of Women Teachers (NUWT), the National Association of Local Government Workers (NALGO) and the Union of Post Office Workers (UPOW), among others, campaigned during the early 1950s for equal pay.[6]

The campaign lasted four years, from 1951 to 1955, and focused largely on the government taking action because employers refused to grant equal pay until the government had done so. Eventually, after a sustained campaign, the government agreed and announced a staged introduction of equal pay for civil servants over the next six years. Public sector employers shortly followed suit. However, as Boston points out, this was a decisive yet limited victory. The award only applied to a group of skilled, professional women. It did not cover manual grades in the Civil Service and local government. Cooks, cleaners and canteen workers were still deemed to be doing women's work even if the work could be seen to be of equal value. Typists in government departments were excluded for the same reason. Similarly, the Post Office refused to concede equal pay except for postal and telegraph officers. Nursing was excluded too because it was regarded as women's work and therefore commanded less pay.[7] Despite the victory on equal pay for a minority of women workers, Lewis states that women's pay in relation to men's fell from the 1950s to the mid-1960s so that women, on average, earned 59 per cent of men's wages.[8] Sex segregation was at the root of much of the pay disparity between men and women. Lewis states that sex segregation had persisted throughout the twentieth century and had suppressed women's wages. In 1951, 86 per cent of women workers were employed in gender-segregated jobs, a trend that continued throughout the 1950s and 1960s.[9]

The debate on married women working

There is little doubt that the war acted as a defining moment in women's employment and that the female workforce changed in its profile, although this was tempered by the continuing segregation of women into so-called 'women's work'. It is interesting to note that the female workforce was older in the post-war period. Young women under the age of 25 represent around a third of the female workforce in 1951 compared to around half in 1931.[10] Thanks to the marriage bar, both formal and informal, it had been largely a single workforce too. By the time the 1951 Census had taken place, women formed 31 per cent of the labour force; this rose to 36 per cent if the focus is on women aged 20 to 64. Part-time work accounted for 12 per cent of these women and 26 per cent of all working women aged 15 to 59 were married.[11] By 1959, the number of married women workers had risen to 52 per cent of part time workers. By the early 1970s, the percentage of married women workers had risen dramatically to 49 per cent of all women workers and 35 per cent of women workers worked part-time.[12] The rise in married women working was striking. In 1921, only 9 per cent of married women were recorded as working, rising slightly to 10 per cent in 1931.[13] However, figures varied from region to region. In heavy industrial areas such as South Wales, central Scotland and the north of England, women were less likely to be employed, counting as less that 20 per cent of the labour force. However marked regional differences decreased during the 1950s and 1960s.[14] In areas such as Lancashire and Greater London there were more women working, especially in the expanding service sector.[15] Table 11.1 demonstrates the increase in married women in the labour force since the Second World War. Of course, numbers are under-recorded as many married women had congregated in low-paid casual work which would not be counted in the census. However, the recording of part-time work indicates that this type of work had moved into the mainstream although it still tended to be located in the low-paid, low-status, low-skilled jobs.[16] Furthermore, it indicated that married women were not so reluctant to admit to undertaking paid work as they had been earlier in the century.

Table 11.1 Women in the labour force, Great Britain 1951–81[17]

	1951	*1961*	*1971*	*1981*
Women in labour force (% of the total labour force)	31	33	37	40
Women in labour force (% of women aged 20–64)	36	42	52	61
Women employed part-time (% of the total labour force)	12	26	35	42
Married women in labour force (% of all married women aged 15–59)	26	35	49	62

The increase of married women working led to a debate that began in the 1950s about when, in their life cycle, women should work, how this affected their primary role as homemaker and whether in fact it was possible or desirable for married women to work. Tellingly, married working women were referred to as 'working wives', thus keeping their perceived primary function well to the fore. Supporters of the move towards women continuing to work envisaged women taking on a dual role where marriage and work became compatible. Indeed, a pattern was emerging where young women were continuing full-time work on marriage, leaving work for full-time childcare on the birth of the first child and returning to part-time work when the children were all at school. This pattern is called the two-phase or bi-modal pattern of female employment.[18]

However, there was still an expectation that women with small children would not work outside the home. It was also hoped that women would have more than the 2.2 children that was the statistical average at the time. The Royal Commission on Population, which had published its findings in 1949, felt that it was imperative for the national interest that women have at least three or four children. Unsurprisingly, the report focused on making motherhood more attractive than wage earning and therefore is regarded as part of the pronatalist discourse of the 1940s and 1950s.[19] The report had a contradictory position concerning post-war marriage. It blamed feminism for encouraging women's paid employment and weakening the man's role as breadwinner. This, it reasoned, had led to companionate marriages where the marriage was viewed as an equal but complementary partnership rather than a patriarchal dictatorship. In this new idealized version of marriage, the husband was more considerate to his wife and did not want her to suffer continual childbirth.[20] The state was in favour of couples being committed to concentrating their efforts on building a stable family unit for children. However, couples often reasoned that fewer children better provided for was their goal, thus undermining state requirements for larger families. In addition, there were fears that if a marriage did not live up to expectations, divorce would be seen as a solution. This anxiety has to be assessed in the context of the rising number of divorces in the post-war era. From a feminist perspective, Finch and Summerfield argue that this approach to motherhood and family life led to a narrowing of a woman's role by advocating that her sole concern should be her family and, in particular, her children.[21]

The socialization of children and the importance of the mothering role were also issues that affected the debate around married women's work. Fears about the dislocation of the family during the war years, with husbands absent, children evacuated, mothers working and homes literally destroyed, led to a panoply of reports, articles and books by various childcare specialists and others who wrote about the needs of the child and the importance of the family in developing good citizens. Bowlby is the most well known of these writers but there were many others too, popularizing pronatalist ideas in newspapers, magazines and on the radio.[22] The message impressed upon women's minds was that they were primarily responsible for their children's welfare and that this had to be their first priority. On a practical level, this was not always possible and many women felt that they had no choice but to work whether they wanted to or not. Part-time work went some way to providing a compromise between the stay-at-home mother and a working one. The Report of the Royal Commission on Population was not totally opposed to married women working. It welcomed the possibility of women combining paid and domestic work and therefore favoured married women doing part-time work. Both the government and many employers regarded part-time work as the way forward. Married women could fulfil their responsibilities as wives and mothers and contribute to the economy. Lewis states that an economic survey in 1947 had recommended that employers adjust working conditions to accommodate part-time married women workers. To aid this flexibility, the government brought in the Factories (Evening Employment) Order in 1950. This allowed women to work the 'twilight', i.e. early evening, shift.[23] Useful as this may have been to married working women, it tended to fix the notion that married women's paid work was peripheral, both to her other duties and to employers who could use married women as a temporary workforce as and when they were needed.

Others felt that part-time work was not the answer and looked to the women's life cycle for a solution. Two sociologists, Alva Myrdal and Viola Klein, partially challenged the assumption that women had to choose between a family and a career in their famous text *Women's Two Roles.*[24] Lewis states that the book developed from an invitation that Myrdal received from the International Federation of University Women to survey the needs of women wanting to combine a family with a professional life.[25] The book, therefore, was primarily focused on educated, professional women. They argued that women, especially professional women such as teachers, should be encouraged to return to their previous careers once the children were grown. They advocated a model of employment for women, which in reality, was already being played out to some extent in a broader context than the professions. This model suggested that women work up to the birth of their first child and then return once the children had started school.[26] Like other commentators, they did not challenge the assumption that the home was primarily the woman's responsibility. Companionate marriage was assumed to embody complementarity rather than equality. There was no attempt to suggest that men should prioritize their roles as husbands and fathers. There was also an assumption that professional married women could rely on domestic help in order to carry out their dual role, a luxury that poorer women could not afford. As Table 11.1 indicates, women were working whether the government and experts thought it was a good idea or not and they were doing so in increasingly large numbers. Whether they needed the money for essentials or luxuries or whether they worked for the social company only, married women continued to find ways in which they could combine paid and unpaid work despite any obstacles put in their way. However, importantly, Myrdal and Klein helped to redefine the married woman's role. No longer was a married woman solely defined by maternity; motherhood was regarded as a stage in a woman's life rather than, as in earlier periods, the whole of it. The idea that marriage meant full-time housework was also losing favour as more women returned to work when the children were grown, especially if their husbands were not advocates of the stay-at-home-wife school of thought. Indeed, Klein reported in 1960 that attitudes were definitely changing:

> It is no longer thought virtuous but, on the contrary, to be a sign of
> lack of organising ability to spend your whole day doing housework
> . . . I think this is a change of attitude – they [married women] feel it
> is "lazy" to stay at home. I have heard it said in so many words that if
> she has no small children a woman is wasting her time if she does not
> do a job.[27]

This is an overstatement possibly, but the price paid for the shift to the
dual-role model was a strengthening of the assumption that women were
less serious than men in the career stakes as they would give up work for
a certain number of years at the crucial stage of most career structures. This
assumption was reflected both in women's wages generally and in their
ability to move up the career ladder in the professions.

Contradictory attitudes towards women, especially married women, as
workers were also manifested in the thinking behind the Beveridge Report
and its implementation as the new Welfare State. As we have already seen,
throughout the short-lived baby boom of the 1940s and into the 1950s,
there was an ever-present anxiety about the falling birth rate and consequent national decline. Beveridge was a pronatalist, so the state's desire
for larger families was reflected in the new Welfare State. For example,
Family Allowance was only payable for the second and subsequent children. Rathbone's idea that the benefit should be an endowment recognizing
the value of women's work as mothers was lost in the Act. The level
of family allowance was much less than either Rathbone or Beveridge had
recommended and, consequently, could not in any way be regarded as
a 'wage', although it was paid to the mother rather than the father due to
protests from feminists in Parliament. Wilson argues that it was never
intended that women should be treated equally with men in the Welfare
System.[28] Briar adds that this is because women's economic well-being was
still regarded as vested in her male partner.[29] The welfare system was based
on the assumption that married women would not be breadwinners in
the conventional patriarchal sense of the word. Any entitlement a married
woman received was seen as coming from her husband's contributions;
like the children, she was his dependant. A married woman could opt
in to paying full contributions if she wished but even then would receive
lower rates of benefit. Normally married women paid the 'married
woman's stamp', a nominal amount that brought no independent benefits.
Single women, too, received less benefit than men as it was assumed they
had no dependants. This assumption ignored the many single women,
widows, divorced and separated women who were the primary breadwinners in their families. This gender difference was picked up by women's
organizations. For example, the Co-operative Women's Guild had campaigned for married women to be insured on the same terms as workers
rather than be classed with their husbands.[30] This time the protest was a

non-starter as there was no political will to identify married women as primarily workers, whereas paying mothers family allowance fitted in with dominant thinking about women's role in the companionate marriage. Even the social security safety net discriminated against women, regarding them as dependent on their husbands or partners so that they could not claim in their own right if they lived with a man. Wilson states that Beveridge proposed a special maternity benefit that was 50 per cent higher than normal unemployment or disability benefit and that women be paid the equivalent reduction in unemployment and disability benefit. This was another tactic to encourage a higher birth rate.[31] However, the scheme only lasted for five years when payment was reduced to male unemployment rates. Indeed, the only women who clearly gained from the new benefits structure were single mothers who, for the first time, could claim benefit in their own right for themselves and their children. This enabled single women to keep their children rather than having them adopted, an unseen consequence rather than deliberate policy and one which would become an issue later in the century as divorce and single motherhood became of greater national concern.

Educating girls in the 1950s and 1960s

The concern about women's role as mothers also influenced debate and policy concerning girls' and young women's education. Finch and Summerfield argue that much of the discussion about girls' education in the 1940s and 1950s was so reactionary that it did not even address the idea that marriage was a partnership. They assert that no consideration of a boy's future role as a father and husband was given. They were regarded primarily as workers, albeit workers who needed enough education to command an income that would allow them to maintain a wife and family. It is indisputable that the debate around girls' education was couched in a discourse that assumed that a girl's primary role was to be a wife and mother. The Norwood Report suggested in 1943 that all girls should be taught domestic science because they were all potential homemakers. In 1948 Newsom, in his book *The Education of Girls*, disagreed that girl should be taught domestic skills at school, arguing that they would forget what they had learned by the time they were married, although he still wanted their education to focus on preparing them for marriage. He suggested that they should attend continuation evening classes before they married.[32] Briar asserts that Newsom also thought that only clever girls should be educated to their full potential and receive the same training as boys, while the rest needed an education that trained them for marriage.[33] Newsome's ideas were reflected in the Crowther Report, which also dismissed the notion that women's work was as valuable as that performed by men and argued that paid work for women was just a stop-gap before marriage.[34] It is hardly surprising, given the general climate concerning women and work, that policy makers thought that girls' primary role was as homemaker. Even if the discourse was glossed over by the concept of companionate marriage, the underlying message was the old patriarchal one that a woman's place was primarily in the home while a man's place was primarily in the workplace. The construction of the new tripartite secondary education system focused on boys' needs rather than girls'[35] and even grammar schools taught girls to defer to men.[36]

Briar argues that there was another strand to the discourse. Not only was there an assumption that women were primarily homemakers, there was active discrimination against women and girls in training and education policy. This was cloaked in a rhetoric claiming equality of access. She adds that there was also a claim that there was a lack of demand from women and girls for appropriate training in, for example, engineering.[37] However, Wightman has shown how women were discouraged from applying for training by the Engineering Employers Forum because it assumed that women would leave to marry and, even for women who managed to obtain the training required, their promotion to higher grades was not seriously considered.[38]

Further evidence of discrimination towards young women can be seen in the attitudes towards those entering higher education. Women still failed to make much progress in the professions and Pugh argues that this was because they failed to gain wider access to higher education. Women comprised around 27 per cent of university undergraduates, a figure very little changed since the 1920s.[39] This charge of failure is a harsh judgement as there was overt discrimination against women entering university in the post-war years. In 1946, George Isaacs, the Minister of Labour, persuaded the vice-chancellors of British universities not to accept female school-leavers unless they were exceptional, in order to prioritize ex-servicemen.[40] This ruling held for three years yet even when the ban was lifted, it was difficult for young women to obtain financial assistance from their Local Education Authority to attend university. Instead, young women were offered financial assistance to take a two-year teacher training course. In addition, women's grants were less than men's.[41] These restrictions were felt particularly by bright young working-class women who found it difficult enough to attend grammar school and could not progress to university without a grant. Many went to teacher training colleges because that was the only way they could continue with their education. However, during the 1960s the differential between girls and boys entering higher education was diminishing as the growth of the university and polytechnic sector, coupled with the introduction of maintenance grants, allowed more girls, especially middle-class girls, to continue their education. Unsurprisingly, given their previous educational experience, they tended to choose humanities and social science subjects over science subjects.[42]

Indeed, women's access to education and training at any level was treated differently to men's. Briar states that 93,777 men but only 10,572 women trained under the Vocational and Disabled Training Scheme between 1946 and 1952. Further, between 1943 and 1952 203,401 men but only 15,346 women took courses under the Further Education and Training Schemes. Women's access to these schemes was further curtailed in 1947 when the schemes were restricted to women who had undertaken at least one year's work of national importance. Briar points out that this mainly affected the same group of young women who were excluded from universities.[43]

The type of work that young women were able to train for was generally of a less skilled, lower-paid variety, reflecting the normative assumption of what sort of work a woman should undertake. Young women were offered training as hairdressers, shorthand typists, dressmakers, textile workers and canteen cooks. A few were offered training as engineers or draughtswomen. In comparison, young men were offered training in skilled occupations that attracted higher wages.[44] By 1957, the government was worried about the skills shortage in the country. It published a white paper, *Technical Education*, which stated that only about one-fifth of girls undertook any form of further education and of those who did, most took courses in nursing, home craft or secretarial skills. Very few girls went to university.[45] This was hardly surprising given the effective obstacles put in place in order to channel girls into these very areas. The report went on to suggest that girls should be encouraged to train in the areas of science and technology. However, not wanting to make any truly radical changes to the balance of women in the workplace, it argued:

> Much needs to be done to stimulate among girls a greater demand for further education if only to bring the numbers up to what they should be in subjects traditionally regarded as suitable for girls. But an even greater problem confronts us in tapping the resources of talent and labour available among girls in the strictly technical occupations.[46]

The propaganda had worked too well and girls were adhering to the path laid out for them, regarding paid work as an interlude before marriage just as their mothers had done. No attempt was made to make science a more central part of the school curriculum. Even in the grammar schools art subjects were more highly prized, so it is difficult to know how the government thought girls would be encouraged to follow a career in science or technology.[47] The decline in young women taking up places on training courses, whether science based or not, continued into the 1960s. During this period a high proportion of girls went from school straight into lower-paid, lower-skilled jobs in the retail or clerical sector. Far fewer girls went into jobs with opportunities for training. Young men on day-release schemes outnumbered young women by about four to one. Briar reports that in 1956–7, 148,700 boys were on day-release schemes from work, whereas only 36,000 girls were on such schemes. By 1961–2, there were 199,600 boys and only 50,000 girls on such schemes.[48] Consequently, it comes as no surprise that numbers of women in skilled work were declining in this period from around 15.5 per cent in 1951 to 13.9 per cent in 1961.[49] By 1968, there was a belated recognition that girls and young women needed to be better trained to help stop the decline in the economy. Again, the concern was with ensuring that women helped meet the needs of the economy when it was under pressure, rather than any concern for women's own needs. The Donovan Report, recognizing that women were able to undertake the work required yet were lacking the appropriate skills, warned that:

> Lack of skilled labour has consistently provided a brake to our economic expansion since the war, and yet the capacity of women to do skilled work has been neglected . . . women provide the only substantial source from which extra labour, and especially skilled labour, can be drawn during this period.[50]

There were attempts to modify policy in the 1970s, but post-war training policy reflected the wide consensus that women inhabited a secondary role in the workforce and was all too successful at maintaining this assumption.

Immigrant women

After a period of austerity, the post-war years saw the arrival of an economic boom that highlighted the acute labour shortage that Britain was facing. As discussed in the previous chapter, the government's attempts to encourage married women back into the workforce in specific sectors was not entirely successful as women either chose to stay at home or found more acceptable work elsewhere. The government, therefore, found another way to address the labour shortage question. Between 1946 and 1949, nearly one million people came to Britain to work in industries that were failing to recruit British workers.[51] The first tranche of these workers – called European Volunteer Workers – came from displaced persons camps in Europe. Balt Cygnet was the first of the schemes to send workers to Britain, which sent single women from camps in Germany who were then employed to do domestic work in general and mental hospitals. The second scheme was Westward Ho: men and women of various nationalities were sent to work in a variety of industries where there were shortages, especially textiles for the women. Under yet another group of schemes, women workers were brought to Britain. These women were regarded, like their British counterparts, as filling a temporary shortage. There were no plans for them to settle permanently in Britain. They also worked in textiles and domestic service. In all, more than 17,000 women came to work in Britain under these schemes. Women from Germany, Austria and Italy returned home when the schemes ended, but most women from Eastern Europe stayed on in this country.[52] Contracts were for two years and, whatever skills they had, workers were directed to manual work. Domestic service became a key area of work for migrant women beyond these schemes. Briar states that by 1951 commercial agencies brought in 36,570 workers, mainly women, to work in private homes in Britain.[53] Pay and conditions were poor and the women had little opportunity to redress this, partly because they were regarded as temporary workers and partly because domestic service was an unregulated occupation.

By the 1960s, a new group of immigrant women were brought in to help resolve the shortage of workers in domestic service. These workers were au pairs. Briar states that in 1964 there was an estimated 20,000 women brought to Britain by private agencies to work as au pairs, some of them as young as 15.[54] These mainly young women were easily exploited, as they did not have to obtain work permits. They were not even classed as employees and existed in a grey zone, half-way between a domestic servant and an unpaid housewife. The ease with which women could be brought into the country to work as au pairs meant that the number of workers brought in using work permits declined so that, although there were still around 100,000 people being brought in to work as servants on work permits in 1967–8, this had declined to less than 8,000 by 1972. The influx of cheap unregulated workers also brought an end to the National Institute of Houseworkers in 1971.[55] The availability of these girls to do domestic work for middle-class women meant that these women could, of course, consider returning to work without the double burden of paid and unpaid work. Once more, some middle-class women were able forego domestic duties at the expense of other women.

The women who came from Europe on various work schemes were white and many were from middle-class or educated backgrounds. Consequently, they were seen as ideal immigrants, unlike the black women who later arrived from the Caribbean.[56] However, McDowell argues that although these women were white they were still marked out as foreign because of language problems; they had no citizenship rights; and they were a hybrid category of refugee and economic migrant. They were also alone in an alien culture. Importantly, because they were young and single, they were constructed by British immigrant policy as workers rather than dependants and potential mothers.[57] Almost one-third of a million British citizens from the Caribbean were also encouraged to come to Britain in order to ease the labour shortage. While most of the immigrants from the Caribbean in the 1950s were men, some women also came to Britain and were affected both by gender and race discrimination. Webster argues that black women workers have a very different history of work in this country to white women:

> A focus on white women produces a story of the period which emphasizes the way in which maternity ruled, involving immurement with family and submergence in domesticity. A focus on black women produces a very different story – of poorly paid, low-status full-time employment, separation from family through the process of migration, search for accommodation in which the sign "no coloureds" was repeatedly encountered. The first view emphasizes patriarchy and sees the family as a main site of women's oppression. The second empha-sizes colonialism and racism and sees the family as a main support and resistance to it.[58]

For black women and other migrant workers, being constructed primarily as a worker presented problems because when they married and had children, or if they had children back in their homeland, they still had responsibilities as mothers and these demands were not taken into account. These groups of women were constructed as 'other' and, con-sequently, their predicament was not considered in the discourse around married women workers. Not only were they congregated in low-paid, low-status, non-unionized work, even if they had qualifications, they continued in full-time paid work even when their children were small, without official comment or recognition.[59] There has not been much research undertaken on how these women managed the dual roles of wife/mother and full-time worker; this would make an interesting research project.[60]

There was much resentment of immigrant workers who were seen to be taking jobs from the indigenous community. This was not helped by official discourse that used the language of 'them and us' when discussing immigrant workers.[61] Black women were particularly affected by this resentment because of racist notions embedded in colonialist thinking, especially around the notion of 'suitable immigrants'. There seems little basis in this resentment. As we have seen, there was an acute labour shortage in Britain in the post-war years. Further, the type of work that these women were undertaking was the work that indigenous women were refusing to do wherever possible – textiles, the clothing industry and various forms of domestic service, often working shifts that made com-bining home and work even more difficult.[62] The growing shortage of workers was exacerbated by a large number of people emigrating during this period, either as war brides to America or as 'The Ten Pound Poms' who went to Australia on assisted emigration schemes.[63] However, the idea that emigrating white people were being replaced immigrating black people did nothing to allay fears about the decline of the race.[64]

Black and other women immigrants had an even greater struggle than indigenous women if they wanted employment mobility. Very few were able to move out of unskilled, low-paid work even if they had qualifications. Webster quotes black women's oral testimony about how they were denied work relating to their qualifications. Cecilia Wade arrived in London in 1956 and went to her local labour exchange:

> I took my references from home saying I was a teacher. This woman at the counter said, "Oh, you were a teacher back home were you? Well, you won't get teaching here!" . . . The following Monday I went and she looked at me up and down again and said, "All I have to offer you is 'Lyon's Tea Shops', or there is a job going at the hospital in Clacton? Which would you prefer?" I said, ". . . I was a teacher and I'm looking for clerical work." "Oh! You won't get clerical work here." She was positive.[65]

The only profession open to black women was nursing, but even then they were restricted to the lower grades and lower-status work such as mental health and geriatric nursing.

Webster argues that immigrant women were treated differently to indigenous women. Whereas indigenous women were seen as 'working wives', with all the problems that attached to this identity, immigrant women were not recognized in this role. Consequently, there was never the expectation that they would subordinate their working identities to those of their familial ones.[66] The double burden of work and family fell particularly heavily on immigrant women's shoulders. The different treatment of indigenous women and black women would have repercussions for the later women's liberation movement, which tended to reflect official views of working women as being defined by their roles as wives and mothers. This is explored further in the next chapter.

Chapter Twelve

ะ

Women's work in the age of equal opportunities

1969 to the end of the century

Trends in women's work in the late twentieth century

> The typical woman worker, at the turn of the century, was . . . a city dweller; a widow or a spinster aged 25 years, employed as a domestic servant or in a textile factory. By the seventies, the typical female worker, aged 40 years, is married, has returned to work after some years of economic inactivity, and works part-time in a clerical job.[1]

Although this comment correctly suggests that there have been significant changes in the profile of the typical woman worker over the span of the twentieth century, these changes have not brought women into an equal relation with their male counterparts. Briar argues that, contrary to official proclamations, it is an overstatement to suggest that attitudes to women workers had substantially changed. She suggests that employment policies in the post-war period reinforced rather that challenged gender in-equalities in both paid and unpaid work.[2] Up until the Equal Pay Act and the Sex Discrimination Act, it was still possible for employers to have a male and female rate of pay for the job in most sectors. As a young under-writer in the insurance sector in the early 1970s, I seethed with resentment because I earned three-quarters of the pay that young men received for doing the same work. To add insult to injury, I often trained up young men to be my superiors. Resentment such as I felt fuelled the women involved in the Dagenham Ford Strike in 1968 and was part of the impetus of the subsequent Women's Liberation Movement.

However, the last third of the twentieth century saw rapid change in the employment sector as the introduction of an information technology revolution changed the nature of work and the pace of life for most workers. The period was also one of economic decline for the country, especially in the manufacturing sector. The 1970s were marked by industrial unrest which culminated in the Miner's Strike in the 1980s. This strike symbolized a political struggle between the old Left and the new Right, represented by Thatcherism. The strike was lost and, consequently, the unions' power rapidly diminished during the 1980s and 1990s. Significantly, Britain joined the European Economic Community in 1973 and this also led to changes in employment legislation. During these years, the number of women participating in the workforce continued to increase. Between 1971 and 1981 women's participation in the labour force increased from 52 per cent to 61 per cent. At the same time men's participation in the workforce declined from 97 per cent to 90 per cent[3] and fell even further to 73 per cent in 1991[4] as heavy industry gave way to the burgeoning service sector. Between 1975 and 1997, women's participation in the workforce increased from 60 per cent to 71 per cent, and is still rising. As forecasted, it has begun to overtake male employment in the twenty-first century.[5] Women's participation varied locally and for the very poor, paid work was not viable, except through the unrecorded black economy, e.g. homework, cleaning and other forms of casual labour, as state benefits were a stable substitute for an uncertain and irregular income. As most single women already worked, this increase in women workers can only be explained by a significant rise in the number of married women undertaking paid work. By 1991, more than half of all married women were in work of some kind.[6] One of the key growth areas in participation in paid work is amongst mothers with children under the age of five. This is surprising given the appalling lack of childcare provision in Britain and that working mothers with small children are still largely frowned upon by society. We shall return to working mothers later.

Women still tended to be segregated into female-dominated sectors during this period whether they worked in the retail, factory, clerical or caring sectors. Even in a profession like teaching where women outnumbered men, men tended to be head teachers or heads of departments. Further, women who managed to find work in better-paid professions found they reached a point on the career ladder that was aptly named 'the glass ceiling' because there was a barrier to career advancement that could not be seen. Briar states that in 1901, 88 per cent of women worked in female-dominated occupations. By 1971, the figure was 74 per cent.[7] Although the occupations had changed somewhat, the pattern of discrimination had not. Unsurprisingly, women-dominated sectors were lower paid than sectors where men prevailed and, therefore, undermined the spirit of the 1975 Equal Pay Act. Moreover, black women were more likely to work in low-status jobs in the health services and were less likely to be employed in relatively high-status clerical work.[8]

The history of women's work in the last thirty years of the twentieth century has yet to be written and it is hard, at this close quarter, to discuss the debates in any detail. However, as shown in this brief introduction, it is possible to trace some key issues and characteristics emerging during this period. These fall into the following areas:

- The effect of the emergence of feminism on women's perceptions of themselves and their abilities;
- The resumption of the campaign for equal pay and the inclusion of the demand for equal opportunities;
- The way that the gendered nature of work has persisted despite the equality laws;
- The impact of welfare policies on perceptions of women as workers.

Underpinning all these issues was the pervasive and enduring understanding that a woman's primary duty was her domestic role. This understanding shaped welfare policy and coloured perceptions of employers, unions, the state and women themselves. This meant that women were constantly struggling to either challenge or accommodate this understanding. In short, patriarchy persisted and women needed to renew their challenge to it.

Feminism and work: the rise of 'women's lib'

Some of the old equal rights feminist groups from before the war were still extant in the 1960s, e.g. the Fawcett Society and The Six Point Group. The main aims of these groups were equal pay and opportunities but also equal taxation and better treatment of single mothers. To this end, the older feminists' groups formed alliances with various professional bodies such as the British Federation of Business and Professional Women, the Association of Headmistresses, the Women's Employment Federation and the Women's Advisory Committee of the TUC. They also made alliances with more general organizations, such as the National Council of Married Women and the National Council for Civil Liberties.[9] Continuing with the aims of the old Industrial Women's Movement from earlier in the century, these groups urged women to join unions to protect their rights and to campaign for an extension of these rights. For example, they supported the Ford women at Dagenham in their struggle to be recognized as skilled workers. In 1969 women from the left and right of the women's rights movement joined to form the National Joint Action Committee for Women's Equal Rights. This organization held a national demonstration in May 1969 that was hailed as the first major event of second-wave feminism and acted as a bridge between the old feminist movement of the earlier part of the century and the new Women's Liberation Movement (WLM).[10]

The origins of the WLM are still the subject of debate as the definitive history of the movement has yet to be written.[11] Pugh argues that the problem for women in the post-war years was not the political structure but lay in cultural attitudes, the structure of marriage and the family and economic conditions. He argues that during the 1960s a raft of legislation served to raise women's expectations without satisfying them. Further, the Wilson Government included several women, including Barbara Castle. However, Pugh argues that the Wilson Government was only superficially progressive. Its values, particularly concerning women, were rooted in the pre-war period.[12] Further, Betty Friedan's book, *The Feminist Mystique*, struck a chord with many well-educated young women who were not finding domesticity the idyll they had been led to expect.[13] The view that young women growing up in the 1950s and 1960s had their expectations dashed as they reached adulthood is supported by the life histories of women who grew up in the 1950s and reflected on their lives in books such as *Truth, Dare, Promise* and *Once a Feminist*.[14] A recurring theme in these books is the growing awareness of the gap between the progressive expectations fostered at grammar schools and the reality of living in a society that still expected a young woman's goal in life to be marriage, children and the primacy of domesticity. There is also situated in this discourse a struggle for autonomy, with young women wanting something more out of their lives than their mothers had experienced.[15] However, these books tend to focus on women activists in the WLM. More research is needed on other women's expectations in the 1960s before we can reach more than general conclusions about the reasons for the popularity of the WLM at that time.

The campaigns that the movement engaged in were a mixture of liberal, socialist and radical feminisms. These differing strands of feminism looked to different causes for women's oppression. In broad and rather crude terms, liberal feminists believed that legislation helped women bring about changes in the way they were regarded by society. Socialist feminists looked to capitalism as the site of oppression although this position was modified over time and an analysis developed that encompassed both capitalism and patriarchy as sites of oppression. Radical feminists tended to privilege patriarchy over class but this view was also modified as more complex theories developed.[16] Whatever the stance taken by feminists, they all regarded women as an oppressed group. Some of their campaigns are beyond the scope of this book, but two of the seven demands of the movement were equal access to education and to employment.[17] From the earliest days, some women identified with the WLM were involved in campaigns concerning women's work.[18] The main campaign that is considered in the next section is the campaign for equal pay and equal employment rights.

The campaign for equal rights

Following the limited concession to equal pay for women working in the public services, the government prevaricated over extending this right to women working in the private sector. It was precipitated into action by the women machinists' strike in Dagenham, which highlighted the complaints that women had been making for nearly 100 years – that their work was deemed inferior to men's. Britain's forthcoming entry into the European Economic Community in 1973 also put pressure on the government to act.[19] Further, women's organizations across the spectrum of beliefs united behind this cause. Meehan argues that between 1970 and 1972 they co-operated to bring attention to wider sexual discrimination than just equal pay and gave substantial evidence to the House of Lords Select Committee on this issue.[20] The Equal Pay Act was passed in 1970 but was phased in over five years. In the terms of the Act, equal pay meant for the same or equivalent work or work that had been rated as equivalent under an evaluation scheme. Briar states that some politicians considered the Act a progressive measure, but she argues that it was poorly enforced. First, because employers were given time to find ways of separating male and female workers and reclassifying the work by gender, and second, the government made little effort to encourage employers to work towards equal pay in the years up to 1975.[21] In short, the government went through the motions of passing the legislation but lacked the political will to ensure that it was properly enforced. However, Meehan argues that Barbara Castle, the minister who brought in the legislation, had constructed the Act in this way as a compromise that would bring the Confederation of British Industry and the TUC on board.[22]

It is interesting to note that the Dagenham strike was a catalyst for the Act because the strike had been about recognition of women's work as skilled work and therefore worth the pay increase they were demanding. They wanted their gendered work as machinists to be valued in the same way that equivalent male work was valued. The Equal Pay Act only covered women doing the same work as men or work that had been evaluated as equivalent. These terms had been included on an assumption that employers would either be supportive of the spirit of the law and would seek to play fair by women or, as Briar argues, that it was never meant to do more than pay lip service to equality and therefore offered employers ways of avoiding the Act.[23]

Briar states that there were two methods available to enforce the Act. It could either be enforced through collective wage agreements, wages councils and employers pay structures or there was provision for women to take individual cases to an industrial tribunal. The former method was the most successful although employers found ways round the Act by redefining jobs so that women's work occupied the lower grades or by paying men bonuses. Further, unions were reluctant to fight the women's corner as it would decrease wage differentials between male and female workers and erode the treasured notion of the male breadwinner. Tribunals were long-winded affairs and largely run by men. Further, the onus was on the woman to prove discrimination and cases were not covered by legal aid. All these factors weighed against women making inroads into pay differentials.[24] What women needed was legislation that enforced gender equality in the employment sector. In 1975 the Sex Discrimination Act (SDA) was passed in order to address this need:

> In the theory, the 1975 Sex Discrimination Act should have effectively compensated for a deficiency in the 1970 Equal Pay Act, which denied equal pay to women not doing the same work as men. A major aim of the 1975 Act was to break down occupational segregation, so that men and women would be doing the same work and be entitled to the same pay.[25]

Before the SDA, women could, in theory, undertake most occupations. However, centuries of prejudice against women as workers had meant that discrimination could take place without any legal redress. As already discussed, during wartime, for instance, women had proved themselves capable of undertaking any task if they were allowed to do it. However, the government, employers and male trade unionists had always looked on women's incursions into male-defined work as a temporary measure and when the emergency was over, assumed that the status quo would be restored. An act that would make it illegal to refuse someone access to training, work or promotion because of their gender was, indeed, a departure from normal practice and was unsurprisingly vigorously resisted by all the usual male interest groups.[26] So why was the Act passed?

Briar argues that the SDA was adopted at this particular time partly because of the pressure brought to bear by the coalition of feminists mentioned above and partly because the European Economic Community put pressure on the government to conform to the EEC's own anti-discriminatory policies.[27] However, the government was slow to act and was extremely sensitive about accusations that, as an employer, it too discriminated against women. Between 1968 and 1972 four private member bills and a proposal for an equal opportunities commission were introduced and defeated. Both the Conservative Government and Labour opposition committed themselves to bringing in the legislation. However, it was only when the Labour Government took office in 1974 that the Bill proceeded through the committee stage, finally becoming law in 1975. The SDA promised to offer revolutionary change to British life. The Act obliged employers to recruit, train and promote employees based on their qualifications and qualities rather than by gender. Indeed, Briar states that there was even limited provision for positive discrimination in training in order to allow women to enter male-dominated employment sectors.[28] The SDA did not revolutionize the work place although it did empower the most determined women to gain access to training and employment in areas from which they had previously been excluded. As with the Equal Pay Act, the onus was on women to prove that discrimination had taken place and the Act was enforced through tribunals. However, case studies demonstrate that discrimination is complex and not always easy to prove.[29] Further, Briar states that there were several exclusions from the Act that disadvantaged women. These included childbirth, retirement pensions, taxation, social security payments, employment in a private house, employment where there were fewer than ten (later five) employees, personal and intimate relationships, the clergy and religious orders and charities, occupations where being of one sex was a genuine occupational qualification (e.g. single-sex schools or acting).[30] It can be seen from this list that women were hardly being treated as equals to men. Beyond these exclusions, it still did not help women who were working in sectors that were female dominated and therefore paid at the lower end of the wage scale.

By 1982 it was obvious that, apart from a rapid rise of women's wages to around 73 per cent of the male wage when the Acts were first implemented, the Acts were not as effective at bringing about equality as had been hoped.[31] There were several amendments to the equality laws during the 1970s and 1980s. The most important of these was the 1983 extension of the Equal Pay Act to cover work of equal value. This came about following pressure from the European Commission and meant that work undertaken by women that was of equivalent value to the work that men did would be entitled to equal pay.[32] Changes were also made to broaden the scope of the SDA in 1986. Further, in 1988 gender-specific protective legislation was removed by the Employment Act. This meant that women could work nights, on oilrigs, underground in mines or cleaning machines in factories, thus reversing much of the legislation that equal rights feminists had bitterly opposed earlier in the century.[33]

Briar argues that the problems faced in creating and enforcing equal opportunities legislation can be traced to the underlying principle of the legislation. She argues that this was the notion of creating equal opportunities to become unequal. By this, she means that the legislation was concerned with the equality of access, not of outcomes, and was wedded to the 'merit' principle, i.e. if women do not secure the most attractive jobs, it is seen that this is a result of their shortcomings, not because of discrimination.[34] Positive discrimination was never a feature of the legislation and no account was given to the cumulative discrimination women had experienced in the years before the Acts were implemented or to the fact that women were still seen to be primarily responsible for childcare and other domestic duties. Further, it has been possible for men to claim successfully that they were unfairly discriminated against in some cases and even challenge the legislation itself. Moreover, women are still congregated in low-paid, low-status work. Sex segregation is still endemic in the British employment sector and it is to this issue we shall now turn.

Flexible work – a mixed blessing? The gendered nature of work in the late twentieth century

As we have observed, since the Second World War the age profile of women workers has steadily risen as more women have continued to work after marriage and having children, or at least they have returned to work as the children have grown. However, women's working patterns do not fit into the male-defined norm. Traditionally, male employment has involved full-time employment from leaving school until retirement. The development of the bi-modal pattern in the post-war period might have suited both women and employers, but women who choose this pattern or who work part-time have been regarded as less committed workers and often as inferior workers. Career breaks taken to raise a family are not considered favourably in job interviews or promotion panels. This has implications both for women's pay and their opportunities for promotion to more officially acknowledged, responsible work. In recent decades, the traditional 'male' model of a working life being forty years of continuous labour in one or a series of permanent full-time jobs has been in decline and work of a 'non-standard' structure has increased. 'Non-standard' embraces work that is part-time, self-employment, short contract or sub-contracted. Homework also falls into this category, although new technologies have given this type of work a new and wider meaning. The rise in this type of employment arises partly from the needs of women who want to work but have to consider their domestic duties too, and partly from the deregulation of the employment sector by the Conservative Government in the late 1970s and 1980s. The aim of deregulation was to improve economic efficiency by promoting employment flexibility. Crompton states that the expansion of the service sector also led to the rise of non-standard employment especially in the caring services, leisure and entertainment industries and the retail sector. These are all areas that employ large numbers of women. Further, Crompton argues that women are more likely to work part-time than men and are more likely to be employed on temporary contracts, although men are more likely to be self-employed than women.[35] This type of flexible, casualized work fits well with women's domestic duties but does little to enhance their reputation as skilled committed workers. Further, Briar argues that flexibility itself is gendered. For men, it means full-time fixed-term contracts but the flexibility is contained within the work, meaning an expectation of overtime and geographical mobility.[36] Both expectations would be difficult or impossible for a woman with domestic responsibilities. Flexibility for women, especially those with children, means shorter hours, less prospect of promotion and usually low pay.

There are other benefits beyond a flexible workforce for employers too. Paying more women to work shorter hours in low-paid, low-skilled work meant that employers could keep employees under the National Insurance threshold and therefore avoid paying National Insurance contributions for these workers. This of course affected pension and unemployment benefit rights. However, even better from the employer's perspective, if women worked less than sixteen hours per week, they were excluded from protection from unfair dismissal, maternity benefits and statutory redundancy payments.[37] As we have seen, women's recorded part-time work increased steadily from the 1950s onwards from 12 per cent in 1951 to 26 per cent in 1961, 35 per cent by 1971, 42 per cent in 1981 and 44 per cent by 1987.[38] This translates into 750,000 part-time women workers in 1951 to 4,117,000 in 1984 when the part-time workforce represented 46.4 per cent of the total workforce.[39] This rate accelerated in the subsequent period and Crompton states that although since 1981 the rate of acceleration has been steeper for men than women, in 1994 78 per cent of all part-time workers were women.[40] Moreover, most part-time workers are still married women.

These factors all served to undermine the SDA. Women were not operating on a level playing field with men and the legislation did little to change underlying patriarchal assumptions about women's role in the workplace. One of the main problems for women with children wanting to work is the appalling lack of affordable childcare both for children under school age and children at school. Further, an acceptance that men should participate in domestic work and childcare has been very slow to take hold. Briar states that in 1988 women who worked part-time were responsible for general domestic responsibilities in 88 per cent of households surveyed. Women who were in full-time employment with a partner also in full-time employment were responsible for housework in 72 per cent of respondents and, in unemployed households, they were responsible in 76 per cent of households. Men were more likely to look after children than participate in mundane chores such as cooking, cleaning and laundry.[41] There has probably been little change in the intervening years.

The re-entry of women into the labour force after a break for child-rearing is often accompanied by occupational downgrading, especially if the children are still young and the part-time work involves few hours. This often means that women returners take work in the low-paid service sector or less responsible work in the clerical sector or the professions rather than the job they had before the break. However, whether part-time work is regarded as a positive choice by married women or whether employers have seen part-time work as an opportunity to exploit women as cheap, casual labour is a debatable point. Some writers have argued that part-time work has been deliberately constructed as low grade because it is seen as women's work, while others have argued that women have demanded work that fits in with their domestic responsibilities and that employers have merely responded to this demand.[42] Further, Briar argues that flexibility, i.e. part-time work, has been presented by the government as offering women choice and has been presented in a discourse of equal opportunities. For example, she says that the lack of employment protection for part-time workers was construed as being to women's advantage because it opened up employment opportunities for women.[43] However, the government was pressurized by the European Commission to rectify the unfair treatment of part-time workers and, in 1995, part-time employees gained the same statutory rights as full-time workers but these didn't extend to casual workers.[44] It is difficult to put any historical perspective on this debate at the moment and the nature of part-time work and the gendered nature of the work is constantly changing with the social context. For example, in recent years, a new group of part-time workers has emerged: since the abolition of mandatory maintenance grants, there has been an increasing trend for students of both sexes to take part-time casual work that fits around their timetable.

Of course, not all women are married and not all married women work part-time, so how have full-time women workers benefited from the Equal Pay and Sex Discrimination Acts? In theory, women can now do any job and can reach the top of the occupational ladder. In practice, gender segregation is still in operation for full-time women workers as well as part-time workers, although it is not the result of the blatant discrimination of the past. Crompton uses the banking sector as an example of how employment legislation has transformed the sector from the most backward of employers in terms of sex equality to a sector that is at the cutting edge of equal opportunities practice. However, she notes that the changing nature of work in banking and the introduction of information technology has meant a change in the career structure. Now, instead of employees being recruited at the same level and being promoted through the career structure, there is a two-tier recruiting system with staff being recruited to different areas of work such as general clerical, management trainees and graduate trainees. Women predominate in the lower-grade work, such as jobs in call and processing centres, and have therefore lost the opportunity of working up through the ranks to the top jobs even if, in practice, few women have had achieved this. They are excluded not by gendered promotions practices but by the type of jobs they are recruited into in the first place and in the context of banking this means success is measured by the ability to sell products and behave competitively.[45]

Cockburn suggests that there is a never-ending articulation of work into new horizontal and vertical subdivisions and that although new opportunities open up to women, men tend to move on to other areas taking their higher status with them.[46] This harks back to the double helix theory discussed earlier, where women's position does improve but only relatively to men's so they retain a subordinate position. Perhaps, as Crompton suggests, theories that address structural explanations only address part of the problem. She argues that we also need to examine how gender is constructed in the contemporary workplace through demonstrating how particular discourses of gender are constructed within the workplace. By this, she means that we need to examine the way that the characteristics that are designated 'male ' or 'female' in wider society are inscribed in particular occupations. In this approach, organizations are viewed as processes rather than structures and as such reflect wider cultural meanings in a range of ways. So for example, as society is to all intents and purposes based on certain patriarchal assumptions, it is not surprising if workplace cultures reflect these wider assumptions.[47] She argues that this takes us away from the classic models of bureaucracies (and it is office work she is focusing on here) as impersonal structures peopled by sexless workers. Postmodernist theories, she argues, helps us to avoid generalizing about 'all men' or 'all women' by helping us recognize the diversity of images that make up the concepts of 'male' and 'female'. However, she warns against placing all our trust in post-structuralist approaches as structures play a part too.[48] Post-structural analyses add a dimension to our understanding but discourse analyses do not replace materialist analyses entirely and should be used in tandem.

Conclusion to Part Four

So what conclusions can we reach about women in paid employment since the Second World War? On the positive side, one of the first observations we can make is that since the war, women workers have been growing in numbers and are an increasingly visible part of the workforce; married women workers are no longer pariahs although those with small children are still made to feel guilty about leaving their children with others. However, women still earn around 80 per cent of a man's wage; they are clustered in female-dominated occupations and they find that although women are now able to rise up the career ladder, they are confronted by a glass ceiling and rarely reach the same levels of seniority as their male counterparts. Further, the double burden of domestic and paid work has persisted even though new technologies have made both less physically demanding.

In the years immediately following the Second World War, it was assumed that married women would leave paid work to resume homemaking and indeed many did, relieved to be released from the double burden of long hours at paid work compounded by the difficulties of running a home during war. This release was short-lived as the acute post-war labour shortage meant that the government was obliged to attempt to persuade married women back into the workforce. However, these labour shortages meant that women had choice and many chose not to work in the sectors where shortages were particularly acute, such as textiles and cleaning. These areas were filled with immigrant women either from the Caribbean or from the refugee camps of war-torn Europe. Immigrant women brought another dimension to the debates about women workers because whereas indigenous women were primarily conceived of as mothers, immigrant women were regarded primarily as workers. This had implications for both groups of women, even though the assumptions were different, because their dual roles were not adequately considered. The problem of dual roles is one that persisted throughout the period and is now a focus for both trade unions, women's organizations and more progressive employers trying to address the work–life balance for both men and women.

The marriage bar was lifted during the war and never returned in any systematic way during the post-war period, although there are isolated examples of the practice up to the introduction of the SDA in 1975. The lifting of the marriage bar was for pragmatic reasons rather than any sea change in society's thinking about men as the breadwinner. Women were expected to work full-time up to and after marriage but their wages after marriage were seen as a supplement rather than a major source. Further, women were still expected to give up work on the birth of their first child. Whether or not, and when, they should return to work was the focus of much debate. Pronatalists were keen on women staying at home and producing an ideal four children. Supporters of the companionate marriage tended to support smaller families and women returning to part-time work when the children were older, in order to supplement the bread-winner's wage rather than usurp it. Some feminists and sociologists, such as Myrdal and Klein, were keen that women, especially professional women, should return to their career full-time when the children were grown. Part-time work was increasingly an option for married women with children although this brought its own problems.

Government policy in the immediate post-war years was crucial in shaping women's opportunities. Built into the Beveridge Report was the assumption that the man was the breadwinner with a dependent wife and children. This had serious implications for married women who were not given equal access to benefits and pensions even when working full-time. It also had implications for single women with dependants as there was little recognition of their needs. The male breadwinner with dependent wife model also informed education policy and although reform of the state education system meant that more girls could attend grammar schools, the underlying assumption that a young woman's main aim in life was to marry and have children meant that girls were channelled into a narrow range of caring professions – teaching, nursing or social work or into clerical work. Shop work declined in status and, along with hairdressing and other service industry jobs, was seen as appropriate for the respectable but not very well-educated young woman. Factory work, catering and cleaning was seen as suitable for the rest, including immigrant women, despite their level of education and training.

The campaign for equal pay had rumbled on during the war but it was not until the 1950s that there was a concerted campaign to obtain equal pay, at least for women working in certain areas of the public sector. Equal pay was implemented in the 1960s. However, it was grudgingly awarded after sustained pressure from women's organizations and the trade unions (although not without a struggle with male union members) and was not followed by the private sector. Encouraged by Britain's forthcoming entry into the EEC and the success of the Dagenham Ford women machinists' strike, by the end of the 1960s, women began to organize to extend equal pay legislation to all women workers. The campaign included women from the old equality feminism organizations, trade unionists and the burgeoning Women's Liberation Movement, which did much to encourage women to demand far more than just equal pay. The WLM can, justifiably, be credited with encouraging women generally, not just those who identified with feminism, to question the sexual politics of the late twentieth century, both in private relationships as well as the workplace and the public sphere more generally. In the parlance of the time, it raised women's consciousness.

The Equal Pay Act 1970 was not as far-reaching as women had hoped although it did lay down the principle of equality. In 1975, the Sex Discrimination Act extended this notion of equality beyond the issue of pay and meant, in theory at least, that women had access to practically any work and could not be discriminated against in the career structure of any company, subject to certain exclusions. However, the state benefits system still worked against women, making it preferable for example, for single mothers not to take regular work as it affected their benefit adversely. This pushed many single mothers into enforced unemployment or exploitation in the black economy. It also encouraged employers to use women as part-time, casual workers as, for example, employees working less than 16 hours per week were not subject to National Insurance contributions and other protective legislation. The effect was that these women appeared to be an expendable workforce and it did nothing to promote married women's perception of themselves as anything but a reserve pool of labour.

During the last third of the twentieth century, change in the workplace accelerated, partly due to new technologies but also due to responses to wider changes in the economy and shifts in the British economy from a manufacturing to a service-dominated market. Many of the 'male' jobs in unionized heavy industry disappeared during this period to be replaced by lower-paid, less stable non-unionized work deemed more suitable for women in the service sector. Flexible working lives were promoted as a positive outcome of the changing structure of the workplace in the 1980s and 1990s, but this was gendered too with flexibility often meaning self-employment, overtime and geographical mobility for male workers and casualized, part-time, low-status work for women.

Various theories are being offered to explain why women are still paid less than men and tend to work in female-dominated sectors throughout the economy. The period 1969–1999 is too recent for historians to be able to make any informed judgement. More research is needed into both documentary and oral evidence before this period can be put into a historical context. What can be said is that the workplace has continued to change over the period covered by this book and that women's relationship to work has changed accordingly.

Chapter Thirteen

ও▲

Women's work since the 1840s
Continuity and change

In the introduction to this book, I discussed Walby's theory concerning the forms that patriarchy took. I would now like to return to this theory in order to ascertain whether all or some of these patriarchal forms still apply as we enter the twenty-first century. To recap, Walby argues that rather than there being one source of male domination, patriarchy is present in six forms of social structures: patriarchal production relations in the household; patriarchal relations in paid labour; the state; male violence against women; patriarchal sexual relations and patriarchal cultural institutions.[1] We have seen that during the period covered by this book, women's primary role has been seen as domestic, although class, race and ethnicity have always tempered this. An unspoken, and spoken, assumption has been present that women have domestic responsibilities that will affect their performances as workers. The double burden of paid work and domestic labour has been seen as uniquely a 'woman's problem'. Even the most radical of feminists in the nineteenth and early decades of the twentieth century failed to theorize about men participating in domestic labour. The strength of this assumption of the primacy of domesticity for women has changed over time but it has always been present. For example, in the nineteenth and early twentieth century, working-class women's role as mother informed the debates around protective legislation. Later, during the Second World War, the double burden was again an issue for women workers and some rather half-hearted attempts were made to lighten the load, such as nurseries and shopping schemes. The most enduring solution to women's double burden was the introduction of part-time work in most employment sectors. Part-time work has continued up to the present day to be regarded as the ideal solution for married women wanting or needing to work. However, part-time work has always been seen to mean part-time commitment, which has consequently contributed to the strengthening of women's subordinate status in the workplace and has adversely affected women's wages and promotion opportunities.

In recent years though, there has been a challenge to the assumption that women are primarily responsible for domestic work. In the 1970s, women involved with the WLM saw the patriarchal production relations in the household as one of the primary causes of women's oppression and sought ways of ameliorating it. One of their demands was wages for housework but others argued that this was still accepting primary responsibility for domestic work. Others wanted 24-hour nurseries so that women could be relieved of some of the burdens of childcare, but again this assumed that childcare was primarily a woman's responsibility. However, as the traditional male structure of employment, i.e. full-time, life-long careers, is breaking down some younger couples want to share childcare and are demanding a better work–life balance. This trend is still in its early stages, and we have yet to see men sharing domestic responsibilities on an equal basis, but this could be an interesting challenge to patriarchal production relations in the household.

We have seen that since 1840 women's participation in the workforce has increased dramatically, not only in numbers, but also in the breadth of occupations they have entered. One of the early successes was opening up the world of work to middle-class women in occupations other than governessing, needlework or unpaid work behind the scenes in the family business. How far this opening up of work to middle-class women was caused through the needs of the market or was the result of the campaigns of women's groups and other social reformers concerned with the plight of the unmarried middle-class woman in need of employment is still being debated. However, it is evident that there were limitations to this success as the dominant ideology of separate spheres contributed to occupational segregation. This meant that women were not usually in direct competition with men. This was particularly true in the burgeoning clerical sector where women were segregated in low-paid, low-status although not necessarily low-skilled, work. The underlying assumption about the primacy of women's domestic role informed decisions about what sort of work women could and should do. Low pay and a lack of career structure was informed by the assumption that women were not the main breadwinners and that their incursion into the world of work was temporary, as they would leave to marry after a few years. This assumption has persisted until the present day, albeit in a weaker form, as women no longer give up work on marriage. However, the assumption that women do not need to earn as much as men persists to some degree. Even during the two World Wars, when women took over many tasks normally considered as men's work, they were only tolerated for being there for the duration of the war. To ensure that women returned to their own sphere at the end of hostilities, various measures were put in place that served to reinforce the fact that women would be expected to return to feminine occupations or the home. In recent years, part-time work has tended to be low paid, low status and often temporary and in occupations segregated from full-time workers. As women form the majority of part-time workers, this too has led to reinforcing women's subordinate position in the workforce. Occupational segregation also meant that the Equal Pay Act 1970 was easily evaded by unscrupulous employers who could easily argue, as had happened in both World Wars, that women were not doing the same work as men and could therefore justify paying them less.

State policies have consistently served to reinforce patriarchal notions of women's place in society throughout this period. In the mid-nineteenth century, various Royal Commissions into labour were underpinned by the notion that women's paid work was necessary if not welcome. This meant that the government sought to regulate the type of work that women could undertake and limit the ways in which women could participate in that work. During the World Wars and in the following years, the government sought to regulate women, pulling them into the workforce when they were needed and attempting to force them out again when they were no longer required. The Beveridge Report also sought to reinforce patriarchal ideas about the family by enshrining the notion of the male breadwinner and dependent family in the structure of the Welfare State. Even the equality legislation of the 1970s did not bring women the equal opportunities that they demanded. Up to the introduction of the Beveridge Report, women still earned less than men and proportionally were less likely to reach the highest positions in their occupation, even in female-dominated professions such as teaching. This is because little has been done to counter the years of discrimination that women have suffered and the problems that women still face with juggling work and family life. For example, although maternity leave is paid for a limited period, the government still resists facilitating affordable childcare. This forces women who need to work to either spend most of their salary on private childcare or reduce their working hours to fit around any childcare they can find and afford. Childcare is still an issue that affects women's opportunities to work far more than men's, despite the media coverage of stay-at-home fathers.

Gendered education policies throughout the period have also reinforced the assumption that a woman's primary role is domestic and therefore offered limited possibility for girls to train in so-called 'male' trades. The debates and campaigns around work have always been closely related to those around education. The campaign to improve the standard of middle-class girls' education emanated from the discovery that middle-class girls were ill-equipped to take paid work if they needed it. At the end of the nineteenth century, there was resistance to including domestic training in the curriculum for girls. More important in some respects was the resistance by men, particularly in the skilled unions, to opening up training for women. The print trade is a particular example of this, where men resorted to threats and actual violence to women involved in the Women's Printing Society. During the First World War, members of the various engineering unions fought hard to ensure that not only would women be tolerated only for the duration of the war but that jobs would be diluted in an effort to protect men from the incursion of cheap, semi-skilled female labour. After the Second World War, girls and young women were actively discriminated against in the education system and often unofficially excluded from certain sections of the curriculum deemed male, that is, science and technology. Inevitably, girls turned to the humanities and social science subjects, which directed them towards the caring professions – teaching, social work and nursing. Others were guided towards commercial colleges where they learned clerical and secretarial skills or to technical colleges where the emphasis for girls was on hairdressing, childcare and catering, and later, the lower-status grades of the tourist industry. Many other young women left school with no qualifications whatsoever and worked on assembly lines and in shops. These girls had no expectations beyond working full-time for a few years before marriage and having a family and then returning as part-time workers once the children reached school age. Since the 1970s, feminists and others have worked hard to encourage young women to take up some form of further or higher education and there were many campaigns to open up so-called male work to women, for example in the building trade or in science. We have now reached the position were more than half the undergraduates at university are women, although they still tend to predominate in the humanities and social science subjects. Some areas of the sciences have a large proportion of women students, for example life sciences, but they are still very much a minority in engineering and physics, despite the best efforts of women activists in these fields. Further, in the area of post-graduate study, the proportions reverse with more male students than women. This is an area that activists must address as postgraduate qualifications lead to more senior positions in many sectors.

Male violence against women has been a feature throughout the period studied. In the early days, when women were excluded from most trade unions, men attacked women who replaced them when they were in dispute with their employers. Sometimes the abuse was verbal but at other times physical violence was used. Rather than putting class interests first at these times, by including women in the unions, male workers left women in a vulnerable unorganized position at the mercy of employers only too willing to exploit their vulnerability by employing them on lower wages than men. Campaigns to encourage women to join unions through-out the nineteenth and early twentieth centuries were, at worst, resisted by male unionists and, at best, tepidly welcomed. When welcomed, it was often as a strategy to protect male workers, for example, during the First World War when women munitions workers were unionized. Once in the unions, women found that they had very little power, even in unions where they were numerically powerful. Again, women were regarded as second-class temporary workers who had to adapt to a male-dominated union structure that did little to encourage them, other than to pay their subscriptions. Meetings were held at inconvenient times and women's issues were ignored or paid lip service to at the Trades Union Congress. After the First World War, the absorption of the WTUL and NFWW into their male counterparts did nothing to improve women's status within the movement as they lost any small amount of autonomy they had enjoyed. It is only in recent years that women have been regarded as workers, although the double burden of paid work and domestic responsibilities is acknowledged. Through the work of women activists and some sympathetic male trade unionists, women's issues now receive support. In some unions, separate women's groups work to ensure that equal opportunities for women are near the top of the agenda. Sexual harassment is another manifestation of male abuse in the workplace. In the nineteenth and early twentieth centuries, sexual harassment was the 'problem with no name' and was hidden under a plethora of euphemisms often employed as reasons why women should be segregated from male workers. Harassment was also used as the subject for jokes in popular culture. The WLM took this issue on board and exposed the range of 'harmless' practices that constituted sexual harassment, from bottom pinching to sexual blackmail, which were still prevalent well into the 1970s and beyond. It is one of the areas where the SDA has served women well and it is no longer considered the 'problem with no name' or a joke as employers have been taken to task for tolerating the practice in their company.

Although patriarchal ideology and practice have continued to persist, it would be wrong to look on the past 140 years too pessimistically. We have progressed a long way from the days when the main occupation for working-class women was live-in domestic service and for middle-class women live-in governessing. If compared with men over the same period, we can fairly say that women's access to education, training and opportunities have increased hugely, although men are still advantaged because patriarchal structures and ways of thinking continue to persist. The separation of the public world of production from the private world of reproduction continues to disadvantage women although there is a growing recognition that action needs to be taken over the work–life balance in Britain and that this will benefit both men and women. Perhaps we shall know that we have reached equilibrium when young men, as well as women, have to take into account whether or not they intend to have a family when choosing a career or, better still, that young women no longer have to factor in whether they want a family when choosing their career. Until then women will not be seen as such committed workers as men, the qualities they bring to their work will be seen as inferior to men's, they will not be recognized in promotion panels and very few will reach the top of their profession or realize their full potential in whatever work they undertake.

The history of women's employment in Britain is intrinsically linked to women's struggle for independence, citizenship and equality. There have been setbacks as well as progress and the challenge continues. Some groups of women have been advantaged at the expense of others. In the nineteenth century middle-class women often thought that they knew what was best for working-class women and sought to speak for them rather than enable working-class women to articulate their own ideas. Factory inspectors, welfare superintendents and trade union activists were often middle-class women earning their living by representing working-class women. Middle-class women activists also enjoyed some authority as they were listened to at Royal Commissions and in the media. These women were well-intentioned and hoped to breach class difference through a rhetoric of sisterhood. However, sisterhood is not necessarily an equal relationship and there can be power differences between big sisters and little sisters. Patriarchy is not the only source of oppression experienced by women, although it is arguably the most persistent. In the twenty-first century debates about disadvantaged groups of women will persist. Globalization brings to our doorstep the problems of women workers in the developing world, exploited to support our lifestyle, immigrant women being employed to undertake the tasks that we have shunned and the attraction of the burgeoning sex industry for women who would otherwise be consigned to the lowest-paid work are all questions for consideration. Poverty as well as patriarchy continues to be a challenge and women will have to continue the struggle using the lessons that they can learn from the changes that occurred in the past to offer hope to women in the future.

So what has most affected women's work during this period? Was it women's refusal to be consigned to a limited domestic role of unpaid labour? Was it the changing nature of industrial and post-industrial society? Was it the upheaval of two World Wars? It is, of course, a combination of all these things. Industrialization, coupled with the rise of the British Empire, over time, transformed the working landscape of Britain. As capital needed more labour than the male workforce could provide, it was obvious that women could never be completely restricted to the domestic sphere. The competing pressures of patriarchy and capital shaped women's role in the workplace. However, women were agents in their own lives and the demands of feminists, women trade unionists and, later, women MPs shaped government policy which, in turn, shaped workplace practice both in times of war and peace. Further, as advances in contraceptive technology enabled women to control their fertility, the years that most women spent in childrearing were drastically reduced, enabling women to understand work as something more than an interlude between childhood and childrearing. This, more than anything else, has impacted on women's life choices and although women still struggle with the double burden of paid and unpaid work in the twenty-first century, they are less at the mercy of their biology.

The challenges for women in the twenty-first century are in many ways very different to the challenges that women faced in the mid-nineteenth century. Equal pay and sex discrimination legislation has gone some way to redressing injustices in employment, but women need to continue the debate around whether we want to be treated the same as men by following male-defined working practices or whether we are going to demand new ways of working that address our broader roles as workers and carers. Working lives have changed greatly and the norm has moved from life-long full-time employment to more flexible, less permanent working patterns which could benefit women wanting both a career and childrearing. Workplaces have changed too with the advent of the age of information technology. This gives a new meaning to homework and could well work in women's favour. We have yet to see whether the ever-changing needs of capital and patriarchy will favour women or offer more challenges that need to be addressed.

ह♠

Chronology of important dates

1841   Governesses Benevolent Institutes established.

1842   Mines Act banned women and children from underground work.

1844   Factory Act reduced working hours to twelve per day. Women classified as protected persons.

1847   Ten Hours Act.

1853   Series of Factory Acts extended protection to women outside the textile industry (pottery, paper, tobacco, etc.).

1854   First mixed sex trade unions in the textile industry formed as the Blackburn Weavers' Association.

1857   Select Committee on employment of women and children in bleaching and dyeing trades.
        Barbara Leigh Smith publishes *Women and Work*.

1858   *English Woman's Journal* founded by Barbara Leigh Smith and Bessie Rayner Parkes.

1859   Society for Promoting the Employment of Women (SPEW) established.
        Harriet Martineau publishes 'Female Industry' in the *Edinburgh Review*.

1860   Nightingale Fund School of Nursing founded at St Thomas's Hospital in London.
        Emily Faithfull establishes the Victoria Press.

1862   Female Middle-Class Emigration Society established.
        Female Medical Society (midwives) established.

1865   Ladies Medical College (midwives) established.

1866   *Englishwoman's Review* first published.

1867   Factory and Workshop Act defined a factory as any establishment employing more than 50 employees.
        Report of Royal Commission on Employment of Children, Young Persons and Women in Agriculture. Regulation of gangs.

1869   Bleaching and Dyeing Act.

1870   National Union of Teachers founded.

1871   Women clerks introduced at the Prudential Assurance Company.

1874   Emma Paterson publishes 'The Position of Working Women and How to Improve It' in *Labour News*.
        Women's Protective and Provident League (WPPL) established.
        National Union of Women Workers established.
        Union of Women Bookbinders established.
        Jane Nassau Senior appointed to the workhouse inspectorate.
        Women clerks employed at the National Savings Bank.

1875   Society of Dressmakers, Milliners and Mantlemakers; Union of Women Upholsteresses; Union of Women Shirt and Collar Makers all formed in London, with others forming outside of the capital, e.g. Dewsbury, Batley and Surrounding District Heavy Woollen Weavers' Association and the Benefit Society for Glasgow Working Women.
        Emma Paterson and Edith Simcox attended the Trades Union Congress.

1876   Emma Paterson established the Women's Printing Society.
        Women's Union Journal founded.
        Report of the Royal Commission on Factories and Workshops.
        Women employed by the Post Office.

1877   Tailoresses Union established.

1878   Factory and Workshop Act.
        Women's Halfpenny Bank founded.
        Women's Union Swimming Club established.

1879   London Tailoresses Union formed following a successful women's trade dispute in Pimlico.

1881   Working Women's Benefit Society founded in Oxford.
        New Civil Service grade for women introduced.
        General Union of Textile Workers established.

1882   Report to the House of Commons on White Lead Works.
        London Women's Trades Council established.

1883   Factory and Workshop Act.
        Women's Co-operative Guild established.

1885   Women allowed to join the National Union of Boot and Shoe
        Operatives but excluded from certain areas of the trade.

1886   Amalgamated Association of Card and Blowing Room Operatives
        established. Women members allowed from the outset.
        Shop Act restricted working hours to seventy-four hours per
        week.

1887   Royal British Nurses Association founded.
        WPPL and Council for Women's Trade established in Scotland.

1888   Bryant and May (Match Girls') strike led to the formation of more
        women's unions around the country, e.g. the Women's Industrial
        Council in Liverpool and the Society of Workwomen in Leeds.

1889   WPPL became the Women's Trade Union and Provident League
        (WTUPL) and the Women's Trade Union Association (WTUA) was
        established.
        Scottish Mill and Factory Workers Association established.

1890   National Union of Clerks formed. Women members allowed from
        the outset.
        Amalgamated Association of Beamers, Twisters, Drawers-in
        formed. Women members allowed from the outset.

1891   Factory and Workshop Act excluded mothers from working within
        four weeks of confinement.
        Amalgamated Society of Laundresses formed and fights for
        regulation of the trade. Jessie Boucherett and Helen Blackburn
        form the Women's Employment Defence League (WEDL) and
        oppose regulation of laundry work.
        WTUPL becomes Women's Trade Union League (WTUL) and
        Women's Union Journal becomes *Women's Trade Union Review*.
        National Amalgamated Union of Shop Assistants, Warehousemen
        and Clerks formed. Women members allowed from the outset.
        Women assistant commissioners appointed to Labour
        Commission.

1892   Shop Act. Allowed local authorities to employ inspectors.

1893   First women factory inspectors appointed.
        Women's Industrial Defence Committee formed to oppose
        legislation affecting women's work.

1894   Labour Commission Report on women's work.
Report on the Condition of Labour in Lead Industries.
Women's Industrial Council (WIC) replaced WTUA and founded the *Women's Industrial News*.
Manchester Women's Trades Union Council founded.

1895   Factory and Workshop Act attempted to extending protection to women in small workshops and sweats shops, leading to an increase in outworking.
National Union of Women Workers in Great Britain and Ireland established in Nottingham.
Shop Act imposed fines on employers not conforming to the 1886 Act.

1896   Margaret Bondfield went undercover to investigate shop work for the WIC. Truck Act passed.

1897   WEDL is renamed Freedom of Labour Defence Association.
Association of Post Office Women Clerks established.

1898   *Women's Industrial News* first published.

1899   Seats for Female Shop Assistants Act.
Women's Sanitary Officers Association established.

1900   National Union of Women Teachers established.
Women join the Amalgamated Society of Tailors and Tailoresses but excluded from certain areas of the trade.

1901   Factory and Workshop Act.
Association of Women Clerks in the Post Office formed.

1903   Association of Shorthand Writers and Typists; the Civil Service Typist Association and Women Sorter's Association formed.
Mary Macarthur became the secretary of the WTUL.

1904   Women finally allowed to join the National Union of Printing and Paper Workers but not as compositors or machine operatives.
Early Closing Act passed.

1906   National Women Workers Federation (NFWW) established.
Amalgamated Society for Male and Female Pottery Workers formed.
Sweated Trades Exhibition and formation of the Anti-Sweating League.
Cadbury, Matheson and Shann published *Women's Work and Wages*.

1907   Factory and Workshop Act.
The Woman Worker established.

1909   Trades Board Act passed affecting lacemaking, chainmaking, paper box making and tailoring.

1910   Cradley Heath Chainmakers' strike.

1911   National Health Insurance Act.
Series of strikes in Bermondsey and the East End of London in the canning and food making industries.
Shop Act regulated working hours and holidays.

1912   Association of Women Clerks and Secretaries replaced Association of Shorthand Writers and Typists.
Shop Act incorporated all previous Acts (1886, 1892, 1893, 1895, 1899, 1904 and 1911).

1913   Extension of the Trades Boards Act and Shop Act.

1914   War Emergency Workers' National Committee formed.
Queen Mary's Work for Women Fund established.

1915   Central Committee on Women's Employment established.

1916   Standing Joint Committee of Womens' Industrial Organizations formed.

1917   National Union of Bookbinders and Machine Rulers allowed women members but not in the skilled branches of bookbinding.

1918   Representation of the People Act enfranchised women householders over the age of 30.
Parliamentary Qualification of Women Act allowed women to be elected as members of Parliament.
Restoration of Pre-War Practices Act passed.
Further extension of the Trades Boards Act.

1919   Sex Disqualification (Removal) Act abolished all existing restrictions upon the admission of women into professions and civic positions, such as jury service or becoming a magistrate.
Nurses Registration Act required registration of all nurses.
Reports from the War Cabinet on Women in Industry.
Report of the Women's Advisory Committee on the Domestic Service Problem.
'Women's Right to Work' conference in Manchester.

1920   Employment of Women, Young Persons and Children Act prohibits women from night work in certain industries.
Time and Tide first published.
Council of Women Civil Servants formed.
Union of Post Office clerks formed. Women members allowed from the outset.

1920   Married Women's Property (Scotland) Act extended these rights to Scotland.

1921   NFWW merged with the National Union of General Workers and the WTUL was absorbed by the TUC.
Six Point Group formed.

1923   Report to the Minister of Labour of the Committee Appointed into the Present Conditions as to the Supply of Female Domestic Servants.

1926   Open Door Council formed. Focus on equal rights in employment issues.

1928   Equal Franchise Act gave all women the same voting rights as men.

1931   Anomalies Act passed which restricted married women's access to unemployment benefit.

1940   Woman-Power Committee formed.
Extended Employment of Women Agreement drawn up.

1941   National Service (No 2) Act allowed for single women aged 20–30 liable for conscription to undertake war work.

1942   Restoration of Pre-War Practices Act passed.
Beveridge Report published.

1943   Women allowed to join the Amalgamated Society of Engineers, which was first established in 1851.

1944   Equal Pay Campaign Committee formed.
Education Act passed.

1944   Marriage bar for women teachers formally abolished.

1945   Royal Commission on Equal Pay.

1946   National Insurance Act enshrined married women as dependent on their husbands and all men as breadwinners in terms of benefits.
Marriage bar for women civil servants formally abolished.

1947   Markham Report on Domestic Employment recommends the establishment of the National Institute of Houseworkers.

1949   Royal Commission on Population report published. It welcomed the possibility of women having dual roles as housewife and paid worker.

1950   Factories (Evening Employment) Order enables women to work evening shift work.

1956   Alva Myrdal and Viola Klien published *Women's Two Roles, Home and Work.*

1968   Ford machinists at Dagenham strike for recognition as skilled workers and a pay increase.

1970   Equal Pay Act passed.

1975   Sex Discrimination Act, Employment Protection and Social Security Pensions Act passed.

1977   Grunwick strike in North London.

1983   Equal Value (Amendment) Regulations passed.

1989   Employment Act raised retirement age for women to 65.

ใ๑

Brief biographies of some key women

Clementina Black (1853–1922)

Black was the eldest daughter of a solicitor and when her mother died she took over caring for the family and business apprentices. She worked for a while as a teacher, during which time she met and befriended Eleanor Marx. She was also a novelist. In the 1880s she moved to London with two of her sisters and through Marx became involved with radical groups. Through this connection, she became interested in questions concerning working-class women's work. She became the secretary of the Women's Trade Union League but, possibly because of her involvement with the Match Girls' strike, she left and became a founding member of the Women's Trade Union Association (WTUA) which was later superseded by the Women's Industrial Council (WIC). Black was pivotal in the WIC and working and serving as its president for many years. A keen advocate of protective legislation, she came into conflict with older feminists, such as Boucherett, and wrote an essay defending the Factory Acts. She was also a member of the Executive Committee of the Anti-Sweating League and fought long and hard for the Trades Boards Act. This issue caused a split in the WIC with Black on the opposite side to Margaret McDonald. The split caused her to resign the presidency for a time while she concentrated on campaigning for the Trades Boards legislation. As a writer, she produced many books and articles on the problems that women workers faced, based on her work with the WTUA and WIC. She was also the acting editor of the suffrage newspaper *The Common Cause* from 1912–13. Black was never wealthy and had to support herself and her niece by writing which she continued to do until her death. Her written non-fiction work includes many articles in the *Fortnightly Review*, *The Common Cause*,

Women's Industrial News and numerous other WIC publications including *Sweated Industry and the Minimum Wage*, 1907; *A Case for the Trades Boards*, 1909; *Married Women's Work*, 1915; and *A New Way of Housekeeping*, 1918.

Helen Blackburn (1842–1903)

Blackburn was an editor of the *Englishwoman's Review* and a suffrage organizer. Like Boucherett, she was strongly opposed to protective legislation aimed at women and was a co-founder with Boucherett of the Labour Defence Association. Her written work includes, with Boucherett, *The Condition of Working Women and the Factory Acts*, 1896; and, with Nora Vynne, *Women under the Factory Acts*, 1903.

Margaret Bondfield (1873–1953)

Bondfield started work at age 13 as a pupil-teacher at Chard, Somerset but a year later she became an apprentice shop assistant in Brighton. Whilst there, she met and was influenced by Louisa Martindale, a local suffragist who taught young shop workers about women's rights. Having moved to London in 1894, Bondfield, through her trade unionist brother, became involved in union activity as a member of the National Union of Shop Assistants, Warehouseman and Clerks. In 1896 she joined a two-year investigation of the conditions of shop workers organized by the Women's Industrial Council (WIC). This led eventually to a Select Committee being set up to investigate shop working hours. In 1898 she was appointed assistant secretary of the union and represented the union at the 1899 TUC – she was the only woman present. She was an active member of the Women's Trade Union League (WTUL) and nominated her friend Mary Macarthur for the post of secretary of the WTUL. She worked closely with Macarthur in the WTUL and the National Federation of Women Workers (NFWW). Both women supported adult rather than women's suffrage. Bondfield worked with Clementina Black on the investigation into married women's work, using her working-class background to get close to the women she was interviewing in ways that the other investigators were unable to do. During the First World War she was a member of various committees including the War Emergency Workers' National Committee. In the post-war years she became a Labour MP and, in 1923, the first woman cabinet minister. She was responsible for unemployed women workers. She became less involved in women's employment issues in the late 1920s and up to her retirement in 1938. Her written works include a chapter in C. Black (ed.) *Married Women's Work*, 1915 and her autobiography *A Life's Work*, 1949.

Jessie Boucherett (1825–1905)

Boucherett was from a landed background in Lincolnshire. She moved to London in 1859 to become involved with the campaign to promote women's employment. With Bessie Rayner Parkes and Emily Faithfull, she formed the Society for Promoting the Employment of Women (SPEW) and, like them, she was also on the committee of the National Association for the Promotion of Social Science. She contributed articles on women's employment to the *English Woman's Journal* and when this was superseded by the *Englishwoman's Review* she became its editor until 1897. A keen liberal in the widest sense, she vociferously opposed all legislation aimed specifically at women and was a member of the Freedom of Labour Defence Society which campaigned against protective legislation. Alongside her commitment to opening up employment opportunities for women, she was a keen supporter of women's suffrage.

Her writings include her many articles in the *English Woman's Journal*, the *Englishwomen's Review* and various suffrage journals. She also contributed a chapter to Josephine Butler's *Woman's Work and Woman's Culture*, 1869 and co-wrote with Helen Blackburn *The Condition of Working Women and the Factory Acts*, 1896.

Ada Nield Chew (1870–1945)

Chew was the second born in a family of thirteen. Her childhood experiences of being the eldest daughter in a poor family informed her politics in later life. Having worked in a series of unskilled jobs, Chew embarked on her political career after being discovered as the author of a series of letters to the *Crewe Chronicle*, written under the pseudonym 'A Crewe Factory Girl'. She was, at first, a speaker for the Independent Labour Party and in 1895 became a Poor Law Guardian, one of the first working-class women to hold this position. In 1896, she became a member of the *Clarion*'s campaign to introduce socialism into country districts and travelled around the country with fellow missionaries. She met her husband George at this time. After the birth of her daughter, Chew became an organizer for the Women's Trade Union League (WTUL) and travelled the country organizing women in trade unions and reporting on the conditions she found in various industries in the *Women's Trade Union Review*. During her time at the WTUL she became involved in its Pottery Fund Committee, reporting on the terrible conditions in this industry. She kept up this work even when she had left the WTUL to work as an organizer for the National Union of Women's Suffrage Societies. During her years as a suffrage organizer she kept her interest in working-class women's lives, writing in the *Common Cause* and other feminist publications about the needs and demands of working women, especially working mothers. Her various articles are gathered in her daughter's book *Ada Nield Chew: Writings of a Working Woman Remembered and Collected* by Doris Nield Chew, 1982.

Lady Emily Dilke (1840–1904)

Emily Strong was educated at home and attended the South Kensington School of Art in 1859. She eventually became an art editor for the journal *Academy*. Her first marriage was to an Oxford don and it is said that she was George Eliot's inspiration for the character Dorothea in *Middlemarch*. She was involved with suffrage from 1869 onwards and through this work met Emma Paterson who encouraged her to become a founder member of the Women's Protective and Provident League (WPPL). As a speaker for the WPPL, she travelled the country encouraging women to set up or join unions. She set up a branch of the league in Oxford and organized the tailoresses there. After the death of her first husband she married the Liberal MP Charles Dilke who was a great supporter of the WPPL and later the Women's Trade Union League (WTUL). After the death of Paterson, Dilke became the leading light in the women's trade union movement. She helped expand the WTUL and update its policy in the light of the move towards new unionism and the acceptance of protective legislation, something Paterson had always opposed. She also worked for the closer association of women's unions with male unions as she believed this would strengthen the women's movement. From 1889 up to her death in 1904, Lady Dilke represented the WTUL at the Trades Union Congresses, keeping the promotion of women's involvement in trades unions to the fore. From the end of the nineteenth century up to her death she also campaigned with her husband on behalf of shop workers and championed sweated workers. Articles she wrote concerning women workers can be found in the *Women's Trade Union Review* and the *Fortnightly Review*. She also wrote the introduction to A. A. Bulley and M. Whitley *Women's Work*, 1894.

Emily Faithfull (1835–95)

Faithfull was one of the founding members of the Society for Promoting the Employment of Women (SPEW) and was on the committee of the National Association for the Promotion of Social Science. In 1860, she undertook some typesetting training and set up a printing office, the Victoria Press, in which all the compositors were women. In 1863, she founded the *Victoria Magazine* but was involved in a scandalous divorce case and had to withdraw from both the press and magazine. She became a member of the Women's Protective and Provident League (WPPL) and continued her work for women's employment through this organization and helped Paterson set up the Women's Printing Society in 1876.

Isabella Ford (1855–1924)

Ford came from a Quaker family based in Leeds. As a young woman, she taught young women factory workers in evening classes at a school established by her parents. Through her mother, she knew Emma Paterson and was encouraged by Paterson to establish a Tailoresses' Society. This union was short-lived but it brought her into contact with members of the Leeds Trade Council. In 1888, she set up the Workwomen's Society, a benefit society that did not support strikes and which was open to all women, but specifically aimed at tailoresses working in factories. She became known as a trade union activist and women's rights advocate in the West Riding in the late 1880s when there was widespread industrial unrest in Leeds where she supported the striking women. In 1889, Ford established the Tailoresses' Union and became involved with the Socialist League, a move away from her Liberal past. She joined the central committee of the WTUL at this time. Throughout the 1890s, she concentrated her energies on organizing the tailoresses and textile workers in Leeds and the West Riding although she also worked with Varley during the Manningham Mill strike of 1890–1. In 1896, she was the West Riding of Yorkshire Tailoresses' representative at the TUC. She also supported a paid organizer for the union and with her established a Women's Trade Union Club in 1897. The Tailoresses' Union merged with the male union in 1899.

Throughout her career as an activist she championed working women in her writings, both fiction and non-fiction, supported married women workers against their detractors and opposed those who thought philanthropy was the answer to women's poverty. She was not automatically in support of protective legislation if she felt it would restrict women's ability to work and felt that it was not useful if women were not organized. During the early years of the twentieth century, she was active in the Independent Labour Party and she and her sisters entertained many international socialists at their Leeds home. She was a constitutional suffragist but was among the pacifist suffragists who split from the National Union of Women's Suffrage Societies during the First World War and focused on bringing about an early end to the war. Ford wrote numerous articles in journals and newspapers such as the Women's *Trade Union Review*, the *Humane Review, Englishwoman, Common Cause* and the *Labour Leader*.

Dame Florence Hancock (1893–1974)

Hancock began her working life as a kitchen assistant at the age of 12. She later became a factory worker and became involved in trade unionism. In 1917, she became an organizer for the Workers' Union in Wiltshire. In 1929, when the Workers' Union amalgamated with the Transport and General Workers' Union, she became the woman's officer in Bristol, representing the burgeoning number of women working in the light engineering trades. She also helped to establish the Women's Advisory Committee of the TUC. Throughout her career in the trade union movement she supported women. In 1935, she spoke out against stopping the unemployment benefit of young women who refused to move to London to find work. She also supported protective legislation aimed at women and young people expected to undertake long hours of over-time. She worked on behalf of laundry workers and women employed in the tobacco and confectionery industries in the Bristol area. During the Second World War she was made chief women's officer of the Transport and General Workers' Union (TGWU) and was chair of the TUC Women's Advisory Committee from 1941 to 1944. Again, she was concerned with the welfare of women workers and argued against long hours in munitions factories. She supported the notion of equal pay at the Royal Commission on Equal Pay but backed down when the Labour Party were reluctant to accept the findings immediately after the war, arguing that national needs must come first. However, she continued to support the notion of equal pay. After the war, she argued that nurseries would enable women to return to work. Also, working with Violet Markham, she prepared the report on private domestic workers, calling for these low-paid, non-unionized workers to be covered by the unemployment benefit scheme and to receive proper training. She was made a dame in 1951 and retired in 1958.

Amie Hicks (1839/40?–1917)

Hicks was a socialist who became involved with the Social Democratic Federation in 1883. In 1889, along with Black, she was one of the found-ing members of the Women's Trade Union Association (WTUA). Her daughter Frances was also a member. Hicks senior organized women rope makers, a trade of which she had experience. Along with Clara James, who represented the confectioner's union, she gave evidence at the Royal Commission on Labour in 1891 and asked for working women factory inspectors rather than the Lady Inspectors who were eventually appointed from 1893 onwards. She also represented women rope makers on the London Trades Council for a short while. In 1894, she became a founder member of the Women's Industrial Council (WIC) which superseded the

241

WTUA. Amie's daughter Frances was the secretary of the WIC until her marriage and Hicks senior served on several of the WIC's committees. Hicks senior was especially interested in the Clubs Industrial Association, founded in 1898. This association organized working girls' clubs. It sought to educate working girls in industrial social questions and gave them an opportunity to socialize after a long working day. She remained with the WIC until 1910 and continued to be involved with Girls' Clubs.

Susan Lawrence (1871–1947)

Lawrence came from a legal background and studied Maths at Newnham College, Cambridge, until her father died and she was obliged to leave. She worked in local government, serving on the London School Board and becoming the vice chair for the education committee of London County Council. Here she became interested in the plight of low-paid women school cleaners and this brought her into contact with Mary Macarthur. Macarthur persuaded her to become involved in Labour politics and during the First World War Lawrence became involved with the Women's Trade Union League (WTUL) and she represented workers on several trades boards. She also served as the Fabian Society's representative on the War Emergency Workers' National Committee. With Bondfield, she was one of the first women Labour MPs. She was not particularly involved with women workers after the First World War.

Barbara Leigh Smith Bodichon (1827–91)

Leigh Smith was the illegitimate daughter of a radical MP and a milliner. Her father was progressive in his ideas about his daughters and gave them far more freedom and money than most young women of the day. Leigh Smith put her money and opportunities to good use. In 1854 she wrote an important text on married women's property as it stood in law. In 1857 she wrote another important essay on women and work in which she made a cogent argument for women's right to work whether they needed the money or not. She also used her own money to good effect by starting up the *English Woman's Journal* where many of the economic, social and political issues that affected women were discussed. She was a founder member of the Langham Place Group where many of the early feminist campaigns for women's economic and political independence were discussed and acted upon. Following her marriage, Bodichon spent half the year in Britain and the other half in Algeria where she pursued her career as an artist. However, she followed the progress of the women's movement and used her money to bank-roll several feminist projects, including the construction of Girton College, Cambridge.

Mary Macarthur (1880–1921)

Macarthur came from a well-to-do background although she worked in her father's shop as a bookkeeper. In 1901 she attended a meeting of the Shop Assistants' Union which converted her to trade unionism and she soon became the first chairman of the Ayr branch of the union. She met Margaret Bondfield at a union conference in 1902 and, in 1903, with help from Bondfield, moved to London and became secretary of the Women's Trade Union League (WTUL). Under her direction and personality, the WTUL was revitalized and the membership grew. In 1906, she established the National Federation for Women Workers (NFWW). She also joined the Anti-Sweating League in the same year. In 1907, she launched the women's paper *Woman Worker* and edited it for a year. She was on the opposing side to MacDonald in the debate around homework and the Trades Boards Act. She helped Varley ensure that women chain makers came under the Act and helped to set up the trade board in Nottingham for the women lace makers there. In 1911, with help from Marion Phillips, she helped to organize a number of strikes amongst women factory workers in Bermondsey and used strikes to encourage the women to unionize. During the war, she was a member of the War Emergency Workers' National Committee as the WTUL representative. Her role was to ensure that women were treated fairly in the exceptional conditions of war work and that trade union standards were maintained. With the support of Queen Mary, she established the Queen's Work for Women Fund – a contentious organization because many activists felt that women were being treated as cheap labour. However, out of this organization developed the Central Committee on Women's Training and Employment. After the war her main aim was to oversee the amalgamation of the NFWW with the Women Worker's Section of the National Union of General Workers. This happened on 1 January 1921, the day she died.

Her written work can be found in the *Christian Commonwealth, Daily News, Labour Leader, Women's Trade Union Review* and the *Woman Worker*. She also contributed essays to collections such as G. M. Tuckwell (ed.) *Women in Industry from Seven Points of View*, 1908 and M. Phillips (ed.) *Women and the Labour Party*, 1918.

Margaret MacDonald (née Gladstone) (1870–1911)

MacDonald studied political economy under Millicent Fawcett at King's College. She taught in Sunday Schools as well as servant girls at the Nassau Training School. Later, she managed several Board Schools in London, was secretary of the Hoxton and Haggerston Nursing Association and worked as a visitor for the Charity Organization Society. Influenced by the writings of F. D. Maurice and Charles Kingsley, she moved towards Fabian socialism in the 1890s. She joined the Women's Industrial Council (WIC) in 1894 and became the secretary of its Legal and Statistical Committee. She met and married Ramsay MacDonald and joined the Independent Labour Party in 1895. In 1906, she gave evidence to the Select Committee on Homework, opposing the introduction of the Wages Board and supporting the notion of the male breadwinner and dependent wife and children. Her opposition to the Wages Board led eventually to a split in the WIC with MacDonald and Black on opposing sides. She was also a member of the National Union of Women Workers where she campaigned for a wide range of women's employment issues including the registration of midwives and nurses, police court matrons, women probation officers, restaurants for women workers, early closing of shops and florists' working hours. She was vociferous in her campaign to prevent young women being employed as barmaids. She was also involved in the campaign to provide women and girls with industrial education and helped establish the first trade school for girls at the Borough Polytechnic in 1904. She was also part of a WIC deputation to establish a training centre for children's nurses in Hackney. In the last years of her life her work centred on the Women's Labour League, the women's section of the Labour Party. Her writings, often written with others, include *Home Industries for Women*, 1897; *Women as Barmaids*, 1904; *Wage Earning Mothers*, 1911; *Married Women's Work*, 1915; plus many articles and reports in journals such as *Women's Industrial News*

Emma Paterson (1848–86)

Paterson began an apprenticeship as a bookbinder at the age of 16 but the early death of her schoolteacher father meant that she and her mother had to seek employment. First, they set up a private school but when that failed Emma became a secretary to a lady clerk at the Working Men's Club and Institute Union in 1866. In 1872, she left the institute to become a secretary for the Women's Suffrage Association but left on her marriage to Thomas Paterson, a cabinet maker. Following their honeymoon in America, where they studied women's trade unions, she returned to set up the Women's Protective and Provident League (WPPL) with like-minded people from the institute, suffrage movement and other like-minded liberals. The first trades she organized were women bookbinders, milliners and mantlemakers, hat trimmers, upholsterers and shirt makers. Between 1875 and her death in 1886, she attended every Trades Union Congress except for 1882 when her husband died. Amongst other roles, she was an early advocate of women factory inspectors although she thought these should be practical working women rather than the ladies that were eventually employed. She worked with Emily Faithfull at the Victoria Press, a women's press, and set up the Women's Printing Society in 1876. She also edited the *Women's Union Journal* and set up various initiatives for women under the auspices of the WPPL, e.g. a savings bank and a swimming club. Her writings can be found in the *Women's Union Journal* and the *Transactions of the National Association for the Promotion of Social Sciences*.

Sarah Reddish (1850–1928)

Although Reddish's main focus of activity was in the Women's Co-operative Guild, she was also one of the working-class organizers of the Women's Trade Union League (WTUL). Her personal experience of industrial conditions stemmed from her work as a cotton mill worker and as a supervisor in a hosiery factory. She was also actively involved in the suffrage petition of women textile workers in 1901 and the Lancashire and Cheshire Women Textile and other Workers Representation Committee which developed out of this campaign. She continued to work with this group until the outbreak of the First World War.

Edith Summerskill (Baroness Summerskill) (1901–80)

Summerskill came from a middle-class family and was encouraged to train as a doctor. She was a feminist who continued to practise as a doctor after marriage and motherhood. Having become a Labour MP in 1938, she campaigned against the marriage bar, for equal pay and against discrimination against women in tribunals for conscientious objectors. She also campaigned for male wage earners to be compelled to reveal their earnings to their wives. During the war, she campaigned for equal compensation for women who had suffered war injuries. She also argued for the better use of women's skills and helped secure women's right to serve as auxilliaries in the Home Guard. She opposed the conscription of women into war work because the scheme did not offer women equal pay with men. After the war she was involved in the campaign for equal pay for teachers and civil servants and once this was granted she argued for equal pay for women industrial workers. In the 1960s, she focused more on other feminist issues such as divorce and abortion.

May Tennant (née Abraham) (1869–1946)

A friend of Lady Dilke, May Abraham began her career as the secretary and treasurer of the Women's Trade Union League (WTUL). She became involved in the campaign for protective legislation for laundry workers and, in 1891, she became one of the four Lady Assistant Commissioners who undertook field inquiries for the Royal Commission on Labour. Her areas of responsibility were the textile industries in Lancashire, the Midlands and Yorkshire and the effects of the white lead industry. In 1893 she became the first woman factory inspector at the age of 24. She gave up this work on her marriage to the politician Jack Tennant in 1896. She continued to campaign for more legislation and acted as chairman of the Industrial Law Committee. She also supported the Anti-Sweating League and the implementation of the Trades Boards Act. Throughout her work as an activist, she supported protective legislation and was opposed to married women working. During the First World War, Tennant was on the Central Committee on Women's Employment that was set up to deal with women's unemployment at the outset of the war. She was also a director of the women's section of the National Service Department and chief adviser on women's welfare to the Ministry of War. She continued to serve on the Central Committee on Women's Employment, which focused on retraining unemployed women after the war, until 1939.

Gertrude Tuckwell (1861–1951)

Tuckwell was Lady Dilke's niece. Brought up in a radical Christian family, she met members of the Women's Trade Union League (WTUL) through her aunt. On the advice of activists in the WTUL, she trained as a teacher in Liverpool where she came into direct contact with severe poverty and the slums. From 1884 to the early 1890s, she worked as an elementary teacher in London. She tried to be progressive but found this difficult in large classes crammed with malnourished, exhausted children. She left teaching through ill health and worked as her aunt's (Lady Dilke's) secretary at the WTUL. She became the editor of the *Women's Trade Union Review* and stayed in this post until 1905. A supporter of protective legislation, in the 1890s she investigated the pottery industry and the white lead mills and campaigned for the use of leadless glaze on pottery. She also worked with Chew on the Potteries Fund campaign before the First World War. She supported the campaign for a minimum wage for industrial workers and was a secretary for the Christian Social Union Research Committee which investigated low-paid women's trades such as laundry work, food manufacture, fish curing, brush making and tea packing from 1896 onwards. Consequently, she took part in the formation of the Anti-Sweating League in 1906 and appeared with Mary Macarthur before the Select Committee on Home Work. After the death of her aunt, she became the president of the WTUL in 1905 and the president of the National Federation of Women Workers (NFWW) in 1908; she remained active in both organizations until she retired from both in 1918. However, she continued to be active on behalf of women workers after the war on various advisory panels focused on women's work. After the war, she was an advocate of equal pay for women which she regarded as the only fair system for both men and women. She also supported Eleanor Rathbone's campaign for family allowance. She became less involved with women's employment issues in the final decades of her life but she still worked for the disadvantaged in society. Her writings include a piece on regulation of women's work in G. M. Tuckwell (ed.) *Women in Industry from Seven Points of View* and articles in *Fortnightly Review*. The Gertrude Tuckwell Collection at the TUC Library is a wonderful collection of cuttings about the Industrial Women's Movement before the First World War.

Julia Varley (1871–1952)

Varley was the eldest child of a mill worker. She left school at the age of 12 to become a part-time mill worker. At 15 she became secretary of the Weavers' and Textile Workers' Union and although she gave up work to look after her siblings when her mother died, she remained active in the union. She was involved in the Manningham Mill strike in 1890–91 and eventually became the first woman member of the Bradford Trades Council between 1899–1906. In 1903, she was appointed to inquire into employment conditions in Bradford and from 1904–7 she worked on the Bradford Board of Guardians. During this time, she undertook an under-cover operation to investigate the conditions that very poor tramping women (i.e. homeless women) experienced. She disguised herself as a wife looking for her husband and tramped from Leeds to Liverpool. She also investigated London common lodging houses. Varley was a suffragette and served two periods of imprisonment in 1907. She also worked for the Women's Trade Union League (WTUL) and the National Federation for Women Workers (NFWW). With Mary Macarthur, she established a branch of the NFWW amongst the women small chainmakers at Cradley Heath and campaigned with the Anti-Sweating League to ensure that small chainmakers were included in the Trades Boards Act of 1909. In 1909, she moved to Birmingham and became the secretary of the Birmingham Women's Organization Committee, as well as working for the NFWW, and organized the card box workers at Bournville. From here she went on to be the first woman member of the Birmingham Trades Council. This position led her into working on behalf of the Associated Bakers and Confectioners' Union to raise low wages and reduce working hours from 90 to 54 hours a week. She also campaigned with the small chainworkers to ensure that employers could not evade the provisions of the Trades Boards Act. She worked to establish the Workers Union (WU) in the

Birmingham area and, following a whole range of committee work on the Trades Council, she became the Women's Officer of the WU for Birmingham and continued her campaigning work. She was the only woman organizer for the WU during the crucial early months of the First World War and continued to organize women throughout the war despite ill health. She also served on various advisory committees during the war. After the war she continued to work for the WU and was on the council of the Industrial Welfare Society as well as serving on various advisory committees. In 1929, she became the women's organizer of the Transport and General Workers' Union, which had merged with the Workers Union, until her retirement in 1936.

ᴓ

Notes

1 Introduction

1 S. Rowbotham *Hidden From History: Three Hundred Years of Women's Oppression* London, Pluto 1973.

2 Useful texts which deal with the earlier period include D. Valenze *The First Industrial Woman* Oxford, Oxford University Press 1995; P. Sharpe (ed.) *Women's Work: The English Experience, 1650–1914* London, Arnold 1998; K. Honeyman *Women, Gender and Industrialisation in England, 1700–1870* Basingstoke, Macmillan 2000; and in a wider European context, D. Simonton *A History of European Women's Work, 1700 to the Present* London, Routledge 1998.

3 For women's work in coal mining, see A. V. John *By the Sweat of Their Brow: Women Workers at Victorian Coal Mines* London, Routledge Kegan Paul 1984.

4 A useful introduction to 'The Woman Question' can be found in C. Bolt *Feminist Ferment: 'The Woman Question' in the USA and England, 1870–1940* London, UCL Press 1995.

5 See Sharpe, op. cit., Section 1 'Debating Women's Work' which discusses this debate comprehensively.

6 For examples of earlier periods, see A. Clark *Working Life of Women in the Seventeenth Century London* Routledge and Kegan Paul 1982 edn; L. Charles and L. Duffin (eds) *Women and Work in Pre-Industrial England* Kent, Croom Helm 1985 and the work of B. Hill, especially *Women, Work and Sexual Politics in Eighteenth Century England* Oxford, Blackwell 1985.

7 See in particular C. Hall *White, Male and Middle-class: Explorations in Feminism and History* Cambridge, Polity Press 1992, Part II 'Gender and Class'.

8 A. Vickery, 'Golden Age to Separate Spheres? A Review of the Categories and Chronology of English Women's History', *The Historical Journal*, 36, 2 1993 383–414.

9 For unpaid work, see L. Davidoff and C. Hall *Family Fortunes: Men and Women of the Middle Class, 1780–1850* London, Routledge 1987, but see also Vickery's critique of the text op. cit., and J. Gerard *Country House Life: Family and Servants, 1815–1914* Oxford, Blackwell 1994; P. Branca *Silent Sisterhood: Middle-class Women in the Victorian Home* London, Croom Helm 1977.

10 J. D. Milne *The Industrial and Social Position of Women* 1857, 1870 edn quoted in P. Hollis Women in *Public: Documents of the Victorian Women's Movement* London, George Allen and Unwin 1979 p. 60.

11 P. Horn *The Rise and Fall of the Victorian Servant* Dublin, Gill and Macmillan 1975. See Appendix A for the range of wage rates for different levels of domestic service throughout the nineteenth century.

12 For an example of a fairly typical employment life history for a domestic servant in the mid-nineteenth century, see Liz Stanley (ed.) *The Diaries of Hannah Culwick, Victorian Maidservant* London,Virago 1984.

13 Horn op. cit., chapter 2 discusses the problem of obtaining and keeping servants.

14 For the relationship between mistresses and servants and the implications that this had for wider class relationships between women, see A. Summers 'A Home from Home: Women's Philanthropic Work in the Nineteenth Century' in S. Burman (ed.) *Fit Work for Women*, London, Croom Helm 1979 pp. 33–63.

15 Horn op. cit., p. 17.

16 E. Roberts *Women's Work, 1840–1940*, Cambridge, Cambridge University Press 1988 p. 2.

17 For an in-depth discussion of the problems women faced if they needed to work for money, see E. Jordan *The Women's Movement and Women's Employment in Nineteenth Century Britain* London, Routledge 1999, chapter 2 'The Constraints of Gentility', pp. 23–41.

18 J. Rendall *Women in an Industrializing Society: England, 1750–1880* Oxford, Blackwell 1990, especially chapter 2.

19 See for example, R. Gray 'Factory legislation and the Gendering of Jobs in the North of England, 1830–1860', *Gender and History*, 5, 1 Spring 1993 56–80.

20 See G. Braybon *Women Workers in the First World War* London, Routledge 1981; D. Beddoe *Back to Home and Duty: Women between the Wars, 1918–1939* London, Pandora 1989 and P. Summerfield *Women Workers in the Second World War: Production and Patriarchy in Conflict* London, Croom Helm 1984 for this discussion.

21 For an example of this, see E. Jordan 'The Lady Clerks at the Prudential: The Beginning of Vertical Segregation by Sex in Clerical Work in Nineteenth Century Britain', *Gender and History*, 8, 1 April 1996 65–81.

22 For an overview of working-class girls' and women's education, see J. McDermid 'Women and Education' in J. Purvis (ed.) *Women's History: Britain, 1850–1945* London, UCL Press 1995 and J. Purvis *A History of Women's Education in England* Milton Keynes, Open University 1991.

23 Davidoff and Hall op. cit., analyses how women contributed to the middle-class family economy.

24 For the history of women's education, see M. Bryant *The Unexpected Revolution: A Study in Development of Women and Girls' Education in the Nineteenth Century* London, University of London, Institute of Education 1979; Felicity Hunt (ed.) *Lessons for Life: The Schooling of Girls and Women* Oxford, Blackwell 1987 and Purvis 1991 op. cit.

25 For an in-depth discussion of this theory, see H. Hartmann 'Capitalism, patriarchy and job segregation by sex' in Z. Eisentein (ed.) *Capitalist Patriarchy* New York, Monthly Review Press 1979.

26 S. Walby *Theorizing Patriarchy* (Oxford, Basil Blackwell 1990, especially the introduction and chapter 2.

27 S. Walby *Patriarchy at Work: Patriarchal and Capitalist Relations in Employment* Cambridge, Polity 1986 p. 2.

28 See, for example, J. Lown *Women and Industrialization: Gender at Work in Nineteenth Century England* Cambridge, Polity Press 1990; C. Cockburn *In the Way of Women: Men's Resistance to Sex Equality in Organizations* London, Macmillan 1991; S. O. Rose *Limited Livelihood: Gender and Class in Nineteenth Century England* London, Routledge 1992.

29 Beddoe op. cit.

30 C. Steedman *Landscape for a Good Woman* London, Virago 1985.

31 S. Bruley *Women in Britain since 1900* London, Macmillan 1999.

Part One 1840–70

1 For a useful local study which illustrates the complexity of studying working-class women's waged work, see S. Alexander 'Women's Work in Nineteenth Century London: A Study of the Years 1820–1860' in S. Alexander (ed.) *Becoming a Woman and Other Essays in 19th and 20th Century Feminist History* London, Virago 1976, 1994. For an indication of the range of work that working-class women undertook, see Sharpe (ed.) *Women's Work: the English Experience, 1650–1914* Basingstoke, Macmillan 1998 and S. Pennington and B. Westover *A Hidden Workforce: Homeworkers in England, 1850–1985* London, Macmillan 1989.

2 'Fit work for women' working-class women and paid work in the mid-nineteenth century

2 This is the title of a very useful book: S. Burman (ed.) *Fit Work for Women* London, Croom Helm 1979.

3 Although see A. Vickery 'Golden Age to Separate Spheres? A Review of the Categories and Chronology of English Women's History', *The Historical Journal*, 36, 2 1993 383–414 for a discussion of how the golden age view of pre-nineteenth-century history needs to be treated with caution.

4 For a discussion of the uneven development of industrialization, see P. Sharpe 'Continuity and Change: Women's History and Economic History in Britain', *Economic History Review*, 48, 1995 and K. Honeyman *Women, Gender and Industrialisation in England, 1700–1870* Basingstoke, Macmillan 2000 pp. 10–14.

5 I. Pinchbeck *Women Workers and the Industrial Revolution, 1750–1850* London, Virago 1931, 1981 discusses this in depth, part 2. But also see Vickery op. cit., 401–12.

6 Although there was an increase in girls' apprenticeships in domestic work during the eighteenth century, see Honeyman op. cit., p. 26.

7 S. Walby *Patriarchy at Work: Patriarchal and Capitalist relations in Employment* Cambridge, Polity Press 1986 p. 92.

8 For an example, see case study at Courtaulds in J. Lown *Women and Industrialization: Gender at Work in Nineteenth Century England* Cambridge, Polity Press 1990.

9 For discussions on the representations of working women in Royal Commissions, see S. Hamilton 'Images of Femininity in the Royal Commissions of the 1830s and 1840s' in E. Janes Yeo (ed.) *Radical Femininity: Women's Self-representation in the Public Sphere* Manchester, Manchester University Press 1998 pp. 79–105; A. V. John *By the Sweat of Their Brow: Women Workers at Victorian Coal Mines* London, Routledge Kegan Paul 1984 and K. Sayer *Women of the Fields: Representations of Rural Women in the Nineteenth Century* Manchester, Manchester University Press 1995. See also D. Valenze *The First Industrial Woman* Oxford,

Oxford University Press 1995 for a discussion of how women were increasingly regarded in contemporary debates as victims of industrialization rather than workers in their own right in the early nineteenth century.

10 S. Walby *Patriarchy at Work: Patriarchal and Capitalist Relations in Employment* Cambridge, Polity 1986 p. 100.

11 Sayer op. cit., p. 75 and John op. cit., pp. 51–5.

12 P. Hollis *Women in Public: Documents of the Victorian Women's Movement* London, George Allen and Unwin 1979 p. 53 and E. Roberts *Women's Work, 1840–1940*, Cambridge, Cambridge University Press, 1988 p. 19.

13 E. Higgs 'Women's Occupations and Work in the Nineteenth Century Censuses', *History Workshop Journal* 23 1987.

14 P. Horn *The Rise and Fall of the Victorian Servant* Dublin, Gill and Macmillan 1975.

15 E. Higgs 'Domestic Service and Household Production' in A. V. John (ed.) *Unequal Opportunities: Women's Employment in England, 1800–1918* Oxford, Blackwell 1986 125–50. See also Higgs op. cit., 71.

16 There have been some works on domestic service beyond those already mentioned, e.g. T. McBride *The Domestic Revolution: The Modernisation of Household Service in England and France, 1820–1920* London, Croom Helm 1976 and J. Gerard *Country House Life: Family and Servants, 1815–1914* Oxford, Blackwell 1994. However, there is plenty of scope for more research given the numbers of women involved in this sector.

17 G. Lerner, *The Majority Finds Its Past: Placing Women in History*, Oxford, Oxford University Press 1979.

18 A useful book to consult before embarking on a local study is D. Beddoe *Discovering Women's History: A Practical Guide to the Sources of Women's History, 1800–1945* London, Longman, 1998. Chapter 1 is entitled 'Doing a research project: writing a dissertation'.

19 Honeyman op. cit., p. 77.

20 See P. Horn *The Rise and Fall of the Victorian Servant* Dublin, Gill and Macmillan 1975, especially chapter 7. See also L. Davidoff 'Mastered for Life: Servant and Wife in Victorian and Edwardian England' in L. Davidoff (ed.) *Worlds Between: Historical Perspectives on Gender and Class* Cambridge, Polity Press 1995 pp. 18–40 for an exploration of the relationship between employer and servant.

21 For example, as previously mentioned, pit brow women spurned domestic service as alternative employment during the campaigns to exclude women from pit brow work. See John op. cit., pp. 51–5.

22 C. Black 'The Dislike of Domestic Service' *Nineteenth Century* March 1893, quoted in J. Horowitz Murray (ed.) *Strong-minded Women and Other Lost Voices from Nineteenth Century England* Harmondsworth, Penguin 1982 pp. 338–9.

23 However, in many rural areas it was the only work available. Young Welsh women, in particular, were regarded as good servant material. See A. V. John (ed.) *Our Mother's Land: Chapters in Welsh Women's History, 1830–1939* Cardiff, University of Wales Press 1991. See also Horn op. cit., chapter 7; Roberts op. cit., p. 21 and Higgs op. cit., 145–6.

24 Patricia E. Malcolmson *English Laundresses, A Social History, 1850–1930* Illinois, University of Illinois Press 1986 p. 7.

25 Malcolmson op. cit., p. 8.

26 Malcolmson ibid.

27 Hollis op. cit., p. 46.

28 Alexander op. cit., p. 28.

29 For more on the variations in the tailoring trade see J. Morris 'The Characteristics of Sweating: The Late Nineteenth-Century London and Leeds Tailoring Trade' in John op. cit., 1986, pp. 96–121; D. Bythell *The Sweated Trades* London, Batsford 1978; J. Smeichen *Sweated Industries and Sweated Labour* London, Croom Helm and Alexander 1976.

30 Pennington and Westover op. cit., pp. 20–1.

31 Henry Mayhew's interviews with young needlewomen suggest that prostitution was often the other work these women engaged in. H. Mayhew *London Labour and the London Poor* London, Griffin Behn 1861.

32 John op. cit., p. 11.

33 For a discussion of how men's work was seen as skilled and women's unskilled, see A. Phillips and B. Taylor 'Sex and Skill: Notes towards a Feminist Economics', *Feminist Review*, 6 1980.

34 Pennington and Westover op. cit., p. 34.

35 Alexander op. cit., 33–8 and Pennington and Westover op. cit., chapter 4 discuss other types of home work carried out by women, some of it skilled and comparatively well paid.

36 H. Rogers '"The Good are not Always Powerful, nor the Powerful Always Good": The Politics of Women's Work in the London Needle Trades, 1841–1864', *Women's History Notebooks*, 1 1994 3–25. Also published as '"The Good are not Always Powerful, nor the Powerful Always Good": The Politics of Women's Needlework in Mid-Victorian London', *Victorian Studies*, 40 1997 589–623.

37 H. Mayhew 'Labour and the Poor, *Morning Chronicle* November 9, 1849 quoted in Horowitz Murray op. cit., 352–6.

38 *Punch* December 1843, quoted in Horowitz Murray op. cit., 351–2.

39 Rogers op. cit., p. 5.

40 Rogers ibid., p. 7.

41 See also Walby op. cit., who argues that protective legislation can be seen as patriarchal rather than reformist, p. 101.

42 Pennington and Westover op. cit., p. 45.

43 I. Pinchbeck op. cit., appendix.

44 Pennington and Westover op. cit., p. 46.

45 Pennington and Westover ibid., p. 45.

46 Pennington and Westover ibid., p. 44.

47 Hollis op. cit., p. 53.

48 Walby op. cit., p. 98.

49 See P. Hudson *The Industrial Revolution* London, Edward Arnold 1992 for a discussion of the gendered nature of skill in this context.

50 S. Horrell and J. Humphries 'Women's Labour Force Participation and the Transition to the Male Breadwinner Family, 1790–1860' in Sharpe (ed.) op. cit., 172–206. The concept of the male breadwinner is discussed in more detail in Part Two.

51 See J. Lown op. cit., for an in-depth discussion of the gender relations in factory work. Also S. O. Rose *Limited Livelihood: Gender and Class in Nineteenth Century England* London, Routledge 1992, which has a good analysis of the concept of gender and examines home-based as well as factory-based manufacture.

52 For a discussion of how women responded to these issues, see C. E. Morgan 'Women, Work, and Consciousness in Mid-nineteenth-century English Cotton Industry', *Social History*, 17 1992 23–41 and Walby op. cit., pp. 109–26.

53 Pinchbeck op. cit., p. 194.

54 Pinchbeck ibid., p. 187.

55 Walby op. cit., pp. 110–11.

56 Honeyman op. cit., p. 129.

57 For a detailed discussion of the industrialization process, see J. Rendall *Women in an Industrializing Society: England 1750–1880* Oxford, Basil Blackwell 1990 and Honeyman op. cit.

58 Pennington and Westover op. cit., chapter 3.

59 Walby op. cit., p. 97.

60 Hollis op. cit., p. 46. For a discussion of women's reactions to the Acts in a particular industry, see C. E. Morgan op. cit.

61 R. Gray 'Factory legislation and the Gendering of Jobs in the North of England, 1830–1860', *Gender and History*, 5, 1 Spring 1993 56–80.

62 Lord Shaftesbury's Speech on the Ten Hours Factory Bill, House of Commons, *Hansard*, 15 March 1844, quoted in Hollis op. cit., Gray op. cit., 76–7.

63 For a discussion of sexual harassment in factories, see J. Lambertz 'Sexual Harassment in the Nineteenth Century English Cotton Industry', *History Workshop Journal*, 19 1985 29–61.

64 For analyses of the language of the Royal Commissions and the language of reform, see Hamilton op. cit., 79–105 and R. Gray 'The Language of Factory Reform' in P. Joyce (ed.) *The Historical Meanings of Work* Cambridge, Cambridge University Press 1987.

65 Horn op. cit., p. 148.

66 See Higgs who suggests that, in total, that the number of agricultural workers should be increased by around one third. Edward Higgs 'Occupational Censuses and the Agricultural Workforce in Victorian England and Wales', *Economic History Review*, 48 1995 700–2.

67 Dairy work was often the unpaid labour of the farmer's wife although she was often assisted by paid female labour. See Sayer op. cit., p. 6.

68 For more details of the gang system, see Pinchbeck (op. cit., pp. 86–90 and Sayer op. cit., chapters 2, 4 and 5. The 1867 Report has accounts of workers which give a vivid impression of the work and conditions but also see the account of Mrs Burrows 'A Childhood in the Fens about 1850–1860' in M. Llewellyn Davies (ed.) *Life As We Have Known It* London, Virago 1931 109–14.

69 Sayer op. cit., pp. 44–6 and K. Sayer 'Field-faring Women: the Resistance of Women who Worked in the Fields of Nineteenth-Century England', *Women's History Review* 2 1993. For bondaging in Scotland, see B. W. Robertson 'In Bondage: The Female Farm Worker in South-East Scotland' in E. Gordon and E. Breitenbach (eds) *The World is Ill-Divided: Women's Work in Scotland in the Nineteenth and Twentieth Centuries* Edinburgh, Edinburgh University Press 1990 117–19.

70 *Sixth Report of Children's Employment Commission*, PP 1867 XVI pp. 83–4, quoted in Beddoe op. cit., p. 107.

71 *First Report of Commission on Children's, Young Person's and Women's Employment in Agriculture*, PP 1867–8 XVI pp. 53–4, quoted in Beddoe ibid., p. 108.

72 See K. D. M. Snell *Annals of the Labouring Poor: Social Change and Agrarian England, 1600–1900* Cambridge, Cambridge University Press 1985, especially chapter 1 for a discussion of women's declining participation in agricultural work.

73 See Pennington and Westover op. cit., especially chapter 4; P. Horn *Victorian Countrywomen* Oxford, Basil Blackwell 1991, which also outlines a wide range of

work undertaken by countrywomen of all classes, and Pinchbeck op. cit., chapter IV which discusses agricultural employment and conditions in this period in great detail.

74 For a discussion of how representations of countrywomen draw on discourses of femininity, class and national identity, see Sayer op. cit., passim.

75 See for example PP 1867–70, XVII op. cit., p. 198.

76 Sayer op. cit., pp. 92–3.

77 The best text for the study of women working in mines is John op. cit.

78 John ibid., p. 38.

79 'Report by S. S. Scriven (on part of the West Riding of Yorkshire), Children's Employment Commission', *First Report of the Commissioners. Mines*, Appendix, pt II, *British Parliamentary Papers* 1842 XVII p. 75 quoted in Hamilton op. cit, 87.

80 Hamilton op. cit., 88–9.

81 Quoted in Walby op. cit., p. 118.

82 John op. cit., pp. 52–60.

3 The problem of the 'superfluous women'

1 'Queen Bees or Working Bees', *Saturday Review*, 12 November 1859, quoted in P. Hollis *Women in Public: Documents of the Victorian Women's Movement* London, George Allen and Unwin 1979 p. 11.

2 For the range of work undertaken by middle-class women, see L. Holcombe *Victorian Ladies at Work: Middle-class Working Women in England and Wales 1850–1914* Newton Abbot, David & Charles 1973.

3 There are examples of women living by their writing, e.g. Mrs Oliphant and Harriet Martineau, but they would be women of exceptional talent rather than ordinary women, especially given the quality of most women's education.

4 For example, a recent useful regional study is H. Wojtczak *Women of Victorian Sussex* Hastings, Hastings Press 2003 which, for example, shows that around 40 per cent of all shops in Sussex listed a woman as the proprietor, p. 59.

5 For women working in family enterprises, see C. Hall *White, Male and Middle-class: Explorations in Feminism and History* Cambridge, Polity Press 1992; and see L. Davidoff and C. Hall *Family Fortunes: Men and Women of the Middle Class, 1780–1850* London, Routledge 1987 and K. Gleadle *British Women in the Nineteenth Century* Basingstoke, Palgrave 2001 pp. 56–63. See also the work of the Courtauld women in factory welfare in J. Lown *Women and Industrialization: Gender at Work in Nineteenth Century* England Cambridge, Polity Press 1990. For a Welsh example, see A. V. John 'Beyond Paternalism: The Ironmaster's Wife in the Industrial Community' in A. V. John (ed.) *Our Mother's Land: Chapters in Welsh Women's History* Cardiff, University of Wales Press 1991. Women working in shops will be dealt with in Part Two.

6 Horowitz Murray op. cit., p. 48. See also M. Vicinus *Independent Women: Work and Community for Single Women, 1850–1920* London, Virago 1985, chapter 1 'The Revolt against Redundancy'.

7 W. R. Greg 'Why are Women Redundant?' *National Review*, April 1862, quoted in Horowitz Murray op. cit., p. 51.

8 For an account of middle-class women's emigration, see A. J. Hammerton *Emigrant Gentlewomen: Genteel Poverty and Female Emigration* London, Croom Helm 1979.

9 One of the best accounts of the role of the governess is K. Hughes *The Victorian Governess* London, Hambledon Press 1993.

10 W. Neff *Victorian Working Women* New York, AMS Press 1966 p. 153.

11 K. Hughes op. cit., discusses the governess in the novel.

12 Neff op. cit., pp. 158–9.

13 Vicinus op. cit., p. 23.

14 'The Governess Question', *English Woman's Journal*, November 1860, quoted in Hollis op. cit., p. 90.

15 J. Purvis *A History of Women's Education in England* Milton Keynes, Open University Press 1991.

16 The most useful text on teaching training in the elementary school sector and the class dynamics of this sector is F. Widdowson *Going up into the Next Class: Women and Elementary Teacher Training 1840–1914* London, Hutchinson 1983.

17 Widdowson op. cit., p. 15. For debate around the dangers of too much intellectual work for middle-class girls in the context of higher education, see Hollis op. cit., section 4.3 pp. 142–6.

18 A. Burdett-Coutts letter to the *English Journal of Education*, April 1858, quoted in Hollis op. cit., p. 91.

19 *English Journal of Education*, April 1858, quoted in Hollis op. cit., pp. 91–2.

20 Hollis op. cit., pp. 92–3.

21 Widdowson op. cit., p. 18.

22 For the writings of the Langham Place Group, see C. Lacey (ed.) *Barbara Leigh Smith Bodichon and the Langham Place Group* London, Routledge Kegan Paul 1987.

23 For a useful biography of Barbara Leigh Smith, see P. Hirsch *Barbara Leigh Smith Bodichon: Feminist, Artist, Rebel* London, Pimlico 1999. For a discussion of the political work of the Langham Place Group, see B. Caine *English Feminism, 1780–1980* Oxford, Oxford University Press 1997 pp. 93–115.

24 Barbara Leigh Smith 'Women and Work' 1857 in Lacey op. cit., pp. 38, 41 and 61.

25 A useful account of SPEW can be found in E. Jordan *The Women's Movement and Women's Employment in Nineteenth Century Britain* London, Routledge 1999, pp. 170–97. For an examination of the role of women in NAPSS, see E. Janes Yeo Social Motherhood and the Sexual Communion of Labour in British Social Science, 1850–1950', *Women's History Review*, 1, 1 1992 63–87.

26 See 'Twentieth Anniversary of the Foundation of the Society for Promoting the Employment of Women', *Englishwoman's Review*, 10 July 1879 291.

27 P. Levine *Victorian Feminism 1850–1900* London, Hutchinson 1987 p. 87.

28 See B. Rayner Parkes 'A Year's Experience in Women's Work', *English Woman's Journal*, 6 November 1860 115.

29 C. Cockburn *Brothers: Male Dominance and Technological Change* London, Pluto 1983 pp. 152–9.

30 'Twentieth Anniversary of the Foundation of the Society for Promoting the Employment of Women', *Englishwoman's Review*, 9 August 1882 377; for a study of the development of women as clerical workers, see M. Zimmeck 'Jobs for the Girls: The Expansion of Clerical Work for Women, 1850–1914' in A. V. John (ed.) *Unequal Opportunities: Women's Employment in England, 1800–1918* Oxford, Blackwell 1986 pp. 153–77.

31 'Report of the Society for Promoting the Employment of Women', *English Woman's Journal*, 9 August 1862 377.

32 For an account of women and the print trade in London, see F. Hunt Opportunities

Lost and Gained: Mechanization and Women's Work in the London Bookbinding and Printing Trades in John op. cit., pp. 70–93. For Scotland, see Sian Reynolds *Britannica's Typesetters: Women Compositors in Edwardian Edinburgh* Edinburgh University Press 1989 and Cockburn op. cit.

33 For a full account of the Victoria Press, see W. E. Fredeman 'Emily Faithfull and the Victoria Press: An Experiment in Sociological Bibliography', *The Library*, June, xxix, 1974.

34 These women must have come from outside London as the all-male London Society of Compositors had a stranglehold on the trade. See John op. cit., pp. 77–8.

35 John op. cit., p. 79.

36 [Matilda Hays], 'A Ramble with Mrs. Grundy – A Visit to the Victoria Printing Press', *English Woman's Journal*, 5 June 1860 271; 'Victoria Press', *English Woman's Journal*, 6 October 1860 122.

37 Fredeman op. cit., p. 149.

38 Cockburn op. cit., p. 203.

39 John op. cit., pp. 72–82.

40 E. Faithfull *Three Visits to America* Edinburgh, 1884 pp. 24–5.

41 S. Walby *Patriarchy at Work: Patriarchal and Capitalist relations in Employment* Cambridge, Polity Press 1986 Appendix I.

42 For an analysis of working-class male attitudes to women workers in the 1830s, see B. Taylor, '"The Men Are as Bad as Their Masters. . .": Socialism, Feminism and Sexual Antagonism in the London Tailoring Trade in the 1830s', *Feminist Studies*, 5, 1 1979.

43 Jordan op. cit., pp. 184–93.

44 See *Englishwoman's Review*, October 1866 12–26 for a discussion of the servant problem.

45 For a discussion of the debate around domestic work in the early twentieth century, see Carol Dyhouse *Feminism and the Family, 1880–1939* Oxford, Blackwell 1989, chapter 4.

46 For example, *Englishwoman's Review*, April 1867 30–1. SPEW offered to pay the premium for girls to become apprentice dressmakers, an area of women's work under threat by skilled men. There was an appeal to wealthy women to subscribe to a fund to make this possible.

47 For a discussion of the extent to which women's work and ladies' work was redefined in the latter part of the nineteenth century, see Jordan op. cit., part IV.

48 See K. Sayer *Women of the Fields: Representations of Rural Women in the Nineteenth Century* Manchester, Manchester University Press 1995 for a full discussion of this language.

49 'Employment of Women in Agriculture', *Englishwoman's Review*, 1869 155–76.

50 Ibid.

51 'SPEW Annual Report', *Englishwoman's Review*, 1879 295.

52 Holcombe op. cit., p. 18 and Levine op. cit., p. 100.

53 Jordan op. cit., pp. 184–5.

54 Sylvia Walby op. cit., see chapter 5.

Part Two 1870–1914

1 An Old Oriental, 'The woman at work', *Englishwoman's Review*, 35 1904 pp. 151–2, quoted in David Rubenstein *Before the Suffragettes: Women's Emancipation in the 1890s* Brighton, Harvester Press 1986 pp. 72–3.

2 There were several local studies carried out in this period, which are useful in gaining a picture of the extent and type of women's employment. They include C. Booth *Life and Labour of the People of London* London, Macmillan 1905; E. Cadbury, M. C. Matheson and G. Shann *Women's Work and Wages: A Phase of Life in an Industrial City* London, Fisher Unwin 1906; C. Black, (ed.) *Married Women's Work Being the Report of an Inquiry by the Women's Industrial Council* London, G. Bell 1915, reprinted London, Virago 1983. See also B. L. Hutchins *Women's Wages in England in the Nineteenth Century* London, G. Bell 1908.

3 E. Roberts *Women's Work, 1840–1940*, Cambridge, Cambridge University Press 1988 p. 22.

4 L. Holcombe *Victorian Ladies at Work: Middle-class Working Women in England and Wales 1850–1914* Newton Abbot, David and Charles 1973 p. 216.

5 Rubenstein op. cit., p. 70.

6 Research needs to be done on women researchers such as Clara Collet who began her work as a researcher with Charles Booth, served on the Royal Commission on Labour and then joined the Board of Trade; see B. Harrison *'Not only the Dangerous Trades': Women's Work and Health in Britain, 1880–1914* London, Taylor & Francis 1996 p. 205.

7 Clara Collet 'Report by Miss Colett on the statistics of employment of women and girls in England and Wales', *Bulletin of the Department of Labour*, 1 November 1895–6, 1 1896.

8 Catherine Hakim *Occupational Segregation: A Comparative Study of the Degree and Pattern of Differentiation between Men and Women's Work in Britain, the United States and other Countries* London, Research Paper No. 9, Department of Employment 1979.

9 Holcombe op. cit., p. 217.

10 Collet op. cit.

11 Ellen Jordan 'Female Unemployment in England and Wales: 1851–1911: An Examination of the Census Figures for 15–19 Year Olds' *Social History*, 13 1988 175–90.

12 Although shop and clerical work was not restricted to the middle classes, for example, aspirant upper working-class girls also worked in shops and offices. For an example of young upper working-class women's lives in this period, see T. Thompson (ed.) *Dear Girl: The Diaries of Two Working Women 1897–1917* London, The Women's Press 1987.

4 Women organizing: trade unions and other industrial organizations

13 See C. E. Morgan 'Women, Work and Consciousness in the Mid Nineteenth Century English Cotton Industry', *Social History* 17 1992. See also A. Clarke *The Struggle for the Breeches: Gender and the Making of the British Working-Class* London, Rivers Oram 1995 pp. 239–41 and M. Bottomley 'Women and Industrial Militancy' in J. A. Jowitt and A. J. McIvor (eds) *Employers and Labour in the English Textile Industries* London, Routledge 1988.

14 E. Paterson 'The Position of Working Women and How to Improve It', *Labour News* June 1874, also reproduced in H. Goldman *Emma Paterson* Lawrence & Wishart 1974.

15 For biographical details of Emma Paterson, see Goldman op. cit., and J. Bellamy and J. Schmiechen 'Emma Anne Paterson (1848–1886) Trade Unionist and Feminist' in *Dictionary of Labour Biography* vol. IV Macmillan 1977 167–70.

16 Paterson op. cit.

17 Paterson ibid.

18 Paterson ibid.

19 A general union was established in Bristol. However, a women's national general union was not achieved until 1906 when Mary Macarthur established the National Federation of Women Workers. See B. Drake *Women in Trade Unions* London, Labour Research Department 1920 p. 12.

20 See R. Fuerer 'The Meaning of "Sisterhood": The British Women's Movement and Protective Labour Legislation, 1870–1900', *Victorian Studies* 31, 2 Winter 1988 240, who argues that the WPPL reflected feminist-philanthropic biases.

21 E. Paterson 'The Industrial Position of Women engaged in Handicrafts and other Industrial Pursuits' *Englishwoman's Review* January XXI (NS) 1875 3.

22 Paterson op. cit., 4–5.

23 However, it was one of the successes of the WPPL that they were eventually allowed to represent working women at the Trades Union Congress.

24 For a discussion of women's reluctance to join unions because they could not perceive any personal benefits, see J. Bornat '"What About That Lass of Yours Being in the Union": Textile Workers and Their Union in Yorkshire, 1888–1922' in Leonore Davidoff and Belinda Westover (eds) *Our Work, Our Lives, Our Worlds* Basingstoke, Macmillan 1986.

25 For further discussion of why women were difficult to organize, see P. Levine *Victorian Feminism 1850–1900* London, Hutchinson 1987; S. Lewenhak *Women in Trade Unions* London, Ernest Benn 1977; J. Bornat 'Lost Leaders: Women's Trade Unionism and the Case of the General Union of Textile Workers 1875–1914' and D. Thom 'The Bundle of Sticks: Women Trade Unionists and Collective Organization before 1918' both in A. V. John (ed.) *Unequal Opportunities: Women's Employment in England, 1800–1918* Oxford, Blackwell 1986.

26 K. A. Mackenzie *Edith Simcox and George Eliot* Oxford, Oxford University Press 1961.

27 For an account of this struggle, see *Women's Union Journal* October 1886; C. Tsukuki *The Life of Eleanor Marx* Oxford, Oxford University Press 1967 p. 61. For an argument that centres on the protective legislation debate as crucial to this struggle, see Fuerer op. cit.

28 M. Cameron 'Clementina Black: A Character Sketch', *Young Woman* 1 June 1892 315–16 and F. E. Willard 'Questions of the Day: An Interview with Clementina Black' *Women's Signal* IV, 87, 29 August 1895.

29 See Barbara Caine *Victorian Feminists* Oxford, Oxford University Press 1992 pp. 224–5 for a discussion of Millicent Fawcett and Josephine Butler's distaste of trade unions although they both supported the WPPL.

30 *Women's Union Journal* July 1888 and WPPL *Annual Report* 1889 5. Also Edith Simcox represented the Matchworkers Union at the International Trades Union Congress in London in November 1888. A. H. Nethercott *The First Five Lives of Annie Besant* London, Hart Davies 1961 pp. 269–75.

31 WTUL *Twentieth Annual Report* 1895.

32 Drake op. cit., p. 30 and Table I.

33 WTUL *Twenty-Sixth Annual Report* 1899.

34 A. Bulley and A. Whiteley *Woman's Work* London, Methuen 1894 pp. 81–2.

35 For a discussion of this, see Thom's article in John op. cit., 261–89.

36 *Women's Union Journal* October 1886.

37 See Rubinstein op. cit., p. 125.

38 *Women's Trade Union Review* October 1896.

39 J. Liddington and J. Norris *One Hand Tied Behind Us: The Rise of the Women's Suffrage Movement* London, Virago, 1978 p. 98.

40 O. Banks *Becoming A Feminist: The Social Origins of 'First Wave' Feminism* Brighton, Harvester 1986. For a study of women involved in British Socialism during this period, see J. Hannam and K. Hunt *Socialist Women, Britain, 1880s to 1920s* London, Routledge 2002.

41 For a definition of social feminism, see O. Banks *Faces of Feminism: A Study of Feminism as a Social Movement* Oxford, Martin Robertson 1981 pp. 80–4; and Mappen in John op. cit., p. 256, n. 1.

42 See Fabian Women's Group 'Three Years' Work, 1908–1911' in S. Alexander (ed.) *Women's Fabian Tracts* London, Routledge 1988 p. 153.

43 C. Black 'The Organization of Working Women' *Fortnightly Review* XLVI November 1889 704.

44 WTUA *First Annual Report* 1889–90 3–4 in E. Mappen *Helping Women at Work: the Women's Industrial Council 1889–1914* London, Hutchinson 1985. A similar organization had been set up earlier in Liverpool in January 1889 by the Liverpool Trades Union Council called the Women's Industrial Council of Liverpool and led by a wealthy London socialist, Mrs Mole. The most famous member of this organization was Eleanor Rathbone.

45 See, for example, C. Black 'Some Current objections to Factory Legislation for Women' in B. Webb (ed.) *The Case for the Factory Acts, 1802–1895* London, Grant Richards 1901 192–223 and J. Boucherett 'The Fall in Women's Wages', *Englishwoman's Review* April 1898 for the opposing arguments.

46 Ellen Mappen op. cit., p. 16.

47 WTUA *First Annual Report* 1889–90 in Mappen op. cit.

48 See C. Black, 'The Chocolate Makers' Strike', *Fortnightly Review* XLVII August 1890 305–14; also in Mappen op. cit., pp. 49–59 .

49 See T. Olcott 'Dead Centre: The Women's Trade Union Movement in London, 1874–1914' *The London Journal* 2 1976 for a discussion of why the attempts to organize London women failed. See also M. Llewellyn Davies (ed.) *Life As We Have Known It By Co-operative Working Women* London, Virago, reprinted 1984 39–40 for Mrs Layton's account of the difficulties working-class women had in getting to meetings.

50 WTUA *Fifth Annual Report* 1893–4 3.

51 Ibid.

52 Ibid., 4.

53 Ibid., 12–13.

54 Mappen op. cit., pp. 60–1.

55 L. Papworth-Wyatt 'The Women's Industrial Council: A Survey', *Women's Industrial News* 64 January 1914, p. 204.

56 The argument centres on the proposed incorporation of the WIC, which would increase the power of the executive committee. Amie Hicks and Lily Montagu of the CIA resigned from the WIC over this issue. See E. Mappen 'New Introduction' to C. Black *Married Women's Work* London, Virago 1983 p. viii.

57 For a discussion on WIC's use of its investigative work to promote girls' training, see J. Goodman 'Social Investigation and Economic Empowerment: The Women's Industrial Council and the LCC Trade Schools for Girls,1892–1914', *History of Education* 27, 3 1998.

58 Papworth-Wyatt op. cit., p. 204.

59 Ibid., p. 205.

60 WIC *First Annual Report*, 1894–5 3.

61 Papworth-Wyatt op. cit., p. 207.

62 C. Webb 'The Organization of Women Workers: Women's Industrial Council', in *Reformer's Yearbook* London 1902 62.

63 See Thompson (ed.) op. cit., Ruth Slate joined the WIC and was on its investigation committee for a while but found it impossible to combine full-time work as a post office clerk and domestic work at home with a commitment to social investigation. One would imagine that other working women would have found it equally difficult.

64 For the Fabian Women's Group see 'Introduction' to Alexander op. cit.; C. Dyhouse Feminism and the Family in England, 1880–1939 Oxford, Blackwell 1989 and S. Alexander's 'Introduction' to M. Pember Reeves *Round about a Pound a Week* London, Virago, reprinted 1979.

65 For a similar situation in the settlement movement, see M. Vicinus *Independent Women: Work and Community for Single Women, 1850–1920* London, Virago 1985 pp. 225–8.

66 Thom in John op. cit., p. 277.

67 Papworth-Wyatt op. cit., p. 210.

68 *Reformer's Yearbook* London 1902 62.

69 WTUL *Twenty-Ninth Annual Report* 1902.

70 *Reformer's Yearbook* London 1903 108.

71 The WPPL had sent middle-class women to the TUC but this had caused resentment so the WTUL revised its policy. See C. Tsukuki op. cit.

72 D. E. Martin 'Mary Macarthur (1880–1921) Trade Union Organiser' in *Dictionary of Labour Biography* op. cit., II 256. Drake op. cit. claims that by 1906 there were 118,000 women trade union members, over 80 per cent of them working in textiles, p. 30.

73 Martin op. cit., p. 255.

74 See Drake op. cit., Table I. See Thom in John op. cit., Table 9.1 'Trade Union Membership' 270. For her arguments on why trade unionism amongst women increased rapidly between these years see pp. 272–5; see also Olcott op. cit., pp. 46–8.

75 Thom in John op. cit., p. 268.

76 M. Macarthur in *Women in Industry from Seven Points of View* London, Duckworth 1908 73–5.

77 Martin op. cit., p. 256.

78 S. Boston *Women Workers and the Trade Unions* London, Davis Pointer 1980 p. 61.

79 Boston op. cit., p. 80.

80 For women teachers, see H. Keen *Deed not Words: The Lives of Suffragette Teachers* London, Pluto 1990.

81 Drake op. cit., pp. 46–8.

82 *Reformer's Yearbook* London 1909 194.

83 In particular, Margaret MacDonald opposed this policy favouring licensing of

homework. For a full discussion of this issue, see E. F. Mappen 'Strategists for Change: Social Feminist Approaches to the Problems of Women's Work' in John op. cit.

84 Thom in John op. cit., pp. 273–5.

85 Boston op. cit., pp. 65–7.

86 Ibid., p. 31.

87 Drake op. cit., p. 46; Thom in John op. cit., 277–8.

88 Thom in John op. cit., passim.

5 Equal or different? Divisive issues in the industrial women's movement

1 For the full history of the campaign to open Cambridge to women, see R. McWilliams Tullberg *Women at Cambridge*, Cambridge, Cambridge University Press 1975. For a clear outline of this debate, see chapter 4 and appendix A. See also F. Hunt 'Divided Aims: the Educational Implications of Opposing Ideologies in Girls' Secondary Schooling, 1850–1940' in Felicity Hunt (ed.) *Lessons for Life: The Schooling of Girls and Women* Oxford, Blackwell 1987 pp. 3–21.

2 For example, see F. Hunt 'Opportunities Lost and Gained: Mechanization and Women's Work in the London Bookbinding and Printing Trades' in A. V. John (ed.) *Unequal Opportunities: Women's Employment in England, 1800–1918* Oxford, Blackwell 1986 78, for the print trade.

3 S. Walby *Patriarchy at Work: Patriarchal and Capitalist Relations in Employment* Cambridge, Polity Press 1986 pp. 61–6.

4 *Englishwoman's Review* January 1875 37–9. In fact the Kidderminster Power Loom, Carpet Weaving and Textile Workers' Association did not let women join the union until 1917; see John op. cit., pp. 22–3 and Walby op. cit., appendix I.

5 For a useful discussion on how middle-class women gained agency through using their cultural capital to forward their cause, see in E. Jordan *The Women's Movement and Women's Employment in Nineteenth Century Britain* London, Routledge 1999 pp. 18–19. This is crucial to her argument throughout the book.

6 For examples see B. Drake *Women in Trade Unions* London, Labour Research Department 1920 and S. Boston *Women Workers and the Trade Unions* London, Davis Pointer 1980.

7 E. Roberts *Women's Work, 1840–1940*, Cambridge, Cambridge University Press, 1988 p. 50.

8 S. Walby *Theorizing Patriarchy* Oxford, Blackwell 1990 p. 111.

9 Many articles were written concerning different aspects of the lives of married working women. See '"Let the Women be Alive!" The Construction of the Married Working Woman in the Industrial Women's Movement, 1890–1914' in E. Janes Yeo (ed.) *Radical Femininity: Women's Self-representation in the Public Sphere* Manchester, Manchester University Press 1998 p. 191 n. 3 for examples.

10 For a discussion of this report, see A. A. Bulley 'The Lady Assistant Commissioners' Report', *Fortnightly Review* LV January 1894 39. See also E. F. S. Dilke 'Women and the Royal Commission' *Fortnightly Review* 50 1891.

11 For a comprehensive discussion of this issue, see A. Davin 'Imperialism and Motherhood', *History Workshop Journal* 5 Spring 1978 9–65.

12 C. Dyhouse, 'Working-class Mothers and Infant Mortality in England, 1895–1914' in C. Webster (ed.) *Biology, Medicine and Society, 1840–1940* Cambridge, Cambridge University Press 1981 p. 73.

13 Mrs Sumner 'The Responsibilities of Mothers' in A. Baroness Burdett-Coutts (ed.) *Woman's Mission* London, 1893 pp. 68–9.

14 M. Llewellyn Davies (ed.) *Life As We Have Known It by Co-operative Working Women* London, Virago 1931 p. 40 and J. Lewis 'The Working-Class Wife and Mother and State Intervention, 1870–1918' in J. Lewis (ed.) *Labour and Love: Women's Experience of Home and Family, 1850–1940* Oxford, Blackwell 1986 pp. 99–122.

15 Ada Nield Chew wrote a wonderful short story about the well-intentioned intrusion of the middle-class health visitor in the working-class home. See A. Nield Chew 'All in a Day's Work: Mrs Turpin' *Englishwoman* July 1912, reproduced in D. Nield Chew *Ada Nield Chew: The Life and Writings of a Working Woman* London, Virago 1982 pp. 152–60.

16 See, for example, Anna Martin 'The Married Working Woman', *Nineteenth Century* December 1910 and M. Pember Reeves *Round about a Pound a Week* London, Virago 1979.

17 B. Harrison *'Not only the Dangerous Trades': Women's Work and Health in Britain, 1880–1914* London, Taylor & Francis 1996 p. 84.

18 *Report of the Proceedings of the National Conference on Infantile Mortality . . . with Address by the Right Honourable John Burns, MP* London 1906; and *Report of the Proceedings of the Second National Conference on Infantile Mortality* Westminster 1908.

19 See Dyhouse op. cit., pp. 85/6 which states that in 1908, the Medical Officer of Health in Birmingham carried out an investigation that demonstrated that infant mortality was lower amongst working mothers than those who did not undertake paid work in the poorest wards.

20 Fabian Women's Group pamphlet 'Three Years Work of the Women's Group 1908–1911' in S. Alexander (ed.) *Women's Fabian Tracts* London, Routledge 1988 pp. 145–63. For a useful discussion on the economic independence of women in vis-à-vis their families, see C. Dyhouse *Feminism and the Family in England, 1880–1939* Oxford, Blackwell 1989 chapter 2. For a discussion of how the married working woman was represented in these debates at the time, see Holloway in Yeo op. cit., pp. 172–95.

21 For example, see M. Pember Reeves *Round about a Pound a Week*. London, Virago 1979.

22 Llewellyn Davies op. cit., introduction.

23 Martin op. cit., pp. 3, 10 and 43.

24 Ibid., pp. 40–1.

25 Ibid., p. 45.

26 For discussions concerning the concept of the family wage, see for example S. Horrell and J. Humphries 'Women's labour force participation and the transition to the male-breadwinner family, 1790–1865' in P. Sharpe (ed.) *Women's Work: The English Experience, 1650–1914* London, Arnold 1998; and J. Humphries 'Class Struggle and the Persistence of the Working-class Family', *Cambridge Journal of Economics* I 1977. Also M. Barrett and M. McIntosh 'The "Family Wage" – Some Problems for Socialists and Feminists', *Capital and Class* 2 1980 51–72 and 'The Family Wage', *Feminist Review* 6, 55–77. See also Walby op. cit., chapter 1 for a critique of the various arguments about the family wage.

27 H. Swanwick *The Future of the Women's Movement* London, Bell & Son 1913 pp. 86–7.

28 For detailed discussions on the endowment of motherhood question, see E. Rathbone *The Disinherited Family* London, Edward Arnold 1924; M. Stocks

Eleanor Rathbone: A Biography London, Victor Gollancz 1949; M. Stocks *My Commonplace Book* London, Davies 1970 pp. 120–2; H. Land 'Eleanor Rathbone and the Economy of the Family' in H. L. Smith *British Feminism in the Twentieth Century* Amherst, University Press of Massachusetts 1990 pp. 104–23; and Dyhouse op. cit., pp. 88–104.

29 M. A. (1914) in Alexander op. cit., pp. 278–9.

30 A. Nield Chew 'The Problem of the Married Working Woman' *Common Cause* 6 March 1914.

31 Ibid.

32 For a discussion of the debates that occurred at this time around Gilman's ideas concerning domestic work, see Dyhouse op. cit., chapter 3.

33 Barrett and McIntosh op. cit., pp. 51–72; see also Walby op. cit., especially pp. 104–8.

34 Rowan in Rowan and Brunt op. cit., p. 66.

35 M. Macarthur 'The Woman Trade-Unionists Point of View' in M. Phillips (ed.) *Women and the Labour Party* London, Headley Bros 1918 18.

36 Thom in John op. cit., pp. 282–3.

37 Mrs Player and Mrs J. R. MacDonald 'Wage-Earning Mothers', *The League Leaflet* 3, March 1911, p. 3.

38 Ibid., p. 2.

39 C. Black *A New Way of Housekeeping* London, Collins 1918.

40 *Sussex Daily News* 21 July 1908.

41 See, for example, M. Bondfield *A Life's Work* London, Hutchinson 1948 pp. 38–43.

42 The reasons for dissension in the WIC are discussed in Mappen's introduction to the Virago reprint of C. Black *Married Women's Work* London, Virago 1983 p. ix and in her essay in John op. cit.

43 Black op. cit., p. v.

44 Black ibid., pp. 2–7.

45 Black ibid., p. 14.

46 Chew op. cit.

47 A. Nield Chew 'The Mother-Interest and Child Training', *Common Cause* 6 March 1914 in Chew op. cit., pp. 248–55.

48 Although this was only partially caused by the impact of legislation, the numbers of women involved in agriculture dropped from 44,319 in 1851 to 24,150 in 1891 in England and Wales and from 26,151 to 22,046 in Scotland in the same period. Roberts op. cit., p. 34. A similar decrease can be seen among women working in the mining industry; see A. V. John *By the Sweat of their Brow: Women Workers at Victorian Coal Mines* London, Routledge Kegan Paul 1984 part III.

49 For details of homeworkers in England, see S. Pennington and B. Westover *A Hidden Workforce: Homeworkers in England, 1850–1985* Basingstoke, Macmillan 1989.

50 See studies mentioned in note 1 above and also Mappen op. cit. and J. Lewis *Women and Social Action in Victorian and Edwardian England* Stanford, Stanford University Press 1991 chapter 1 and Sally Alexander op. cit., especially introduction.

51 S. Hall and B. Schwarz 'State and Society, 1880–1930' in M. Langan and B. Schwarz (eds) *Crisis in the British State, 1880–1930* London, Hutchinson 1986 pp. 14–15.

52 For a discussion of the term 'social feminist', see Naomi Black *Social Feminism* Ithaca, Cornell University Press 1989, especially part I.

53 R. Fuerer 'The Meaning of "Sisterhood": The British Women's Movement and Protective Labour Legislation, 1870–1900', *Victorian Studies* 31, 2 Winter 1988.

54 Philippa Levine *Victorian Feminism, 1850–1900* Florida, University Press of Florida 1994 p. 119.

55 For information about the *Review*, see D. Doughan 'Periodicals by, for, and about Women in Britain', *Women's Studies International Forum* 10 (3) 1987 261–76 and J. Horowitz Murray and A. H. Clarke *The Englishwoman's Review of Social and Industrial Questions: An Index (with Introduction)* New York, Garland 1985.

56 For their case against legislation, see J. Boucherett and H. Blackburn *The Condition of Working Women and the Factory Acts* London, Grant Richard 1896 and for the pro response, see C. Black 'Some Current Objections to Factory Legislation for Women' in B. Webb (ed.) *The Case for the Factory Acts 1802–1895* London, Grant Richards 1901.

57 For this discussion, see A. V. John 1984, op. cit.; part III.

58 Ibid., p. 149.

59 Ray Strachey *The Cause: A Short History of the Women's Movement in Great Britain* London, Bell 1929 p. 238.

60 P. Levine *Feminist Lives in Victorian England: Private Roles and Public Commitment* Oxford, Blackwell 1990, p. 163.

61 For a discussion of male trade unionists', labour men's and co-operative men's attitudes towards women organizing and becoming active on their own behalf see, for example, John 1986, op. cit., pp. 71–94; Boston op. cit., chapter 11; C. Collette *For Labour and For Women: The Women's Labour League, 1906–1918* Manchester, Manchester University Press 1989 chapter 1; G. Scott *Feminism and the Politics of Working Women: The Women's Co-operative Guild, 1880s to the Second World War* London, UCL Press 1998 chapter 1 and Davies op. cit., p. 41.

62 For an example in agriculture, see K. Sayer *Women of the Fields: Representations of Rural Women in the Nineteenth Century* Manchester, Manchester University Press 1995 passim.

63 Evidence to the *Royal Commission on Factory and Workshops Acts* 1876 XXX q. 435.

64 Ibid., q. 435.

65 For examples of women objecting to legislation, see John 1984 op. cit., especially part III.

66 Black 1901 op. cit., pp. 192–3. The standard sources for the sweated labour debate are D. Bythell *The Sweated Trades* London, Batsford 1978; J. Schmiechen *Sweated Industries and Sweated Labour: The London Clothing Trades 1860–1914*, London, Croom Helm 1984 and J. Morris *Women Workers and the Sweated Trades* London, Gower 1986.

67 Mappen op. cit.

68 M. Drake McFeely *Lady Inspectors: The Campaign for a Better Workplace, 1893–1921* London, University of Georgia Press 1991 p. 12. For the work of the women factory inspectors, see also Harrison op. cit. and A. Anderson *Women in the Factory: An Administrative Adventure 1893–1921* London, John Murray 1922. For a comparative study of women factory inspectors in Britain and the colonies, see B. Harrison and M. Nolan 'Reflections in Colonial Glass? Women Factory Inspectors in Britain and New Zealand', *Women's History Review* 13, 2 2004.

69 *Annual Report of the Chief Inspector of Factories and Workshops for 1879* p. 98, quoted in Anderson op. cit., p. 190.

70   E. F. S. Dilke 'Women and the Royal Commission', *Fortnightly Review* 50 October 1891 536–8.

71   There are no biographies on any of these women but for discussions of the Royal Commission, see Drake McFeely op. cit.; Harrison op. cit.; Anderson op. cit.; Rubenstein op. cit.; P. E. Malcolmson *English Laundresses, A Social History, 1850–1930* Illinois, University of Illinois Press 1986; D. Crow *The Victorian Woman* London, Allen and Unwin 1978 and H. Jones 'Women Health Workers: The Case of the First Women Factory Inspectors in Britain', *The Journal of the Society for the Social History of Medicine* 1 1988 165–81.

72   Rubenstein op. cit., p. 106.

73   Royal Commission on Labour *Minutes of Evidence, With Appendices Taken Before Group 'C', in Sessional Papers: House of Commons* XXXIV 1892; reprinted in Irish University Press Series of British Parliamentary Papers 27 *Industrial Relations: Labour Commission* Shannon 1968 p. 455.

74   Amie Hicks was one who pressed for women inspectors. See Drake McFeely op. cit., p. 12.

75   Home Office Memorandum, unsigned, July 1891, PRO, HO45/9818/B8031, quoted in Drake McFeely ibid., p. 12.

76   Anderson op. cit., pp. 8–9.

77   *TUC Annual Report* 1879 p. 30.

78   *TUC Annual Report* 1891 p. 68.

79   Drake McFeely op. cit., pp. 13–14 and Jones op. cit., p. 171.

80   For a full discussion of this, see R. Livesey 'The Politics of Work: Feminism, Professionalisation and Women Inspectors of Factories and Workshops', *Women's History Review* 13, 2 2004. See also Drake McFeely op. cit., p. 14 and Harrison and Nolan op. cit., p. 272.

81   Drake McFeely argues that Lady Dilke wanted women factory inspectors to be the equal or betters of their male colleagues, op. cit., p. 14.

82   L. Middleton (ed.) *Women in the Labour Movement: The British Experience* London, Croom Helm 1977 95.

83   Jones op. cit., p. 171.

84   A. Hicks, Women's Trade Union Association. *How Women Work. I, Being extracts from Evidence Given before Group C of the Labour Commission in Regard to Women Working in the Ropemaking and Other Trades in London*, quoted in Drake McFeely op. cit., p. 12.

85   Livesey op. cit., pp. 235–7.

6   Women's work before the First World War

1   There are many books on the 'New Woman'. See D. Rubinstein *Before the Suffragettes: Women's Emancipation in the 1890s* Brighton, Harvester 1986 chapters 2, 3, 11 and 12 for a discussion of the New Woman. See also S. Mitchell *The New Girl: Girls' Culture in England, 1880–1915* New York, Columbia University Press 1995; S. Ledger *The New Woman: Fiction and Feminism at the fin de siècle* Manchester, Manchester University Press 1997; and D. Gorham 'The Ideology of Femininity and Reading for Girls, 1850–1914' in Felicity Hunt (ed.) *Lessons for Life: The Schooling of Girls and Women, 1850–1950* Oxford, Blackwell 1987 pp. 39–59 for a discussion of the cultural influences on young women of this period. For a discussion of changing attitudes to marriage, see C. Dyhouse *Feminism and the Family in England, 1880–1939* Oxford, Blackwell 1989 chapter 4.

2 For a fascinating insight into the lives of lower middle-class young women in the years before the First World War, see T. Thompson (ed.) *Dear Girl: The Diaries of Two Working Women 1897–1917* London, The Women's Press 1987.

3 Patricia E. Malcolmson *English Laundresses, A Social History, 1850–1930* Illinois, University of Illinois Press 1986 p. 7.

4 Clara Collet (1896) *Statistics of Employment of Women and Girls in England and Wales*, quoted in B. Harrison *'Not only the Dangerous Trades': Women's Work and Health in Britain, 1880–1914* London, Taylor & Francis 1996 p. 6.

5 Malcolmson op. cit., p. 7.

6 L. Papworth-Wyatt and D. Zimmern *The Occupations of Women: According to the Census for England and Wales 1911* London, WIC 1914 table 5 p. 23.

7 Malcolmson op. cit., p. 8.

8 Ibid., p. 44.

9 Ibid., pp. 45 and 47.

10 Ibid., p. 48.

11 Ibid., p. 49. Millicent Fawcett herself was on the committee of the WPLL for some time and was vehemently opposed to industrial legislation. See B. Caine *Victorian Feminists* Oxford, Oxford University Press 1992 p. 243.

12 This group changed its name to the Freedom of Labour Defence Association in 1897.

13 J. Boucherett and H. Blackburn *The Condition of Working Women and the Factory Acts* London, Grant Richards 1896.

14 Malcolmson op. cit., p. 52. See also the previous chapter on the debate around married women's work.

15 Ibid., p. 56.

16 Ibid., p. 52. For the affects of continual childbirth and overwork on working-class women, see M. Llewellyn Davies *Maternity: Letters from Working Women* London, Bell and Son 1915.

17 B. Webb *Women and the Factory Acts* London Fabian Society Fabian Tract No. 67 1896 reprinted in S. Alexander (ed.) *Women's Fabian Tracts* London, Routledge 1988 pp. 17–32.

18 Malcolmson op. cit., p. 106.

19 Ibid., pp. 53–4.

20 Ibid., pp. 55–60 and chapter 4.

21 These figures are, of course, conservative and there were probably many more women involved in some sort of paid domestic work. See E. Roberts *Women's Work, 1840–1940* Cambridge, Cambridge University Press 1988 p. 19.

22 Ibid., p. 20.

23 Harrison op. cit., pp. 106–8. See also *Royal Commission of Labour* 1893–4 PPXXXVII; 'Reform in domestic life as required by scientific sociology' 1893 *Shafts* p. 26 and C.V. Butler *Domestic Service: An Enquiry by the Women's Industrial Council* London, Women's Industrial Council 1916.

24 Butler in Harrison op. cit., pp. 109–10.

25 Ibid., p. 109.

26 Ibid., p. 111.

27 Roberts op. cit., p. 24; P. Hollis *Women in Public: Documents of the Victorian Women's Movement* London, George Allen and Unwin 1979 p. 53; B. Drake *Women in Trade Unions* London, Labour Research Department 1920 table III.

28 Drake op. cit., table I.

29 S. Walby *Patriarchy at Work: Patriarchal and Capitalist Relations in Employment* Cambridge, Polity 1986 p. 133.

30 S. Pennington and B. Westover *A Hidden Workforce: Homeworkers in England, 1850–1985* London, Macmillan 1989 p. 34. This is a most useful text for a discussion of the complex issues involved in homeworking but the focus is limited to England. A similar text is not available for Scotland and Wales but see A. J. Albert 'Fit Work for Women: Sweated Home-workers in Glasgow, c.1875–1914' in E. Gordon and E. Breitenbach (eds) *The World is Ill Divided: Women's Work in Scotland in the Nineteenth and early Twentieth Centuries* Edinburgh, Edinburgh University Press 1990 pp. 158–77.

31 Hollis op. cit., p. 53; Drake op. cit., table I.

32 Drake op. cit., table I.

33 Harrison op. cit., pp. 57–9.

34 Ibid., p. 55. See also Barbara Harrison 'Are Accidents Gender Neutral? The Case of the Industrial Accident in Britain, 1880–1914', *Women's History Review* 2 1993 253–76.

35 For the WIC's Clubs' Industrial Association, see E. Mappen *Helping Women at Work: the Women's Industrial Council 1889–1914* London, Hutchinson 1985 pp. 113–18. For a discussion of Lily Montagu's work in the WIC with Jewish tailoresess in London, see J. Spence 'Working for Jewish Girls: Lily Montagu, Girls' Clubs and Industrial Reform', *Women's History Review* 13, 3 2004.

36 See J. Goodman 'Social Investigation and Economic Empowerment: The Women's Industrial Council and the LCC Trade Schools for Girls, 1892–1914', *History of Education* 27, 3 1998 297–314.

37 'Letters of a "Crewe Factory Girl" to the *Crewe Chronicle*' in D. Nield Chew *Ada Nield Chew: The Life and Writings of a Working Woman* London, Virago 1982 pp. 75–134.

38 Chew op. cit., pp. 75–6.

39 Harrison op. cit., p. 12. But also see Pennington and Westover op. cit., chapter 3 for a more complex analysis of why and where homework developed.

40 The House of Lords Select Committee on Women's Work 1888–9 and the Select Committee on Homework 1907 both sought to define sweated labour.

41 D. Bythell *The Sweated Trades: Outwork in Nineteenth Century Britain* London, Batsford Academic 1978 p. 16.

42 See Pennington and Westover op. cit., p. 45.

43 Harrison op. cit., pp. 92–3. For a useful discussion of various definitions of sweating that caused difficulties for the Lords Select Committee Inquiry, see N. N. Feltes 'Misery or the Production of Misery: Defining Sweated Labour in 1890', *Social History*, 17, 3 1992 pp. 443–52. For the causes of sweating, see also J. Schmiechen *Sweated Industries and Sweated Labour: the London Clothing Trades 1860–1914* London, Croom Helm 1984 and J. Morris 'The Characteristics of Sweating: The Late Nineteenth-Century London and Leeds Tailoring Trade' in A. V. John (ed.) *Unequal Opportunities: Women's Employment in England, 1800–1918* Oxford, Blackwell 1986.

44 See for example, Clementina Black *Sweated Industry and the Minimum Wage* London, Duckworth 1907.

45 Pennington and Westover op. cit., chapter 4 for a detailed discussion on the determinants of sweated labour.

46 Mrs Heatherley (1876) *Royal Commission on Factories and Workshops* quoted in Hollis op. cit., p. 79.

47 Morris in John op. cit., pp. 46–7.

48 Reports on these investigations are found in journals interested in women's work

issues. The ones mentioned here are from *Nineteenth Century*: Mrs Hogg 'The Fur Pullers of South London' Nov. 1897; *Women's Industrial News*: 'Birmingham Pen Trade' June 1900; Mrs Oakeshott 'Women Polishers' March 1902; G. Oakeshott 'Artificial Flowermaking' June 1903; 'Report on Millinery' March 1906; 'Report on Boxmaking Enquiry' Sept. 1908; C. Black 'Recent Evidence on Homework' March 1908; 'Underground Workrooms' October 1912; others can be found in *Women's Trade Union Review and the Englishwoman*. A summary of the investigations can be found in *The Contemporary Review* December 1897 pp. 880–6. For larger investigations, see E. Cadbury, M. C. Matheson and G. Shann *Women's Work and Women's Wages: A Phase of Life in an Industrial City* London, T. Fisher Unwin 1906; Black 1907 and 1915; B. Rowntree Seebohm *Poverty: A Study in Town Life* London, Nelson 1902; and for state instituted investigations, see *Reports of the Select Committee of the House of Lords on the Sweating System* 1886, 1889, 1890; Select Committee on Homework 1908.

49 E. J. Macrosty 'Rate of Women's Wages' *Women's Industrial News* July 1907; B. L. Hutchins 'Homework and Sweating: the Causes and the Remedies' *Fabian Tract* 130 1907; B. L. Hutchins *The Case For and Against a Legal Minimum Wage for Sweated Work* London, WIC 1909; M. Macarthur 'The Working of the Trade Board Acts' *Englishwoman* Sept. 1913 and also note 40 above for other examples.

50 For a detailed discussion of feminist approaches to sweating, see E. F. Mappen 'Strategists for Change: Social Feminist Approaches to the Problems of Women's Work' in John op. cit., pp. 235–59. See also Harrison op. cit., pp. 96–100.

51 For a discussion of the Sweated Industries Exhibitions, see S. Lewenhak *Women and Trade Unions: An Outline History of Women in the British Trade Union Movement* London, Ernest Benn 1977 pp. 119–22 and Schmeichen op. cit., chapter 7.

52 Mappen op. cit., pp. 249–53.

53 Ibid., p. 253.

54 Walby op. cit., pp. 134–5.

55 Ibid., pp. 137–8; Drake op. cit., pp. 115–17.

56 C. Wightman *More than Munitions: Women, Work and the Engineering Industries, 1900–1950* London, Longman 1999 Introduction.

57 Hollis op. cit., p. 47.

58 L. Holcombe *Victorian Ladies at Work: Middle-class Working Women in England and Wales 1850–1914* Newton Abbot, David & Charles 1973 p. 103.

59 Roberts op. cit., p. 26.

60 For a good general history of the retail trade before the First World War, see A. Adburgham *Shops and Shopping, 1800–1914* London, Allen and Unwin 1981.

61 For a discussion of the impact of industrialization on the retail trade, see C. Hall 'The Butcher, the Baker, the Candlestick-maker: the Shop and the Family in the Industrial Revolution' in C. Hall (ed.) *White, Male and Middle Class: Explorations in Feminism and History* Cambridge, Polity Press 1992.

62 Holcombe op. cit., pp. 104–5.

63 Ibid., p. 105.

64 Ibid., p. 107.

65 E. Jordan *The Women's Movement and Women's Employment in Nineteenth Century Britain* London, Routledge 1999 p. 68 and table 4.1 p. 69.

66 Ibid., p. 70

67 See for example studies on the clerical sector: R. Crompton and G. Jones *White*

Collar Proletariat: Deskilling and Gender in the Clerical Labour Process London, Macmillan 1984 and S. Cohn *The Process of Occupational Sex-Typing: The Feminization of Clerical Labour in Great Britain* Philadelphia, Temple University Press, 1985.

68 Holcombe op. cit., p. 109.
69 J. Boucherett 'Sir John Lubbock's Bill', *Englishwoman's Review* October 1873, quoted in Hollis op. cit., p. 86.
70 C. Collett *Report on Conditions of Work in London, 1892–3* PPXXXVII.
71 Her report was published as M. Bondfield 'Conditions under which Shop Assistants Work', *Economics Journal* 9 1899 pp. 277–86. But see also Margaret G. Bondfield *A Life's Work* London, Hutchinson 1948 and Black op. cit., chapter 3.
72 According to Holcombe, the living-in system was not universal and was, indeed, unheard of in Scotland, op. cit., p. 112.
73 *Englishwoman's Review* July 1880, quoted in Harrison op. cit., p. 114.
74 Drake op. cit., states that there were around 500 women shop workers unionized in 1896 table I.
75 Holcombe op. cit., p. 118.
76 Ibid., p. 120 and Drake op. cit., p. 164.
77 Harrison op. cit., p. 115.
78 Ibid., p. 115.
79 Holcombe op. cit., p. 132.
80 Ibid., p. 142.
81 G. Anderson (ed.) *The White Blouse Revolution: Female Office Workers since 1870* Manchester, Manchester University Press 1988, p. 4.
82 Jordan op. cit., pp. 179–84.
83 Roberts op. cit., p. 28.
84 Anderson op. cit., p. 4.
85 H. Jones *Women in British Public Life, 1914–1950: Gender, Power and Social Policy* Longman 2000 p. 11.
86 M. Zimmeck 'Jobs for the Girls: the Expansion of Clerical Work for Women, 1850–1914' in John op. cit., pp. 153–77. For a useful local study of women's clerical work in this period, see R. Guerriero Wilson 'Women's Work in Offices and the Preservation of Men's "Breadwinning" Jobs in Early Twentieth-century Glasgow', *Women's History Review* 10, 3 2001.
87 Roberts op. cit., p. 28 and Holcombe, op. cit., pp. 210–11.
88 Jones op. cit., p. 9.
89 Zimmeck op. cit., p. 157.
90 See Thompson op. cit., for examples of working-class girls doing clerical work.
91 Evidence of Mr Scudamore (1871) *Report on the Re-organization of the Telegraph System* in Hollis op. cit., p. 104.
92 Zimmeck op. cit., pp. 158–9.
93 Ibid., p. 164.
94 Anderson op. cit., p. 7.
95 Harrison op. cit., p. 117.
96 Walby op. cit., pp. 148–53.
97 Cohn op. cit.
98 Walby op. cit., pp. 154–5.
99 Holcombe op. cit., pp. 155–6.
100 Drake op. cit., table I.
101 Holcombe op. cit., pp. 158–9.

102 Walby op. cit., p. 151.

103 For women's access to higher education, see C. Dyhouse *No Distinction of Sex? Women in British Universities, 1870–1939* London, UCL Press 1995.

104 Jones op. cit., p. 9.

105 P. Levine *Victorian Feminism 1850–1900* University of Florida Press 1994 p. 96. See also C. Blake *The Charge of the Parasols: Women's Entry in the Medical Profession* London, The Women's Press 1990.

106 Jones op. cit., p. 9.

107 Ibid., p. 11. For women in the Civil Service, see H. Martindale *Women Servants of the State, 1870–1938: a History of Women in the Civil Service* George Allen and Unwin 1938; Cohn op. cit.; T. Davy '"A Cissy Job for Men; a Nice Job for Girls": Women Shorthand Typists in London, 1900–1939' in L. Davidoff and B. Westover (eds) *Our Work, Our Lives, Our Words: Women's History and Women's Work* Basingstoke, Macmillan 1985; M. Zimmeck '"Get Out and Get Under": the Impact of Demobilization on the Civil Service, 1918–1932' in Anderson op. cit.

108 Jordan op. cit., pp. 219–20.

109 Holcombe op. cit., p. 68.

110 Jordan op. cit., pp. 123–6.

111 For more on philanthropic nursing, see M. Vicinus *Independent Women: Work and Community for Single Women, 1850–1920* London, Virago 1985 chapter 2 and A. Summers 'Ministering Angels: Victorian Ladies and Nursing' in G. Marsden (ed.) *Victorian Values: Personalities and Perspectives in Nineteenth-Century Society* London, Longman 1990.

112 For a discussion of why the changes took place, see Jordan op. cit., chapter 7. For histories of nursing, see M. E. Baly *Nursing and Social Change* London, William Heinemann 1980; F. B. Smith *Florence Nightingale: Reputation and Power* London, Croom Helm 1982; A. Summers *Angels and Citizens: British Women as Military Nurses 1854–1914* London, Routledge and Kegan Paul 1988 especially chapters 1 and 2; for an international perspective, see A. M. Rafferty, J. Robinson and R. Elkan (eds) *Nursing History and the Politics of Welfare* London, Routledge 1997.

113 Jordan op. cit., p. 126.

114 Ibid., pp. 139–40.

115 Ibid., p. 141.

116 See Summers op. cit.

117 Vicinus op. cit., p. 102 and Harrison op. cit., p. 125.

118 Harrison op. cit., p. 125.

119 Jordan op. cit., p. 123; Hollis op. cit., p. 49 and Harrison op. cit., p. 126.

120 Harrison op. cit., p. 126.

121 Vicinus op. cit., pp. 107–8 and 119.

122 Ibid., pp. 108–9.

123 Holcombe op. cit., pp. 96–102.

124 For a discussion of the professionalization of midwifery, see J. Hannam 'Rosalind Paget: the Midwife, the Women's Movement and Reform before 1914', in H. Marland and A. M. Rafferty (eds) *Midwives, Society and Childbirth: Debates and Controversies in the Early Modern Period* London, Routledge 1997, pp. 81–100.

125 For a fuller discussion of professionalization as a gendered concept, see A. Witz *Professions and Patriarchy* London, Routledge 1992.

126 Jordan op. cit., table 4.4 p. 79.

127 For an account of the campaign to open up the medical profession to women, see Blake op. cit. For biographies of leading women in the campaign, see J. Manton *Elizabeth Garrett Anderson* London, Methuen 1965 and S. Roberts *Sophia Jex-Blake: A Woman Pioneer in Nineteenth-Century Medical Reform* London, Routledge 1993.

128 Holcombe op. cit., p. 37.

129 Ibid., p. 34.

130 Holcombe op. cit., appendix.

131 For a full account of this campaign, see F. Widdowson *Going Up into the Next Class: Women and Elementary Teacher Training 1840–1914* London, Hutchinson 1983 section IIIi.

132 Ibid., p. 29.

133 Ibid., pp. 31–3.

134 Ibid., pp. 40–1.

135 A. Oram *Women Teachers and Feminist Politics, 1900–1939* Manchester, Manchester University Press 1996 chapter 2.

136 Harrison op. cit., p. 121.

137 Vicinus op. cit.

138 Widdowson op. cit., p. 57.

139 Holcombe op. cit., p. 38.

140 Oram op. cit., p. 2.

141 Ibid., p. 3. See also H. Kean *Deeds not Words: the Lives of Suffragette Teachers* London, Pluto Press 1990.

142 For an in-depth discussion of theories around gender segregation, see Sylvia Walby *Theorizing Patriarchy Oxford*, Blackwell 1990 chapter 2.

143 Oram op. cit., introduction.

144 Harrison op. cit., pp. 120–4 for the health implications of the sector.

145 For London, see Mappen op. cit. and Spence op. cit. For Manchester, see J. Goodman 'Girls' clubs in late Victorian and early Edwardian Manchester', *History of Education Society Bulletin* 60 1997.

Part Three 1914–45

1 Millicent Fawcett *The Women's Victory and After* Sidgwick and Jackson 1920 p. 106.

2 This discussion is based on P. Summerfield 'Women and War in the Twentieth Century' in J. Purvis (ed.) *Women's History: Britain, 1850–1945* London, UCL Press 1995 pp. 307–32.

3 Summerfield op. cit., pp. 308–9.

4 G. Braybon and P. Summerfield *Out of the Cage: Women's Experiences in Two World Wars* London, Pandora 1987 p. 107; G. Braybon *Women Workers in the First World War: the British Experience* London, Routledge 1989 chapter 5.

5 Summerfield op. cit., p. 313.

6 For a discussion of DORA, see L. A. Hall *Sex, Gender and Social Change in Britain since 1880* Basingstoke, Macmillan 2000 chapter 5; S. R. Grayzel *Women and the First World War* London, Longman 2002 chapter 5.

7 For the argument that the vote was a reward for women's war work, see A. Marwick *The Deluge: British Society and the First World War* London, Bodley Head 1965.

8 M. Pugh *Women and the Women's Movement in Britain, 1914–1999* Basingstoke, Macmillan 2000 chapter 2.

7 Out of the cage? Women's experience of work during the First World War

9 Title borrowed from G. Braybon and P. Summerfield op. cit.

10 Catherine Hakim *Occupational Segregation* research paper 9 table 13 1979, quoted in J. Lewis *Women in England, 1870–1950: Sexual Divisions and Social Change* Brighton, Wheatsheaf Books 1984 p. 147 for England and Wales and E. Roberts *Women's Work, 1840–1940* Cambridge, Cambridge University Press 1988 p. 11.

11 Braybon and Summerfield op. cit., p. 38.

12 E. James (1962) 'Women and Work in Twentieth Century Britain', *Manchester School of Economics and Social Science* XXX figure 2 in Lewis op. cit., p. 156.

13 Braybon *Women Workers in the First World War* London, Routledge 1989 p. 48.

14 Ibid., p. 44.

15 Braybon and Summerfield op. cit., p. 32.

16 E. S. Pankhurst *The Home Front: a Mirror to Life in England during the First World War* London, Hutchinson 1932 p. 58. Clementina Black was also critical of well-to-do women volunteering to do work that working-class women would normally be paid to perform, then employing poor women through workshops at a fraction of their usual wage. See *Women's Industrial News* XVIII 67 1914 298.

17 M. Pugh op. cit.

18 Ibid., p. 19.

19 Braybon and Summerfield op. cit., p. 34.

20 Pugh op. cit., p. 20.

21 Ibid., p. 20.

22 Braybon op. cit., pp. 47–8.

23 Partial extract of main employers of women from Pugh op. cit., p. 20 based on Board of Trade *Report on the State of Employment in all Occupations in the United Kingdom in July 1918.*

24 D. Thom *Nice Girls and Rude Girls: Women Workers in World War I* London, I. B. Tauris 2000 p. 32.

25 H. Jones *Women in British Public Life, 1914–1950: Gender, Power and Social Policy* London, Longman 2000 pp. 15–16.

26 Pugh op. cit., p. 20.

27 Ibid., p. 31.

28 Ibid., p. 21.

29 S. Pennington and B. Westover *A Hidden Workforce: Homeworkers in England, 1850–1985* London, Macmillan 1989 states that homeworkers made lightweight army clothes and kit from their homes for a pittance, pp. 133–5.

30 Thom op. cit., p. 24. For an international perspective of the war see Grayzel op. cit.

31 Braybon op. cit., chapter 9 and passim.

32 Pugh op. cit., p. 83.

33 D. Beddoe *Back to Home and Duty: Women between the Wars, 1918–1939* London, Pandora 1989 chapter 1 discusses the way women workers were represented in the press at the close of the war.

34 For an analysis of how this came about, see J. de Vries 'Gendering Patriotism: Emmeline Pankhurst and Christabel Pankhurst and World War One' in S. Oldfield (ed.) *This Working Day World* London, Taylor and Francis 1994. See also Grayzel op. cit., pp. 20–2.

35 Pugh op. cit., pp. 24–5.
36 For a full discussion of employer and trade union attitudes to women entering so-called male areas of work, see Braybon op. cit., chapter 3; Walby op. cit., pp. 158–64.
37 Pugh op. cit., p. 25.
38 Braybon op. cit., p. 90.
39 Wightman *More than Munitions: Women, Work and the Engineering Industries, 1900–1950* London, Longman 1999 chapter 3 discusses this in detail.
40 Braybon op. cit., p. 61.
41 Thom op. cit., p. 59.
42 Ibid., p. 33.
43 Braybon op. cit., chapter 3.
44 Pugh op. cit., pp. 26–7.
45 For autobiographical writings of the First World War, see, for example, V. Brittain *Testament of Youth: an Autobiographical Study of the Years 1900–1925* London, Victor Gollancz 1933; P. Hamilton *Three Years or the Duration: Memoirs of a Munition Worker* London, Peter Owen 1978 for the view of a middle-class munitions worker; E. S. Pankhurst op. cit. There are few accounts written by working-class women during this period.
46 Braybon and Summerfield op. cit., use women's testimony of life during the two World Wars throughout, much of it taken from the tapes and autobiographies stored at the Imperial War Museum and Southampton City Museum.
47 Thom op. cit., p. 35.
48 Braybon and Summerfield op. cit., pp. 60–71; for an in-depth account of life in the munitions factory, see also D. Thom 'Tommy's Sister: Women in World War I' in Thom op. cit.
49 Pugh op. cit., pp. 22–3.
50 Ibid., p. 24.
51 For example, Hamilton op. cit.
52 Braybon and Summerfield op. cit., p. 79.
53 Ibid., p. 80.
54 Thom op. cit., p. 58.
55 Braybon and Summerfield op. cit., pp. 86–7.
56 Thom op. cit., pp. xi–xv.
57 Braybon and Summerfield op. cit., pp. 87–8.
58 Thom op. cit., p. 153.
59 Although Thom op. cit., says that class differed in different factories and included policemen's wives, untrained ladies, forewomen, school mistresses and other women used to controlling young women's behaviour. For a more in-depth discussion of welfare supervisors, see A. Woollacott *On Her Their Lives: Munition Workers in the Great War* California, University of California Press 1994 pp. 71–5 and 167–70.
60 Thom op. cit., p. 152.
61 Braybon and Summerfield op. cit., p. 90.
62 Lillian Barker quoted in Thom op. cit., p. 152.
63 'Women after the War' in *National News* 8 March 1917 quoted in Braybon op. cit., p. 146.
64 See Pugh op. cit., pp. 32–4; Braybon and Summerfield op. cit., pp. 109–10 and Hall op. cit., chapter 5 for a discussion of the worries around morality and the implementation of the Defence of the Realm Act (DORA).

65 Braybon and Summerfield op. cit., pp. 95–6 and Thom op. cit., chapter 6 'TNT Poisoning and the Employment of Women in the First World War'.

8 Women's work in the inter-war period

1 M. Macarthur 'The Woman Trade-Unionists Point of View' in M. Phillips (ed.) *Women and the Labour Party* London, Headley Bros 1918 p. 18.
2 3,277,000 according to D. Thom *Nice Girls and Rude Girls: Women Workers in World War I* London, I. B. Tauris 2000 p. 47, or 3,276,00 according to M. Pugh *Women and the Women's Movement in Britain, 1914–1999* Basingstoke, Macmillan 2000 p. 20.
3 S. Bruley *Women in Britain since 1900* Basingstoke, Macmillan 1999 p. 42 draws on figures taken from S. Lewenhak *Women and Trade Unions: an Outline History of Women in the British Trade Union Movement* London, E. Benn 1977. Thom op. cit., p. 140 and so does Pugh op. cit., p. 100.
4 Thom op. cit., p. 44 and S. Boston *Women Workers and the Trade Unions* London, Davis-Poynter 1980 p. 127.
5 G. Braybon and P. Summerfield *Out of the Cage: Women's Experiences in Two World Wars* London, Pandora 1987 p. 122.
6 Ibid., p. 121.
7 Thom op. cit., p. 189. C. Wightman *More than Munitions: Women, Work and the Engineering Industries, 1900–1950* London, Longman 1999 does not discuss this group of workers.
8 M. Zimmeck '"Get Out and Get Under": the Impact of Demobilisation on the Civil Service, 1918–32' in G. Anderson (ed.) *The White Blouse Revolution: Female Office Workers since 1870* Manchester, Manchester University Press 1988 p. 89.
9 I. O. Andrews (2nd edition) *The Economic Effects of the World War upon Women and Children in Great Britain* Oxford, Oxford University Press 1921, quoted in G. Braybon *Women Workers in the First World War: the British experience* London, Routledge 1989 p. 174.
10 Pugh op. cit., p. 80.
11 Thom op. cit., p. 193.
12 D. Beddoe *Back Home to Duty: Women between the Wars, 1918–1939* London, Pandora 1989 p. 48 and Braybon and Summerfield op. cit., p. 121.
13 *Daily News* 15 February 1919, quoted in Beddoe op. cit., p. 49.
14 For a full discussion of the way the media treated unemployed women, see Beddoe op. cit., chapter 1.
15 *Woman Worker* February 1919 p. 6, quoted in Thom op. cit., p. 192.
16 Ibid., p. 192.
17 Ibid., pp. 188–90.
18 Macarthur quoted in ibid., p. 187.
19 Pugh op. cit., table 4.2 and 4.3 p. 91, extracted from A. H. Halsey (ed.) *British Social Trends since 1900* 1988 p. 106 and pp. 166–72.
20 M. Glucksmann *Women Assemble: Women Workers and the New Industries in the Inter-War Years* London, Routledge 1990 table 3 pp. 44–6.
21 Pugh op. cit., pp. 91–2.
22 For a discussion of the limited career pathways open to graduates during this period, see P. Thane 'Girton Graduates: earning and learning, 1920s–1980s', *Women's History Review* 13, 3 2004.
23 M. Glucksmann op. cit., p. 41.

24 Taken from Catherine Hakim *Occupational Segregation* research paper 9 Department of Employment table 6 1979.
25 Taken from C. Hakim op. cit., table 7.
26 Ibid., 1990 p. 41.
27 Glucksmann (1990) explores this in detail for the new assembly line industries.
28 Pugh op. cit., p. 96.
29 P. Summerfield *Women Workers in the Second World War: Production and Patriarchy in Conflict* London, Croom Helm 1984 pp. 14–15.
30 Pugh op. cit., p. 96. For teaching, see A. Oram *Women Teachers and Feminist Politics, 1900–1939* Manchester, Manchester University Press, 1996 chapters 3 and 4 and for the Civil Service, see M. Zimmick 'Strategies and Stratagems for the Employment of Women in the British Civil Service, 1919–1939', *The Historical Journal* 27, 4 1984 901–23. For both, see also H. Jones *Women in British Public Life, 1914–1950: Gender, Power and Social Policy* London, Longman 2000.
31 H. L. Smith 'British Feminism and the Equal Pay Issue in the 1930s', *Women's History Review* 5, 1 1996 98.
32 Smith op. cit., p. 98.
33 Ibid., p. 99.
34 Ibid., p. 100.
35 Ibid., p. 102.
36 See S. Pennington and B. Westover *A Hidden Workforce: Homeworkers in England, 1850–1985* London, Macmillan 1989 chapter 8.
37 For an in-depth discussion of how the decline in textiles affected women workers, see S. Bruley 'Gender, Class and Party, the Communist Party and the Crisis in the Cotton Industry between the Two World Wars', *Women's History Review* 2, 1, 1993.
38 See Glucksmann op. cit., chapter 5 for a full discussion of this. For an oral history account of life on the assembly line, see S. Bruley 'Sorters, Pressers, Pippers and Packers: Women in Light Industry in South London, 1920–1960', *Oral History* Spring 25, 1 1997.
39 Glucksmann op. cit., p. 42.
40 M. Glucksmann 'In a Class of their Own? Women Workers in the New Industries in Inter-war Britain', *Feminist Review* 24 1986 20.
41 Anderson op. cit., p. 13 and Zimmick op. cit., 1984.
42 Bruley 1999 op. cit., p. 69. For a discussion of men's fears about women taking work from them, see S. Alexander 'Men's Fears and Women's Work: Responses to Unemployment between the Wars', *Gender and History* 12, 2 2000.
43 Women's Advisory Committee Report 1919 p. 36.
44 Pennington and Westover op. cit., p. 143.
45 Wightman op. cit., p. 39 table 2.2.
46 Beddoe op. cit., p. 77 table 7.
47 E. James 'Women and Work in Twentieth Century Britain', *Manchester School of Economics and Social Science* XXX Sept. figure 2 1962 291.
48 For a discussion of how women were marginalized when the design industry was professionalized, see J. Seddon 'Mentioned but Denied Significance: Women Designers and the Professionalization of Design in Britain, 1920–1951', *Gender and History* 12, 2 2000.
49 Figures derived from Beddoe op. cit., p. 77 table 7.
50 S. Walby *Patriarchy at Work: Patriarchal and Capitalist Relations in Employment* Cambridge, Polity Press 1986 p. 167.

51 E. Roberts *A Woman's Place: an Oral History of Working-class Women, 1890–1940* Oxford, Blackwell 1984.

52 Ray Strachey *Careers and Openings for Women: A Survey of Women's Employment and a Guide for Those Seeking Work* 1937, quoted in Jones op. cit., p. 52.

53 Pugh op. cit., p. 89 shows that the crude birth rate for England and Wales fell from 28.2 births per thousand of the population in 1901 to 15.8 by 1931.

54 For the case for endowment, see E. Rathbone *The Disinherited Family* London, Edward Arnold 1924. For a useful discussion of the endowment issue in this period, see C. Dyhouse *Feminism and the Family, 1880–1939* Oxford, Blackwell 1989 pp. 88–103 and H. Land 'Eleanor Rathbone and the Economy of the Family' in H. L. Smith (ed.) *British Feminism in the Twentieth Century* Massachusetts, Massachusetts University Press, 1990.

55 Pugh op. cit., p. 115.

56 Ibid., p. 116.

57 For a discussion of women's attitudes towards unemployment in this period, see S. Bruley 'A Woman's Right to Work? The Role of Women in the Unemployed Movement Between the Wars' in S. Oldfield (ed.) *This Working-Day World: Women's Lives and Culture(s) in Britain 1914–1945* London, Taylor and Francis 1994 pp. 40–53.

58 Alexander 2000 op. cit., p. 403.

59 See Oram op. cit., pp. 58–9 for a discussion of how the notion of the male breadwinner affected women teachers in this period.

60 Ibid., p. 110.

61 For an in-depth discussion of the equal pay issue during and after the war, see H. Smith 'The issue of "equal pay for equal work" in Great Britain, 1914–1919', *Societas* viii 1 39–47 1978 and Smith 1996 op. cit.

62 Pugh op. cit., p. 96.

63 E. Rathbone *Wages Plus Family Allowances* 1925 p. 2, quoted in Pugh op. cit., p. 97.

64 See for example Zimmeck in Anderson op. cit., pp. 88–120 and Walby op. cit., pp. 185–8.

65 F. W. Fox 'Introduction of Machinery into Government Departments', Institute of Public Administration 1956, quoted in Walby op. cit., p. 187.

66 Glucksmann op. cit., pp. 198–202.

67 Ibid., pp. 203–8.

68 Ibid., p. 208.

69 For a discussion of attitudes towards women in the engineering unions, see Wightman op. cit., chapter 6. For the motor industry during this period, see S. Tolliday 'Militancy and Organization: Women Workers and Trade Unions in the Motor Trades in the 1930s', *Oral history* 11, 2 Autumn 1983.

70 Pugh op. cit., p. 100.

71 Glucksmann op. cit., pp. 190–4.

72 Ibid., p. 224.

73 H. L. Smith 'British Feminism in the 1920s' in H. L. Smith (ed.) *British Feminism in the Twentieth Century* Massachusetts, Massachusetts, University Press 1990 p. 58.

74 Pugh op. cit., p. 99.

75 Smith 1990 op. cit., p. 61.

76 Pugh op. cit., p. 100.

9 Women's employment in the Second World War

1 See A. Marwick *War and Social Change in the Twentieth Century: a Comparative study of Britain, France, Germany, Russia and the US* London, Macmillan 1974.

2 P. Summerfield *Women Workers in the Second World War: Production and Patriarchy in Conflict* London, Croom Helm 1984; H. L. Smith 'The Effect of the War on the Status of Women' in H. L. Smith (ed.) *War and Social Change: British Society in the Second World War* Manchester, Manchester University Press 1986. See also S. Lewenhak *Women and Trade Unions: an Outline History of Women in the British Trade Union Movement* London, E. Benn 1977 and S. Boston *Women Workers and the Trade Unions* London, Davis-Poynter 1980 for a discussion of the effect of war on women's employment.

3 Smith op. cit., p. 211.

4 Summerfield op. cit., appendix B, table B.1.

5 Smith op. cit., p. 211.

6 G. Braybon and P. Summerfield *Out of the Cage: Women's Experiences in Two World Wars* London, Pandora p. 187.

7 Ibid., p. 155.

8 For a discussion of the role of propaganda in recruiting women to war work and especially the contradictory messages sent out by the government, see S. Carruthers 'Manning the Factories: Propaganda and Policy, 1939–1947', *History* 75, 244 1990.

9 Smith op. cit., p. 212; Summerfield op. cit., chapter 3 gives a full account of the mobilization process.

10 Smith op. cit., pp. 212–13.

11 Summerfield op. cit., p. 35.

12 Ibid., p. 29.

13 *Time and Tide* 6 December 1941.

14 Summerfield op. cit., p. 35.

15 Smith op. cit., p. 215.

16 For a discussion of how little power women had to influence government thinking during the war, see H. Jones *Women in British Public Life, 1914–1950: Gender, Power and Social Policy* London, Longman 2000 chapter 8.

17 Braybon and Summerfield op. cit., p. 170.

18 Summerfield op. cit., p. 151.

19 Ibid., chapter 7 for her discussion of dilution. See also Boston op. cit., chapter 7.

20 Summerfield op. cit., p. 179.

21 C. Wightman *More than Munitions: Women, Work and the Engineering Industries, 1900–1950* London, Longman 1999 p. 171.

22 Wightman op. cit., p. 132.

23 Ibid., p. 153.

24 Pugh op. cit., p. 274. For an in-depth discussion of equal pay during the war, see H. Smith 'The Problem of "Equal Pay for Equal Work" in Great Britain during World War II', *Journal of Modern History* 53 Dec. 1981.

25 Boston op. cit., pp. 192–3.

26 Pugh op. cit., p. 273.

27 S. Bruley *Women in Britain since 1900* Basingstoke, Macmillan 1999 p. 102.

28 Bruley ibid., p. 102. See also P. Summerfield 'The Patriarchal Discourse of Human Capital: Women's Work and Training in World War Two', *Journal of Gender Studies* 2, 2 1993 189–205.

29 See M. Higgonet and P. L-R. Higgonet 'The Double Helix' in M. Higgonet, J. Jenson, S. Michel and M. C. Weitz (eds) *Behind the Lines: Gender and the Two World Wars* New Haven and London, Yale University Press, 1987 for a full discussion of this idea.

30 Bruley op. cit., p. 103.

31 T. Stone 'Creating a (Gendered?) Military Identity: the Women's Auxillary Air Force in Great Britain in the Second World War', *Women's History Review* 8, 4 1999.

32 Smith op. cit., p. 216.

33 For the war experiences of the female correspondents to Mass-Observation, see D. Sheridan (ed.) *Wartime Women: A Mass-Observation Anthology* London, Phoenix Press 2000.

34 Smith op. cit., p. 213.

35 Bruley op. cit., p. 96.

36 Smith op. cit., p. 216.

37 Summerfield op. cit., p. 145.

38 Ibid., p. 146.

39 Ibid., p. 145.

40 Ibid., p. 146.

41 Ibid., chapter 8 'Conclusions' for the whole of this section.

42 Mass-Observation *People in Production* London, John Murray pp. 227–8 1942, quoted in ibid., chapter 5 discusses the issue of shopping in depth.

43 Bruley op. cit., p. 27.

44 *News Chronicle* 16 July 1941, quoted in Summerfield op. cit., pp. 102–3.

45 Braybon and Summerfield op. cit., p. 200.

46 Smith op. cit., p. 215. See also Penny Summerfield 'The "levelling of class"' in ibid., pp. 193–4.

47 Mass-Observation Archive TC32 'Women in Wartime' Box 3, File E, 25 April 1941, quoted in Braybon and Summerfield op. cit., p. 198.

48 Braybon and Summerfield op. cit., p. 198.

49 It is not possible to go into detail about the richness of oral history as a source for women's history. An excellent book that focuses on this period is P. Summerfield *Reconstructing Women's Wartime Lives: Discourse and Subjectivity in Oral Histories of the Second World War* Manchester, Manchester University Press, 1998.

50 Wightman op. cit., p. 154.

51 Dorothy Sheridan op. cit., chapter 20.

52 Ibid., p. 215.

53 Ibid., p. 216.

54 Ibid., p. 225.

55 P. Summerfield '"It Did Me Good in Lots of Ways": British Women in Transition from War to Peace' in C. Duchen and I. Bandhauer-Schøffmann *When the War Was Over: Women, War and Peace in Europe, 1940–1956* Leicester, Leicester University Press 2000 pp. 13–28.

56 For a discussion of the split in the women's suffrage movement, see J. Vellacott 'Feminist Conciousness and the First World War', *History Workshop Journal* 23, 1987.

57 Braybon and Summerfield op. cit., p. 158.

58 Boston op. cit., pp. 136–8.

59 Ibid., p. 150.

Part Four 1945 to the end of the century

1 G. Braybon and P. Summerfield *Out of the Cage: Women's Experiences in Two World Wars* London, Pandora 1987 p. 259.
2 M-O *People in Production* 1942, quoted in ibid.
3 J. Lewis *Women in Britain since 1945: Women, Family, Work and the State in the Post-war Years* Oxford, Blackwell 1992 p. 2.
4 N. Soldon *Women in British Trade Unions 1874–1976* Dublin, Gill and Macmillan 1978 p. 148.
5 S. Lewenhak *Women and Trade Unions: An Outline History of Women in the British Trade Union Movement* London, E. Benn 1977 pp. 262–5.
6 S. Bruley *Women in Britain since 1900* Basingstoke, Macmillan 1999 p. 168.
7 S. Boston *Women Workers and the Trade Unions* London, Davis-Poynter 1980 pp. 278–80.
8 For a fuller discussion of this campaign, see S. Alexander *Becoming a Woman and other Essays in 19th and 20th Century Feminist History* London, Virago 1994 Appendix pp. 257–68, reprinted from *Red Rag* 6 1973.
9 B. Bryan, S. Dadzie and S. Scafe *The Heart of the Race: Black Women's Lives in Britain* London, Virago 1985 p. 36.
10 S. Rowbotham *The Past is Before Us: Feminism in Action since the 1960s* London, Pandora 1989 p. 227.
11 Bryan *et al.* op. cit., p. 36.
12 See E. Wilson *Women and the Welfare State* London, Tavistock 1977.
13 C. Briar *Working for Women? Gendered Work and Welfare Policies in Twentieth Century Britain* London, UCL Press 1997 chapter 8.

10 Back to home and duty again? The women and work debate, 1945–50

14 G. Thomas *Women at Work: Wartime Social Survey. An Enquiry Made for the Office of the Ministry of Reconstruction* 1944, quoted in C. Wightman *More than Munitions: Women, Work and the Engineering Industries, 1900–1950* London, Longman 1999 p. 170. See also P. Summerfield *Women Workers in the Second World War: Production and Patriarchy in Conflict* London, Croom Helm 1984 for a discussion of what women wanted to do at the end of the war.
15 S. L. Carruthers '"Manning the factories": Propaganda and Policy on the Employment of Women, 1939–1947', *History* 75, 244 1990 248.
16 For a discussion of the debates to encourage women back into domestic service after the war, see J. Giles 'Help for Housewives: Domestic Service and the Reconstruction of Domesticity in Britain, 1914–1950', *Women's History Review* 10, 2 2001 299–323.
17 Giles op. cit., 300–1.
18 M. Pugh *Women and the Women's Movement in Britain, 1914–1999* Basingstoke, Macmillan 2000 p. 287.
19 Ibid., p. 287.
20 Braybon and Summerfield op. cit., pp. 261–2.
21 Pugh op. cit., p. 287.
22 Braybon and Summerfield op. cit., pp. 265–7.
23 Ibid., p. 261.
24 Wightman op. cit., p. 171 and also see Carruthers op. cit.
25 Braybon and Summerfield op. cit., p. 260.

26 See, for example, Braybon and Summerfield op. cit.; Bruley op. cit.; P. Summerfield '"It did me good in lots of ways": British Women in Transition from War to Peace' in C. Duchen and I. Bandhauer-Schoffmann (eds) *When the War was Over: Women, War and Peace in Europe, 1940–1956* Leicester, Leicester University Press, 2000.

27 Pugh op. cit., p. 287.

28 Ibid., p. 288.

29 Summerfield 2000 op. cit., pp. 15–16.

30 See S. Pennington and B. Westover *A Hidden Workforce: Homeworkers in England, 1850–1985* London, Macmillan 1989 chapter 9 for a discussion of homework in this period.

31 Pennington and Westover op. cit., pp. 156–7.

32 Pugh op. cit., p. 286.

33 Wightman op. cit., p. 174 and H. L. Smith 'The Womanpower Problem in Britain during the Second World War', *Historical Journal* 27, 4 1984.

34 For discussions on the Attlee Government's campaigns to attract women workers after the war, see Carruthers op. cit., and W. Croft 'The Attlee Government's Pursuit of Women', *History Today* August 1986. See also D. Riley 'The Free Mothers: Pronatalism and Working Women in Industry at the End of the Last War', *History Workshop* 11, 1981.

35 Carruthers op. cit., P. 252.

36 Briar op. cit., p. 94.

37 Wightman op. cit., p. 174.

38 Carruthers op. cit., p. 248.

39 Croft op. cit., p. 31.

40 Ibid., p. 30.

41 Briar op. cit., p. 94.

42 Lewis op. cit., p. 72.

43 Croft op. cit., p. 31.

44 Carruthers op. cit., p. 250.

45 Croft op. cit., p. 32.

46 Carruthers op. cit., p. 251.

47 Giles op. cit., p. 308.

48 Ibid., p. 308.

49 Ibid., p. 312.

50 Lewenhak op. cit., p. 246.

51 Briar op. cit., p. 96.

52 Carruthers op. cit., p. 251.

53 Croft op. cit., p. 32.

54 Pugh op. cit., p. 287.

55 Croft op. cit., p. 35.

56 Carruthers op. cit., p. 252.

57 Quoted in Denise Riley *War in the Nursery; Theories of the Child and Mother* London, Virago 1983 p. 134.

58 R. Crompton 'The Feminisation of the Clerical Labour Force since the Second World War' in G. Anderson (ed.) *The White Blouse Revolution: Female Office Workers since 1870* Manchester, Manchester University Press, p. 123, taken from census data.

59 Pugh op. cit., p. 287.

60 Anderson op. cit., p. 11, taken from census returns.

61 For a collection of oral histories that highlight this point of view, see E. Roberts *Women and Families, An Oral History, 1940–1970* Oxford, Blackwell 1995 especially chapters 7 and 8.

62 Wightman op. cit., pp. 171–2.

63 See, for example, Summerfield 2000 op. cit. and Elizabeth Roberts op. cit.

64 For discussions on issues raised in oral history and life history writing, see T. Cosslett, C. Lury and P. Summerfield (eds) *Feminism and Autobiography: Texts, Theories, Methods* London, Routledge 2000.

65 Summerfield 2000 op. cit., pp. 15–16.

66 Mass-Observation *The Journey Home: A Mass-Observation Report on the Problems of Demobilisation* London, Murray 1944.

67 Mass-Observation op. cit., p. 55.

68 Ibid., p. 117.

69 Summerfield 2000 op. cit., p. 18.

70 Ibid., pp. 20–1.

71 Ibid., p. 22.

72 Briar op. cit., p. 109.

11 Women's employment in the 1950s and 1960s

1 M. Pugh *Women and the Women's Movement in Britain, 1914–1999* Basingstoke, Macmillan 2000 chapter 10.

2 S. Boston *Women Workers and the Trade Unions* London, Davis-Poynter 1980 p. 224.

3 See D. Riley *War in the Nursery: Theories of the Child and Mother* London, Virago 1983 for a full discussion of the pronatalist debate.

4 For a full discussion of the equal pay campaign, see H. Smith 'The Problem of "Equal Pay for Equal work" in Great Britain during World War II', *Journal of Modern History* 53 1981 657–8 and P. Summerfield *Women Workers in the Second World War: Production and Patriarchy in Conflict* London, Croom Helm 1984 pp. 174–8.

5 S. Bruley *Women in Britain since 1900* Basingstoke, Macmillan 1999 p. 102.

6 Boston op. cit., pp. 248–51.

7 Ibid., p. 251.

8 J. Lewis *Women in Britain since 1945: Women, Family, Work and the State in the Post-war Years* Oxford, Blackwell 1992 p. 80.

9 Ibid., p. 81.

10 Pugh op. cit., p. 288.

11 Lewis op. cit., p. 65.

12 G. Braybon and P. Summerfield *Out of the Cage: Women's Experiences in Two World Wars* London, Pandora 1987 p. 100.

13 E. Wilson *Only Halfway to Paradise: Women in Post War Britain, 1945–1968* London, Tavistock 1980 p. 65.

14 S. Walby *Patriarchy at Work: Patriarchal and Capitalist Relations in Employment* Cambridge, Polity 1986 p. 202.

15 Linda McDowell 'Narratives of Family, Community and Waged Work: Latvian European Volunteer Worker Women in Post-war Britain', *Women's History Review* 13, 1 2004 30.

16 Lewis op. cit., p. 66.

17 Ibid., p. 65, taken from O. Robinson 'The Changing Labour Market: Growth of Part-

time Employment and Labour Market Segregation in Britain' in S. Walby (ed.) *Gender Segregation at Work* Milton Keynes, Open University Press 1988 pp. 114–34.

18 J. Lewis 'Myrdal and Klein, *Women's Two Roles* and Post War Feminism, 1945–1960' in H. L. Smith (ed.) *British Feminism in the Twentieth Century* Massachusetts, Massachusetts University Press 1990 p. 167.

19 Riley op. cit., for the debate on pronatalism.

20 Lewis op. cit., p. 17.

21 For a discussion of the pros and cons of the concept of companionate marriage of this period, see J. Finch and P. Summerfield 'Social Reconstruction and the Emergence of the Companionate Marriage, 1945–49' in D. Clark (ed.) *Marriage, Domestic Life and Social Change: Writings for Jacqueline Burgoyne (1944–1988)* London, Routledge 1991.

22 Lewis op. cit., pp. 16–26.

23 Ibid., p. 72.

24 Alva Myrdal and Viola Klein *Women's Two Roles, Home and Work* London, Routledge and Kegan Paul 1956. Another useful text that focused on professional women is Judith Hubback *Wives who went to College* London, Heinemann 1957. See also O. Campbell *The Report of a Conference on the Feminine Point of View* London, Williams and Norgate 1952.

25 Lewis op. cit., p. 177.

26 For a detailed analysis of this book, see ibid., pp. 167–88.

27 Viola Klein 'Working Wives' in National Society of Children's Nurseries *Working Wives: What of the Children?* 1960, quoted in W. Webster *Imagining Home: Gender, 'Race' and National Identity, 1945–64* London, UCL Press 1998 p. 136.

28 E. Wilson *Women and the Welfare State* London, Tavistock 1977 p. 150. See also Lewis op. cit., chapter 4.

29 C. Briar *Working for Women? Gendered Work and Welfare Policies in Twentieth Century Britain* London, UCL Press p. 106.

30 Pugh op. cit., p. 295.

31 Wilson 1977 op. cit., p. 151.

32 Finch and Summerfield op. cit., p. 14.

33 Briar op. cit., p. 111.

34 Finch and Summerfield op. cit., p. 15.

35 M. David *The State, the Family and Education* London, Routledge 1980, quoted in Bruley op. cit., p. 127.

36 For girls' experiences of the grammar school system, see L. Heron (ed.) *Truth, Dare, Promise: Girls Growing Up in the 1950s* London, Virago 1985.

37 Briar op. cit., p. 97.

38 Wightman op. cit., p. 186.

39 Pugh op. cit., p. 288.

40 Briar op. cit., p. 97.

41 Ibid., p. 111.

42 Bruley op. cit., p. 128.

43 Briar op. cit., p. 97.

44 L. Mackie and P. Patullo *Women who Work* London, Tavistock 1977, quoted in ibid., p. 97.

45 Briar ibid., p. 98.

46 *Technical Education* 1957, quoted in ibid., p. 112.

47 Bruley op. cit., p. 128.

48 Briar op. cit., n. 56 p. 112.
49 Ibid., p. 99.
50 Donovan Report 1967/8, quoted in ibid., p. 99.
51 For an in-depth discussion of these workers, drawing on their oral testimony, see McDowell op. cit. See also W. Webster 'Defining Boundaries: European Volunteer Worker Women in Britain and Narratives of Community', *Women's History Review* 9, 4 1997 257–76.
52 McDowell op. cit., p. 25.
53 Briar op. cit., p. 96.
54 Ibid., p. 96.
55 Ibid., pp. 111 and 96.
56 Webster 1998 op. cit., pp. 32–40 discusses the report of the Royal Commission on Population's notion of 'suitable immigrants' in depth.
57 McDowell op. cit., p. 27.
58 Webster 1998 op. cit., pp. x–xi. See also H. Carby '"White Women Listen!" Black Feminism and the Boundaries of Sisterhood' in Centre for Contemporary Cultural Studies *The Empire Strikes Back* London, Hutchinson 1982.
59 McDowell op. cit., p. 43.
60 Ibid., and Webster 1998 and 2000 have produced the most recent research at present, although there has been some interesting sociological work on black women workers in Britain. See B. Bryan, S. Dadzie and S. Scaife *The Heart of the Race: Black Women's Lives in Britain* London, Virago 1985 especially chapter 1 and G. Lewis 'Black Women's Employment and the British Economy' in W. James and C. Harris (eds) *Inside Babylon: the Caribbean diaspora in Britain* London, Verso 1993.
61 See Webster 1998 op. cit., chapter 2 for an in-depth analysis of this issue.
62 Webster 1998 op. cit. notes that women from the Caribbean were not recruited into the textile mills because they were considered unsuited to the climate and were also thought, erroneously, to be illiterate, p. 35.
63 Bruley op. cit., p. 118.
64 Webster 1998 op. cit., pp. 28–31.
65 Cecilia Wade in *'Sorry No Vacancies': Life Stories of Senior Citizens from the Caribbean* Notting Dale Urban Studies Centre 1992, quoted in Webster 1998 op. cit., p. 146.
66 Ibid., pp. 146–7.

12 Women's work in the age of equal opportunities: 1969 to the end of the century

1 G. Joseph *Women at Work: the British Experience* Oxford, Phillip Allan 1983, quoted in J. Lewis *Women in Britain since 1945: Women, Family, Work and the State in the Post-war Years* Oxford, Blackwell 1992 p. 66.
2 C. Briar *Working for Women? Gendered Work and Welfare Policies in Twentieth Century Britain* London, UCL Press 1997 p. 93.
3 Lewis op. cit., p. 65.
4 R. Crompton *Women and Work in Modern Britain* Oxford, Oxford University Press 1997 p. 25.
5 S. Bruley *Women in Britain since 1900* Basingstoke, Macmillan 1999 p. 193 and M. Pugh *Women and the Women's Movement in Britain, 1914–1999* Basingstoke, Macmillan 2000 p. 341.

6 Crompton op. cit., p. 27.

7 Briar op. cit., p. 164.

8 For details of black women's occupations during this period, see R. Bhavani *Black Women in the Labour Market: a Research Review* Manchester, Equal Opportunities Commission 1994.

9 For a fuller discussion of these, see E. Meehan 'British Feminism from the 1960s to the 1980s' in H. L. Smith (ed.) *British Feminism in the Twentieth Century* Massachusetts, Massachusetts University Press 1990 pp. 189–204.

10 Meehan op. cit., p. 193.

11 The best account of the WLM to date is B. Campbell and A. Coote *Sweet Freedom: The Struggle for Women's Liberation* Oxford, Blackwell 1987 but it does not have the distance needed for a definitive history.

12 Pugh op. cit., pp. 312–13.

13 B. Friedan *The Feminine Mystique* London, Gollancz 1963. Friedan called the depression that many middle-class, college-educated housewives in the USA experienced 'the problem that has no name'.

14 L. Heron (ed.) *Truth, Dare, Promise: Girls Growing Up in the 50s* London, Virago 1985; M. Wandor (ed.) *Once a Feminist: Stories of a Generation* London, Virago 1990. For other texts based on women's life stories of this period, see S. Maitland (ed.) *Very Heaven: Looking Back to the 1960s* London, Virago 1988 and A. Sebestyn (ed.) *68. 78. 88: From Women's Liberation to Feminism* Bridport, Prism Press 1988.

15 Pugh op. cit., p. 314 states that in 1965 one in four university students were women. This had increased to one in three by 1981. By the year 2000 women students outnumbered men although this varied from discipline to discipline.

16 For a useful discussion of the various threads of feminist thought, see M. Maynard 'Beyond the "Big Three": the Development of Feminist Theory into the 1990s', *Women's History Review* 4, 3 1995.

17 The Seven Demands were: equal pay; equal opportunities and education; 24-hour nurseries; fee contraception and abortion on demand; legal and financial independence; no discrimination against lesbians and freedom from intimidation by violence or sexual coercion.

18 See, for example, S. Alexander *Becoming a Woman and Other Essays in 19th and 20th Century Feminist History* London, Virago 1994 pp. 257–68 and S. Rowbotham *The Past is Before Us: Feminism in Action since the 1960s*. London, Pandora 1989 p. 227.

19 Lewis op. cit., p. 117.

20 Meehan in Smith op. cit., p. 196.

21 Briar op. cit., p. 101.

22 Meehan in Smith op. cit., p. 196.

23 Briar op. cit., p. 101.

24 Ibid., p. 101.

25 Ibid., p. 139.

26 The SDA had a broader focus than just employment and training. It also made it illegal for a woman to be treated less favourably than a man in the areas of housing and the provision of goods and services, but these are beyond the scope of this book.

27 Briar op. cit., p. 116.

28 Ibid., p. 117.

29 Campbell & Coote op. cit., pp. 122–3.

30 Briar p. 118.
31 Meehan in Smith op. cit., p. 197.
32 Ibid., p. 197.
33 Briar op. cit., p. 118.
34 Ibid., p. 119.
35 Crompton op. cit., pp. 30–1.
36 Briar op. cit., p. 121.
37 Ibid., pp. 121–2.
38 Lewis op. cit., p. 75.
39 Briar op. cit., p. 122.
40 Crompton op. cit., pp. 32.
41 Briar op. cit., quoting figures from the British Social Attitudes survey, 1989 p. 142.
42 For a deeper discussion of this debate, see V. Beechey and T. Perkins *A Matter of Hours* Cambridge, Polity 1987 pp. 145–6 and C. Hakim *Key Issues in Women's Work* London, Athlone Press 1996, both quoted in Crompton op. cit., p. 33.
43 Briar op. cit., p. 123.
44 Ibid., p. 124.
45 Crompton op. cit., pp. 108–9.
46 C. Cockburn *Machinery of Dominance: Women, Men and Technical Know-how* London, Pluto 1985, p. 232.
47 Crompton op. cit., pp. 109–10.
48 Ibid., p. 111.

13 Women's work since the 1840s: continuity and change

1 S. Walby *Patriarchy at Work: Patriarchal and Capitalist Relations in Employment* Cambridge, Polity Press 1986.

ह

Further reading

This is a guide for readers new to the subject. It is divided into key primary and secondary sources. For a complete list of all the works used, see the notes section for each chapter.

Key primary sources

Annual Reports of the Chief Inspector of Factories and Workshops.

Autobiographies, e.g. Bondfield, M. *A Life's Work* London, Hutchinson 1953; Brittain, V. *Testament of Youth* London, Gollancz 1933; Pankhurst, E. S. *The Home Front: A Mirror to Life in England during the First World War* London, Hutchinson 1932.

Beveridge and Webb Collections at British Library of Political and Economic Science for the development of the Welfare State.

Census Schedules and *Reports* from 1841 (indicate a limited range of women's employment).

Domestic diaries (for day-to-day details of servants' and mistresses' lives, e.g. L. Stanley *The Diaries of Hannah Cullwick: Victorian Maidservant* London, Virago 1984).

Estate Records (for agricultural and domestic workers), e.g. the University of Hull has a wide collection of these, see www.hull.ac.uk/arc/

Imperial War Museum, Women's Work Collection (includes taped oral history interviews and photograph collection).

Journals, e.g. *English Woman's Journal; Englishwoman's Review of Social and Industrial Questions; Labour Woman; Time and Tide; Spare Rib; Women's Trade Union Review*, all archived at the Women's Library, London.

Mass Observation Archive, University of Sussex – for the responses of ordinary people to all aspects of British life.

Mayhew, H. *London Labour and the London Poor* 4 vols. London, Cass 1861, 1967 (classic survey of labouring people based on interviews with working people).

Special interest newspapers, e.g. *Common Cause; The Engineer; The Woman Worker; Woolwich Pioneer; The Women's Dreadnought.*

Parliamentary Papers and Government Reports e.g.:

Report of Commissioners, Children's Employment Commission: First Report (Mines), PP 1842 XV; *Appendix*, PP 1842 XVI; *Part II*, PP 1842 XVII.

Report from Commissioners on the Employment of Women and Children in Agriculture, PP 1843 XII.

Report of Commissioners on Children's, Young Persons' and Women's Employment in Agriculture: 1st Report and 2nd Report, England PP 1867–8 XVII and PP 1868–69 XIII; 3rd Report, Wales PP 1870 XIII; 4th Report, Scotland PP 1870 XIII.

Royal Commission on Factory and Workshops Acts 1876.

Royal Commission on Labour, Minutes of Evidence, With Appendices Taken Before Group 'C'.

Commissioners' Reports on Women in Industry and on the Domestic Service Problem (First World War).

Reports of the Central Committee on Women's Employment (First World War).

Reports of the Health of Munition Worker's Committee (First World War).

Records of the Ministries of Labour, Munitions and Supply and Works (1914–19), all at Public Records Office.

Records of private businesses (e.g. Cadburys, Clarks, Courtaulds) found in company archives and local Records Offices.

Trades Union Congress Library Collection (records of both mixed and women only unions, especially the Gertrude Tuckwell Collection which charts most of the union activity that went on up to the First World War).

Women's organizations' records, e.g.:

Women's Trade Union Association Papers (London School of Economics).

Women's Co-operative Guild Papers (University of Hull and London School of Economics).

Women's Industrial Council Papers (London School of Economics).

Women's Trade Union League Collection (TUC Library).

See also the Women's Library for material on the Women's Liberation Movement, Fawcett Society, Six Point Group and other women's organizations of the twentieth century.

Key secondary texts

Alexander, S. *Becoming a Woman and Other Essays in 19th and 20th Century Feminist History* London, Virago 1994.
A useful collection on women's skilled and casual work.

Anderson, G. (ed.) *The White Blouse Revolution* Manchester, Manchester University Press 1988.
A collection of essays on the clerical sector and women's roles within it.

Beddoe, D. *Back to Home and Duty: Women Between the Wars* London, Pandora 1989.
A useful survey of the period.

Boston, S. *Women Workers and the Trade Unions* London, Davies-Poynter 1980.
This study is useful for equal pay debates and trade union attitudes towards women workers.

Braybon, G. *Women Workers in the First World War* London, Croom Helm 1981.
The basic text for this topic.

Braybon, G. and Summerfield, P. *Out of the Cage: Women's Experiences in Two World Wars* London, Pandora 1987.
Draws on women's personal experiences of war.

Briar, C. *Working for Women? Gendered Work and Welfare Policies in Twentieth-Century Britain* London, UCL Press 1997.
Analyses women's work from a welfare perspective.

Bruley, S. *Women in Britain since 1900* London, Macmillan 1999.
A useful overview of the period.

Bryan, B., Dadzie, S. and Scafe, S. *The Heart of the Race: Black Women's Lives in Britain* London, Virago 1985.
One of the few books that deals with black women workers from black women's perspective.

Burman, S. (ed.) *Fit Work for Women* London, Croom Helm 1979.
Useful essays on class relationships, landladies and trade unions.

Bythell, D. *The Sweated Trades: Outwork in Nineteenth Century Britain* London, Batsford 1978.
The main text on the subject.

Chew, D. N. (ed.) *The Life and Writings of Ada Nield Chew* London, Virago 1982.
A rare account from a working-class perspective.

Clark, D. (ed.) *Marriage, Domestic Life and Social Change: Writings for Jacqueline Burgoyne (1944–1988)* London, Routledge 1991.
Includes an essay by Finch and Summerfield on the companionate marriage.

Crompton, R. *Women and Work in Modern Britain* Oxford, Oxford University Press 1997.
Useful for recent trends in women's work.

Davidoff, L. & Westover, B. *Our Work, Our Lives, Our Words: Women's History, Women's Work* New Jersey, Barnes and Noble 1986.
Life histories of working women and their relationship with trades unions.

Drake McFeely, M. *Lady Inspectors: The Campaign for a Better Workplace* Georgia, Georgia University Press 1988.
Focuses on working conditions, class relations and protective legislation.

Duchen, C. & Bandhauer-Schoffmann, I. (ed.) *When the War was Over: Women, War and Peace in Europe, 1940–1956* Leicester, Leicester University Press 2000.
This collection includes useful essays by Summerfield and Tinkler.

Dyhouse, C. *Girls Growing Up in Late Victorian and Edwardian England* London, Routledge 1981.
An analysis of separate spheres and its implications for girls' education.

Dyhouse, C. *No Distinction of Sex? Women in British Universities, 1870–1939* London, UCL Press 1995.
Focuses on the opening up of education for women and its implications for women's employment.

Glucksmann, M. *Women Assemble: Women Workers and the New Industries in Inter-war Britain* London, Routledge 1990.
In-depth study of factory work in the inter-war period.

Gordon, E. and Breitenbach, E. (eds) *The World is Ill-Divided: Women's Work in Scotland in the Nineteenth and Early Twentieth Centuries* Edinburgh, Edinburgh University Press 1990.
Informative collection of essays on Scottish women's work.

Hall, C. *White, Male and Middle Class: Explorations in Feminism and History* Oxford, Polity 1992.
Collection of essays focusing on gender, class and 'race'.

Harrison, B. *Not Only the Dangerous Trades: Women's Work and Health in Britain, 1880–1914* London, Taylor and Francis 1996.
An important study of occupational health issues and protective legislation.

Heron, L. (ed.) *Truth, Dare, Promise: Girls Growing Up in the 1950s* London, Virago 1985.
Life histories of young women's aspirations and where these led them.

Higgs, E. *Making Sense of the Census: The Manuscript Returns for England and Wales, 1801–1901* London, HMSO 1989.
A useful guide to interpreting census material.

Hilton, M. & Hirsch, P. (eds) *Practical Visionaries: Women, Education and Social Progress, 1790–1930* Harlow, Longman 2000.
This collection contains useful chapters on widening work opportunities for middle-class women.

Holcombe, L. *Victorian Ladies at Work: Middle-class Working Women in England and Wales 1850–1914* Newton Abbott, David & Charles 1973.
Surveys of the various employment possibilities for middle-class women.

Honeyman, K. *Women, Gender and Industrialisation in England, 1700–1870* Basingstoke, Macmillan 2000.
An analysis of how gender and class interacted during industrialization; also has a good survey of the literature on industrialization.

Horn, P. *The Rise and Fall of the Victorian Servant* Stroud, Alan Sutton 1975, 1997.
Good analysis of class and working conditions for servants.

Horn, P. *Victorian Countrywomen* Oxford, Basil Blackwell 1991.
This study focuses on agricultural work, rural crafts and trades, teachers and nurses.

Hughes, K. *Victorian Governesses* London, Hambledon Press 1993.
The essential text on the problems of the governess.

John, A. V. *By The Sweat of Their Brow: Women Workers at Victorian Coal Mines* London, Routledge and Kegan Paul 1984.
The definitive study of women in mining.

John, A. V. (ed.) *Unequal Opportunities: Women's Employment in England, 1800–1918* Oxford, Blackwell 1986.
Focuses on various women's trades, local studies, trade unions.

John, A. V. (ed.) *Our Mothers' Land: Chapters in Welsh Women's History, 1830–1939* Cardiff, University of Wales Press 1998.
Focuses on Welsh women's lives, including employment.

Jones, H. *Women in British Public Life, 1914–1950* London, Longman 2000.
Very good analysis of women's role in policymaking, including employment policy, for this period. Comparisons with some European countries, Australia and USA.

Jordan, E. *Women's Movement and Women's Employment in Britain in the Nineteenth Century Britain* London, Routledge 1999.
Very useful study of middle-class women's work especially teaching, nursing, clerical work and professions generally.

Klein, V. *Britain's Married Women Workers* London, Routledge and Kegan Paul 1965.
A fairly rare but useful empirical study of the period and subject.

Lewis, J. *Women in England 1870–1950* Brighton, Wheatsheaf 1971.
Useful overview of the period.

Lewis, J. *Women in Britain since 1945* Oxford, Blackwell 1992.
One of the few books that deals with the history of women's work for this period.

Lown, J. *Women and Industrialization: Gender and Work in Nineteenth Century England* Cambridge, Polity Press 1990.
A very useful local case study of Essex silk workers.

Malcolmson, P. *English Laundresses: A Social History, 1850–1930* Illinois, Illinois University Press 1986.
A comprehensive case study that focuses on married women's work and protective legislation in this trade.

Mappen, E. *Helping Women at Work: The Women's Industrial Council, 1889–1914* London, Hutchinson 1985.
Focuses on the Women's Trade Union Association, Women's Industrial Council, protective legislation debate and minimum wage debate.

Mitchell, S. *The New Girl: Girls Culture in England, 1880–1915* New York, Columbia University Press 1995.
An analysis of the cultural aspects of middle-class girls' education and their employment opportunities and changing ideas of femininity.

Myrdal, A. and Klein, V. *Women's Two Roles, Home and Work* London, Routledge and Kegan Paul 1956.
Seminal work on women's role as worker and wife and mother in post war Britain.

Pennington, S. and Westover, B. *A Hidden Workforce: Homeworkers in England, 1850–1985* Basingstoke Macmillan, 1989.
An overview of homeworking for the whole period of this book.

Pinchbeck, I. *Women Workers and the Industrial Revolution* London, Virago 1930, 1981.
A classic study and a good background on women in agriculture, industry, crafts and trades.

Pugh, M. *Women and the Women's Movement in Britain, 1914–1999* London, Macmillan 2000.
An overview of the women's movement and women's work in this period.

Purvis, J. (ed.) *Women's History: Britain, 1850–1945, An Introduction* London, UCL Press 1995.
Contains chapters on women and work and is a useful overview of the debates.

Rendall, J. *Women in an Industrializing Society, 1750–1880* Oxford, Blackwell 1990.
A useful background reading on the period.

Riley, D. *War in the Nursery: Theories of the Child and Mother* London, Virago 1983.
The best text on pronatalist thinking in post war Britain.

Roberts, E. *Women's Waged Work, 1840–1970* Basingstoke, Macmillan 1988.
An overview of most of the period.

Roberts, E. *Women and Families, 1940–1970* Oxford, Blackwell 1995.
An oral history of the period that focuses on women's home and working lives.

Rose, S. O. *Limited Livelihoods: Gender and Class in Nineteenth Century England* London, Routledge 1992.
A useful analysis of the gendered implications of women's work.

Rowbotham, S. *The Past Is before Us: Feminism in Action since the 1960s* London, Pandora 1989.
A good source for 'second wave' feminism.

Sayer, K. *Women of the Fields: Representations of Rural Women in the Nineteenth Century* Manchester, Manchester University Press 1995.
Focuses on representations of femininity of women agricultural workers.

Sharpe, P. (ed.) *Women's Work: The English Experience, 1650–1914* Basingstoke, Macmillan 1998.
Essays on suitable work and general debates.

Smith, H. L. (ed.) *British Feminism in the Twentieth Century* Massachusetts, Massachusetts University Press 1990.
A collection of essays that addresses key issues for feminism in the twentieth century.

Summerfield, P. *Women Workers in the Second World War* London, Croom Helm 1984.
The basic text for this topic.

Thom, D. *Nice Girls and Rude Girls: Women Workers in World War I* London, I. B. Tauris 2000.
A collection of Thom's essays on this period.

Vicinus, M. *Independent Women: Work and Community for Single Women* London, Virago 1985.
Good analysis of the widening employment opportunities for single women in the nineteenth and early twentieth centuries.

Walby, S. *Patriarchy at Work: Patriarchal and Capitalist Relations in Employment* Cambridge, Polity Press, 1986.
Feminist analysis of women and work.

Webster, W. *Imagining Home: Gender, 'Race' and National Identity, 1945–64* London, UCL Press 1998.
A cultural history with a chapter on black women and work.

Widdowson, F. *Going Up into the Next Class: Women and Elementary Teacher Training 1840–1914* London, Hutchinson 1983.
Focuses on working-class and middle-class women teachers.

Wightman, C. *More than Munitions: Women, Work and the Engineering Industries, 1900–1950* London, Longman 1999.
A useful study of this particular trade.

Wilson, E. *Only Half Way to Paradise: Women in Postwar Britain: 1945–1968* London, Tavistock 1980.
A cultural history including a discussion on women and work.

Yeo, E. (ed.) *Radical Femininity: Women's Self-representation in the Public Sphere* Manchester, Manchester University Press 1998.
Useful analyses of women's challenges to dominant constructions of femininity.

Index

INDEX

3; feminine behaviour of 11; and
globalization 227; and health/welfare
12, 13; infantilization of 25, 142; and
loss of status 24, 41; male violence
against 225; moral anxieties
concerning 25-6, 48; moral
character of 5; and patriarchal
oppression 227; and poverty 2, 32,
78, 227; power of 17; regulation/
control of sexuality/private lives
127-8; and right to work 43-4;
sexual harassment of 60; as skilled
workers 137-8; study of 1;
subordinate position of 160, 161, 166
women factory inspectors 55, 79, 125,
142; campaign for 91-5; and class
issues 95; education requirements for
94; and infringements of law 104;
male opposition to 92; middle class
vs working women 92, 93-4; as
protectors of vulnerable sisters/
daughters 94; and Royal Commission
on Labour 93; worker resentments
94-5
Women's Advisory Committee, Report
(1919) 154
Women's Army Auxiliary Corps (WAAC)
134
Women's Auxiliary Air Force (WAAF)
167
Women's Auxiliary services 165
Women's Co-operative Guild 86
Women's Employment Committee 141,
177
Women's Employment Federation 210
Women's Engineering Society 145
Women's Freedom League (WFL) 151
Women's Industrial council (WIC) 12,
47, 55, 64, 66-70, 80, 84, 85-7, 88,
91, 97, 99, 101, 107, 125, 177
Women's Industrial News 69
Women's Institute 189
Women's International League 145
Women's Labour League (WLL) 69, 84,
131, 177
Women's Land Army 134, 167
Women's Liberal Federation 62, 94
Women's Liberation Movement (WLM)
207, 220, 223; campaigns of 211; and
equal rights campaign 212-15;
impetus for 208; popularity of 211;
rise of 210-11; seven demands 211,
see also feminists

women's movement 2, 14, 43, 46, 48;
and factory acts 98; revitalized 181;
and socialism 63; split in 160; and
unionization 60-1
Women's Printing Society 46
Women's Protective and Provident
League (WPPL) 12, 46, 55, 58-60, 89,
90
women's role 3, 48; challenges to 49;
industrial 67; natural/primary 4, 8,
17, 26, 49, 50, 164, 165, 170-1, 174,
175, 177, 201-2, 210, 215, 223, 224;
patriarchal views on 136-7; shaping
of 227-8
Women's Royal Air Force (WRAF) 134
Women's Royal Naval Service (WRNS)
134, 172
Women's Trade Union Association
(WTUA) 12, 55, 61, 63-6, 91, 93
Women's Trade Union League (WTUL)
12, 55, 58, 60-3, 64, 70-4, 84, 89,
91, 97, 99, 100, 125, 131, 159, 177
Women's Trade Union and Provident
League (WTUPL) 61
Women's Trade Union Review 70
Women's Union Journal 46, 61
women's unions 8, 148; and cotton
weaving industry 16; decline in 180;
difficulty in organizing 60; and equal
pay 166; equal rights stance 73;
essentialist stance 73-4; feminist
element 73; flourishing of 176;
membership of 71, 72; middle-
class/working-class tensions 73;
sporadic activity involving 57-8,
see also trade unions
Woolwich Arsenal 141, 145
work, access to 211; and advent of new
technologies 158-9; age profile 54,
150, 151, 187, 188, 192, 196, 215;
attitudes toward 2; benefits of equal
pay/sex descrimination acts 217;
continuity/change 2-3, 11; debates
concerning 4; and deregulation 215;
efforts to improve conditions 45-6,
48; and employment rights 2;
exclusions from 4; fitness of 75; and
gender construction 218; and glass
ceiling 181, 209; industrialization of
3, 16; as interlude between
school/marriage 60, 202, 203; lack of
career structure 185; legislation for
48-9; numbers of women employed

307

307